Sewickley: A History of a Valley Community

By Frances C. Hardie

R R D O N N E L L E Y F I N A N C I A L

For my husband, Jim, a big help in this and all my other endeavors.

ISBN 0-9619308-2-9

1st Printing, 1998

Table of Contents

Preface

I would like to thank all of my readers for their useful advice in correcting and improving the manuscript. They are: Elizabeth Mertz; James H. Hardie; Joan Adibi; Mary Lee Grey; and Betty G. Shields. John H. Demmler took the modern photographs of houses mentioned in the text. George Beck, Tom Lowrey and the staff of Donnelley Financial have been extraordinarily helpful. The information from local libraries has been invaluable. The Historical Society of Western Pennsylvania has two important sources: an extensive collection of Sewickley historical papers compiled by Gilbert Hays; and the Way family papers. The Pennsylvania Room of the Carnegie Library in Oakland yielded many treasures. The librarians at the Sewickley Public Library, especially Lynne Schneider, were a big help in locating items in the William C. Robinson Collection. The Sewickley Valley Historical Society and its director, Mrs. B. G. Shields, provided both information and pictures. More recent events in Sewickley history were brought to life by most enjoyable interviews with many residents. I thank them for their time and interest. I thank also Susan Cockrell who joined me in conducting many of the interviews.

People Interviewed

John Alexander	Mary Ann Balldridge
F. Torrance Baker	J. Judson Brooks, Jr.
Charles Butler	Nancy Chalfant
Raymond Connelly	Jane Evans
Virginia Hailstock	Margaret Halpin
Helen Hegner	James H. Higgins
Mary Louise Johnson	Mark Leavitt
Richard McPherson	Jim Munizza
Harriet Orndorff	Joseph Reiser
Roseanne Reiser	Adelaide Ritchey
James Shaughnessy	Charles Stinson
Charles Stinson	Jerry Tignanelli
Josephine Hebst Sybo	Josephine Toia
Bruno Toia	Oliver Ward
Jerry Vescio	Capt. Frederick Way, Jr.
Mary Yankello	

I have retained the original spellings in quotations because it gives a feel for the language.

Introduction

As today's urban planners are searching for the way to design the best possible communities, they might do well to examine the development of the Sewickley area. This includes Sewickley Borough, its three neighbors, Osborne up the Ohio River to the east, Edgeworth down river to the west, and Sewickley Heights to the north. Somehow, over a period of almost 200 years, the area has managed to evolve into a large community which includes blacks, Italians, the super-rich and the not-so-rich. Although there are certainly problems to be faced, most residents seem to agree that there is no better place to live. How did this feeling of community evolve? Was it luck, geography, or careful planning by town residents? This history of Sewickley will explore the question.

A major question facing urban planners is how to design communities with two important requirements: pleasant surroundings and access to jobs. Because the Sewickley area meets both criteria, it provides a good model. Many places have one of these two community requirements. Western Pennsylvania abounds in delightful small towns which beckon invitingly to the passing tourist. Brownsville, on the Monongahela, combines the advantages of a splendid river setting with the tantalizing prospect of historic houses. Somerset and Ligonier are both wonderful small towns where the urban dweller fresh from dealing with traffic jams would love to settle. But the number and range of jobs are limited. On the other hand, where jobs are more available in downtown Pittsburgh or Oakland, it is difficult to find a place to live which has the flavor of a small town.

Why was Pittsburgh not surrounded by a series of communities like Sewickley, all satellite communities to Pittsburgh, but each with its own individuality? An examination of several other suburbs of Pittsburgh will explain. Homestead started out like Sewickley. Some wealthy landowners farmed their estates. Times changed in 1871, when two members of founding families, Abdiel McClure and Lowry West, subdivided their land for development. All went well at first. An early map boasted that "During the three days public sale in September 1871, 447 'Homestead' lots were sold for $385,496, the majority of purchasers intending to become residents." However, the Panic of 1873 halted development. The lots that might have been the beginning of a community similar to Broad Street in Sewickley were snapped up by industry.[1]

The North Side of Pittsburgh, until 1907 a separate city called Allegheny, developed faster than Sewickley. It was similar in being right on the river with a flat plain and hills behind. Like Sewickley, it had a mix of population including all economic groups. But by 1900 it had developed as a much more urban area, with its own industry. Its proximity to Pittsburgh was its undoing, and it was annexed in 1907.

The East End, particularly Shadyside, started out to be similar to Sewickley. It was a suburban retreat for wealthy Pittsburghers who could commute easily by railroad. In the 1870s both Sewickley and Shadyside must have looked alike with wide, shaded streets and large, comfortable houses. Today, Shadyside still retains some of the flavor but, like the North Side, it is too close to Pittsburgh to have the community feel of Sewickley. Because it has no geographical boundaries, being on a large flat plain, it can spread out with no definite beginning or end.

Oakmont, north of Pittsburgh on the Allegheny River, is similar to Sewickley. It has a town center and its inhabitants tend to feel they live in Oakmont, the way Sewickleyites say they are from Sewickley. Like Sewickley, Oakmont has a famous country club and some elegant suburban houses. It is, however, much smaller than the Sewickley area.

Mount Lebanon, south of Pittsburgh, is another suburb to compare with Sewickley. Both were tavern stops on a main road to Pittsburgh. Both have commercial centers. Mount Lebanon developed as a suburb after gaining access to Pittsburgh by railroad in the 1870s and trolley in 1902. Mount Lebanon developed much later than Sewickley but it is similar in having attractive, well-maintained houses. It meets the two requirements sought by urban planners, access to jobs and pleasant surroundings. Mount Lebanon, however, does not have the flavor of a small town with a heterogeneous population. Unlike Sewickley, the population is solidly upper middle class. Moreover, the area developed in terms of housing projects. Franklin Toker in his study of Pittsburgh says,

> The first housing project constructed in Mt. Lebanon, in 1901, was urban rather than suburban in character, and it held close to the projected trolley line on Washington Road. . . . [In later waves,] despite their elevated prices, homes were still part of a "development": most were designed by a half-dozen architects who were retained by the developers.[2]

Mount Lebanon is a group of connected developments. Sewickley grew organically as individuals decided to settle there.

Fox Chapel, across the Allegheny River from Oakmont, is sometimes called a copy of Sewickley Heights. Both are wealthy suburbs of Pittsburgh. Sewickley Heights, however, is in essence part of a larger area of Sewickley Borough, Osborne, and Edgeworth, which includes various kinds of people and housing types. Fox Chapel is all upper middle class. Fox Chapel developed as a suburban community much later than Sewickley. There was no way to commute to Pittsburgh from Fox Chapel until the coming of automobiles. Until then it was a farming community. Another major difference is Sewickley Height's access to a pleasant town for shopping. Fox Chapel has only a mall for full service shopping.

Many suburbs, whose first residents' primary aim in leaving the city was to find privacy and solitude, are finding that they crave community. Tom Dyke, an urban planner said,

> There is a big nostalgic movement right now to the old-fashioned downtown, the New England village, the kind of place where you pass people on sidewalks. People want a sense of place, a feeling that they are part of a bigger whole.[3]

One suburb of Chicago, Schaumburg, is even starting to build an instant town center, complete with a New England style town square. Here people hope to be able to walk around, meet their neighbors, and relax. This will answer a local tavern owner's complaint that, "The only way you can see other people from Schaumburg is through their car windows, as they drive home from work."

People made the decision to move to Sewickley for different reasons at different times. At first, when Sewickley was a stagecoach and riverboat stop, the main occupations of residents were service industries or farming. After the coming of the railroad in 1851, Sewickley became a suburb of Pittsburgh. Many residents commuted daily to jobs of every sort in the city and returned each night to the bucolic charms of a village. Still later, the coming of the automobile enabled commuters to extend the radius of their commute far up into the hills to as great a distance as they wished to drive each day. Each group to come to Sewickley built houses suitable for their time. Fortunately, examples of houses from all these periods remain today. The Lark Inn, built around 1800, remains on Beaver Road. There is a log house on Fern Hollow and Hunt Roads dating from about 1820. The Sewickley Valley is a treasure-trove of houses dating from 1870-1910, looking like the American idea of "Home." Franklin Toker in his book on Pittsburgh calls Sewickley "a virtual museum of mid-Victorian design."[4] Many of the houses in Sewickley and Edgeworth that date from the early twentieth century were designed by famous architects such as Alden & Harlow, Rutan & Russell, and Benno Janssen. A few of the mansions built in Sewickley Heights have been preserved. They give an idea of the enormous wealth and extravagant life style of the early twentieth century.

The first part of this history depends on written sources. From the early part of the twentieth century, oral histories supplement the written record. Fortunately there are many people still living who can remember growing up in the Sewickley Valley prior to World War II. Their memories, recorded in interviews, evoke a lovely, many-faceted village with different groups of people and numerous activities.

[1] Curtis Miner, *Homestead; the Story of a Steel Town*. Pittsburgh, Historical Society of Western Pennsylvania, 1989, p. 1-3.

[2] Franklin Toker, *Pittsburgh: an Urban Portrait*. University Park, Pa, Pennsylvania University Press, 1986, p. 285.

[3] *New York Times*, August 7, 1996, p. 7.

[4] Toker, p.295

Chapter 1
Early Days in the Sewickley Valley

When George Washington paddled down the Ohio River in 1770, he reported that the river "has some ugly rifts and shoals which we found somewhat difficult to pass, whether from inexperience of the Channel or not, I cannot undertake to say. . . . The water is rapid in some places, gliding gently in others, and quite still in others."[1] Imagine being a passenger in Washington's canoe when he reached what is now Sewickley. It would be difficult for all but the keenest eye to recognize the site. Perhaps important landmarks such as Little Sewickley Creek or the wide expanse of flat land along the riverbank might be clues. A canoeist today and Washington would glimpse a road paralleling the river: the modern traveler would see Ohio River Boulevard; Washington, an Indian trail. Today a canoeist could recognize Sewickley by its church steeples and by its green, well-tended yards surrounding attractive houses. But in George Washington's time, the land from the river to the highest hills was covered with dense forests of mixed evergreen and deciduous trees. Oak trees were the most prevalent, followed by sugar maple, then chestnut, walnut, and hickory. On the hills, where the soil was poor, scrub oak, cedar, pine, mountain laurel and rhododendron formed dense thickets, making travel difficult. Indians frequently burned such thickets to facilitate hunting. In the forests where the soil was fertile and trees grew tallest, sunlight did not reach the ground. Here songbirds seldom came. Only eagles, ravens and owls lived in the forest gloom, sharing the space with wolves, mountain lions and lynx, which preyed on deer, elk, bear, and bison. Along rivers and in clearings flew turkeys, woodcock, quail, grouse, pigeons, vultures, bald eagles, and parakeets.[2] Washington reported in his diary, "The River along down abounds in Wild Geese and several kinds of Ducks, but no great quantity. We killed five wild Turkeys today."[3]

F. Cumming, who traveled the River in 1807, noticed other flying creatures.

Deadman's Island [near Sewickley] is small and covered with aquatic shrubs and plants and so low that it must always be inundated in moderate risings. The banks on each side abound in partridges, whose responsive calls are continually heard, interrupted by the buzz of multitudes of large horse flies, which probably attracted by the odour of our provisions, seemed more pleased with our boat than we were with them.[4]

Little is known about the Indians who lived in these forests before the coming of the settlers. Early residents found intriguing traces of their predecessors, but they serve more to fire the imagination than to give real knowledge. The early Indians, members of the Algonquian stock, are known as the Mound Builders. They had a fairly highly developed culture: they raised corn, beans and squash and made clay utensils.[5] There were many mounds around Sewickley; some survived until 1911 when Gilbert Hays described them in an article in the *Sewickley Herald*.

One [mound] is located on the grounds of Mrs. Agnes Graff, at Shields station, close to the railroad. This mound, about twenty-five feet in diameter and five feet high, perfectly round, as they all are, was opened by Dr. John Dickson and others about fifty years ago, but barring traces of human remains, some stone implements, traces of charred wood and rocks discolored by fire, suggestive of sacrificial uses, there was nothing else. This was the condition of all others opened during various periods. . . .

On the site of the handsome residence of Mr. John Marron, at Quaker Valley station, there was a smaller mound, which was removed at the time the Marron house was built [on 617 West Drive, Edgeworth]. Two similar sized mounds were in evidence forty years ago in the meadow on the Shields property between Edgeworth and Shields station, but these have been entirely removed and their exact location forgotten by all except a few of the older residents.

According to an early plan, there was a mound just behind the gardens of Newington on Beaver Road near Shields Lane.

After the Mound Builders left or died out, their place was taken by various Indian tribes including the Shawnee, Delaware, Mingo, and Iroquois, all from an entirely different group of Indians. Many used to camp on the broad plain between the river bank and the steep hills leading to Sewickley Heights. Old-time residents remember finding numerous arrowheads and other artifacts. In 1911, Gilbert Hays wrote of hunting relics in his youth.

Thousands of arrowheads, spearheads, fleshing knives, tomahawks, and other stone implements have been found throughout the valley and can still be found in plowed-up fields. In recent years a handsome stone tomahawk was picked up on Pine Avenue, immediately in front of the residence of Mr. Gilbert A. Hays. The favorite method of finding these interesting relics was to take a corn field, in midsummer, just after a heavy rain, when a group of boys, one to each row, would walk miles in search of these interesting trophies, invariably finding quantities. At one time forty years ago, the writer and his brothers had a soap box filled with flint arrow heads with a large number of larger specimens in tomahawks, etc. In fact Hays & Murphy was a firm of boys which advertised and issued a small catalogue of Indian curiosities for sale at that period. Several large collections of Indian relics are owned in Sewickley Valley, the largest—a wonderful assembly of rare specimens—is that in the residence of Captain Frederick Dippold, at Glen Osborne, the entire family being active enthusiasts in the collection of this class of antiquities.

The name "Sewickley" comes from the Indians, according to each of two conflicting legends. One legend relates that the town was named for the Shawnee word for two creeks, Sawakola (or Sawokle). Sawi means raccoon and ukli means town. Sewickley, therefore, would mean Raccoon Town.[6] According to the other legend, Sewickley means sweetwater in some unspecified Indian language, referring to the sap of maple trees. The land along the river contained many maple trees, remembered today in Maple Lane just south of the Ohio River Boulevard. Here the Indians made maple syrup from the sewickley. Reverend Hopkins' children discovered the Indian's interest in maple syrup when they came to Sewickley in the 1850s and brought home "small quaint stone jars with little bark-covered wooden troughs set in a niche cut in a sugar mapletree for the sweetwater to run into. These trophies were always carried home with joy."[7]

Despite evidence that Sewickley was a popular place among the Indians, they offered to give it to their good friend, Colonel George Morgan, in 1779. Morgan had been a fair and honest dealer with the Indians since 1766, when he built and managed the store and warehouse of the Pittsburgh branch of the Philadelphia firm Bynton, Wharton, and Morgan. He handled trading with the Indians as far away as Illinois. In 1776, he was appointed Indian agent, based in Pittsburgh, with the task of keeping the Indians from joining with the British during the Revolution. He convinced the Delawares, Shawnee, and Seneca to attend a meeting in Pittsburgh in October 1776 where, in return for promises of friendship and neutrality, they received a large present from the Continental Congress.[8] Morgan remained in Pittsburgh until 1779, always attempting to smooth relations with the Indians. The Delaware called him Tamenend, the affable one, after one of their great chiefs. In May 1779, while Morgan was visiting his family, who were living in Princeton, he was met by a delegation of Delaware Indians. Chief Kezlement addressed Morgan as follows:

> The Delaware Nation have experienced great advantages from your wise Councils [sic] and from your Truth and Justice in representing their real sentiments and dispositions to the Congress of the United States. You have at all times studied the good of our Nation and done all in your Power to promote the Happiness of our women and children and of our posterity. You have now entertained a considerable number of us for some time, and you have kindly undertaken the care of some of our children who we have brought here to be educated. We see your own children and we look on them with pleasure as on our own.

> For these considerations and in order to show our love for you and for your family we now give you a tract of Land in our country that you may call your own and which you and your children may possess and enjoy forever. . . . It begins at the mouth of the run, opposite the foot of Montour's Island, we mean the lower end of the island [where Haysville now stands,] and extending down the river Ohio to the run next to Logstown, bounded by the said two runs and the river Ohio, and extending back from the river Ohio to the tops of the highest hills. . . . This tract contains the whole of the Sewickley Bottom, which is very good land, and we desire that you and your children may accept and possess it for ever.[9]

Although the offer was repeated two times, each time Morgan refused. He said he had already been paid by the government for doing his job and if he accepted a free gift, it could lead to claims by others for similar gifts, or it could encourage dishonest white men to get the Indians drunk in order to cheat them of their lands.[10] Morgan advised the Indians never to give away their lands.[11]

As a result of Colonel Morgan's forbearance, Indians remained in Sewickley at least until the end of the eighteenth century. James Steele was interviewed in 1872, when he was 89 years old. He remembered that when he came to Sewickley Bottom in 1796, he saw an Indian village of 14 huts up Big Sewickley Creek. John Way, Jr., writing in 1888, remembered that in his youth there had been "a colony of Indians [which] dwelt up Big Sewickley Creek in wretched huts made of poles, covered with clay; and yet they used the bow and arrow."[12]

Even though the Indians were expelled almost 200 years ago, western Pennsylvanians trace their steps every day as they travel the many roads which follow ancient Indian paths. The Forbes Road, now Route 30, followed the old Raystown Indian path. The Beaver Road, from Pittsburgh to Beaver, was an Indian path before becoming a crude road about 1778. General Anthony Wayne turned it into a military road in 1792, when he used it to drill his troops for battle with the Indians. Wayne's winter quarters were about three miles north of Big Sewickley Creek on the Ohio River in Legionville, described by an early traveler as "a collection of Miserable log Huts [with a] mingling of the Indian Nations and a Parcel of reprobate Indian Traders, which is nevertheless the principall Mart of Trade in the Region and the beginning of all westward journeys."[13] Although Legionville sounds unpleasant, the soldiers must have admired the surrounding area because many remained. Some of the oldest families in the Sewickley area, such as the Merrimans, are descended from soldiers in General Wayne's army who settled there after deserting or after their enlistments ended.

Despite its location on a flat plain right on the river, Sewickley was not settled by whites until after the Revolution. Other towns which seem no more attractive were settled earlier. Brownsville had started in 1759 as a frontier fort. Washington, settled about 1769, had 23,901 inhabitants in 1790. Hannastown, near Greensburg, had 30 log houses when it was burned by the Indians in 1782. The reason Sewickley was so late was political, not geographical. Until after 1784, Indians owned the land north of the Allegheny and Ohio rivers and settlement was forbidden. The English tried to enforce this ban by a law stating,

> Whereas many disorderly people in violation of his majesty's proclamation have presumed to settle upon the lands not yet purchased from the Indians, [any settler] being legally convicted was to be punished with death without benefit of clergy.[14]

In 1784 the Commonwealth of Pennsylvania purchased all the land north of the Ohio River. The Commonwealth decided to use its newly acquired land to fulfill two promises it had made in order to encourage enlistment in the Revolutionary War: to pay soldiers in a sound currency and to reward them with free land. The northern part of the new territory, running to Lake Erie, was set aside as Donation Lands. Revolutionary War veterans received free land in relation to their rank: a major general received four 500 acre lots; a lieutenant, two 200 acre lots; and a private, one 200 acre lot. The southern part of the newly purchased land, including all of the Sewickley area, became the Depreciation Lands. Certificates to purchase the Depreciation Lands were issued to soldiers of the Pennsylvania line who had been paid in Continental certificates which, it turned out, were not "worth a Continental." Their value in relation to gold had plummeted. In 1777 the ratio was 3 to 1. By 1780 it had risen to 75 to 1. When the Commonwealth lacked cash to make up the difference, Benjamin Franklin suggested giving the soldiers certificates which, for purposes of buying Depreciation Lands, were equal to gold or silver for land in the newly acquired territory.

The Commonwealth directed that the Depreciation Lands be surveyed and laid out in lots of 200 to 350 acres. As soon as 100 lots had been surveyed, they were to be sold, the full sum to be paid in gold, silver, or depreciation certificates.[15] Four surveyors were appointed. The western part of the Sewickley area was surveyed by Daniel Leet and the eastern part by Nathaniel Breading (sometimes spelled Braden). A north-south line divided the two districts. This imaginary line became Division Street, which ran diagonally through the town.

Lots in Daniel Leet's district were the first and the last of the Depreciation Lands to be sold. The first sales of 32,000 acres were made in Philadelphia in 1785. The next sales, also of 32,000 acres, were in Nathaniel Breading's district. Seventeen thousand of these acres were returned and had to be resold the next year, "the original purchasers having failed to comply with the terms of sale." Two hundred tracts in Leet's district were returned and resold but, according to a report to the Supreme Executive Council of Pennsylvania, the resale was a failure. "To my great surprise and mortification, the 27 lots which were sold on that day averaged only £5 8s 4d per 100 acres."[16]

Sales did not go well because most of the Revolutionary soldiers who received certificates were from the eastern part of the state and did not want to move out to the wilderness. They sold their certificates to speculators who hoped to make a quick profit. By 1787, when sales were discontinued, less than half of the Depreciation Lands had been sold, for an average price of 28 cents an acre.

Although the Commonwealth and the soldiers did not gain much from the sales, some of the surveyors did. According to Judge Agnew in his book on the Depreciation Lands, the surveyors were not supposed to give or act on information about the quality of the lots because their inside information gave them unfair advantage. They did anyway, as an early history relates. "There were not wanting those among the surveyors who took advantage of the county to secure good tracts for themselves."[17] One who took advantage was Sewickley's surveyor, Daniel Leet, according to Judge Agnew. "Daniel Leet, Surveyor of the Second Depreciation District, got large and valuable land on the Sewickley Bottom."[18] Leet's "large and valuable land" was what is now the western half of Edgeworth Borough. Some of it has remained in the family more than 200 years.

There were two reasons for the lack of interest in settlement of the Depreciation Lands. One was fear of the Indians. Isolated Indian attacks continued in the area until 1794, when Mad Anthony Wayne won the battle of Fallen Timbers. His victory cleared the way for the settlers to move to land in Pittsburgh and the West. The other reason was the likelihood of disputes over land titles. In 1792 the General Assembly of Pennsylvania, anxious to promote the settlement of its western lands, passed an act offering warrants to all land north of the Allegheny and Ohio rivers to "persons who will cultivate and improve the same . . . within two years" and to persons who had already settled on a piece of land. The second part of this act encouraged squatters. People who tried to settle or sell their land found that squatters had been issued warrants for the same tract by right of settlement. The conflicts continued for years. Land title cases were the most frequent and important matters to come before the courts, causing what Judge Daniel Agnew called in 1887 "the greatest litigation and uncertainty of title which ever ruined the prosperity of a new country."[19]

[1] Hugh Cleland, *George Washington in the Ohio Valley*. Pittsburgh, University Press, 1955, p. 250.

[2] Solon J. and Elizabeth Hawthorn Buck, *The Planting of Civilization in Western Pennsylvania*. Pittsburgh: The University Press, 1939, p. 7-13.

[3] Cleland, p. 251.

[4] F. Cumming, *Sketches of a Tour of the Western Country*, Pittsburgh, Cramer, Spear, Eichbaum, 1810, p. 251.

[5] Ibid., p. 20-21.

[6] *History of Pittsburgh and Environs*. American Historical Society, 1922, v.3, p. 764.

[7] Letter from Mary Gardiner Lipp to Gilbert Hays, 26 Feb. 1913, in Hays collection.

[8] Buck, p. 185.

[9] Joseph A. Bausman, *History of Beaver County, Pennsylvania*, N.Y., Knickerbocker, 1904, v.l, p. 68.

[10] *Fiftieth Anniversary Exercises of the Presbyterian Church, Sewickley, Pennsylvania, 1838-1888*. Pittsburgh. W.W. Water, n.d., p. 13-14.

[11] Max Saville, *George Morgan, Colony Builder*. New York: Columbia Univ. Press, 1932, p. 164.

[12] *History of the Presbyterian Church of Sewickley*, 1888, p. 107.

[13] Stefan Lorant, *Pittsburgh the Story of an American City*. Pittsburgh, The University Press, 1964, p. 8.

[14] *Laws of Commonwealth of Pennsylvania*. Republished, Philadelphia: John Bioren, 1810, v.2, p. 124.

[15] Ibid., p. 6.

[16] Pennsylvania Land Office, *Report of Internal Affairs*, 1892, p. 768.

[17] *History of Allegheny County Pennsylvania*. A. Warner, 1889, v.2, p. 112.

[18] Daniel Agnew, *A History of the Region of Pennsylvania North of the Ohio and West of the Allegheny River*. Philadelphia, Kay & Bro., 1887

[19] Ibid., p. 119.

Chapter 2
Settlement Before the Railroad

Despite troubles getting and keeping good title to land, Sewickley was gradually settled during the first half of the nineteenth century. A modern resident, however, would have great trouble recognizing the area as it was in 1850. Some of the original forest was cleared for field and pasture by 1850. A discerning modern eye could pick out Newington, David Shields' house on the river in what is now Edgeworth. Otherwise, the landscape was sparsely dotted with houses and farms.

Population Figures

The 1820 and 1850 censuses give very general pictures of the area. Specific information on the modern subdivisions, Sewickley, Edgeworth, Osborne, and Sewickley Heights, is lacking. They were all part of the larger Ohio Township. In 1820 the total population of Ohio Township was 1,145. There were 201 listings of heads of households. The only information given in this very early census is the age, sex and race of members of the household. The average size of each household was 5.7 people. This is almost double the average size in Pennsylvania in 1980 (2.74). More astonishing is the number of outsized households. For example, John Way had ten others living with him.

John Way's Household in 1820

Age:	Under 10	10-16	16-25	26-45	45-
Males		1	1	1	1
Females	2		3		1
Colored				1	

James Merriman had 12 in his household. His was the largest of six Merriman households with a total of 48 members. The first Merriman, Frederick, had come to Sewickley with Mad Anthony Wayne's expedition against the Indians. Frederick settled in Sewickley and started a population explosion of his own.

There were 21 households in Ohio Township-Sewickley with ten or more members; 31 with nine or more. The largest household listed was Nathan McFerson's, a misspelling of McPherson. He had 15 people living with him:

Nathan McPherson's Household in 1820

Age:	Under 10	10-16	16-25	26-45	45-
Males	3	2	4	2	
Females	3	1		1	

Two members of this household were engaged in commerce. The McPherson family remains in the area and includes Richard McPherson, Jr. who lives in Murrysville near Pittsburgh.

Fourteen households were headed by women. These must have been widows because unmarried women of the time lived with relatives. The only woman who lived alone was Betsey Boring, aged between 26 and 45, but she was near John Boring and his wife, also between 26 and 45. Other women headed large households. Addy Beer lived near Robert Beer in an eight-person household. Patty Frampton headed a household of 10:

Patty Frampton's Household.

Age:	10-16	16-25	26-45	45-
Males	2	4	1	
Females	1		1	1

Two members of this household were engaged in commerce.

There are only two black families listed in the 1820 census. One was headed by Daniel Mulron, or Mulson. His family of "free colored persons" included one male under 26, one female under 26, and one colored female over 45. The other black family was headed by Prisila [sic] Wallace.

The 1850 census gives more information on each household. All household heads were of English, Scotch-Irish, or German extraction. In 1850 there were 800 people in 380 households in the whole area. Thirty percent (114) possessed taxable property. Two-thirds of those with taxable property were native-born and the others were first generation from the British Isles or Germany.[1]

Transportation

The census figures give numbers but not the idea of what it was like to live in the Sewickley area in the early nineteenth century. Families had to be fairly self-sufficient because of the remoteness of the area. Sewickley was isolated from the rest of the world.

A stagecoach going from Pittsburgh to Wooster, Ohio stopped each day in Sewickley, but the 14 miles from Sewickley to Pittsburgh by stage took about three hours. An advertisement in a Pittsburgh paper in 1835 stated:

> The Western Mail Line for Beaver, New Lisbon, Canton, Wooster leaves daily at 4:00 A.M. Through Economy to Beaver in 6 hours, fare $1.50 Leaves from General Stage Office, 42 Wood Street.[2]

The stagecoach was slowed by traffic problems unknown to modern travelers, according to "Uncle Joe," who recalled,

> You can hardly realize what our town was like in the days of long ago [in the 1840s]. Droves of cattle, sheep and horses passed up our main street almost daily, and, would you believe it, sometimes a large drove of turkeys being taken in that way from one city to another.[3]

Because roads were poor, the Ohio River provided the best link between Sewickley and other places. The first packet boat providing regular service between Cincinnati and Pittsburgh started in 1793. It made the round trip in four weeks. An advertisement promised an adventurous voyage:

> The proprietor of thefe boats having maturely considered the many inconveniences and dangers incident to the common method hitherto adopted of navigating the Ohio, and being influenced by love of philanthropy, and defire to be fervicable to the public, has taken great pains to render the accommodations on board the boats as agreeable and convenient as they could poffibly be made.

> No danger need be apprehended from the enemy, as every perfon on board will be under cover, made proof againft rifle or musquet balls and convenient port holes for firing out of. Each of the boats are armed with fix pieces carrying a pound ball; alfo a number of good mufkets and amply fupplied with plenty of ammunition, ftrongly manned with choice hands, and the mafters of approved knowledge.[4]

The first boat powered by steam to pass Sewickley was the "New Orleans," which made the first run from Pittsburgh to New Orleans in 1811. Soon daily steamboat service on the Ohio River was the best connection with Pittsburgh. It must have been around 1850 that Miss Agnes Ellis employed an early form of hitchhiking to get to Pittsburgh by steamboat. She waited on the boat landing of a house down by the river and, when she saw a boat coming, waved her handkerchief to get it to pick her up.[5] "Uncle Joe" told a similar story.

> An occasional steamboat going up and down the Ohio river was our only means of reaching the adjacent cities and towns. A large frame house near the boat landing was our waiting place for the oft-times long-delayed boat. All who came to the house were given a hearty welcome, and many times there were hours of waiting, when the hostess insisted upon giving food as well as rest. What warm and lasting friendships were formed during those hours of waiting and travel.[6]

River transportation was unreliable, however, because of variations in the river. In times of drought, ice, or flood the river was impassable. For about fifteen weeks a year the water was too low for traffic. General Anthony Wayne's campaign against the Indians in 1792-93 was stalled by the river. His difficulties moving men and supplies are documented in his letters to Secretary of War Henry Knox.

> August 24, 1792. The Water of the Ohio is too low for Navigation but I hope it will not long be the case.

> August 31. At present nothing can be done by Water—the Ohio has never been so low in the memory of the Oldest Inhabitants.

September 7. [Supplies for the troops could not be replenished.] Some of the provisions are not fit for use. We were fed but from hand to mouth. It's true that the rivers are not navigable, which is the only excuse that can with propriety be made.

October 12. We have a favorable prospect of the River being up from a heavy and constant fall of rain all Night, which continues to encrease [sic].

November 29. I have the honor to inform you that the Legion embark'd at Pittsburgh yesterday morning and encamped at this place [Legionville] last evening without any accidents.

[Wayne suspected the Indians of using the river as a weapon of war. If they could drag out peace negotiations long enough into the summer, Wayne would not have time to launch a campaign before the river closed. The Indians hoped the water would get] too low for navigation and to prevent us from making the necessary arrangements in season for Offensive Operations.[7]

Wayne's problems were not unusual. In 1849, for instance, traffic was blocked from the middle of summer until the first week of October. At these times commerce stalled. Merchants could not send their products down the river for sale. Unemployment rose. Prices of coal in Cincinnati and other river towns skyrocketed.[8]

Even when the river was open, travel was risky. Zadoc Cramer offered advice and admonitions to settlers going west.

The first thing to be attended to by emigrants or traders wanting to descend the river is to procure a boat, to be ready so as to take advantage of the times of floods and to be careful that the boat be a good one: for many of the accidents that happen in navigating the Ohio and the Mississippi, are owing to the unpardonable carelessness or penuriousness of the boat builder, who will frequently slight his work, or make it of injured plank. . . .

The best seasons for navigating the Ohio are in spring and autumn. The spring season commences at the breaking up of the ice, which generally happens about the middle of February, and continues good for about three months. The fall season generally commences in October, and continues until about the 1st of December, when the ice frequently begins to form.

But freshes in the rivers are not entirely confined to spring and fall. Freshes however are not to be depended on, and when they occur, must be taken immediate advantage of, as the waters subside rapidly.[9]

In the dry season, riverboats were stuck in port, waiting for higher water. Meanwhile, men could wade across in many places and a horse and wagon could carry cargo with no need for ferries. Sometimes traffic accidents might involve two unlikely parties. Captain Way, a Sewickley native and the foremost historian of the inland waterways, remembered a story of a steamboat going slowly through the fog that nearly crashed into a farmer's wagon in the middle of the river. Produce crossing the river by wagon often included the delicious asparagus grown on Neville Island and served at the Waldorf Astoria in New York City.

In winter, if the water was low, the river froze. Then sleds replaced boats. Helen Hegner remembered, "Before the dams were built, the river froze over. They hauled hay and straw in the winter across the ice—didn't have to use the ferry."

Sometimes there was too much water in the river. Floods were a constant worry in the spring and fall until the flood control dams were built after 1936. Firsthand accounts of early floods in Sewickley itself are not available but an anonymous author living in a cabin down the Ohio River from Fort Duquesne recalled a flood in 1757.

We had formed a sort of little village composed of about 60 cabins of wood, where a part of the garrison lodged; I had also set up there a little cottage where it sometimes happened that I slept. . . . I had the curiosity to pass the night of the flood there the better to see the effect. . . . I threw myself completely dressed on my bed. [Later], seeing neither fire nor light, I reached my arm out to the ground and felt the water; I immediately mounted to the loft where I saw by the loft window many people in boats in the plain with torches to lead people onto higher ground; then I took the course of calling out; a man came to me with a boat who guided me to the ground like the others; there were already a number of cabins carried off. . . . I was surprised like the others to see the water subside as quickly as it had come, for at eight o'clock in the morning it was no longer on the bank.[10]

Many remembered when the frightening 1936 flood reached Sewickley. Charles Butler watched the river rise.

We saw houses come down, hit the piers of the bridge. Chickens were on top of the chicken houses; dogs on top of dog houses. Oh, it was a pitiful sight. We were in it down on Chadwick Street. They had to come get us in a boat. The water came up so fast—in half an hour. We had one and a half feet in the first floor. In Edgeworth, too, the water came clear up to Sand Hill.

Roseanne Reiser lived on Challis Lane. She remembered preparations for the 1936 flood.

My father took the motor out of the washing machine. We moved all the furniture up to the second floor. Then, the flood stopped: it only flooded our basement. We were the only house [on Challis Lane] that didn't get the first floor flooded.

Anne Stolzenbach remembered her experience of the 1936 flood:

[When] I came home on the train, I said to my father, "I think there is going to be a flood." Father said, "You always exaggerate so." Next morning, I went to Herbst Gas Station. He said, "Where are you going?" "To town." "You can't get there." "But I go the back way." "Millvale is closed too. Go home and enjoy yourself." I was home for a week. Had to go into safe deposit boxes and hang out certificates to dry.

Flood 1936. An Osborne woman escaping from the second floor of her house by rowboat. *The Sewickley Herald.*

Captain Way moved into his house on 121 River Avenue just before the 1936 flood. "We were greeted by the flood. The water came up and made ponds on each side of the house, but didn't reach us. There was no way to tell how high it was going to go." Captain Way owned an 18-foot rowboat, "Lady Grace", which was pressed into service for rescues. They were called to recover the contents of the Duquesne Foundry safe, left behind when the water flooded the plant. They loaded the rowboat on the company truck, but first they had to evacuate a family in Osborne. Then, according to Captain Way, "there was a dire need of a rowboat in Edgeworth on Pine, between Hazel and Orchard, to remove valuables from the homes in that section. So the 'Lady Grace' was borrowed for that task."

The substation of the Duquesne Light Company was flooded, shutting off power in the Valley except for Edgeworth which had emergency pumps. Radios did not function, nor did the printing press of the *Herald*. The editor, Ross W. Buck, ordered print set on the old hand press, and managed to bring out an extra edition dated Thursday, March 19, the day after the flood crested. It described conditions in Edgeworth.

At the peak Wednesday night, water reached Meadow and Chestnut in Edgeworth, with Challis Lane, School St., lower Quaker, Orchard Lane, Orchard Place, Elm Street and Hazel Lane under water. Edgeworth Volunteer Firemen worked all day and all night, rescuing people from houses and stalled cars. The bottom fell out of an old flat-bottomed boat they were using to transport two ladies to safety, and they were thrown into nine feet of water. Charles Singer, John McCrea and Jim Reno swam to their aid and rescued them. They were taken to the Elmhurst Inn.

Paul Griffin, Woodland Road, was stalled in his car in water on the Ohio River Boulevard with water up to his chest. He was rescued by "Honey" Hatton, John McCrea and Ray Singer in a row boat.[11]

After the water subsided, there was "a lot of cleaning to do," according to Charles Butler. John Alexander remembered that books, carpets, and furniture were all ruined but most of the houses remained.

Even when the river was navigable, it presented problems. One was finding a channel. The river was obstructed throughout its entire length by snags, rocks, and gravel or sand bars. The depth over bars at extreme low water was about one foot. Dead Man's Island and ripple near Edgeworth, now drowned by the Dashields Dam and Locks, was troublesome. Zadoc Cramer explained how to navigate it in 1808.

Dead Man's island and ripple.

In high water this island is covered—you pass it on the right; the channel is very serpentine. Being in the middle of the river at its head, where there is a ripple, you must pull for the right shore, and again to the right shore, thence towards the island, then again to the right shore, and again toward the left, which will put you clear of Dead Man's ripple just below the island, where the water is very rough and looks dangerous.[12]

One early Sewickley entrepreneur used navigation problems to his advantage. Henry Ulery built a house on riverfront land he bought in 1798. He noticed that in times of low water, keelboats had great difficulty getting up through the swift and narrow channel below the present U.S. Coast Guard Station. Mr. Ulery fixed a rope for the keelboatmen to use to pull themselves through the chute. Because his charge for the aid varied according to whim, the shoals became known as Ulery's Trap.[13]

Oil-burning lights along the River aided navigation. In 1880 there were 600 lights between Pittsburgh and the Mississippi River. The Edgeworth light, located 50 yards west of Edgeworth Lane, burned from dusk to dawn and all day long if the weather was foggy. George Gibb, Sr., aided by his nine sons and one daughter, tended the light from 1878 to 1928. The tender "Lilly" brought a new supply of oil every three months.

The river aided transportation to Pittsburgh and Ohio, but blocked commerce from the north and south. There was no sure way to cross the river until the ferries started operations sometime after 1847.

A Self-Sufficient Life

Like transportation, communication was primitive and unreliable. There was no paper or magazine in Sewickley. No Pittsburgh paper was delivered until 1848 when the *Chronicle* was mailed to David Shields. There were no clubs and no government to encourage people to get together. The only public gathering places were the inns where people could hear news of the outside world. One unifying force was religion, but the population was so spread out that churches were too far from many who would have welcomed both the chance to practice their religion and to socialize among themselves.

Because of this isolation, the settlers were dependent on the forest to provide many of the raw materials for necessities: hickory for making tool handles and ox yokes; walnut for fence posts and buildings; dogwood for tool handles; locust and chestnut for fence posts; beech for charcoal; oak for fence posts, firewood, shingles and cabins; white pine for frame buildings and maple for furniture. Some trees provided food: fruit from wild plum and crab apple; nuts from walnut and hickory. The forest also provided a habitat for animals to hunt. Other food came directly from the Ohio River: perch, pike, catfish, sturgeon, bass, turtle and eel. To supplement nature's bounty, settlers had to clear land for planting a vegetable garden and raising grain for the family cow and horse.

More specific information on the natural history of Sewickley in the 1830s comes from David Shields' diary.

December 16, 1830: It may be worthy of notice for the inquisitive eye of a future reader that of the original wild game of this country, there are red deer and turkies on the hills immediately back of Sewickley Bottom [Edgeworth]. A wolf was killed near this place some five or six years hence. None have been since. Opossums, foxes, mink, raccoons are numerous here at all times.

November 8, 1834: A bear was killed yesterday by one of the Scotts, about two miles up the creek [Little Sewickley]. Bears have been strangers in this part of the country for many years. This autumn, there have been several seen, who probably have come from the north, there being no nuts or acorns in the country.[14]

Captain John Anderson, born in 1828, remembered Sewickley when he was a boy. His conversation on July 12, 1923 with Bayard Christy was recorded by a stenographer.

"Do you remember, Mr. Anderson, that there were Wild [Passenger] Pigeons about here?"

"Yes, I remember when there used to be lots of them in the woods. They were in the white-oak trees and ate the acorns; sometimes there would be so many get on the limb they would almost break it off. . . . They came in the latter part of September and October and some would stay all year round."

"How large were the flocks?"

"I would say some of them would have thousands of them in, or more."

"They were pretty good eating?"

"Yes, they were right good."

"Did you ever see turkey in the woods here?"

"Oh, yes, I remember lots of turkeys. . . . I would see the turkeys up what is called the Camp-meeting Road. The land there belonged to the Shields estate and the Economites. That's where the white oaks and chestnuts were. Very little timber had been cut out on it. After the weather would begin to get snow on the ground, we would find them [the turkeys] in the corn fields. The country farther back [from the hills beyond the river] was more settled. The nearer hills were not. There used to be immense woods there. It wasn't half cleared out when I was a boy and that is where the turkeys were."

"I suppose lots of them were shot?"

"Yes, and squirrels, too. We always would kill a few Pigeons when we went after squirrels. There were a great many deer. The deer would stay up on the flat that I sold to Mr. Oliver, up there on the branch of Hoey's Run. Where the two branches come together, near Mrs. Rea's stables, that was a great place for deer."

The abundant wildlife described by Captain Anderson and David Shields was soon reduced by competition with settlers. John James Audubon remembered seeing the fall migration of passenger pigeons in 1814.

The air was literally filled with pigeons, and the noonday light was obscured as by an eclipse. The dung fell in spots not unlike melting flakes of snow, and the continuous buzz of wings tended to lull my senses.[15]

Audubon estimated that each flock had over a billion birds, and he counted 160 flocks in 21 minutes. Men clubbed the pigeons to death and fed them to the hogs. The last survivor died in the Cincinnati zoo in 1914.

Bounty laws encouraged destruction of wildlife. When Pennsylvania adopted its first bounty law in 1683, it was for wolves only. In 1724 it added foxes; in 1740, squirrels. Later puma and bobcat were included. The 1819 bounty law provided twelve dollars for the scalp of a grown wolf or panther; five dollars for an immature panther or wolf puppy. All the animals included in the bounty law except squirrels were extirpated in Pennsylvania before 1900.[16]

[1] Mary Florence Brown, *The Sewickley Valley in the Nineteenth Century.* Paper, University of Pittsburgh, 1970, p. 9.

[2] *Statesman*, January 31, 1835, p. 1.

[3] Uncle Joe, *Memories of Sweet Valley: or 40 Years Ago and Now.* Pittsburgh, Murdoch, Kerr, 1890, p. 17.

[4] *Ohio River Handbook*, Cincinnati, Young & Klein, 1950. n.p.

[5] Agnes Ellis, *Lights and Shadows of Sewickley Life.* Philadelphia, J.B. Lippincott, 1893, p. 36.

[6] Uncle Joe, p. 6.

[7] Anthony Wayne, *A Name in Arms.* University of Pittsburgh Press, 1960, pp. 79-230.

[8] E. Douglas Branch, "Success to the Railroad." In *Western Pennsylvania Historical Magazine*, March 1937, v. 20 # 1, p. 10.

[9] Zadoc Cramer, *Ohio and Mississippi Navigator*, 1802 and 1904. Repiir & Karl Yost Morrison, 1987, p. 9-10.

[10] John W Harpster, ed., *Pen Pictures of Western Pennsylvania.* University of Pittsburgh Press, 1938, p. 40.

[11] *The Sewickley Herald*, March 12, 1986, p. 4 and 6.

[12] Zadoc Cramer, "The Navigator." In *Ohio River Handbook and Picture Album.* Cincinnati, Young & Ke, 1950, p.z-4.

[13] Frederick Way Jr., "The Trap" in *S&D Reflector*, v. 18, no. 1, page 45.

[14] Quoted by B. G. Shields in the *Sewickley Herald*, 1993.

[15] Walter Havighurst, *River to the West*, N.Y., Putnam, 1970, p. 153.

[16] Stanley P. Young and Edward A. Goldman, *The Wolves of North America.* New York, Dover, 1944, v.1, p. 257.

Chapter 3
Life in the Sewickley Valley as seen in the Way Family Papers

The interview with Captain Anderson, a rare example of oral history, provides a glimpse of early Sewickley in his day. More than a glimpse, perhaps a stare, comes from a more traditional source, four boxes of the personal papers of the Way family. The Ways were among the first settlers of the area that is now Edgeworth, just west of Sewickley on the Ohio River. The Way family remained in the area until 1991. John Way's great-grandson, Captain Frederick Way, Jr., born in 1901, lived on River Avenue. He spent his career on the river, becoming captain of the "Betsy Anne," a working steamboat on the three rivers. He wrote several books on riverboats.

Captain Frederick Way, Jr. gave the voluminous Way papers to the Historical Society of Western Pennsylvania in 1934. The papers are not well arranged and are difficult to impossible to read. Some are scraps of paper as small as two by three inches with a scrawled note saying something like "I owe you $2.50." Because paper was very expensive at the time, a whole page was not wasted on a short note. It seems strange to see such a scrap of paper dated 1805. The Way papers are important because of their inclusiveness. They contain a wealth of information on the details of living in the early nineteenth century. The letters are fascinating because they were not written with an eye to history. They were written to give information or to direct actions. After spending some time with the Way papers, the reader gets a good idea of the pleasures and problems of living in "olden times."

Most of the papers concern John Way but other family members are introduced through letters, deeds, and wills. John's father, Caleb, of Chester County, Pennsylvania, enters the scene briefly and is seen no more. In 1785 Caleb Way bought a 200-acre tract for £225 in what is now Edgeworth. It was called it Way's Desire. Caleb did not move to the new property but he sold it to his son, John, for 60 cents in 1810. John had moved west in 1797 with his wife, Mary Clark Way, to settle. His grandson, John Way Jr., describes him in a handwritten memo:

> John was a watchmaker by trade. He and laborers cleared a portion of his father's purchase west of Pittsburg, built a house (log) and settled here. He became land agent and surveyor for the wild tracts of land for many miles around, was one of the first justices of the peace appointed by the governor of the county of Allegheny, and held the appointment until his death.

The Way papers include correspondence of John and his three sons and one daughter: Nicholas was a farmer in Sewickley; James became a merchant in St. Louis; Rebecca married Able Townsend. The other son, Abishai, a successful wholesale and retail merchant in Pittsburgh, was the local agent for the Harmony Society in Economy, handling their trade in large quantities of wool and other products.

Like many early settlers, John Way used his log house on the river for only a short time. In 1810 he built what is thought to be the first brick house in the area. It is still standing on Beaver Road in Edgeworth.

Health Matters

The letters are mostly about business transactions; details of personal affairs are few. There is some mention of health. In cases of sickness, family communication always improves. Sickness and death were always lurking and diagnoses and remedies were scarce. Nicholas sums up the attitude to sickness in a letter to Abishai in 1836.

> I have a bad cold, or rather the influenza, the scarlet fever is in the neighborhood. Elias Grimes' only child aged about 4 died this morning, a very interesting little boy. I fear our family will have to contend with it 'ere long.

In the early nineteenth century there was not much doctors could do to cure sickness. Some were not even trusted to help at all, as John Way complains in a letter to William Vicary.

> The Doctor Miller you mentioned lives adjoining me above. He is here called a poor Quack rather much quackery in many things. He has engaged to pay $55 rent next April. I know not how he is to pay it.

John Way's own last illness is well chronicled. He must have foreseen problems when he left for a visit in Chester County. He writes his son, Nicholas, on August 15, 1825:

> Now remember the care of our property and ourselves devolves principally on thee, being the head of the family, and request that the residue of the family will be governed accordingly. The eyes of your neibours will be upon your conduct— and not only so but the great father of all good that sees in secret knows not only every act of the creature but their very

thoughts. We hope and pray that you may all act with dignity and temperance in all things here, and hereafter [the great father] may say well done good and faithful steward thou shalt be rewarded tenfold. It seems to me that thou should be last up and first up in the morning [to] see that the house is shut up and the fire secured. The main thing is to save what we have that no waste may be negligence etc. etc.

[Signed] JW

We soon hear that John Way's premonitions were correct. On Oct. 11, 1825, Abishai reports on a visit his clerk paid John Way,

He says that on the friday before he was with father who was quite clear of his fever and getting better fast but on monday he was attacked with an inflammation of the urinary canal with an obstruction of urine which became very alarming. Another Physician was called from Downingtown and on Thursday. They operated on him and produced a discharge of urine and blood which gave him considerable ease but the case is considered dangerous nor do they [give] us much hope of his recovery. A.W.

James Way, John's son, seems to have been either sickly or something of a hypochondriac. His letters dwell on sickness. He writes Nicholas on Sept. 29, 1827:

Mary Ann [Abishai's wife] continues dangerously ill. Dr. Moury attends her. Dr. says there are yet good symptoms of recovery but I think it very doubtful indeed whether she will ever rise again from her bed. She is excessively weak and a continued high fever, her head is so weak on the least agitation, she becomes quite flighty. Abishai is not well, he is distressed and fatigued, being up day and night.

Yr Bro Jas Way.

Mary Ann did recover but James continued to fret. He writes Nicholas in September, 1832: "I hope the Asiatic Scourge may not touch in Sewickley." When not worrying about the health of others, he could always think of his own. In a January, 1831 letter to Nicholas he writes:

Say to Mother that with the exception of this 10 days, my constitution is improving by change of air, scene. Living the active life I am now engaged in [my constitution]—which I do contend was once good but was much impaired during the 4 or 5 last years of my stay in Pittsburg. Had I remained there, I would now have been "one foot in the grave."

Despite this improved constitution, he was careful about his health. He writes Nicholas in July 1833:

Abishai may leave for Pittsburg in a week but I dislike travelling much in that direction until I hear the country is perfectly restored to health. Not that I fear contagion but the heat of stage travelling or confinement on a little shoal waterboat will create bile. Too much violent exercise or confinement or riding at night are equally bad. I find by the public paper that cholera had at length visited Pittsburg. It behooves you to be careful of your family as the disease has proved fatal in the villages in the interior of Kentucky. It will be well to abstain as much as possible from all fruits and vegetables, potatoes excepted. Be careful in the case of dysentery amongst your children. If it is allowed to run even a few hours, death will be the consequence.

James gives advice on the care of his elderly mother. First in a letter to Nicholas on October 1833:

I write a few lines to mother as it is almost impossible for me to make her hear owing to her deafness. I enclose a letter for her. I hope you and Abishai will both bear with our mother; she is getting old and frail. [Later in a letter to his brother-in-law, A. Townsend, dated May 30, 1837.] It is with feelings of regret I hear of the dilapidated state of Mother's health. Could it be possible for her to divest herself of the habit of "all work" it would prove beneficial for her health, but the force of habit is irresistible I suppose. At her time of life every unnecessary exertion and exposure makes rapid inroads upon the constitution and cuts years from many a useful life and adds to the few remaining years not but pain and misery.

The Squire's Work

Such are the only glimpses of personal life reflected in the Way papers. In contrast, the business affairs of the family are detailed at extraordinary length. John Way was involved in just about everything that went on in the Sewickley Valley from crime to real-estate deals. The most important facet of his career for historical purposes is his long-standing service as justice of the peace. Justices of the peace, usually addressed as Squire, were involved in all sorts of local happenings. Justices were appointed by the governor and held office "during good behaviour." Because the justices were not elected, they were above the fray of local politics. John Way remained justice until his death in 1825.

Justices of the peace had many duties, according to *Binn's Justice*, 1840.

Every criminal offense is presumed to be within the scope of their authority to inquire into, take bail, to commit the accused unless the justices' jurisdiction was bonded by the common law, or has been limited or taken away by our Constitution or acts of Assembly. In civil matters . . . they, in most cases, hold the place, and exercise the authority of both court and jury. They pass on the law and the facts.[1]

Squire John Way was the local judge where wrangling citizens came to have quarrels adjudicated. Most of his cases mentioned in the papers are summarized but some are sufficiently detailed to be re-enacted on television soap operas. Consider the following plot. In 1807 Mary Boyd came before Squire Way to bring a civil suit against Sarah Wright. Mary Boyd complained:

One cross-barred wool and cotton gown woven last spring [was] taken from her house and there is just cause to suspect and that she doth suspect that some part of the said gown are in the lining of a bedquilt and concealed in the house of Jeremiah Wright.

Many witnesses were called to testify in this case. Jeremiah Wright, the defendant's husband, said he was "generally home since April last and has never seen Sarah Wright have any such a thing as Mary Boyd's gown and saith such a thing could not be about his house as there is no lock on the Bureau." Another witness, Ann Wright, said "Sarah Wright never had Mary Boyd's gown."

Testifying for the plaintiff, Ruth Hinkel swore that she "saw a petticoat and it was Mary's." Moreover, Mary Dickson under oath said she spent the night with Sarah and "saw the lower part of a petticoat . . . but did not distinguish it as it was fire light. Sarah appeared to avoid her seeing it and she had not fortitude to ask to see it." Penina Veal said she saw "the material on a little girl and that girl was Levina Wright."

Several other witnesses testified, but Squire Way was not satisfied. He directed the constable, William McDonald, to seize two witnesses who had not appeared and to "make diligent search in the Day time in the house of the said Jeremiah Wright for the said goods and to . . . bring the person in whose custody you find the same before the said John Way." The worthy constable did not wish to conduct the search, complaining that it was "the first thing of the kind he ever done."

Mary Boyd lost the case and was required to pay all costs. The costs included:

Subpoena—$1.15
Wilson attendance 1 day—$1.22
4 days attendance of 2 others—$2.00 each
Mary Dickerson + mileage 24 miles—$.97

Mary Boyd was either unable or unwilling to pay. Nine years later, in 1816, she at least agreed she owed the money. Unable to sign a document admitting the debt, she did put her mark on it.

Mary Boyd

X

her mark

Squire Way presided in another case involving a quarrel between Thomas Backhouse and Alex Duff. Thomas Backhouse was a respectable citizen, serving as a member of the Session of the Presbyterian church. On at least one occasion, however, he lost his temper in a fracas recorded in the Way papers. The first hearing was on April 25, 1816.

W. Clelcon Wood [? the name unreadable] on oath saith that Mr. Duff would not consent to pay for any but one lamb (Mr. Backhouse wanted him to pay for 5 sheep). They both had a good deal of Ruff language and Mr. Duff stript to fite Backhouse who said he did not come there to fight . . . .They had more Ruff words Mr. Duff said he was not afraid to take him in any manly way fisticuff, or pistol.

Mr. Way heard and recorded the testimony. He noted on the back of the report that Mr. Duff paid Way $4.50 on April 25. This was not the end of the matter. On May 8, 1816 the parties were back at Squire Way's office.

John Boggs on oath [said] on first day of Woods Raising [barn raising] Backhouse had a handspike under a log. Duff came as if to take one end thereof. Backhouse stepped back and said he wondered he was not afraid to come. He said he was not. Backhouse said you certainly must when you swore your life against me. Duff said he had not sworn his life against Backhouse. Backhouse said he had or he was wrong informed. Duff said it was a darned lie, he was not afraid of him as a man but as a darned Raskle. Duff advanced toward Backhouse who told him to stand off for he was certainly in danger, or at least said Backhouse would consider myself in danger if I had sworn my life against you. A good deal of conversation was had and Duff said he was not and wood take satisfaction of him. He advanced some steps nigher to Backhouse who told him on his peril not to come any nigher to him. Backhouse said if he came within a yard of him he might be in danger of his life. Duff [offered] to fight Backhouse as a Gentleman with Sword and Pistol then or at any other time. Backhouse did not appear to advance but rather [was] on the Retreat. Duff [brandished] his hands or fists and appeared pretty much in a fiting manner and advanced toward Backhouse but not very near.

Another witness, James Scott, "saith as above and further saith that Backhouse said to Duff, I now give way and call witnesses that he did give way."

Squire Way bound Backhouse and Duff for $100 and Boggs and Scott for $50 as witnesses. Evidently matters were smoothed over because on August 12, 1816, Backhouse and Duff signed this affidavit:

We the undersigned are desirous to leave all matters in variance and controversy between us to the final determination of William ? [illegible] John Dickson, and Joseph Dickson whereof we have hereunto set our hands.

A justice of the peace not only acted as judge and jury, he also had to make sure that the procedural parts of the law went smoothly. He had to issue subpoenas for witnesses:

August 4, 1824. To Mathias re E. Jones Estate. You are hereby Required to lay all business aside and appear before Arbitrators at the house of George Beal in the City of Pittsburgh on 28 August at 2 P.M. to give evidence in a case of which Estate of Ephraim Jones is Plaintiff and John ? [illegible] Defendant. Enclosed a Map of Pittsburgh herein. Fail not on pain of $10 each.

[Signed] J. Way

He had to make sure that the costs of the trials were paid by the proper party. If plaintiffs lost a case, they had to pay the costs incurred. Squire Way was asked to collect the costs when S. Wardan sued Thomas Mitchel for:

Damage for unjust Suit brought before John M. Michael, Esq. in 1816 to deter family from removing to Ohio. $2.50 per week.
Journey from Ohio in winter 1817-18: $15
Journey in August 1820: $15
January 10, 1818. Cash paid Esquire Michael unjustly: $9

Squire Way was responsible for collecting fees for witnesses called to testify. James Merriman billed $5.16 to the Commissioners of Allegheny County.

Please give John Way a warrant for my fees as witness for Attending on behalf of the Commonwealth against Nathan McPherson for an alleged Assault and Battery on John Flowers. Bill filed with prothonotary.

James Merriman, his mark

If a judgment were entered against a person who was unable or unwilling to pay, the justice of the peace would instruct the constable to seize and sell any valuables of the debtor. If this still did not settle the amount, the debtor went to jail. In 1805 John Way instructed his constable how to proceed.

I command you to Levy Distress on [seize and sell] the goods and chattels of the said William Sutten and Samuel Merriman and make sale thereof . . . and for want of goods and chattels whereon to Levy you are to take the Body of said William Sutten and Samuel Merriman to the Goal of said County and deliver them to the Keeper who is hereby required to receive them in safe custody and keep them until the debt and costs are paid or until otherwise discharged by due process of Law.

[Signed] John Way

The constable was not authorized to arrest the debtor unless there was a "want of sufficient distress." If the debtor could give the constable "goods and chattels or valuables of any kind out of which he is satisfied he can make the debt, interest, and costs, then the constable has no right to take the debtor into custody." Some things owned by the debtor could not be seized for debts: "household utensils; tools of trade; wearing apparel; 4 beds and bedding; spinning wheel; stove; one cow, two hogs, and six sheep; some food; 10 pounds of flax; and all Bibles and school books."[2] These exceptions were made to provide minimal sustenance for the family of the imprisoned debtor. Imprisonment for debt ended in Pennsylvania in 1842.[3]

A number of John Way's duties as justice of the peace were not litigious. Because many of the people he dealt with were illiterate, they needed someone they could trust to read and explain business matters for them. Like current justices of the peace, Squire Way often certified sworn statements. For example, during the War of 1812, he reviewed the documents for John Fouzer, "a substitute for John Dixon of Ohio Township, he being drafted in the service of the United States for six months commencing the 21st of May 1813, that the said Fouzer has faithfully and honorably performed the duties required of him." Fouzer, in turn, appointed Abishai Way to receive his $37.67 pay. Abishai signed a receipt. All of these documents were examined and certified by John Way.

Among Squire Way's more pleasant duties was performing an occasional marriage. Because most people were married in church, only one is recorded in the Way papers.

> Be it remembered that on the 28th Day of August, 1823 before me William Long of Ohio Township, Blacksmith, and Mary Oliver of said place were legally joined in marriage, both being of age and free.
>
> [Signed] J. Way

Another of John Way's duties as justice of the peace was monitoring apprenticeship agreements. This was desirable because very small children were sometimes apprenticed and they could easily have become permanent servants if their rights had not been protected. Apprentice agreements were required to be "certified by the Justice, or at least expressed in writing before him and attached to the instrument at the time of the assignment. Parol proof [given by word of mouth], afterwards, will not suffice."[4] If a dispute arose between master and apprentice, the aggrieved party applied to the justice of the peace for redress.

A master undertook moral duties for an apprentice. They are described in *Binn's Justice* in 1840.

> Remember you are not only the Master but you are also Parent, Guardian, and next friend of your apprentice. Do not permit them to be wronged. Superintend them with a watchful eye, but with a loving heart; so shall your own conscience speak peace. Your apprentice will speak well of you, and your neighbors will speak well of you, and peace and plenty shall be within your walls . . . and thy Father who seeth in secret, himself shall reward thee openly.[5]

The Way papers contain many articles of apprenticeship. One is for an apprentice for Squire Way's own family.

> Indenture made 27 day of September in the year of our Lord 1806. Witness that Henry Willson of Ohio Township County of Allegheny hath put Margaret Willson a girl of 10 years and 6 months old to John Way Esq. of Sewickley Township with him and his wife Mary to serve after that maner of an Apprentice until she arrives at the full age of 18. During all which term the said Apprentice her said Master and Mistress faithfully shall serve . . . and the said Master and Mistress [shall teach] the art and Mistery of housekeeping . . . and will allow competent and sufficient meat, dining, washing, Lodging and weaving, [and will teach her to] Read the Bible and write and also other things fitting for an apprentice. At the end, she will keep her clothing and one suit of new clothing, one spinning wheel, four sheep and perhaps money.
>
> [Signed] Henry Wilson
> John Way

The Ways agreed to train Margaret Flowers, another apprentice, in January, 1813. At the end of her term she was to get one new set of clothing and one cow. Being an apprentice for the Ways taught both girls to be excellent wives and mothers, able to perform all the "household mysteries," and even able to read and write. Apprenticeship was a form of training school. The Ways, for their part, received helpers around the house who, as the apprentices learned their new skills, became more and more useful.

Squire Way recorded a similar apprenticeship agreement between Mary Jane Hanselman, 9 years, 9 months "by act of her mother to Joseph Douglass." At the end of her term she was to get "2 shirts, 1 spinning wheel, 1 Bible, 1 feather bed and bedding of the value $10."

Sometimes a guardian arranged for his ward to be an apprentice. John Way placed his ward, Zephemia Oliver, with a blacksmith.

A sadder tale can be deduced from the apprentice agreement of Robert Barnhil, "son of Joseph Barnhil (deceased)". Robert was only four when he was apprenticed to Andrew Watt, wheelwright, until he was 21. His mother must have believed that this was the best way for her son to learn how to make a decent living. Watt promised that he would see that the boy received "two years of schooling, one after 10 years old, and also to present him to church for baptism and teach him the Christian religion." When he was 21, Robert was to get two suits of clothes. The agreement was signed by Eleanor, her mark, and Andrew Watt, and was witnessed by John Way.

Apprenticeship was sometimes started at what seems like a ridiculously young age. In some cases, it served to cut costs on social services for the poor. In 1808, two "overseers of the poor" apprenticed Elizabeth Cox, age 5 years 6 months, to William Wall until she was 18. She was to learn housekeeping and to read and write.

When Squire Way died he had an apprentice, Andrew Fouzer. The following notation appeared in the account book, dated April 8, 1826, of Nicholas Way, the son and executor named in John's will.

> Received of Nicholas Way the indentures of Andrew Fouzer, an apprentice bound to John Way which I agree to release the heirs and Executors of Said Way from all obligations to myself and my son.
>
> [signed] John Fouzer

The apprentice agreement did not automatically stop upon the death of the master, but, when it became impossible for him to continue teaching, it was often terminated by mutual agreement.

As one of the Sewickley area's most important people, John Way was often called upon to be a financial adviser for the living and an executor for the dead. His duties as executor of the will of William Semple give a glimpse of more features of life at the time. Colonel Semple states in his will: "I now live in Ohio Township, lately a resident of Beaver County on Big Sewickley [Creek] formerly from Paisley in the Kingdom of Scotland, and heretofore a merchant in Philadelphia." Despite this prosperous-sounding biography, the Colonel had financial difficulties. In 1812 John Way instructed his constable, William McDonald, "Whereas judgment against William Semple for $1.32 plus $1.24 costs was had before John Way, you are requested to Levy Distress on goods and chattles of said Semple . . . or take the Body to the Gaol." A memo on the bottom of the same instructions notes that the bill was paid: "Levied on Corn and Buckwheat in the barn of Hugh Scott left in the care of Scott. Debt $1.32: Interest .30; Cost 1.24; Miles .36; Satisfaction .06."

We next meet Colonel Semple in the Way papers during his last illness. When he fell sick on June 11, 1815, Dr. Milo Adams paid a house call, charging $11.25 for the "journey and attendance." Adams returned three times in June with charges for "journey and medicine" ranging from $8.00 to $8.75. On June 22, Dr. Adams called in his father, Dr. Samuel Adams, for consultation. The father's bill tells us that the diagnosis was kidney stones or gallstones: "Travil to help case of gravel. $5.00. Consultation with Doctor Adams. $5.00." The last visit of Dr. Milo Adams cost only $1.25 and included no medicine. Perhaps he had given up.

A man named Andrew Russell claimed to have taken care of Colonel Semple. He did "one month's attendance in his [Semple's] last illness except 3 or 4 days." How much Russell was paid is unknown because John Way and he agreed "to leave the price per day and night to the determination of John Jackson and Robert Rowland . . . who will hear the parties and make report in writing."

Colonel Semple died July 8th and was buried on the 10th in a coffin costing $5.00. The will directs the executors, John Way and his son, Abishai Way, "to sell my estate both real and personal and divide the residue among the lawful children of my brother James Semple of Scotland and my sister Jane Cochran and my sister Peggy Patterson and sister Ann Elizabeth Wilson. I wish my History to be published by subscription."

The "Inventory and Appraisement of William Semple, New Sewickley Township, Beaver County" gives a good idea of what kinds of things an ordinary person would have had and of their relative worth.

1 Mare	$30.00
1 Red Bull	9.00
2 year old colt	25.00
Oats	8.00
Yearling colt	20.00

Wheat	6.00
3 Black and White cows	46.00
Rice	4.00
Cow with suckling calf	18.00
[Assorted heifers]	32.50
Hay 3 tons in mow	20.00
in stock	5.00
Pewter knives and forks and dish .	2.00
Hoes and ax	3.00
Gun	1.00
10 Sugar kettles	25.00
2 pots and gridiron and knife	3.00
Buckwheat in ground	4.00
8 barrels opened and 2 kegs	2.50
Nursery of apple trees	3.00
1 pair shoes	1.00
Hen and chickens	.50
Pillow and old clothes	.25
Hand saw	1.25
19 or 20 logs	27.50
2 sheep	3.00
Chest and clothes	15.00
Regimental coat	.50
Bed clothes and blankets	2.50

The vendue, or auction, was held in August, 1815, at Colonel Semple's house. Sales totaled $466.80. Buyers paid cash for articles costing less than one dollar but had until January 1, 1816 to pay for everything else.

Squire Way's duties as justice of the peace were so varied and so numerous that they could have taken all his time. This was not the case, however. The next sections will show that John Way found time to be involved in many other matters in the Sewickley Valley.

---

[1] *Binns Justice: Digest of the Laws and Judicial Decisions of Pennsylvania.* Philadelphia: James Kay, 1840, p. 63.

[2] Ibid., pp. 83-85.

[3] *Law of the General Assembly*, 1842, p. 339.

[4] *Binn's Justice*, p. 114.

[5] Ibid., p. 122.

Chapter 4
The Ways' Business Interests

Serving as a justice of the peace was only one of many activities of John Way. He was also involved in several business ventures. He was able to do this despite some difficulties in doing business that would be distressing to today's entrepreneurs. The most serious of these were lack of money and excessively slow and unreliable mail service.

The mails were a constant source of frustration. There was no universal way of addressing correspondence. Letters for John Way could read "John Way, Sewickley bottom," or "Sewickley," or "On the Ohio River below Pittsburgh," or "c/o Abishai Way, Pittsburgh." Because of the inadequacy of mail service, correspondents preferred to entrust letters to travelers going in the direction of Sewickley. Mark Willcox sent a letter to John Way in 1812. "As James Mendinghall is going your way, I trouble you to inform me by a Line when the maine Leace is out." In 1823, Way writes Willcox, "My son, A. Way, is now in Philadelphia. If this come to hand before he leaves there, likely John Wilson could see him and send per him." Sometimes mail delivery was entirely fortuitous. James Way reports to Nicholas in 1834, "I happened to pick up a Jackson [Mississippi] newspaper which had a list of letters remaining in the post office uncalled for, and there beheld a letter for myself. How long it had been in the office I know not". Many letters today begin, "Sorry I haven't written sooner, but . . . ." Letters in the Way file are similar and include many different excuses. The most legitimate is in a letter to John Way from a man in Baltimore in October, 1812.

> The Deed of conveyance was executed on 23 August and should have been forwarded in due season. But on the following day the battle of Bladinsburg took place in which action I had a brother wounded (his leg broken by a musket ball) and taken prisoner. My attending to him and the other urgent duties which the subsequent attack on this place by the British occasioned has put it out of my power to find any private conveyance by which to forward the papers.

Problems with mail delivery slowed business transactions; problems with sufficient and stable currency complicated them. Around 1800 the currency was changing from pounds, shillings and pence to dollars and cents. Some of Squire Way's accounts are rendered in dollars and some in pounds. In 1790, for example, Way charged William Semple "for Sundries, 17 shillings 11 pence" and "for Supper and Horse to Hay, 3 shillings." Way's account book of 1802 lists Mr. Boyd's debts.

> June 18. 1 barrel of whiskey containing 32 ½ gals. 7 pounds, 63 shillings.

> November 3. 1 barrel of whiskey. 7 pounds, 12 shillings, 9 pence. 1 empty barrel. 6 shillings.

On the other hand, in an appraisal of property of Thomas Boyd's estate in 1805, the accounts are entirely in dollars.

2 feather beds	$16
8 quilts	16
1 bay mare	50
1 mare	40

The currency, whether pounds or dollars, was difficult to transfer. Today a bank deposit in Pittsburgh, Philadelphia or New York is worth the same amount. Transactions take milliseconds to complete. In John Way's time there was no central banking system. Each bank could issue notes, the value of which varied. Once a price was set, say, for a piece of real estate, it was necessary to decide how to pay. In 1817 Mark Wilcox cautions John Way on finding the proper currency in Western Pennsylvania.

> Be careful for there is so much trouble with your country money. Would thank you to take none without they will pay the discount. It is now here [in Eastern Pennsylvania] 6% and hard to get it at that. It could be changed by you and lodged in the branch bank of the Pennsylvania Bank at Pittsburg for me.

One year later John Way writes Fred Beates:

> If they don't feel willing to buy Philadelphia paper, likely you will take Pennsylvania Charter paper at the usual discount in your city. We can always know the discount of different banks by the price current which my son [Abishai] receives weekly from Philadelphia.

Much later, in 1839, Mary Way, John's widow, left $20 to a relative in Chester, Pennsylvania. Nicholas writes,

> I have enclosed $20 on Bank of Pittsburgh, not being able to get a draft on the bank of Chester. I could of got one on a Philadelphia bank but would have had to pay a percentage which would of been more than the postage, and then the postage besides.

Lack of sufficient cash or credit made it difficult to conduct business. Today we are moving toward a cashless society with the expanded use of computer and wire transfers. The Ways achieved similar results using a modified barter system. Goods were not traded item by item but purchases were recorded in the Ways' account books. The debt was paid with other goods, with services rendered, or with cash. In 1813, for example, Squire Way charged John Frazer for six plates, muslin, shirten [shirting to make shirts], linen, cotton, bacon, beef, and salt. Frazer paid for all this with 10½ days of work ($4.20); ½ day hoeing corn (25 cents); and six months and 15 days serving as a substitute in the army ($20).

In 1814, when Alexander Young bought a mare from John Way for $40, he paid by working for $10 a month beginning May 1. Mr. Young worked when it was convenient for him; he did not follow the regular five-day, nine to five work week. The account books record his time:

> May 12, 1 day lost; May 16, a day lost at Review; May 16-31 Lost Pittsburgh; June 7 and 8 Lost at Wilson's raisen [barn raising]; June 29 Lost going to Moors; July 4 lost digging McDonald's grave; July 5 lost digging Smith's grave.

Some transactions involved turning a raw material into a finished product. Isaac Feree bought 51 bushels of rye from Way for $20.40. Way received 11 gallons of whiskey in return. A tanner named Philip Hoope owed Way for one steer, one heifer, three calf skins, one steer that died, and one heifer hide. For payment he returned some of the skins to Way as leather. The others, he sold for a profit.

John Way sometimes acted as a banker, making small loans, holding cash, and disbursing it upon request. The papers contain many notes referring to these transactions.

> 20 January 1819. Received of E. Blair by John Way, $5. [Signed] Samuel Wade

> September 20 1819. John Way Esquire: Please let the bearer Samuel Wade have $4 and oblige your friend. [Signed] Thomas Allen

> 21 August 1823. Received of John Way, Esq. $76. George Smith left with said Way the 19th Instant. [Signed] Jacob Frey

Because of the scarcity of cash, road taxes were often paid by working on the roads. Pennsylvania law required that "every township and borough is bound to open and keep in good repair the public roads and bridges."[1] In 1839, when Nicholas Way was supervisor of roads, taxes were assessed at five mills per dollar of real estate value. There was a choice between paying cash and working at the rate of one dollar per day for an eight-hour day. Nicholas Way recorded the tax collections in his account book. The book is useful because the amount of tax levied indicates how much land each person owned and because it shows who was sufficiently wealthy to afford to hire people to work off his or her taxes. Extracts from the book's entries follow.

Margaret Boggs	$ 7.00	
John Champ	.50	
Joseph Dickson	.50	
Dr. John Dickson	2.29	By work
John Davis	.25	By work
John Fife	3.30	By work [done by] D. Auger
James Grimes	2.30	Received of Mrs. Grimes in rent of R. Mann
Thomas Hamilton	12.27	By 3½ Hands $3.50 By 3½ Hands $3.37
Nat McPherson Sr.	7.85	By work 1½ days by 3 hands
David Shields	128.92	By work 9 hands 2 teams $12
		8 hands 2 teams $12
		4 hands and cart $5.50
		Auditor $1.00
Nicholas Way	17.15	

Neither the road taxes nor the labor sufficed to make decent roads, according to a plea sent by the Inhabitants of the County of Allegheny to the General Assembly of the Commonwealth.

> The road from Pittsburgh to Beaver, a great part of which is laid on the Bank of the River Ohio being very narrow and cut out of the steep Banks at great expence and many parts of which is often inundated by the waters of said river, said road is and has been for many years of great interest in traveling to and from the state of Ohio, many of your petitioners have spent much labor and money on the same. . . . The road taxes has been each year raised as high as the laws would admit and all is unable to keep up the [road].

> A law was passed some years ago making it a turnpike. The managers used every honorable means to obtain subscribers in order to get a charter but the law called for $20,000 to be subscribed prior to a charter being granted; not having more than $5,000 subscribed, the law was suffered to expire. It is believed that $3,000 well managed with what liberal minded citizens here would contribute would place a road the Greater part of which would be above high water mark which when properly made and in the proper place would be a great national and state benefit being the Great thorofare to the new and northern part of Ohio. And the mail stage passing the same 4 times each week and other carriages to great extent [sharing] the great expence [will] keep the same in repair.

Squire Way did two things to help transportation from Pittsburgh to Ohio. He invested in the first bridge across the Allegheny River at Pittsburgh in 1818. A receipt from the Allegheny Bridge Company records that John Way paid $150 for ten shares of stock. This turned out to be a good investment. Way received dividends and in 1828, after his death, the shares were appraised at $37.50 each

In 1815, Squire Way acted more locally when he contracted with the County Commissioners of Allegheny and Beaver counties to build a bridge over Big Sewickley Creek for $700. It is surprising that this man, involved in many business and professional matters, still found time and expertise to supervise building a bridge. There is no evidence that he had ever built anything but a house before. The bridge specifications are in the agreement.

> The timbers here represented to lie on the plate laid on stone Butment and to be covered over with stone even with the floor of the Bridge and graveled so as to make comfortable access with team. . . . Both piers to be nine feet high of suitable stone, to be flared from the braces upstream to the post next the current, the Mason work all to be compleated in a workmanlike manner.

Paths to Riches? Investing in Real Estate

Squire Way spent much of his time and energy on real estate, which was the popular investment medium of the day. Like Florida real estate, tulip bulbs, or junk bonds in other times and places, western Pennsylvania real estate was thought to be the way to fame and fortune. Fred Beates wrote Squire Way in 1818. "I think it better not to sell any of the lands I hold near Pittsburgh. That place increases so rapidly." Mr. Beates was still bullish in 1822. "I made up my mind not to sell for some time yet as the neighborhood was improving very fast and property in the vicinity was much sought after." As other speculators have learned, there is no sure road to riches. There were problems with western Pennsylvania real estate: troubles getting good title to land; when prices rose, buyers could move farther west where land was still cheap; rents were hard to collect; and it was difficult to find people to work the land because they wanted to buy their own.

Because of these local problems, added to the problems of absentee landlords in general, speculators from the east needed a reliable, honest, and literate person to take care of their interests in western Pennsylvania. John Way was the obvious choice. John Way invested for his own account and as agent for numerous clients. He did well for his own account. At the time of his death in 1825, he had accumulated 3,073 acres. His executors, his sons Abishai and Nicholas, sold his real estate for a total of $16,880.54.

One of Way's clients, William Sheridan from "Upper Ferry, Schuylkill." explains why he employed Way and the kinds if things he wanted Way to do.

> As you live in that Country and you have been well recommended to me as being an honest, faithful man if you will be so obliging and will do it for me as you have mentioned. Arthur Luster I gave a lease [to] 15 August 1809 for 3 years which has and will expire by next August. A Person informed me Arthur was willing to pay.

> Sir if you will be so good and call on him and agree with him and Receive Rents from the time his lease Expired and Rent him the place by the year hereafter as you think Proper, the money you receive you pay yourself well for your trouble and

expense the Balance. You keep in your hands to pay some small taxes for Lot 192—206 acres in Deer township. If you can conveniently, make Inquery Respecting a tract of land it lies in Alexander's District No 3, I believe now in Butler County. . . . . One half of that tract I sold a number of years ago. I was informed the half I held was sold for taxes. . . . If you think there can be anything made out of it I will share the proceeds with you.

Please let me know your luck either Good or bad whenever it Suits.

Direct your letter to Wm Sheridan in Care of Richard Harding No 102 Race Street Philadelphia they shall be duly attended to

I Am your Respectfully friend etc.

William Sheridan

Another of Squire Way's clients was Mark Willcox, an associate judge of Delaware County, Pennsylvania. Mark's father, Thomas Willcox had immigrated to eastern Pennsylvania in 1727 and started the second paper mill in the colonies, Ivy Mills. The mill printed currency for all the colonies, for the Continental Congress, and later for the federal government. Mark inherited the mill on his father's death in 1779.[2]

The Way Papers contain a receipt dated 1785 stating that Mark Willcox paid £2,975 in Depreciation Certificates for 28 tracts of land totaling 6,302 acres in Daniel Leet's District. For 11 of these transactions he was buying for someone else: he resold 601 acres to Thomas Shields less than three weeks later; he sold 859 acres to Levi Hollingsworth; and he sold 716 acres to Daniel Leet, the surveyor. This left Willcox still owning 4,126 acres. Willcox paid the £90 surveying fee to Daniel Leet himself. He bought Lot 1, the lot that now includes the western half of Sewickley from Levi Hollingsworth in 1786. In addition, he owned, or possibly served as surveyor Daniel Leet's straw man, for the 1,000 acres that made up Lots 3 through 7 in Leet's District, now parts of Edgeworth and Leetsdale.

These were only a few of Mark Willcox's many land purchases in the area. John Way and he had a lengthy correspondence. One set of letters gives a good idea of problems with land squatters. Robert Mitchel was already living on Wilcox's land when Wilcox bought it from the state. Evidently Willcox decided it was easier to try to compromise with Mitchel than to try to evict him. The Way papers contain an 1804 memo of agreement between Willcox and Robert Mitchel. Mitchel is to stay on the place he now lives "he paying the taxes, and plant 50 Apple trees in one year from this date. He is Not to commit waist in the timber."

Evidently this plan did not work, as recorded in a letter from Way to J. W. Allison Esq. dated May 1, 1815.

I am requested to forward the enclosed copy of patent No 91 Leet's District (on which Widow Mitshel [sic] now Resides) Requesting you to send Ejectment to Recover for Mark Wilcox Esq. the Sooner the better as I understand they have resided thereon 20 years or more.

Many landowners found it difficult to collect the rent. Way writes John Willcox, Mark's son, in 1819. "Please inform your father there is a general deficit in his land payments and rents—he may expect to Lose some Rents."

Even when rents could be collected, they were low. Way writes about some lots near Sewickley in 1823.

I advise you to make a price if you intend selling—these lands cannot yield more that two or three per cent interest on the sum they sell for. Even the rents they are bound to pay we cannot get, the way the tenants are going on—it is no benefit to you or credit to me to continue in Rent.

One problem of land investors is liquidity. As Mark Willcox grew older, he wrote John Way to ask for help in getting his affairs in order.

Concord. March 14 1823

I would thank you to get my collection as soon as you can, am [in] very middling health. Can't expect to be here long only want a few months of 79 years. If money can't be collected, would wish it secured by Mortgage on interest. On looking over the Sailes made by you. No. 87 Braydon District interest from April 1819. No. 81 Braydon District sold to Thomas Allison 312 acres at $3 per acre/Recd first payment $300 [then 4 more] $310 still due and interest. No, 80 Braydon's District. 300 acres. Received $310 the remainder to be paid within 2 years with interest. Balance due July 1 1820. Please collect or get mortgage from land. . . . Lodge the money in the U.S. Branch at Pittsburgh.

Mark Willcox

N.B. You must know I am getting old having forgot to mention amount of McElheaney Sail $945.

Way himself bought at least one piece of property from Willcox. In 1825, he signed a promise to pay "one hundred dollars lawful money of the United States for value Received without Defalcation being the purchase money of Lot No. 26 Alexander's District Butler County."

Another of Squire Way's clients, Thomas McKean, signed the Declaration of Independence, served in the Continental Congress, later became chief justice of the Pennsylvania Supreme Court and then governor from 1799 to 1808. While McKean was chief justice, he and Francis Johnson received eight tracts of Depreciation Land in Breading's district, a total of 2,266 acres.[3] Of these acres, 1,641 were in what is now Sewickley Heights. McKean bought Johnson's interest in 1803 for $1 per acre. The lands were not valuable at the time because they were inaccessible; they were far from the river and high up in the hills.

The Way papers contain an inventory of McKean's property in 1810. He owned 17 tracts of from 200 to 334 acres each in Leet's District; ten tracts (200-325 acres) in Breading's district; one in Cunningham's district; and four in Alexander's district.

McKean was too busy to visit or even to devote much time to managing his Pennsylvania land. He was infuriated to find, however, that some of his trees had been cut down. His letter, dated October 5, 1815, to Henry Baldwin, justice of the peace, with a copy to John Way, sounds like the most ardent conservationist today.

> When my grandsons made a tour to Beaver town from Pittsburgh last summer they called at the dwelling of Mr. John Way he told them that three men, tanners in Pittsburgh, namely Thomas Wallace, Lewis Peters, and George Stuff, their servant, had cut down 400 trees on a tract of land belonging to me principally with a view to strip them of their bark. . . .

> I request you after consulting Mr. Way and having proof of the fact, to bring an action of trespass against them without delay and prosecute to judgement and execution, see act of assembly entitled an act about cuting timber-trees passed in 1700 where it appears the trespassers shall forfeit 50 pounds for every tree cut, to the owner. This appears to be a proper punishment of FreeBooters or land pirates enemies of the Human race.

The men, tanners by trade, had cut down the trees because their bark contains tannin used for tanning leather. Large squares of bark were stripped off the trees, girdling them and causing them to die. The rest of the tree was left to rot, leaving hundreds of acres of rotting wood. The hides for making leather were placed in plank boxes which were sunk in the ground, filled with pelts, and covered by crushed bark and water.

Governor McKean's interpretation of the law was correct, although he could not collect £50 per tree. The 1700 act states:

> If any person or persons shall be convicted of cutting or felling any black walnut-trees upon another person's land, without leave, he shall forfeit, to the owner thereof, five pounds for every tree so felled and cut; and for other timber fifty shillings each tree; and for fire or underwood, double the value thereof, to the use aforesaid.[4]

Governor McKean sold some of his land to William Vicary, Gentleman, of Columbia, Lancaster County, Pennsylvania. Mr. Vicary informed John Way in a letter dated July 19, 1813.

> I have purchased half of all Mr. McKean's land in Allegheny, Beaver, Butler and Jefferson Counties as I do not intend to keep them, shall want your assistance to effect Sales. If the people on the lands are inclined to purchase, shall be willing to give preference.

> William Vicary

Please pay yourself $12 out of the rents.

In May, 1812, William Vicary bought a half interest in 1,519 acres in Daniel Leet's district, Numbers 10 through 14 and Number 40. In July, 1813, he bought a half interest in 3,463 acres. If Mr. Vicary wanted to sell his lands for a quick profit, he was not successful. Absentee landlords had their problems, as Mr. Way reported five years later, in May, 1818.

> I have not received any Rents for you this Spring. Oliver is determined to leave your land unless he can have some meadow. ? [name illegible] are gone down the river. Shannon has not paid anything. One other severe flood was 4th March last, not as high as the November flood but much more destructive.

Way's letters often complain of collection problems.

[One man, name illegible] paid only 10$ in 1816 and has gone away into the state of Ohio. One Barbel is now on it [the same tract] a poor, miserable family. Whether anything will be had I know not. Thomas Oliver is dead his widow occupies No. 11 and part of No. 12. I have warned her off. I doubt she cannot pay the Rent. I have very little money for you.

With rents so difficult to collect, Mr. Vicary pursued sales. Squire Way inquires: "Mr. Shields wishes for me to ask you what you would take for your Sewickley land." Mr. Vicary replies:

As Mr. Shields lives near and knows the lands well, I should be glad to know what he will give for the whole in a lump. I shall be satisfied with one quarter on executing the Deed. The remainder to be secured by the lands.

Way reports in January, 1820:

David Shields says he cannot command funds now but will give you $5,000 for your Sewickley property, $1,000 in June 1820 and $1,000 per annum without interest, secured by Mortgage. . . . You can get $1,000 more than David offers. Property has been depreciating here some time.

There the matter rested.

Some of the Vicary-Way correspondence concerns a maple sugar camp on Vicary's Sewickley property. Because cane sugar was a luxury which had to be transported across the mountains from Philadelphia, maple sugar was a useful product. *The Pittsburgh Gazette* reported in 1788, "It is plain that a farmer could raise nothing on his farm with less labor, and nothing from which he could derive more emolument, than the sugar maple tree."[5] Some early settlers continued to gather maple syrup. Among the five most valuable possessions of Colonel William Semple in 1815 were 10 sugar kettles, worth $25.00.

Nevertheless, Mr. Vicary found that scarcity of labor prevented him from reaping the harvest. He says in 1818, "I wish you may permit the Sugar making this year as it would be well to receive some little profit." In 1820, he continues,

I am sorry that no one will on any terms agree to make Maple Sugar. It is not agreeable to me that the Blessings offered by the Almighty should be neglected. If the Trees are not injured it would be more satisfying to have them used than to let them be idle even if we receive no Profit.

The letters between John Way and his clients show that the pursuit of profits in real estate was fraught with frustration. One positive benefit to Way was the chance to keep in touch with various people from all over the state. He avoided the insular life centered on the struggle for survival that engrossed the majority of western Pennsylvanians at the time.

[1] John Reed. *Pennsylvania Blackstone: Laws of Pennsylvania.* Carlisle, George Fleming, 1831, Book 1, p. 182.

[2] *History of Delaware County, Pennsylvania.* Philadelphia, L.H. Everts, 1884, p. 241.

[3] John Emery, "The McKean Tract." In *Western Pennsylvania Historical Magazine.* v.9, No.1, p. 25-26.

[4] *Laws of the Commonwealth of Pennsylvania, 1700 to 1810.* Republished. Philadelphia, John Bioren, 1810, v.1, p. 20.

[5] J.E. Wright and Doris S. Corbett. *Pioneer Life in Western Pennsylvania*, Pittsburgh, University Press, 1940, p. 62.

Chapter 5
The Way Houses

The Walker-Way house, 1890. Courtesy of Susan Jones.

As we have seen, land was a major interest in the Sewickley area in the early nineteenth century. There is much less in the Way papers concerning the houses that were built on the land. Like many early settlers, John Way built a log house for shelter soon after coming west. His house, built in 1797, was right on the river near the foot of Hazel Lane. A traveler, F. Cumming, noticed it on a trip down the Ohio River in 1807.

> A little below the point [of Neville Island] a charmingly situated farm on the right exciting our inquiry, we were informed it was squire Way's. The squire, however, was badly lodged, if he had no better house than the small log hovel we saw on the bank.[1]

The Squire, however, soon improved his lodging, building a larger house more suited to the life of a prosperous citizen. Later his son built a house next door. We can follow the construction of both houses in letters and bills in the Way papers. Both houses remain today, standing as neighbors on Beaver Road in Edgeworth. The John Way house is at the junction of Beaver and Quaker Roads and the other Way house is on 108 Beaver Road.

The first, now called the Walker-Way house, is a large, white, brick house which was constructed in several stages. The oldest part, the western section, was built from 1811 to 1814. It is first mentioned in the Way papers in a receipt from a brickmaker.

> October 23, 1809. Received of John Way $60.00 for molding and burning one kiln of Brick finished this day. 60,000 at 96 cents a thousand. I undertake to say it is well made and burned.

The next bill is dated 27 July, 1811. "$9 for laying brick 12 days." We can follow the progress of the house as the bills continue:

August 1811: Stone work. $29.25

Brick laid $53.50

7 new large arches $4.67

15 Common Arches, window and doors $5.00

7 chimneys $2.33

7 flews $10.50

[Note at bottom of bill.] We engage to paint the stone work and pencil the Brick work without any further cost.

December 1811: Received of John Way Esquire $2.50 for my part of hewing rafters for his house.

January 1812: Settlement for hewing 44 pine rafters for his house $12.54

March: Carpenter work of house $40.

Nov. 30, 1814. Received of John Way, Esquire $28.31 for plastering his house.

The Walker-Way House, Drawing by Susan Gaca.

When John Way died in 1825, Abishai and Nicholas bought the house and farm from the estate. Nicholas lived there with his mother but, according to his daughter Agnes, it was not an amicable arrangement. A memo from Agnes Way explains:

Her father, Nicholas lived in the house with his mother for some years—at least half of his children were born there— Mary, John, Elizabeth, Rebecca, Hannah, and Amanda. The old grandmother lived with him and, being a person of very trying temperament, was always casting up to Nicholas that it was *her* house. He determined to build for himself and, though she continued to live with him, it was his house they occupied.

After completing the new house, Nicholas and Abishai put an addition on the older one, now the middle section of the house. They turned it into an inn. A jury summons in 1827 is addressed to John Way's son as "Nicholas Way, Innkeeper." The problems of adding to an existing structure are detailed by Abishai in a letter to Nicholas dated July 28, 1835:

Put up a new sash for the old kitchen window and a new back door. The stairway from the kitchen in the new house should be put up. . . . [If] fairly moderate weather should come I can get a coat of plaster put on the kitchen and dining room and the bar room. The platform of the main stairs should be level with the second story of the old house as there is to be a door through from that platform.

While fixing up the old house as an inn, it was discovered that the wooden water pipes were rotting. Abishai writes in May, 1835:

I didn't know the water logs were in such bad condition. I wish it to be done well. Put in new logs. Sink the pipe a little lower—they will last longer and the water will be cooler in summer and less liable to freeze in the winter.

Abishai suffered through the perennial problems of getting workmen to keep their promises. In the same letter of July 28, 1835 he complains:

If there is 70,000 bricks made it is as many as I want or care about and should be glad if Rollins gets down that he would set too and set the kiln and burn as soon as possible. He has disappointed me very much and I am now apprehensive that the building will not go up in time for the Season.

The second Way house on 108 Beaver Road is next door to the original. There is some confusion about which brother, Nicholas or Abishai, lived there. Locally it is known as the Abishai Way house. A letter from Nicholas to his aunt dated 1839 supports this position. "Mary A. Way, Abishai's widow, lives here in the mantion farm. She built a new house." The book, *Historic Houses of the Sewickley Valley*, states that Abishai Way started building the house in 1835, but died before it was finished. His widow completed the work in 1838.[2] On the other hand, Charles Stotz in his book, *Early Architecture of Western Pennsylvania*, labels it the Nicholas Way house. Other letters quoted below support this position.

Second Way house, 108 Beaver Road. Built 1835. Photo by John H. Demmler.

In any case, the second Way house must have been under construction at about the same time as the addition to the inn because Abishai suggests in an 1835 letter about replacing the water pipes at the inn, "While the men are there, get *your* water pipe laid.[italics added]" The new house, now 108 Beaver Road, is mentioned first in 1833 in a letter from Abishai to Nicholas advising him to "keep track of cost of the house *you*[italics added] are about to build—it may be necessary for the division of property."

Because the second house is perched on the hill, it required excavation. Abishai writes,

> I would give the digging of that hill back of the house out by the cubic yard and suppose I shall want at least 400 yards excavated, the quarter part of the earth to be placed on the yard in front of the house. [Pennsylvania Main Line] Canal excavation is done for 10 cents a yard and is uphill. This land is easy excavated and is all down hill and money could be made by two industrious men with a horse and a cart who would undertake it at eight cents.

A more practical requirement was an outhouse.

> Joe says he dug the privy well about nine or ten feet deep and that it is now partly filled with water. The water will have to be dipped or pumped out, then walled up.
>
> [Signed] A Way
>
> [P.S.] I got the old and new house insured for six months against fire of which there is much danger.

One problem of building in Sewickley was getting the materials to the building site. No mention of shipment by roads is made in the letters. The roads were primitive and the route to Pittsburgh involved journeying far up in the hills to avoid gullies and stream beds. Everything came by river to be picked up at the Ways' landing. Abishai says,

> I will get a small raft on which I will send down all the flooring boards necessary. [And, in a later letter,] I will have a little raft ready for the hands to take down and may put on it shingles and dry boards. [When things are needed for the house] it will be as cheap to send it from here in a large flat [boat.] [Some of the craftsmen as well as the materials came from Pittsburgh.] May, 1835: Dravo will go down on Wednesday to commence plastering the house. And on that day at about 11:00 there will be 100 bushels of lime in Waggon at the river for you. The lathes and any other articles you want can go down on the flat.

Finally, the end of May, 1835, the house was ready to paint.

> Brother: I sent by the "Beaver" 10 kegs of white lead for the Painter and tomorrow morning. I will send to be left at your landing:
>
> > 1 can Spirits of turpentine
> >
> > 1 keg whiting
> >
> > 1 small jar of green
> >
> > 1 small keg of Paint
>
> All of which you will please get from the river as soon as convenient.

After the new house and the new inn were completed, it was necessary to find someone to operate the inn. Nicholas and Abishai began a long search for a competent manager. Abishai heard of a prospective tenant in December of 1833.

> Irwin who keeps a tavern in Allegheny-town called with me this morning to rent the house and farm where you now are. What do you think we ought to ask him? From his conversation I should infer that he would willingly give 200$ a year but do you think that is enough? I do not for so much ground with all the improvements. It is certainly more than 50$ a year better than Mr. Shields [the Lark Inn, on Beaver Road and Sycamore Street in Leetsdale.] Have you got the new house roofed and can you have it so far completed as to get into it by the first of April?

Mr. Irwin must have decided against taking the inn, for the first manager mentioned in the Way papers was named George Saunders. Abishai writes Nicholas in 1833.

> I have let Saunders stay in the house until Spring for which he will pay quarterly rent $62.50. The man is a stranger to me with a little of the Yankee in his speech. Try him until Spring for it will not do to have the house shut up.

In 1834 the Ways were still looking for an innkeeper. "Henry Wood [wants] to rent the mansion for a public house where he will keep the stage horses. I asked him $250 a year for the house and 20 acres. He offered $200. He is to call again. We will have to do some repairs in the house." He did not call again.

A Mr. Fleming did rent the inn, but he was unsuccessful. Nicholas reports in November 1835:

I have no doubt that Fleming is off not to return unless brought by the creditors. He is largely indebted here — to the Stage proprietor for advances and to others for groceries and liquor all of which he has bought upon credit. He is not much indebted to me. He has boarded my hands during the summer. Get someone else to live in the house and I will advertise for another tenant.

The next tenant was again Mr. Saunders. Nicholas reports,

Saunders has a mind to quit as soon as possible. I heard he has taken a house from Park and is going to farm for Park the coming season. I have my doubts about it. I think more likely he will leave the country the first favorable opportunity.

The Ways decided to get rid of the reluctant Saunders. Abishai sent an eviction notice to be served on him.

Sir: Please take Notice that I require peaceable possession of the "Sewickley Inn" and the premises you now occupy on or before the 1st of April next.

[Signed] Abishai Way

To Mr. George Saunders Pittsburgh. December 30 1835

The Ways problems came because the independent-minded frontiersmen of the period did not want to work for someone else. Most people with the enterprise to move to what was still rather wild country wanted to strike out on their own.

Despite all the problems, the first Way house continued to be run as an inn. Captain Anderson, who celebrated his 100th birthday in Sewickley in 1928 remembered,

Down below Sand Hill was Way's tavern in the brick house, one of the oldest houses here. Old Squire John Way built it, long before my time. The last Way that kept it was Nicholas who kept tavern there for awhile in my earliest recollection. Several people ran it after Way quit.

The inn was successful enough to be too noisy for the elite. When Mr. and Mrs. James Olver were building in the valley in 1835, they needed a place to stay but thought that, "the house of Mr. Way's with its usual inmates and the mail stage stopping there day and night, too, is too noisy for our purposes."

At one time the house was a school. Nicholas Way writes in 1839, "The old mansion house is rented out and is ocupied as an academy for Boys where I am sending my son to school this summer. As I have but one son I wish to give him a liberal education."

The Sewickley valley is fortunate to have the two Way houses as well-preserved examples of early architecture. There is no mention in the Way papers of their employing an architect. This is not surprising, as there were no architects in the Sewickley area in the early days. The first known architect in the area was an Englishman named John Chislett (1800-1869). He designed the Sewickley Presbyterian Church building that was used from 1840 to 1861.

It is possible that the Ways did use a kind of secondhand architect in the later Way house. Books of house plans, called pattern books, by architects or builders were available. At least one pattern book, *House Carpenter and Teacher of Architectural Drawing adapted to the Style of Building in the United States*, by Owen Biddle, was sold in Pittsburgh in 1810. Another pattern book, Minard Lefever's *Builder's Guide*, described how to use elements of Greek architecture and decoration with American materials. This is a possible source for the Greek revival influence in the second Way house.

Both Way houses are much admired by architectural historians and by casual passers-by. The John Way house is a simple, solid building with clean lines. Charles Stotz, an architectural historian, could have had it in mind when he described the virtues of buildings that cannot be classified in a traditional style.

Their quiet lines and excellent mass are wholly satisfying. It seems that in the essential qualities of architectural design their builders, curiously enough, were capable of doing no wrong. . . . Their principal endeavor was to build more substantially but, in conformity with their lives, without ornamentation or display.[3]

The second house, built over 20 years later, is in the more refined Greek revival style, nicknamed Grecian Gusto, which captivated western Pennsylvania from 1830 to 1850. The Ways incorporated some of that gusto in their Way house. It has an elegant Greek revival porch, supported by delicate columns. The front is further embellished with a round window which must have been included for exterior decoration only, because it opens into a closet on the top floor. A large entrance hall runs through the house, providing cool breezes in summer. A delicately carved stairway shows that the Ways' taste and standard of living had risen far from John Way's log cabin on the river.

Charles Stotz says of the second Way house:

[The Way house is] among the most delightful residences built during any period in the district. It has an English basement, half way out of the ground, lighted by large windows with kitchen and dining room and is most livable, light and airy.[4]

The houses reflect a change of taste during the twenty-odd years between them. The John Way house is a simple Pennsylvania farmhouse, with no frills or furbelows. The later Way house is a country gentleman's seat that would be equally suitable for a Virginia planter. Inside, the older house has plain molding. The later house has finely crafted moldings. Even the floor plans reflect changing times. The John Way house has two entrance halls which are practical but not elaborate. The later Way house has an elegant entrance hall with a beautiful stairway curving gracefully upwards. By merely looking at the two houses, a visitor to Sewickley in 1850 could see that both the area and the Way family were thriving. Both houses are pleasing to the eye. One is not necessarily "better" than the other. Their differences make them interesting as reflections of general changes in taste.

[1] F. Cumming, p. 80.

[2] Stephen Neal Dennis, *Historic Houses of the Sewickley Valley*. Sewickley Pa., White Oak Publishing, 1996, p. 27.

[3] Charles Stotz, *The Early Architecture of Western Pennsylvania*. Pittsburgh, The University Press, 1995, p. 17.

[4] Ibid., p. 109-110.

Chapter 6
Edgeworth

The Ways purchased half of the Depreciation Land tracts then known as Sewickley Bottom but now comprising Edgeworth Borough. The remaining half of what is now Edgeworth was purchased by Thomas Shields of Philadelphia in 1785. Thomas Shields' son David, married Eliza, daughter of Daniel Leet. The land has remained in the Leet-Shields family ever since. In 1998 J.J. Brooks, Jr., a great-great-great grandson of David and Eliza Shields, lived in the old family home on Beaver Road. Leet Shields lived in a slightly newer house nearby.

The Leet-Shields and the Way families have had an enduring effect on the development of the Edgeworth area. Edgeworth today is a prosperous, attractive community of mostly well-to-do people living in large houses. The two founding families controlled the land and directed its development. Most of the Sewickley valley and, indeed, the rest of western Pennsylvania was settled by small farmers who moved west, bought a plot of land for individual family farms, and toiled to make a living. They did not have enough land or enough time to worry much about community development. The Way, Leet, and Shields families had the resources and the ability to see the larger picture.

The Ways, as we have seen, bought a large tract of land which they farmed, but they also derived income and prestige from many other activities. Daniel Leet, too, was no common dirt farmer. Like his friend John Way, he was a man of many accomplishments. Unlike Way, whose family had Quaker roots, Leet had a touch of the Virginia aristocrat. Born in New Jersey in 1748, Leet was brought up in Virginia where he studied to become a surveyor at William & Mary College. He served in the English army before the Revolution and under George Washington at Trenton and Valley Forge, where he met Caleb Way. After the Revolution, Leet returned to Washington, Pennsylvania. He did not remain a civilian long. In 1782 he joined William Crawford on an expedition against the Indians in Ohio. Crawford was captured and, after being horribly tortured, burned at the stake. Daniel Leet managed to get his troops home safely.

Leet in cooperation with Thomas Shields obtained a tract of land that is now the western half of Edgeworth. He did not move to his property until 1827, just three years before his death. He did build a mill on Little Sewickley Creek and an inn, now known as the Lark Inn, on Beaver Road. The inn was a convenient stopping place, appropriately called Halfway House because it was equidistant from Pittsburgh and Beaver.

Lark Inn. Photograph about 1905. Courtesy The Sewickley Valley Historical Society.

Daniel Leet sent his daughter, Eliza, east to school at Bethlehem Female Moravian Seminary. This shows an interest in girls' education unusual at the time. Eliza married David Shields in 1803. The Shieldses were a prominent Philadelphia family. David's father, Thomas, was a silversmith. This was a premier occupation in colonial times when silversmiths were much admired and richly rewarded. David Shields came west and settled in Washington, Pennsylvania, where he stayed for a time with Daniel Leet and met Eliza, his future wife. Shields developed an extensive business as a merchant first in Washington, Pennsylvania and later in Sewickley.

Shields kept a Day Book which records all his business transactions from 1820 to 1828. He did many commissions for Abishai Way. For example, the Day Book records 108 transactions for Way between December 15, 1821 and April 3, 1822. These transactions totaled $14,012.24. Because the mail between Philadelphia and Pittsburgh was unreliable, Shields transported cash personally for Abishai Way. He delivered $2,873 in cash and $1,990 in various bank notes to Philadelphia; collected $261.69 for William Woods' sales of butter and granted credit of $165.84 for Wood's groceries. David Shields acted as Abishai Way's personal financial manager. In the same four month period he paid 40 of Way's bills from suppliers.

The Way-Shields connection continued after the death of Abishai, who died intestate. His widow petitioned the court to appoint David Shields guardian for the three minor children under 14. Shields accepted.

Another of David Shields' important clients was the Harmony Society, a communal group with extensive commercial ventures all over the area. The Harmonists had originally settled in 1805 in a place they named Harmony, near Zelionople, Pennsylvania. In 1815 they moved to New Harmony, Indiana, for 10 years. Finding Indiana too remote and too infested with malarial mosquitoes, they sought to return to western Pennsylvania. David Shields suggested possibilities around Sewickley in a letter dated April 7, 1824 to Frederick Rapp, son of the founder and business manager of the Society. The letter gives a good picture of the real estate market at the time.

Squire Way and myself have been busied in getting all the information that with discretion we could arrive at relative to the other land along the river, the amount of which is, that the Bank's tracts may probably be had for four or five doll[ar]s. per ac[re]. The Englishman's 100 as [acres] @ 10 drs. McKee's at seven dolls—Bryan's uncertain, Hazletts at 10 dollars, Blaines at 20 drs. Vickery has declined at present offering his for sale. . . . Squire Way declines selling. Huey's 250 acres may be had but probably will not sell for less than 25 drs. per acre—Beer's the same as Huey's. Park's & Whites we believe may be had, they are but rough land, which is the case with all the land higher up the river.

Shields even offered to sell the Harmonists his own house and extensive property on the Beaver Road in what is now Edgeworth Borough.

Mr. Fred Rapp:

I promised that I would, immediately after conferring with my father in law, write you on the subject of the sale of our Sewickley estate: I am at liberty to sell, and now offer it to you for $40,000. It contains about 1400 acres of patent land.

Later Shields had second thoughts.

It would be very agreeable to me if you could make out your establishment without my property, yet notwithstanding that I now find that I have not duly estimated my estate and its costly and valuable improvement, yet if you deem it necessary or proper to purchase mine also, it shall be yours.

Father Rapp, the sect's leader, rescued Shields from his unwilling sale. He writes Friedrich on April 8, 1824:

About Schielt's [Shields'] land, [which] I would have considered mostly good and useful land, I have a dissatisfaction with it, first of all because it gets flooded, secondly because it is too high in price. You leave it to him. I have already forgotten it: it surprises me only that you have let him go to Washington to speak with his father-in-law. I am quite sick of flooded land.

Newington in 1857. Note additions: gable windows, cupolas on roof, and porch. Courtesy Sewickley Valley Historical Society

Shields Schoolhouse, Edgeworth.
Courtesy Sewickley Library

Newington, the house that Shields rashly offered to sell, is a landmark of western Pennsylvania. The first section, built in 1816, is a small, two-story brick structure. It looked like a typical Pennsylvania farmhouse with a center hall and one room on either side. Oaks cut on the property were sawed by a water wheel at Leet's mill on Sewickley Creek near the Beaver Road. The bricks, also made on the property, are quite soft and must be painted for preservation. Because the first house was small, an addition nearer Beaver Road was built in 1823. The addition is grander than the original house. It has a large central hall with sweeping staircase. On either side of the hall were two rooms.

According to the Day Book, David and Eliza Shields moved in 1823. Accounts dated 2 August, 1823 are from Washington, Pennsylvania; the next entry, dated 6, October, 1823 is from Sewickley Bottom. The Shields Day Book records progress of work on the property.

David Shelah [Shields] CR [credit] 9 days work at Sewickley $5.62¹/₂.

James Kerr. Work for me at Sewickley from 10 November 1821 to 30 April 1823, making 363 days $111.69. 1 May Dec. 31 1823, $56.25.

2d August 1823. Bill of carpenter work, sawing, hewing of house and stable and roofing Sawmill at Sewickley as per bill from James Kerr, carpenter. $1,433.24

Sleds, repairing carts, wheelbarrow and sundry other jobs at Sewickley. $40.

Putting up posts and boarding part of fence at the back of garden (Sewickley) $10.00

Gate and posts at barn $4.

Relaying barn floor $7.

In addition to the main house, there was a laundry, a summer kitchen, an ice house, and housing for those who worked on the plantation. Agnes Hays Gormly remembered Newington which she visited as a child in the 1850s.

Here real plantation life was led, for Mr. Shields built not only the large mansion but had established large barns, a grist-mill, blacksmith shop, and a tavern, all of which served those living in the area or those who travelled the highway. The grist mill was the largest in the surrounding area and served for the neighborhood to turn their grain into flour and meal. The large over-shot wheel stood for many years before the mill was completely demolished. Today the miller's residence is still standing, it being used as a residence. As early as 1837 there were no wagons in this part of the country and the farmers had to bring their grain to the mill on horseback in the summer, and on sleds in the winter.

David and Eliza Shields also built a one-room schoolhouse not far from Newington, a miller's house, and a blacksmith shop and house on Beaver Road and Little Sewickley Creek. David Shield's Day Book records the exact

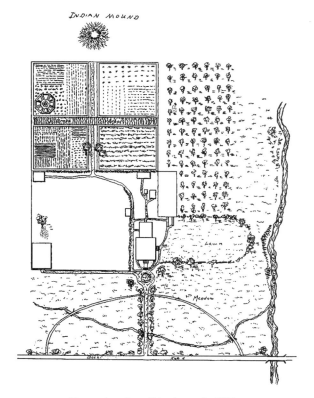

The garden plan of Newington in 1823.
From *Gardens of Colony and State*, by Alice B. Lockwood.

beginning of the smithy's shop: "Cornelius Pascal Credit 3 December 1823. By Digging out foundation for smithshop." The following advertisement appeared in the *Post Gazette* on May 2, 1834.

To Blacksmith

To rent for the ensuing year, from and after the first day of April next, a good Smith Shop with dwelling house, pasturage, etc., situate on the great road, about half way between Pittsburgh and Beaver. Will suit an industrious man of correct habits and a well disposed family and a recommendation to that effect will be required by the applicant.

For further information, apply to the subscriber living near the premises, or by letter addressed to Sewickley Bottom Post Office.

David Shields

Newington is especially well known for its gardens. Charles Stotz, in his book on early Pennsylvania architecture, said that the gardens of Newington "retain in their grounds and gardens much of their original beauty."[1] Mr. Brooks' father, J. Judson Brooks, Jr., tended an especially fine collection of rhododendrons. This careful tending has continued from the beginning, as we can see by examining the plan, dated 1823, included in an account by Sarah E. Bissell, Judson Brooks' third cousin. Sarah Bissell described the gardens in a book published in 1931.

A space was selected for a garden. A clearing was made in the river valley open to the rising and setting sun, and protected by a windbreak of trees listed as Hoop Ash, Black Oak, White Hickory, and a Sychomore of renown. In 1823 the garden took to itself an air of importance, was fenced and hedged about and gated in. The French influence was felt in the garden, and it was blocked out in squares and strips, while paths, bordering narrow beds, led to the eastern corner, where we find a formal garden like a huge cut pie.

The little gate which formed the entrance opened on a long and grassy path broken midway by two cedar trees trimmed to look like huge bushes standing like fat sentinels—a home and a protection for the birds.

The garden was outlined by narrow beds of smaller fruits, raspberries, white, pink and red; gooseberries, strawberries—backed by trellised grapes, white and purple, sharing their sunlight with the herb bed, where grew sage and thyme and sweet marjoram, rosemary and later tarragon. In the midst of the garden flourished all the old-time flowers, growing in a mass of gorgeous bloom. In early spring the Star of Bethlehem forced its way through the mass of leaves, and hyacinths and daffodils and the old red peony took their turns. There all the sweet old roses unfurled their petals—and the hundred-leaved, the moss, red velvet, and the white and yellow Scotch and sweet briar too. Violets, forget-me-nots, lily-of-the-valley, scented the air, and fox-gloves swayed in the breeze near white and blue Canterbury bells, and blazing marigolds. Overhead jasmine and scarlet cypress stretched their graceful vines.

On the southern exposure grew a flourishing orchard, and in the first row to center tree was a Seckel pear, a seedling from the original found in a fence corner by Dr. Seckel, and to this day the only seedling never grafted. And then, to fix the garden with the ancient times, we find an Indian mound. This has been surmounted by a stone-foundationed summer house strong enough to deter marauding hand from disturbing the Indian grave resting quietly below. Beyond this lay the orchard wall above the little Sewickley creek which rippled its sparkling water to the broad Ohio.

The garden at Newington was very closely associated with the garden at Economy laid out in 1827 by that strange community called Harmony Society. . . . Plants and trees were exchanged, dahlias being especially remembered as 'yust so schoen behind as before.'[2]

The Newington gardens have remained spectacular. In the 1870s, Samuel B. Parsons, a landscape architect from Philadelphia, updated the design and included a rose garden. This plan was itself revised by Ezra Stiles, a Pittsburgh landscape architect. Stiles created a formal garden with walls, yews, and azaleas.[3]

Because Newington was well known in the area, it became the location of the first post office. David Shields himself served as the first postmaster from 1824 to 1859. It was vital that the postmaster be familiar with everyone in the community or he would never be able to cope with such addresses as J. and M. Olver, Sewickley, Allegheny County. David Shields' Day Book records what might have been the first postal transaction in the Valley: "January 29, 1824. To James Kerr. Postage letter $.12$\frac{1}{2}$"

The post office was in the eastern corner room of Newington, according to an article in the *Weekly Herald*, 1911. The same room housed a little store: "Many boys of the fifties [1850s] who are living in the Valley today can recall the purchases made from Mr. David Shields, the postmaster. The apples were as inviting as the letters and sweets."[4]

Just after its completion Newington must have been especially impressive when compared with the log cabins and simple farm houses scattered around the area. Later owners of Newington altered the house to suit changing tastes, according to a memo by J. Judson Brooks Jr., the father of the current owner.

> After the Civil War two unmarried daughters took control of the property and the house received its first modernization to bring it into the Victorian Age. Hence the two cupolas on the roof and assorted filigree edgings around the roofs. In the family circle they [the cupolas] are referred to as the "little horrors", but we have all become quite attached to them and for the time being at least have decided that after 100 years they have squatters' rights.

> The second massive renovation came at the turn of the century when the two aunts died and the house passed to the niece, Mrs. L. Halsey Williams. She added various plumbing and made an apartment on the third floor which resulted in the dormer windows being added at that time. Many features of this change were not in keeping with the Colonial character of the house. A terrace with a terra-cotta landing was added on the front and English leaded windows were put in the living room. . . .

> When the Brooks took over Newington in 1960 most of the old accumulation of heavy furniture was moved out regardless of its sentimental value and Mrs. Brooks refurbished the house in the Colonial style. At this time new plumbing and wiring was installed and the interior of the rear wing was completely rebuilt to accommodate a modern kitchen.

Newington has the flavor of a Southern mansion, perhaps reflecting the southern heritage of the Leet family. Like Southern houses, Newington has a large central hall with doors at both ends which encourage summer breezes to waft through the house. This is a characteristic of Southern houses such as Gunston Hall in Virginia.

Southern hospitality was practiced in Pennsylvania, at least at Newington. David Shields noted in his diary on November 10, 1835: "The stage upset last night between Sewickley Bottoms and Sewickley Hotel, one passenger, a Rev. Doct. Kerr seriously hurt." The Rev. Doct. found asylum at Newington where he remained six weeks. It was not until December 29 that Shields could report, "The Rev. Leander Kerr and sister left us. . . . This is the gentleman who was much hurt by the upsetting of the stage."

Other similarities between southern plantation life and Newington in the 1850s appear in the memoir of Agnes Hays Gormly.

> We disembarked at Shousetown Lane [Leetsdale]. A carriage even more magnificent than Mr. Schoenerger's . . . was waiting. The coachman was as black as our Jimmy Stares, and had as ivory a grin. . . . We drew up with a flourish to the doorway where Mr. and Mrs. Shields stood ready to welcome my grandmother. . . . My eyes were riveted on the great fireplace, where Mazeppa, forever bound on his iron steed, was forever pursued by iron wolves. What a real plantation life was lived here; what a majestic presence was Mrs. Shields; what a Quaker gentleman was Mr. Shields! When we retired he handed my grandmother her silver candlestick from the hall table. . . . Next day I saw the great barn, the mill-race, and the big maple tree whence came the sugar eggs that had astonished our Penn street eyes.

> The next day we spent at Mr. John Way Jr.'s, and even then the garden was old and lovely. What good manners we had when we went visiting; one's feet always dangled from the horsehair sofa or chairs; you never volunteered a remark, and always said, "Yes, Ma'am," or "No, Ma'am" and by and by grownups would say something and a little tray of paradisaic cookies and little cut-glass goblets, just big enough for your doll, would come in, and your grandmother would say, "No wine for Aggie, please."

Judson Brooks, Jr. continued the story of Edgeworth as it was when he was a boy in the early 1900s. He was surrounded by family.

Grandmother lived here [at Newington], Uncle Leet lived across the street. When I came home from school, I picked up the mail at the Shields post office [at the foot of Church Lane] for six people, five of them were relatives.

In addition to the family houses, there was the family mausoleum. According to Judson Brooks, the mausoleum was built when the family graveyard was separated from Newington.

During the 1873 crash, an unscrupulous relative with a power of attorney sold property between the house and the graveyard. The aunts could not have that. They built the mausoleum which now contains 7 generations of the Shields family. I roller skated there on rainy days when I was a child.

Because Judson Brooks' grandmother was orphaned when she was very young, she was raised by the two maiden aunts. She told her grandson about her childhood at Newington, giving a picture of upper-class life at the end of the nineteenth century. Mr. Brooks recalled:

Children were brought up to be seen and not heard. The two aunts were entertaining at tea one afternoon. Grandmother came running in. "Aunt! Aunt!" "Don't speak until you are spoken to. Have a cup of tea with the rest of us." After a while, "What were you going to tell us?" "It is probably not interesting now; the damn barn is probably burned to the ground." They took her away, beat her and put her to bed [for swearing]. Then they went down, and sure enough the barn was an ash.

Mr. Brooks' grandmother told him,

I never had a chance to marry anyone but your grandfather. The aunts had heavy shutters on all the windows. These were shut tight every night. A high iron fence surrounded the place. Two large dogs patrolled the premises all night. Fortunately, your grandfather was an excellent horseman, able to jump high fences, and he had a way with dogs.

The Shields family maintained its wealth and social position through marrying well and through fortunate real-estate holdings. David and Eliza Shield's oldest daughter, Maria Leet Shields, is a good illustration. She got a large part of Leetsdale which was later developed for the steel mill. She married John K. Wilson, a successful lawyer and a director of the Pennsylvania Railroad. Wilson was a dignified person around Sewickley who always carried a gold cane and wore a top hat. The Wilsons built a large house on the east side of Beaver Road in present day Leetsdale. Mr. Brooks remembered the house.

It looked like a hospital. It was built like the Rock of Gibralter, to last forever. The world was in pretty good shape and would stay that way.

Amelia Neville Shields married James B. Oliver, the president of Oliver Iron and Steel Company. Their daughter married William J. Crittenden and built a house next to the Wilsons'. The Crittenden house was a copy of Westover in Virginia.

In 1854, Thomas Leet Shields, David and Eliza's son, built a brick house on 436 Beaver Road not far from his parents' house. It was designed by Joseph Kerr, a well-known architect who also designed the present building of The Presbyterian Church of Sewickley. Thomas Shields started an extensive nursery on his flat land which lay south of the Beaver Road between Church Lane and Edgeworth Lane. The size of the business is indicated by an order placed to Hugh Wilson of Washington County for 1,000 arbor vitae and 1,000 quince cuttings. Another order to an Ohio firm was for 91 pear, 98 cherry, and 16 quince trees. Shields & Co. provided plants for James Wardrop's nursery in Manchester on the North Side. One commission in 1859 included "corn seed, rhubarb roots, Lawton blackberry plants, 1,000 strawberry plants, . . . 500 willow cuttings, Osage oranges and clematis."[5]

Leet Shields House, 436 Beaver Road. Photo by John H. Demmler.

Captain David Shields, a grandson of the builders of Newington, lived in the Thomas Shields house. Captain Shields was born in 1844 in Ohio but educated in Pennsylvania. Upon the outbreak of the Civil War, the seventeen-year-old David Shields enlisted in the 63rd Regiment, Pennsylvania Volunteer Infantry. For two years he served as aide to General Alexander Hays, participating in many battles during the war. He was wounded in four of them: first at the Battle of Glendale, Virginia, June 30, 1862; second, at the Battle of Gettysburg, July 3, 1863; third at the Battle of Morton's Ford, Virginia, February 6, 1864 in the morning; and, fourth, at the same battle in the afternoon. Miraculously surviving all, Captain Shields was honorably discharged from the service for disability on his twentieth birthday. Despite the disability, David Shields lived a long life. Judson Brooks remembered that when he was a youth Boy Scouts seeking to become first class scouts were allowed the privilege of seeing the bullet wound in Captain Shields' chest.

Captain David turned the Thomas Shields nursery into a sort of agricultural experiment station, receiving three patents on his work. He reasoned that mixing coal, which is the product of compression of vegetation, with salt water found in oil and gas wells, and local clay should produce a superior fertilizer.

The Edgeworth section of the valley was the most well-to-do and certainly the best documented. Although a visitor in the first half of the nineteenth century might have expected Edgeworth to develop into a town, it has remained a residential area. The pre-eminent position of the two families retarded development. They controlled so much of the property that others who might have started small businesses could not gain a foothold.

Edgeworth was a logical place for a town because it possessed many of the ingredients that usually form the nucleus of a commercial center: an inn; a school; and a church. In addition, it had two other ingredients that might have attracted townsfolk. There was a blacksmith shop, a necessity for anyone with horses. While the horses were being shod, farmers could have replenished supplies. The other attraction was the grist mill, built in 1797 near Newington. Settlers came from miles around to have their crops ground.

Anyone reading Agnes Hays Gormly's description of Edgeworth in the 1850s would think that she was describing the beginnings of a town.

> We rolled past the stone tavern, built by Mr. Shields, past the blacksmith shop, where the red light was streaming across the road, past the grist mill with the great water wheel run by the Little Sewickley Creek, and past the miller's brick house.[6]

Mrs. Gormly did not remark on other features of Edgeworth that would logically have led to the formation of a town: schools and churches. The schools, especially the Shields school and Edgeworth Academy, will be described in a later chapter. Today the only church in Edgeworth is the Shields Presbyterian; in the early days, however, Edgeworth had as many religious institutions as Sewickley Borough. As early as 1798, the Reverend Francis Reno, an Episcopalian, preached at a barn across the river from the Way tavern. Reverend Reno was sent out from Philadelphia by the Bishop White Prayer Book Society to minister to the western settlements. He built a log house in what is now Rochester, Pennsylvania and preached in barns and groves all over the area. Local subscribers around Sewickley agreed to pay for one third of his time for a year for $29.08 cash plus a bushel of wheat and 38 bushels of corn, to be delivered at Leet's grist mill. John Olver, for example, promised to pay three bushels of corn; Henry Ulery, four bushels of corn and one of rye; and John Way, $1.50. Reverend Reno did not hesitate to enforce collection of these promises. In 1801 he enlisted the help of Squire Way in getting judgments against three obdurate subscribers.[7]

The Methodists, too, were in the area early. About 1816, the Trustees of the Methodist Society built a frame chapel on Little Sewickley Creek. Methodists held services here and, later, in the brick schoolhouse built in 1826 by David Shields across Beaver Road from his house.[8]

The Shields schoolhouse served several religions. John Way, Jr. remembered in 1888:

> The building was used for school, prayer meetings, and general church purposes. From time-to-time, as occasion offered, there was preaching there, and prayer meetings: the itinerant preacher always finding at Mr. Shield's house a welcome for himself and his horse.

Mrs. Shields used the same adaptable schoolhouse to teach her afternoon Sunday school from about 1835 to 1844. John Way, Jr. remembered,

> The school began usually as soon as spring weather would admit and continued always until Christmas, when each boy or girl received some suitable present at the hands of the "elect lady" and a bountiful supply of cakes and apples. . . . One of the aids deserves special mention—her carriage driver—a giant African of brawn and muscle who could neither read or write, and whose knowledge of mathematics was limited to four, the number of horses in his farm team. At times when Mrs. Shields was unable from rheumatism to climb the steep hillside to her little Sunday-school, big Jim Robinson would tenderly carry her up in his huge arms.[9]

Edgeworth was a logical place for a town because it possessed many of the ingredients that usually form the nucleus of a commercial center. It would have been logical for Edgeworth or Sewickley to become the commercial center for the area. The two founding families of Edgeworth, however, did not subdivide their land in a way suitable for development. Many of the early landholders of Sewickley did, as we shall see in the next chapter. Sewickley was the quintessential railroad suburb in the nineteenth century. Much of Edgeworth remained relatively unchanged. The 1897 map shows many large plots remaining.

[1] Stotz, p. 30.

[2] Alice B. Lockwood, ed., *Gardens of Colony and State*, comp. and ed for the Garden Club of America. New York, Scribners, 1931, v.1, p. 379-80.

[3] *Sewickley Magazine*, May, 1986, p. 5.

[4] *Weekly Herald*, September 2, 1911, p. 2.

[5] "Edgeworth Preservation," Newsletter, n.d.

[6] Agnes Hays Gormly, "Journey to Newington". In *Old Penn Street*, by Gilbert Hays. Sewickley: The Village Print Shop, 1928.

[7] *Fiftieth Anniversary Exercises of the Presbyterian Church, Sewickley, Pa.*, 1838-1888. Pittsburgh, W.W. Walters, n.d., p. 21.

[8] "Paper in Celebration of the of the Incorporation of the Church." Nov. 16, 1902. Prepared by S.C. Ritchey and J. C. Venning, p. 4.

[9] *The Presbyterian Church, Sewickley, Pa. 1838-1988*, p. 21 and 43.

Chapter 7
Sewickley before the Railroad

Sewickley and Edgeworth are geographically very similar. Both have flat land suitable for farming along the river. Both are cut off from the area to the north by steep hills. Both were sold in two large tracts: Edgeworth to the Way and Leet families; Sewickley to Henry Ulery and Thomas Beer. Ulery, a German sea captain, settled on a 250-acre tract along the river between Edgeworth and Division Street. Thomas Beer bought the other half of what is now Sewickley, between Division Street and Osborne. The Edgeworth owners maintained ownership and control of their land, using it for farming and parting with it slowly. Sewickley owners, on the other hand, were more likely to sell their land any time the price seemed right. Because land was available sooner in what is now Sewickley Borough, development there occurred sooner.

Sewickley became a village where neighboring farmers came to shop, sell their goods, and go to church. But it was more than a village serving farmers. It turned into a thriving town where farmers were joined by travelers going to and from Pittsburgh to points west. F. Cumming's description of road travel in 1810 makes the roads sound almost crowded.

> The traveling on these roads in every direction is truly astonishing, even at this inclement season, but in the spring and fall, I am informed that it is beyond all conception. A European, who had not experienced it, could form no proper idea of the manner of it in this country. The travelers are wagoners, carrying produce to, and bringing back foreign goods from the different shipping ports on the shores of the Atlantick, particularly Philadelphia and Baltimore;—Packers with from one to twenty horses, selling or trucking their wares through the country;—Countrymen, sometimes alone, sometimes in large companies, carrying salt;—Families removing further back into the country, some with cows, oxen, horses, sheep, and hogs, and all their farming implements and domestick utensils, and some without; some with wagons, some with carts and some on foot, according to their abilities:—The residue, who make use of the best accommodations on the roads, are country merchants, judges and lawyers . . . and the better class of settlers removing back.[1]

Captain John Anderson, born in 1828, remembered the Beaver Road, the main road to the west.

> There was immense traffic along the road. Great strings of wagons, Conestogas, with six-horse teams coming in from Ohio and Indiana and going to Philadelphia, I guess. Big, fine horses, with bells on them. And there were droves of cattle, and pigs, and turkeys too. The hogs were the hardest to drive and the turkeys the easiest. Men would run along beside them and scare them so they would crowd together and run. They would drive easier than cattle, but when it began to get dark you couldn't drive them. They would fly up into the trees and roost. I have seen the fence tops all along the road for miles covered with turkeys roosting.[2]

Whether travelers came by river or by road, they could stop at Sewickley for food, lodging and repairs.

Because the river was the main avenue of commerce in the early nineteenth century, the first settlement was near its banks. Both Henry Ulery in Sewickley and John Way in Edgeworth had log houses on the river. Early inns, too, were established to serve river travelers. The river inns were not elegant. Problems with flooding discouraged innkeepers from making large investments. The clientele did not expect or respect elegance. Many customers were settlers using the river to travel to new and fertile lands. Others worked on flatboats or keelboats and were known as the riffraff of the river. Boatmen had a reputation for drunkenness, boasting and violence. There are many accounts in the Pittsburgh papers of savage fights on the Monongahela wharf, where boatmen and draymen (wagoners), natural enemies, congregated before shipping off down the Ohio River.[3] William Winans, an early river traveler, described the flatboatmen.

> The tedious navigation accumulated in them an immense amount of excitability, which had no ordinary and respectable modes of expending itself. This prepared them to yield to any form of excitement within reach of their peculiar condition. This usually leads to drinking, gambling, boxing matches, and other fierce vanities.[4]

In Sewickley these "fierce vanities" might have taken place at Captain John Hay's river tavern or at Thomas Beer's tavern, which he operated out of his house as early as 1805. Here he served "roistering keelboatmen and riffraff of the river".[5] Beer's building was still standing in 1911 when Louise Dippold described it.

> The log part of the dwelling is the upper wing of the building, joined later with a frame addition, and all boarded in later years, making a very compact house of the period. It is owned by Mrs. Margaret McKown Atwell, who can restore it to its former quaintness and make it a finer abode than it is a the present time.[6]

Inns on or near the Beaver Road served a more respectable clientele including farmers going to or from Pittsburgh with their goods, and travelers arriving by the daily stage from Pittsburgh. Sewickley and Osborne had many inns and taverns in addition to the Leet and Way taverns already mentioned. John Little had a tavern on Beaver and Little streets; John Fife's tavern was nearby at Grove and Beaver; John Mitchell's was up Mitchell's glen; James Park's was on the corner of Beaver and Glen Mitchell Roads in what is now Osborne. James Park was a farmer who supplemented his income with the inn. In 1911 his building belonged to Joseph Lambie, according to Louise Dippold, who, like Mrs. Atwell, "will some day restore it to its former quaintness. It is known to be one of the oldest landmarks now standing in our valley." Unhappily, like the Beer tavern, it was never restored quaintly or otherwise.

By 1850 Sewickley was already a town. Agnes Ellis estimated in her book that there were 30 houses in 1846.[7] There were churches, a primary school, and a private secondary school, Sewickley Academy. In 1853, when 82 Sewickley men signed the petition to form a borough, the town was a community of people with varying backgrounds and careers. The first settlers had come from Germany, Scotland or England. Most of the German settlers remained farmers, but the other nationalities entered a variety of occupations. George Starr was postmaster and justice of the peace; Robert Dickson was a builder; Alexander McElwain, a merchant; and Robert Anderson, a silversmith. Some careers required extensive education. William M. Nevin, a teacher at Sewickley Academy, went to Jefferson College. Joseph Travelli, a former missionary to Singapore, was superintendent of Sewickley Academy. He, Daniel Nevin and James Allison, both pastors of the Sewickley Presbyterian Church, attended Jefferson College and the Western Theological Seminary. Dr. William Woods graduated from Jefferson Medical College in Philadelphia. Alexander Hays went to West Point.[8]

Many tradesmen and professionals lived and worked in houses and stores clustered around Beaver Street. Robert and John Green's log house on Grimes and Beaver Streets was the site of the first store.[9] The Greens remained in Sewickley for generations and still owned property on Green and Beaver in 1929. In 1837, John Garrison started another store on what is now 429 Beaver Street. In the 1850s, John Way, Jr. had a combination grocery store and post office on the corner of Beaver and Chestnut Streets. About the same time, the Tracy and Schofield wagon shop was located at 503 Beaver Street. There was at least one physician on Beaver Street. John Dickson started a practice there in 1831, where the Baptist Church stands now.

Of course, where there was so much burgeoning activity, there were churches. Churches were the main social contact in what was a life of hard work. Before there were church buildings, services were held in various places including a log house and Addy Beer's grove of trees, near what is now the nurses' quarters for the hospital. Although the first Episcopalian church building, St. Stephen's, was not completed until 1864, Reverend Francis Reno, an itinerant Episcopalian preacher, held services in Squire Way's barn on the Beaver Road from 1798 to 1809.

As early as 1805 there was Methodist preaching in the Sewickley area at the home of Jesse Fisher on the Shields property. Before 1823 a frame church was erected on Beaver Road near the bridge over Little Sewickley Creek.[10] There were no regular services in Sewickley Borough until the Methodists built their first church building in 1839. This was was a frame building 30 by 40 feet on the same site as the present church, Broad and Thorn Streets. The frame church was replaced by a brick building in 1854; the present building replaced it in 1884. Although there was no organ or choir in the early days, there was plenty of music. A history of the church written in 1902 states:

> People would come before the hour of service and spend the time in singing. Someone would start up a hymn in which all would join; then another hymn would be started, until the minister was ready to begin. All these exercises were very much enjoyed.[11]

Methodism was very successful, according to Daniel Nevin, minister of the Presbyterian Church, who reported with a touch of professional jealousy in a letter to Isaac Cook dated January 9, 1843:

> Deep religious feeling has pervaded the valley through the last month. The Methodists had meetings for a fortnight or more every evening. They numbered (children and backsliders inclusive) 140 conversions. The awakening commenced in their church and several of our young men were among their converts—viz Sam Peebles, James Anderson, Stephen Dickson, and John Way. We commenced a series of meetings three weeks ago in our church [Presbyterian] and I have preached every day.

Later in the century, the Methodists continued their revival meetings, according to *The Valley Gossip, 1881*.

Revival meetings have been held at the Methodist Church every night since the week of prayer, and about 15 accessions to membership were made. Owing to the supply of coal running out, the meetings were discontinued.[12]

The first building of the Presbyterian Church, Sewickley. Photograph 1885.

The Presbyterian Church of Sewickley. 1840 building. Courtesy The Sewickley Valley Historical Society.

The first Presbyterian Church building dates from 1818, but for at least nine years before, Presbyterian services had been held sporadically in the area. In 1809, for instance, the preachers at Sewickley Bottoms (now Edgeworth) were: "Mr. McClain the second Sabbath of January; Mr. McDonald, the fifth Sabbath of January, and Mr. Vennemon the third Sabbath of March."[13] In 1811 Mr. McDonald was hired to spend one third of his time at Sewickley, but his time was decreased to one sixth in 1816, and two years later Sewickley was listed among vacant congregations. Prospects for Presbyterians improved somewhat in the same year when the first meetinghouse was built on Division Street near where the YMCA is today. It did not look much like a church but like a log house with a steep roof, two windows in front and one on the side, and a crude door. There was no chimney. Before its destruction in 1876, the building was used at various times as a school, an undertaker's establishment, and a carpenter's shop, as well as a church.[14] This is a good example of the adaptability of log buildings; the space could be used as needed. In 1822, when John Andrews became part time minister, there were only 12 members, including elders James McLaughlin and Thomas Backhouse. Backhouse was the same person who had the quarrel adjudicated by John Way.

From 1828 to 1834, the Sewickley Presbyterians shared a minister with the Fairmount Presbyterian Church, located in Franklin Borough near Duff City. The Fairmount Church was the more important. Daniel Nevin, called to both churches in 1838, described the arrangement in a letter to his brother.

I have been requested to settle in a Church fourteen or fifteen miles from [Pittsburgh] called Fairmount congregation. It is composed of two branches, one at Sewickley flat embracing Mr. Shields, Mrs. Olver, etc. the other four miles back from the river: this is much the larger branch and would want two thirds of my preaching. They offer to give together five hundred dollars.[15]

For his first three years, Mr. Nevin preached at the Edgeworth Seminary because the log church was not thought fit for occupancy. In 1840 a church was built on 101 Beaver Street, across from the present church. This was a simple but elegant brick building with Gothic windows and a Greek revival pediment and entrance. The architect was John Chislett, an Englishman who had studied architecture at Bath. He became Pittsburgh's first architect and designed the entrance gates to the Allegheny Cemetery and the building on 209 Fourth Avenue, Pittsburgh, that is the headquarters for the Western Pennsylvania Conservancy. The choice of a well-known architect for the Presbyterian Church, Sewickley tells something about the town. More than utility was desired in this new church. The parishioners were willing to spend extra effort and money to obtain a beautiful building.

As Sewickley grew the church building became inadequate despite attempts to adapt it. Dr. James Allison, the minister, remembered:

The Presbyterian Church, Sewickley. Drawing by Susan Gaca.

First new pews were placed in the vacant spaces around the pulpit. Then, all the pews were taken up and placed more close-ly together, . . . and, then, the gallery was erected. . . . But at length a larger house of worship was absolutely necessary.[16]

The congregation chose Joseph W. Kerr, a prominent Pittsburgh architect. The Presbyterian Church, Sewickley, dedicated in 1861, was his first local building to be followed later by the Dixmont Hospital and the Shields Presbyterian Church. Kerr designed the Sewickley church building in the Gothic style, always popular for churches. The stones came from a quarry just above the present Sewickley Hospital. The interior was plain with clear glass windows, in accordance with the beliefs of the old style Presbyterians. In 1898 stained glass windows were allowed. Clear glass gave way to beautiful stained glass creations of master designers Louis Comfort Tiffany and John LaFarge.

Fortunately, surroundings were pleasant, for the services in the early nineteenth century were very long. Sermons were lengthy and there was no organ: Psalm singing and hymns were the only music allowed. The communion services, held outside because of their popularity, lasted for five days with as many as three sermons on Sunday and sermons or fasts on the other days. Only those who could prove that they had attended the preparatory sermons by showing tokens distributed at each event were allowed to take communion.[17]

Sunday school for the Presbyterians was a sometime thing, according to John Way, Jr. James McLaughlin was the leading spirit of the early Sunday school in the log church.

The long distance from his home to the log church, some three miles, was no hindrance to his early and regular attendance each Sabbath morning at the Sunday-school. There he frequently led the devotional exercises. About 1831-32, Colonel Loring Hodge, a New Englander and a Presbyterian, was superintendent of the Sunday-school. He lived in a log house on the river bank. . . . But the glory of being a Sunday-school superintendent did not save the Colonel from the temptations of the world. He kept a small store at his river-side dwelling where he supplied the keel-boatmen and the occupants of the numerous cabins around him with the staple artickles of merchandize, including whiskey. His trade was not large, and, naturally wishing to increase his scanty income, in an evil hour he fell into the snare of all liquor dealers—selling on Sunday. His liquor doubtless was good; his example bad.[18]

Besides the Sunday school, there were two women's groups: the Young Ladies Sewing Society and the Ladies Circle of Industry Society. These were a source of great pleasure for the women, allowing them to socialize without being accused of wasting Presbyterian time.

Most of the buildings in Sewickley Borough constructed before the railroad are gone. A study conducted in 1966 found that thirty structures dating from 1800-1850 remained in Sewickley Borough. Most had been so thoroughly remodeled that they had lost all architectural significance. The house on 601 Hill Street, for example, was built in 1837. By 1937, according to a survey conducted in that year, it had acquired a mansard roof and one-story additions back and front. Fifteen of the thirty pre-1850 structures were originally houses, but some had been turned into commercial buildings. Twenty-two of the thirty structures which remained in 1966 housed commercial businesses on Beaver Street, the center of commercial activity. These structures had been modified to suit changing consumer demands.[19]

A few houses preserve their original appearance. The Garrison-Lewis house (707 Hopkins Street) is a two-story stone and frame vernacular Greek Revival house which dates from 1826.

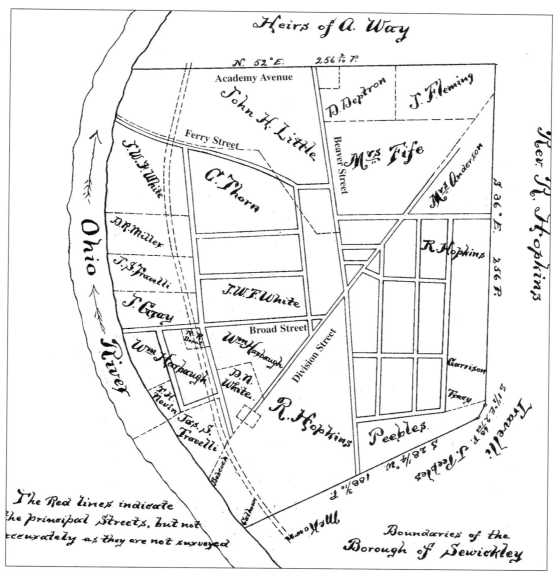

Map accompanying Charter petition, 1853.

What is now Sewickley Borough was settled in various ways by many individuals who bought large tracts of property and divided them, creating a street plan that looks more like a jigsaw puzzle than a grid. There was no master plan. This contrasts with Beaver, only a few miles down the Ohio River. Beaver was surveyed, planned, and carefully laid out by Daniel Leet himself in 1792. The town was designed as a large square, with streets going each way at right angles. There are four large squares in the center of town and one square at the corner of town. All these squares are "reserved for public use". The plan can still be used today to explore Beaver. Compare this tidy arrangement with Sewickley by looking at either the original map included in the petition for incorporation of the Borough in 1853 or a modern map. There is no neat grid with streets intersecting at right angles. The only through street until Ohio River Boulevard was built in the 1930s was Beaver Road, which runs roughly east and west parallel to the Ohio River. Division Street runs north and south because it was the boundary between the Breading and Leet Depreciation Lands districts. Because the two major streets do not cross at right angles, lots are irregularly shaped. Look at the lots around Division and Beaver Streets on the 1897 Sewickley map. They are triangles or irregular quadrilaterals.

Other roads connect haphazardly with the two main streets. All of these haphazard roads remain today and can be retraced on a map or in person. Once a road has been made and houses have been built, it is extremely difficult if not impossible to impose an orderly grid. This is clearly seen in downtown Pittsburgh, which has had to withstand far greater changes than Sewickley. The plots along the Monongahela River, now known as Firstside, were laid out in 1764. When George Woods laid out his plan for Pittsburgh in 1784, he proposed to "new model those small streets and lots so as to make them larger," and to widen Market Street.[20] The lotholders in the early plan refused to have their lots altered, So, Woods retained the original plan and laid out a new grid along the Allegheny River. The 1784 plan can be retraced almost exactly today.

It is interesting to see how the development of Sewickley around the 1850s influenced the way the borough looks today. In some cases, areas developed by the same family were planned in such a way that parts of a large tract would have big, expensive houses and other parts would have modest houses. Samuel and Robert Peebles bought Depreciation Land tract number 126 (234 acres) in 1830. This includes most of Sewickley Borough east of Division Street. The Peebles divided their property. Robert Peebles' share was west of Nevin Avenue and north of Centennial. Instead of developing his property, he farmed it. An idea of the property at the time comes from Robert Peebles' will, dated 1846.

> I give and bequeath to the trustees the farm I now reside on in Ohio Township, together with the household and kitchen furniture and 2 cows, in trust they will let my two sisters to occupy and enjoy the rents and profits of said farm. . . . If my sisters make any claim on my estate, their right to live on the farm will terminate.

Robert Peebles refers to a farm. It remained in a large 43 acre tract when, after the death of the sisters, it was sold to Robert H. Davis in 1855 for $10,000. Mr. Davis kept the land intact. When it was sold in 1906 after his death, it was divided into lots of various sizes. Some bordering Cochrane Lane on the west had over 100 feet of frontage; others had 40 or 50 feet. This would encourage a variety of houses, some large, some small, making up the heterogeneous neighborhood that exists today.

Part of Samuel Peebles' share of the property was developed in a similar way. On November 1, 1848, Samuel Peeble's executor sold 115 acres to Robert Hopkins for $5,100. This is the land labeled Hopkins on the 1853 map of Sewickley. Hopkins was not a real-estate speculator; he was a settler. Born in Kentucky in 1798, Hopkins had been an itinerant Methodist preacher before deciding to settle down in Sewickley. A letter written in 1913 from his descendant, Mary Gardiner Lipp, gives a good idea of his reasons for choosing Sewickley.

> [When Reverend Hopkins came through Sewickley in the mid-1840s on his way to a] preaching appointment, his eyes and heart were caught by the charm and peace of the landscape about him. He decided to secure the land to build a permanent home for his growing family. [He brought his wife to see Sewickley] in a buggy. She too was charmed by the loveliness of hill and vale. Rev. Hopkins bought a large tract from Mr. Peebles, running from the old Peebles home on the river bank where Mr. McWilliams lumber yard now stands [in 1913] and which was also at one time (and for some years) the home of Mr. McKeown. This tract of land included our 120 acres running in various directions and embracing much of the main portion of the bank from the Osborne boundary and railroad to Beaver road, then from Division to Blackburn Street and Broad Street extension to the old stone quarry including the present hospital site and the cemetery hill. In 1849 Mr. Hopkins built a fine colonial home at the foot of this hill [in the block below the hospital and east of the YMCA] in a beautiful grove of oak, chestnut and hickory trees through which ran a brook fed by many springs which had their origin in the

hills above. In 1855 he brought his family from Allegheny by carriage and wagon to the new home. The household goods being transported by boats as at that time there were no steamcars.

Mr. Hopkins built again during the beginning of the Civil War on Bank Street [near what is now the junction of Graham Street and the Boulevard] where he lived until his death in March, 1891.

Mr. Hopkins was a man of great vision. He laid out a large part of the present town on his own land, selling the lots for a mere song, and when the Railway came through his property, he gladly granted a free right of way from Osborne to the present residence of Mrs. H. Gilmore. He sleeps on the hillside above the old home he built and loved.

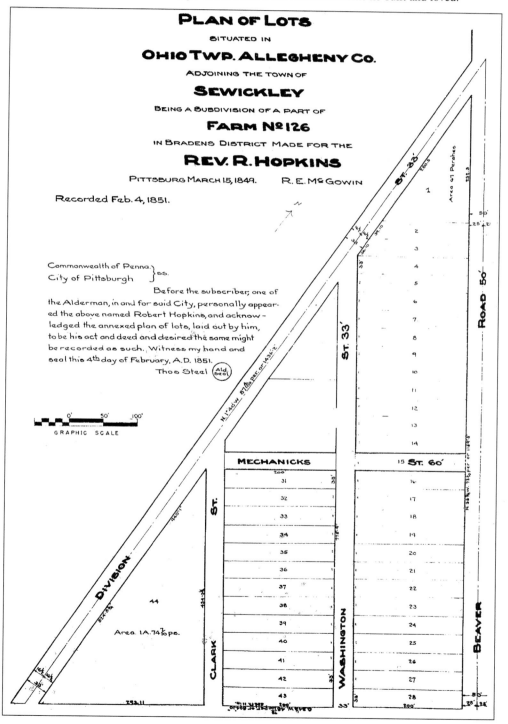

Reverend Hopkins was clearly not a real-estate speculator, but he did sell land. In 1860 he sold 22¼ acres to the Sewickley Cemetery for $1,700. He did not totally resist the giddy speculative fever that accompanied the coming of the railroad in 1851. In 1851 Hopkins laid out the part of Sewickley that lies between Division, Peebles, and Beaver Streets in small lots, encouraging small houses and commercial structures. There were 44 lots; all but six were narrow, 33 by 200 feet. The lots along Beaver Street were quickly used for building. By 1862, there were 12 structures on Beaver Street and 22 buildings on the whole plan. Before 1851, there had been none. The commercial nature of the neighborhood had already been set. There was a blacksmith, a wash shop, three dry goods stores, a meat shop/post office, a carpenter shop, and a justice of the peace/house builder.

Another section of Samuel Peebles' land was subdivided in such a way that it dictated small houses for working class families. In 1851, James Allen laid out a subdivision on two lots of Peebles plan. Allen's plan created 20 new lots, all only 30 feet wide on both sides of Fountain Street. This would dictate either small houses on small lots or the row houses commonly built in New York City and Baltimore. Because row houses were not popular in Pittsburgh suburbs, small houses were chosen. The character of the neighborhood remains today.

Similar development occurred on a section of Samuel Peebles' land bounded by Hill, Beaver, Straight, and Crooked Streets. In 1846, Samuel's executor divided the property into 27 lots of approximately one acre each. On April 6, 1849, he sold 19 of the lots to Dr. John Dickson for $2,575 ($135 per acre.) Dr. Dickson dabbled in real estate. He sold the property off in small parcels, even smaller than the one acre that Samuel Peebles planned. His sales averaged $347 per acre, making him a profit of $212 per acre or $4,028.

Dr. Dickson's lots were further subdivided into smaller parcels. In 1852, for example, he sold James McClelland three one-acre lots bounded by Hill Locust and Fountain and Mulberry Streets for $600. McClelland divided the three lots into 24 lots, each with only 40 feet of frontage. On such small lots it would be necessary to build small houses. Thus, as early as 1852, an observer of the Sewickley scene could have foreseen an urban neighborhood with small houses and people of modest means.

Dr. Dickson and James McClelland were meeting a demand for small lots in Sewickley at the time. By 1862 there were 23 houses on the piece of property described above. By 1906, there were 68. The working class and

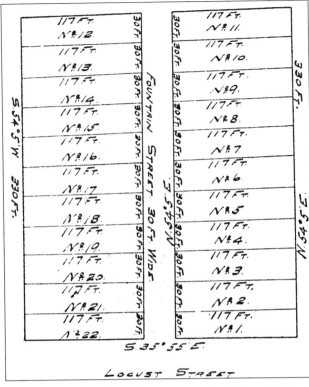

James Allen's Plan of Lots in the Village of Sewickleyville, 1851.

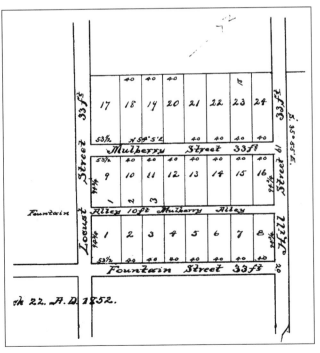

McClelland Plan, 1852

middle class tradesmen, craftsmen and laborers who came to town to provide services to the rapidly developing suburb needed "affordable housing."

Sewickley Borough developed as a town because of its location on transportation routes. On the other hand, Sewickley Heights developed slowly because it was inaccessible. Much of the land was hilly and heavily forested. Two black men took advantage of the woods to make a living as woodchoppers. Pop Reese, a former slave, and Pete Davis, said to be part Indian, worked and lived up in the hills near the present Allegheny Country Club.[21] A few farmers tried to make a living. In 1811, through Squire John Way, Thomas McClelland, Matthew Ingram and Charles Hamilton purchased farms some distance from the river.[22]

Miss Agnes Ellis in her book *Lights and Shadows of Sewickley Life,* written in 1893, says that William McLaughlin was the first white settler in the hills. James Moore, a scout for George Washington during the Revolution, owned 1200 acres in the hills. Moore sold 100 acres at the head of Turkey Foot Run to Frederick Merriman for a gun, an iron kettle, and a sled. This land is now in Bell Acres Boro, northwest of the Sewickley Heights Golf Club. Miss Ellis says that Moore sold another 100 acre tract of land for three hams.[23] It is impossible to tell how equitable either of these transactions was. Frederick Merriman did get a bonus which he might not have known about; two roads in the area carry his name. Merriman descendants remained on the property. A Merriman still owned land next to the Scaifes in 1917.

Some upland farmers owned considerable amounts of land. The Merrimans and the Hamiltons followed the Ways and Shields in total acreage. Perhaps to make up for the remoteness of the Heights, families and nationalities settled close together.[24]

A few early houses remain in the Heights. They are either log houses or farmhouses. Several log houses date from the early decades of the nineteenth century. The most pristine is the one on Fern Hollow and Hunt Roads. This is not a log cabin because it has logs with four flat sides which have been carefully notched at the corners and smoothly chinked. And, unlike log cabins, it has a well-constructed chimney.

Other log houses in the Heights have been adapted in various ways to suit the demands of modern owners. One problem is size. Log houses were only as long and wide as the longest available tree trunk. Usually, they had only one floor plus a loft. This is clearly not large enough for current tastes. The log house on Audubon Road doubled in size when another log house was grafted to it. Another solution to the space problem is shown by the log house on Barberry Road. It has been pretty much engulfed by an addition. The effect is pleasing as parts of the original house emerge from the white of the surrounding structure.

The Henry Oliver house on Blackburn Road shows both types of pre-1850 housing in Sewickley Heights. The main house is a restored farmhouse with an addition in the back. The garage is a log house. Another farmhouse, dating from 1840, is also on Blackburn Road. It is brick with a stone foundation and belongs to Robert McCullough who lives in it and uses the barn and land as a riding stable. An example of an early frame farmhouse which has been only slightly altered is on Barberry Farm on Barberry Road. Instead of destroying the old house to build their mansion, its owners, the Burgwins, left it for use by an employee.

One reason for the slow development of Sewickley Heights is that it was part of the enormous McKean tract. Governor Thomas McKean, Pennsylvania's first governor, and Francis Johnson bought 2,480 acres in 1786. In 1803 Johnson sold his half to McKean. McKean conveyed the tract to his daughter, Sarah Maria Theresa, Marchioness de Casa Yrujo, wife of the Spanish Ambassador to the United States at the close of the Revolution. She left the property to her daughter, Narcissa Maria Louisa Martinez de Yrujo de Pierrard.[25] It was impossible for an absentee landlord from across the ocean to make productive use of a piece of land. In any case, most of the tract was hilly and inaccessible even to markets in Pittsburgh. Therefore, the property lay empty except for squatters. The Spanish owners seldom paid taxes; tenants came and went without paying rent; and the land reverted to wilderness.[26]

There were no commercial or institutional buildings in the Heights except churches and one-room schools. Many of the farmers in the Heights were too far from the valley churches to attend regularly. One of them, Thomas McClelland, an Irishman licensed to be a lay preacher by John Wesley, organized a Methodist class in 1809 and preached from various houses as early as 1811. The congregation built a log chapel in 1833 on the same lot where the Blackburn United Methodist Church is today, on Blackburn Road near Scaife Road.

The Blackburn United Methodist Church evolved from the Hambleton Bible class which met for the first time in 1811. The first log church was replaced by a brick one in 1853, when W.P. Blackburn was the pastor. After a fire in 1890, the congregation built the present frame church.[27]

Another early church, founded in 1822, remains active today. It was originally called the Duff Mill Congregation after one of the first elders, David Duff. Now it is the Fairmount Church, mentioned earlier because of its close connections with the Presbyterian Church, Sewickley.

Several one-room schools were scattered around the countryside. Because the only way to get to school was on foot, all schools had to be located within walking distance of all students. A frame schoolhouse on Fern Hollow Road is a good example.

Sewickley Heights near the turn of the century had changed little since the earliest settlers had started their farms. This contrasts with the Sewickley Valley, which by 1900 had the locations of its houses, streets, churches, and business district well established.

[1] F. Cumming, p. 46.

[2] Franklin Taylor Nevin, *The Village of Sewickley*, The Sewickley Printing Shop, 1929.

[3] Scott Martin, *Leisure in Southwestern Pennsylvania, 1800-1850*. Thesis. University of Pittsburgh, 1990, p. 45.

[4] William Winans, "Recollections of Boyhood Years in Southwestern Pennsylvania." In *Western Pennsylvania Historical Magazine*, v.22, No. 1, March 1939, p. 44.

[5] F. T. Nevin, p. 18.

[6] *Weekly Herald,* Sept. 2 1911, p. 2.

[7] Ellis, p. 35.

[8] Fred Wallhauser, *Upper-Class Society of the Sewickley Valley, 1830-1910*, unpublished paper, University of Pittsburgh, 1964.

[9] F. T. Nevin, p. 18.

[10] *Fiftieth Anniversary of the Presbyterian Church,* p. 22.

[11] S.C. Ritchey and J.C. Venning. "Paper Produced for the Semi-centennial of the Incorporation of the Church, Nov. 16 1902", p. 5.

[12] *Valley Gossip,* February 1, 1881.

[13] *A History of the Presbyterian Church of Sewickley, Pa.*, 1914, p. 2.

[14] Ellis, p. 209.

[15] *A History of the Presbyterian Church of Sewickley, Pa.*, 1914, p. 9.

[16] *The Presbyterian Church, Sewickley, Pennsylvania: The 1988 History of the Church*, n.d., n.p., p. 58.

[17] Ibid., p. 20-21.

[18] *A History of the Presbyterian Church*, 1914, p. 147.

[19] Donald J. Mash, *A Sequent Occupance Study of Sewickley, Pa.* Thesis M.A. University of Pittsburgh, 1966.

[20] Lorant, p. 52.

[21] F. T. Nevin, p. 178.

[22] A. Warner, *History of Allegheny County,* 1889. Chicago, v.2, p. 196-208.

[23] Ellis, p. 33.

[24] Mary Frances Brown, p. 9.

[25] *History of Allegheny County, Pa.* A. Warner, 1889, v.2, p. 196.

[26] Emery, p. 7.

[27] *Sewickley Herald*, Sept. 4, 1996, p. 11.

Chapter 8
The Railroad Comes to Sewickley

The twentieth century is usually considered the time of great technological change, but in Sewickley an enormous change occurred in the middle of the nineteenth century with the coming of the railroad. The population of Sewickley Borough doubled from 1850 to 1860. The arrival of the railroad in 1851 made it possible to commute to Sewickley from Pittsburgh. This was a facilitator but not a reason to move to Sewickley. If people were living in a perfect world, they would not choose to take the trouble to move. Why did so many decide to leave their familiar surroundings and venture off into the country? There are two parts to the answer, the push from the city and the pull toward the country.

Pittsburgh in the middle of the nineteenth century was not a particularly pleasant or safe place to live. It was crowded, hemmed in between the rivers and Grant's Hill, now Grant Street. The streets were muddy, dirty and poorly lit. The unreliable water supply had been insufficient to tame the great fire of 1845, which burned most of the present downtown area. Pittsburgh's perennial nemesis, smoke, horrified visitors. George Ogden remarked in 1821: "Owing to almost the exclusive use of coal, the town presents rather an unpleasant and smoky appearance; and even the complexions of the people are affected by this cause."[1] Willard Glasser visited Pittsburgh in 1883 and reported: "The smoke stinks, and, mingling with the moisture in the air, becomes . . . a consistency which may almost be felt as well as seen. . . . In truth, Pittsburgh is a smoky, dismal city at her best."[2] James Parton, who called the view of Pittsburgh's Strip District "hell with the lid taken off," described Pittsburgh on a summer afternoon in 1866.

> Every street appears to end in a huge black cloud, and there is everywhere the ominous darkness that creeps over the scene when a storm is approaching. When the traveler has satisfied himself that the black clouds are only the smoke-covered hills that rise from each of the three rivers, still he catches himself occasionally quickening his steps, so as to get back to his umbrella before the storm bursts.[3]

Pittsburghers stalwartly defended their city, even claiming that smoke was healthful because "it destroys every property of the atmosphere which is hostile to life. It prevents malaria." Eye diseases were rare, it was said, because smoke "is a perpetual public sunshade and color-subduer."[4]

If, despite such claims, sickness struck, health care was rudimentary. There was no hospital until Mercy opened in 1847. Cholera epidemics struck the city in 1832, 1833, 1834, 1849, 1850, 1854, and 1855. The approved method of avoiding the contagion was by burning coal and pitch in pots on the streets.

These were ample reasons to push people to live outside Pittsburgh. Other reasons pulled them towards Sewickley. Americans in general wanted to live in country houses. This was not true in Europe or South America, where the rich preferred living in the city and having a country house retreat. The poor inhabited the outskirts of cities. The growing ideal for Americans was an elegant villa on a large lot where the businessman could escape from the drudgery of work to a pastoral island of his own. The reasons were perfectly stated as early as 1485, by the Italian architect, Leon Battista Alberti.

> There is a vast deal of satisfaction in a convenient retreat near the town, where a man is at liberty to do just what he pleases. . . . The great beauties of such a retreat are being near the city, upon an open airy road, and on a pleasant spot of ground.[5]

People had long been pushed from the city to seek bucolic pleasure. Bocaccio escaped the dangers and the smells of the plague by fleeing Florence for the beautiful hills of Fiesole. Londoners in Elizabethan times had suburban villas on the Thames as well as their houses in the city. Like so many other ideas in American civilization, the suburban dream crossed the Atlantic. Lewis Mumford says Americans wanted to "create an asylum in which they could, as individuals, overcome the chronic defects of civilization while still commanding at will the privileges and benefits of urban society."[6] Frank J. Scott, America's first writer about suburban landscapes, explained:

> In the neighborhoods of large cities, horse and steam railways and steamers transport in a few minutes their thousands of tired workers to cheerful villages and neighborly suburban homes. . . . They would be villages of a broader, more generous and cosmopolitan character than old-fashioned villages. Post offices, shops, and groceries, butchers, bakers, blacksmiths, shoe makers, and laborers of all kinds must be nearby and part of our community. . . . The attractions of lecture, concert, and dancing halls, and ice-cream resorts cannot be dispensed with.[7]

Sewickley was a popular choice for Pittsburgh businessmen seeking asylum. James Parton, after reflecting on the benefits of smoke, continued:

> Until very recently, in Pittsburgh, it would have boded ill for a man to build a handsome house a few miles out of the smoke. . . . The fashion of living a few miles out of the smoke is beginning to prevail among the people of Pittsburgh. Villages are springing up as far as twenty miles away, to which the business men repair, when, in consequence of having inhaled the smoke all day, they feel able to bear the common country atmosphere through the night. It is probable that, in coming years, the smoky abyss of Pittsburgh will be occupied only by factories and "works", and that nearly the whole population will deny themselves the privilege of living in the smoke.[8]

Sewickley residents gloried in the privilege of avoiding smoke, according to *Sewickley Valley Society*, 1895.

> [Sewickley is] a place beyond the admission of trades and the realm of the vast industries that darken the sky above the Iron City and fill its vicinity with the eternal din of a million noises. There is not a factory in the valley, and the nearest approach thereto is the electric light plant—and its fuel being gas, it sends forth no smoke to dim the purity of the sky that enriches this favored vale. . . . Sewickley being northwest of Pittsburgh, and the prevailing winds of Western Pennsylvania being from the west or northwest, the legacy of smoke from Pittsburgh's myriads of chimneys very seldom drifts Sewickleywards, a blessing which only those who have lived in the eastern portion of the busy city, or within ten miles thereof on the side opposite Sewickley, can appreciate.[9]

Having the blessing of a home with fresh air was important. The nineteenth century worshiped the very idea of Home as an image suggested by the song "Home Sweet Home", the saying "a man's home is his castle", or the prints of Currier and Ives. An editorial in the *Sewickley Herald* expresses the local view.

> Home and home life, synonymous one with the other, is more beautiful than can be pictured in words. It is a place above all places, the dearest when reached, whether radiant with splendor or beautiful in modesty through the maintenance of the income and in conformity with the ideas of the master head of the habitation. It is there that you rest as in no other place and the humbleness does not disturb the feeling of peace, as it is home. . . . In short, the home is what you make it, and when made right, there is no more joyous place on earth.[10]

When the men left to go to work in the city, the women devoted themselves to creating the perfect home. This was considered an important occupation, worthy of concentrated study. Harriet Beecher Stowe and her sister Catherine Beecher promoted the idea in their book *The American Woman's Home*, published in 1869.

> [The housewife's] station and responsibilities in the great drama of life are second to none, either as viewed by her Maker, or in the estimation of all minds whose judgment is most worthy of respect. She who is the mother and housekeeper in a large family is the sovereign of an empire, demanding more varied cares, and involving more difficult duties, than are really exacted of her who wears the crown. . . .
>
> Surely, it is a pernicious and mistaken idea, that the duties which tax a woman's mind are petty, trivial, or unworthy of the highest grade of intellect and moral worth. Instead of allowing this feeling, every woman should imbibe from early youth, the impression that she is in training for the discharge of the most important, the most difficult, and the most sacred and interesting duties that can possibly employ the highest intellect.[11]

The image of Home was clarified and promoted by the famous landscape architect Andrew Jackson Downing and, after his death in 1852, by Frank Scott. Downing said:

> [If you could] place the house in the countryside, in the little world of the family home . . . truthfulness, beauty and order would have dominion. . . . What an unfailing barrier against vice, immorality, and bad habits, are those tastes which lead us to embellish a home, to which at all times and in all places we turn with delight, as being the object and the scene of our fondest cares, labors, and enjoyments; whose humble roof, whose shady porch, whose verdant lawn and smiling flowers, all breathe forth to us in true, earnest tones, a domestic feeling that at once purifies the heart, and binds us more closely to our fellow-beings![12]

Downing provided detailed plans for siting the house and designing the gardens, even including plans for beds with names of flowers to purchase. These plans for houses and gardens presumed a large yard, set back from the street, with an ample lawn for family games.

Downing also planned on a larger scale. In order to make a pleasant landscape for people riding down the road, high fences should be avoided. Winding roads were more pleasing to the eye than the harsh grid of cities.

The villas of Downing were usually set on large lots similar to the grander properties in Sewickley in the nineteenth century. The idea for the smaller suburban lots of half an acre or so, such as the houses on Peebles Street, could have come from Frank J. Scott's 1870 book *The Art of Beautifying the Home Grounds*. His ideal place to live was a suburban community with only enough shops and facilities to provide necessary services to the elegant suburban houses on their well-landscaped lots. Each house's lawn and garden should flow into its neighbor's, making the community look like a park. An example of Scott's ideal is the plate showing five houses with a common lawn which, he said, "will add thousands to their salable value. [The lawn] gives a genteel air to the neighborhood and serves to attract a class of refined people." Each property should add to the overall picturesque scene of the community. Landscaping should never be used to hide the houses. Planting was "the art of picture making and picture framing, by means of the varied forms of vegetable growth." Houses should not be cut off by fences or hedges.[13]

The lawn was to be the center of the landscape plan, according to Scott and Downing. There were two reasons for the popularity of lawns. First, traditional yards had been plowed up, fenced in, and used for growing vegetables. It was a measure of growing wealth that suburbanites could give over a utilitarian vegetable plot for a non-productive lawn. Second, lawns had been difficult to maintain until the invention of the lawn mower in the 1860s. Before that, it had been necessary to use a scythe, a difficult tool which required skill and practice. Now the lawn could be a source of healthful exercise for white-collar businessmen, according to Frank J. Scott.

> Whoever spends the early hours of summer while the dew spangles in the grass, in pushing these grass cutters over a velvety lawn, breathing the fresh sweetness of the morning air and the perfume of the new mown hay, will never rest contented in the city.[14]

After cutting the grass in the morning, the businessman could enjoy it in the evening. Here he could gather with his family after an arduous day in the city.

It was understood that the typical suburban dweller and his good family were likely to be rich. The large lots and attractive houses shown in the Downing and Scott books would not have been for the poor. Scott goes so far as to suggest that large lots were necessary.

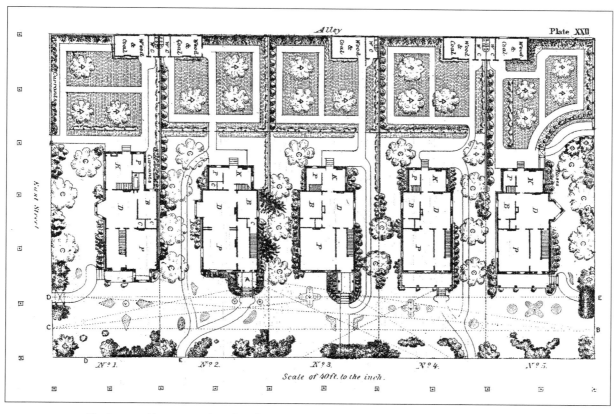

Five houses with a common lawn from Frank J. Scott's *The Art of Beautifying Suburban Home Grounds*.

[Lots just 25 feet by 100 feet] destroy all chance of making true suburban improvements. Such lots will only sell to citizens who are either too poor, too cockneyish, or too ignorant of their own needs, to insist on something more; and cannot be managed so as to attract that class of cultivated and intelligent people who want rurally suburban homes, and not city houses and city habits on the margin of the country.[15]

Scott and Downing were addressing only the suburban part of the Sewickley population. The older residents, both wealthy and poor, already had completed their houses and plantings without benefit of the new landscape philosophy.

The doubling of Sewickley's population between 1850 and 1860 would necessarily cause changes in what was a quiet rural community, even if the new people were similar to the older residents. But the change was magnified because the new people were different. Many were involved with interests in Pittsburgh and brought new ideas and aims for Sewickley. Sometimes these aims conflicted with those of the older residents.

Problems arose in the churches. The Presbyterian church, long governed by a coalition of Scotch-Irish from the hills and the Shields and their neighbors, was enthusiastically invaded by new residents. These included Charles Atwell, George Christy, John Irwin, Jr., Thomas Patterson, and Alexander Robinson. The differences surfaced in 1862 when an organ was donated and installed in the church. The Scotch Presbyterians believed that organ music did not belong in church. Twenty families left the Presbyterian church. At first they held their services in the Methodist Church; later they formed what is now St. Andrew's United Presbyterian Church.

The next divisive event occurred when the conservative minister, James Allison, resigned in 1864. The modernists, lead by Elder Theodore Nevin, proposed Rev. Joseph Bittinger who had been pastor of a "New School" church. Rev. Bittinger was interested in such issues as prison reform and Negro welfare. Dr. Bittinger's appointment is recorded in the latest church history:

Most persons present at the [trial] service conducted by Dr. Bittinger highly approved what they heard and saw. He was requested to return the following Sunday, and again the service appealed to most of those who were present. At the prayer meeting on the following Wednesday evening, a member of the congregation moved that a congregational meeting be hastily called to consider issuing a call to the Rev. Bittinger. The meeting was held four days later, and, a quorum being present, a call was promptly voted. No other candidate was considered. No representative committee on selection had been appointed or consulted. To say that these precipitous actions shocked and offended many members from lower Edgeworth—who had done so much for the Church all these years—is to state the case mildly. They, like the St. Andrew's group, departed from the congregation in high dudgeon.[16]

This group formed the Leetsdale Presbyterian Church, later the Shields Presbyterian Church. In 1868, they built an elegant small church designed, like the Sewickley Presbyterian, by Joseph Kerr. The church was strict "Old-School" with no decorations, and certainly no organ.

The organ question struck the Methodist church almost simultaneously. In the July, 1864 meeting of the Corporation, the Official Board was authorized by a vote of 18 to 10 to "procure a cabinet organ for the church whenever they may deem it proper, and whenever a member of the church can be obtained to play it." When the organ was installed, dissidents took direct measures. In the dead of night, they removed the offending organ and deposited it in the street.[17]

The influence of the new residents extended beyond churches. As we saw, Sewickley in the early nineteenth century lacked groups, clubs or means of social contact. One way of fostering friendship was the railroad itself. Commuters spent nearly one hour each day with each other. This opportunity for informal contact was lost later with the arrival of the automobile, where everyone becomes a rival in the race to the office. New acquaintances made on the train could grow into friendships as commuters became members of the many organizations that have abounded in Sewickley since about 1860. Perhaps in earlier times there were not enough people available to form these groups, other than the obvious religious ones. With the increase in population the critical mass needed to organize social groups was reached. Organized activity also blossomed because the new suburbanites brought ideas with them from the city. They had wanted to escape from the city with its dirt and disorder, but they did not want to leave behind all the amenities the city provided. One of these amenities was social contact. Frank J. Scott worried about the fate of the suburban housewife, left alone while her husband went to work. She needed, he said, "the enlivening influences of easy intercourse with her equals."[18]

With the arrival of the railroad, it was possible to reach Sewickley in less than half an hour; this compares with at least four hours before the railroad. The length of the trip is illustrated by the former name of the Lark Inn: Halfway House. It was a day's journey from Pittsburgh, half way to Beaver.

Many of the old guard residents of the Sewickley Valley did not welcome the changes wrought by the railroad. Large landowners thought their land would be less valuable. Farmers feared the trains would scare the milk right out of the cows. Ezra Young recalled later,

> Being one of the oldest living residents of the valley, I well remember how the introduction of steam railroads here was bitterly opposed in the early 'fifties. My own ancestors, the Andersons, then living on a farm that took in the land now covered by the town of Leetsdale, were among the most bitter opponents. They were somewhat relieved, however, when Mrs. David Shields came to see my grandmother and said, "Don't be alarmed, Auntie, the Economites and Mr. Shields are opposed to the railroad and it won't be built."[19]

Progress was not to be stopped, however. A grand celebration in July, 1851 was planned for the first train, which was run especially for stockholders. The engine, the "Salem", arrived in Pittsburgh on a canal boat, an example of one form of transportation contributing to its own demise. A large crowd gathered at the old canal basin on the Allegheny River to watch the engine go from boat to tracks. As the engine, towing its cars, chugged off towards Sewickley, crowds cheered. Some men on horseback raced the train, according to a newspaper report.

> Some young mad caps on horseback, urged the animals which they rode to the top of their speed, endeavoring to keep up with the iron horse, which of course quickly distanced them, and long before the outer depot was passed, they were far behind.[20]

A letter from one of the passengers later recalled the trip.

> I rode the first train to New Brighton, where we had a free dinner—all on my father's stockholder pass. We stopped at Haysville to wet some of the passenger's whistles—all by order of President William Robinson, who went about begging people to take stock. [Shortly after leaving Haysville, the train passed some men working on the road.] The honest fellows could not restrain the feelings of pleasure they felt, at seeing the practical realization of their labors, but huzzaed loud and lustily.[21]

These "honest fellows" must have been Sewickleyites.

Because the passenger cars were not ready for the train's opening run, small flat cars were fitted with planks from side to side for seating passengers. When the train started, "passengers were thrown into confused heaps, clinging desperately to each other to avoid falling off." The engine burned pitch pine, making black smoke which stung the eyes of the passengers and soiled their clothing. They tried to shield themselves with umbrellas but they got burned and caught fire. "Many of the pleasure-seekers had painful reasons to remember their first ride on a railroad train."

Robert Wardrop started commuting in 1859 from Seminary Station in Edgeworth. He remembered that there was one crew which made two round trips daily between New Brighton and Allegheny, now the North Side. There was a single track with special sidings where two trains could pass. If you failed to meet at a meeting point, you waited 35 minutes, 30 for clearance, and five for variation of watches.

Train service improved. By 1910 there were 49 trains from Sewickley to Allegheny or Pittsburgh. Commuter trains left approximately every ten minutes, taking about half an hour to make the run.[22] Frances McElrath remembered when she was a girl in Sewickley around 1907. "Transportation was excellent, for there were commuter trains and you could go into Pittsburgh almost any time during the day and late evening hours."

Sunday trains sometimes ran afoul of the Pennsylvania Blue Laws. Annie McFadden Hays lived near Old Economy after her husband was killed in the Civil War. She and her children found it difficult to get to church at St. Stephen's in Sewickley until, "General Cass, a high official of the Fort Wayne Railroad . . . directed that a local train would be sent down to Fair Oaks station for their convenience on Sunday."[23]

No complaints about Mrs. Hays have survived but one later complaint ended up in court, according to a newspaper clipping of June 12, 1925.

Whether running a "church train" on Sunday is a necessity will be decided in court, as an appeal is made in the case of George Hood, an engineer who was fined $25 yesterday by Alderman John Edgar of Allegheny for performing "worldly employment" on Sunday. Hood was arrested on information made by James T. Sample of Sewickley.

The commuters enjoyed both the convenience and the beauty of the ride, according to an 1895 publication.

The daily ride to and from the city, along the northern shores of the Ohio, is a daily pleasure that never loses its charms. The windings of "La Belle Riviere" reveal new beauty at every bend, and each season of the year varies the ever-beautiful permanence. The tired man is treated each evening to glimpses of scenic beauty. . . . There is no such scenery, or purity of atmosphere along any road leading from Pittsburgh's heart as is available for Sewickleyans as they occupy the comfortable cars of the P., Ft. W & C.R. Railroad and go to or come from their offices and counting rooms.[24]

Sewickley Valley Station, 1906 photo. Courtesy The Sewickley Valley Historical Society.

The new railroad line had many stops as it traveled along the river. Stops had to be close together because most people walked from their houses. The tracks followed the route which is now Ohio River Boulevard, a route that was convenient for many in the Valley. A train coming from Pittsburgh made its first stop in the Sewickley area at Haysville, named after Captain John Hay who had a road house there; next was Glen Osborne, in honor of Franklin Osburn; then Sewickley; then Roseburg, named for Mrs. Margaret Roseburg Black; then Quaker Valley, named for the early members of the Way family who were Quakers; then Seminary, named for the Olver's Ladies Seminary but later renamed Edgeworth; then Shields; then Leetsdale.[25]

OHIO AND PENNSYLVANIA RAIL ROAD.
TIME TABLE,
No. 3,

Commencing on Monday, 24th of November, 1851.

PITTSBURGH TO ENON STATION—44 MILES.

LEAVES	GOING WEST.		LEAVES	GOING EAST.	
	Express Train.	Accommodation Train.		Express Train.	Accommodation Train.
		A.M. P.M.			
Pittsburgh,.........	8.00 A.M.	10.00 & 4.00	Enon,.............	3.00 P.M.	10.30 A.M.
Courtney's,.........		10.17 & 4.17	Darlington,.........	3.18 "	10.50 A.M.
Haysville,.........		10.30 & 4.30	New Brighton,.......	3.50 "	A.M. P.M.
Sewickley,.........	8.27 Pass.	10.35 & 4.35	Rochester, (Beaver,)..	4.00 "	7.30 & 1.30
Shousetown Lane,.....		10.42 & 4.42	Freedom,...........		7.48 & 1.48
Economy,,.........		10.50 & 4.50	Baden,.............		7.54 & 1.54
Baden,............		11.00 & 5.00	Economy,..........		8.03 & 2.03
Freedom,..........		11.07 & 5.07	Shousetown Lane,.....		8.12 & 2.12
Rochester, (Beaver,)..	9.00 "	11.15 & 5.15	Sewickley,..........	4.35 Pass.	8.19 & 2.19
New Brighton,......	9.15 "	11.30 & 5.30	Haysville,..........		8.27 & 2.27
Darlington,.........	9.45 "	12.05 M.	Courtney's,.........		8.35 & 2.35
Enon,............	10.05 "	12.30 M.	Pittsburgh,........	5.00 P.M.	8.45 & 2.45
	ARRIVES.	ARRIVES.		ARRIVES.	9.00 & 3.00
					ARRIVES.

At 8.27 A.M. and 4.35 P.M. the Express Train and Accommodation Train are to stop and pass at the Sewickley siding. The Accommodation Train is to go on to the siding.

On the completion of the Rail Road to Palestine, in about two weeks from the date of this Time Table, some changes of time will be made.

A Passenger Car will be run at convenient hours between Salem and Alliance, in connection with the Engine of the Construction Train, commencing in a few days.

By authority of the Board of Directors.

S. W. ROBERTS,
Chief Engineer and Superintendent.

Printed by W. S. Haven, Pittsburgh.

Sewickley is fortunate in having two mementos of its railroad years: the two railroad stations. Because the train tracks used to run on what is now Ohio River Boulevard, the station built in 1887 was originally located on what is now the Boulevard. In 1929, when the railroad tracks were moved closer to the river, the station was moved by train to the corner of Chestnut and Chadwick Streets. Here it became the headquarters for American Legion Post 450, the Afro-American post. A community effort in 1993-1995 raised money to restore it.

The building looks like an inn or a large country house in England. This is because architects and engineers in the early days of railroads had no clear conception of what a railroad station should look like. No such building had ever been needed. Designers tended to adopt a style that fit in with the locale. In the case of Sewickley, this would logically be some style of domestic architecture. The 1857 Station was disguised as a house in the Tudor style. If it had been built on Broad Street, it would have blended in well with its surroundings.

Another reason to use domestic styles for railroad buildings, at least in the early days, was to make a traveler who might be nervous about riding in the iron horse feel at home in comfortable surroundings. Moreover, travelers could have their trips enhanced by viewing the picturesque stations along the way. Such stations beguiled landscape architect Andrew Jackson Downing on a trip to England in 1853.

The smaller ones are almost always built in the style of the cottage ornée — and indeed are some of the prettiest and most picturesque rural buildings that I have seen in England. They all have their little flower-gardens, generally a parterre lying open quite to the edge of the rail, and looking like a gay carpet thrown on the greensward.[26]

The former Sewickley Station, 1877. Now the Walter Robinson Post of the American Legion.
Drawing by Susan Gaca.

VIEW ON LOWER BROAD STREET, SEWICKLEY, PA.

E. C. KROPP CO., MILWAUKEE.

View on lower Broad Street showing flower beds maintained by the railroad. Courtesy Sewickley Valley Historical Society.

Sewickley had station gardens, too, where flowers grew to make bouquets for the dining cars on the railroad lines from New York to Pittsburgh. Irene Devine remembered:

Mr. [Robert] Hutchison was a gardener for the railroad. The whole area where the Park Place is now [Kramer Way and Chestnut Street] was gardens and greenhouses. At that time they had enormous jardinieres, two feet around and three feet high, that looked like cloisonnée. They were always filled with fresh flowers. The dahlias were a foot wide.

The gardens and greenhouse were abandoned in May, 1921, according to a rueful article in the *Herald* reporting that there was less interest in the "splendid service given in the past by the Company in keeping the grounds surrounding its stations along the line in attractive shape. The flower beds and neatly-trimmed lawns, that were a pleasure to see, are not so now, and the grass is not cut regularly."

The second railroad station on the corner of Chestnut and Chadwick Streets is no longer in use. It is, however, easily identifiable as a station. A traveler going for the first time to Sewickley would never mistake it for a house. Between the time of the construction of the two buildings, a pattern had been developed. Now people had an idea of what a station should look like, just as they had an idea of what a school or church should look like.

Sewickley in the nineteenth century was a major stop for passengers, water, and fuel because it had a water tank and a fueling station. Wood was the only fuel, so long rows of cordwood stood ready at the Sewickley stop. The first locomotives were very small, able to pull a maximum of 30 freight cars. Each engine had a name, like a ship.

Access to the railroad enabled residents not only to commute to Pittsburgh but also to maintain connections with Chicago, Boston, Philadelphia, and New York. When the famous Boston landscape firm, the Olmsted Brothers, sent a representative to visit James B. Oliver in 1905, he could take the night train to Pittsburgh, arriving early in the morning. After breakfast at the station and a pleasant train ride to Sewickley, he could do a full day's work.[27] The same convenient trains made it possible for Sewickleyites to send their children East to the elite boarding schools and colleges favored by the upper class.

Trains were not only important as a faster way to travel, they also completely changed the fabric of Sewickley society. Sewickley had been a country town several hours' journey from Pittsburgh. Its few stores and inns served local farmers and travelers by boat and river. The railroad made it possible to commute daily from Pittsburgh. People from all trades and professions who had the money to pay the fare could now live in a quiet country atmosphere, far from Pittsburgh's dirt and congestion.

Before the middle of the nineteenth century it was impractical to escape from the city. The only way to get from home to job was on foot. Assuming that half an hour is the maximum time most people are willing to commute, a mile and a half, the distance walked in 30 minutes, was the maximum commuting distance. Because it was impossible to live in the country and work in the city, the best place to live was as close as possible to the city center. In 1850, 78 percent of the Pittsburgh's top businessmen and professionals lived in the center of town.[28] The first technological innovation to expand the range of places to live was the horse-drawn omnibus which came to Pittsburgh in the 1840s. It could accommodate 15 passengers who were picked up at designated stops. The omnibus enabled people to commute in 30 minutes from about two miles from the city center. In the Pittsburgh area it was now possible to live in Oakland or Ridge Avenue. In the 1850s, 60 per cent of Pittsburgh's primary elite lived and worked downtown. Thirty per cent lived in Allegheny City (the North Side).[29] Sewickley was still far beyond the horse car range.

The railroad increased the choice of possible suburbs far more than the horse car. The first train service to Pittsburgh ran through Sewickley. In 1851, the Ohio and Pennsylvania Railroad started service between Enon Valley near Beaver, and Pittsburgh. The next year, service to the East End of Pittsburgh started when trains traveling the Philadelphia-Pittsburgh route stopped in the Eastern suburbs. Expanded service in both directions allowed Pittsburghers a wide choice of places to live. Sewickley and Shadyside developed concurrently as havens for upper middle class families of commuters living in large, comfortable houses on generous lots. By the 1860s, 70 percent of Pittsburgh's primary elite worked downtown, but less than 40 per cent lived there.[30]

The Sewickley valley was almost as convenient as Shadyside for Pittsburgh's wealthier citizens. In half an hour a commuter could travel the 14 miles from Sewickley to Pittsburgh. Moreover, unlike steamboats or stagecoaches, trains could move in almost any weather. One enthusiastic buff exclaimed:

The locomotive was the steamboat that could not be stopped by weather; it was the canal boat with wings. The railway was an artificial river, perennial, always ready.[31]

Sewickley changed from a country town to a busy suburb. In 1850, only 10 or 12 passengers a week traveled to Pittsburgh by steamboat. Five years later, 100 commuted daily by rail. A sociological study by Fred Wallhausser found that 55 upper class families moved to Sewickley between 1850 and 1895. The breadwinner continued to work in Pittsburgh. Most of these families had come from the East End, but a sizable group, 22 per cent, came from Allegheny City.[32] Among the new suburbanites were: General George Cass and Charles Atwell, both presidents of the railroads; George Christy, lawyer and editor of the *Commercial Journal*; F. M. Hutchinson, treasurer of the railroad; Charles McKnight and Robert Nevin, both authors and editors; Theodore Nevin, banker and businessman; Robert Patterson, attorney and editor; Robert Wardrop, bank president; and William Harbaugh, pork and wool producer.

A book published in 1889 gives a good idea of Sewickley after the commuters had changed the area.

Sewickley borough is not an industrial center. It is the most beautiful suburb in Allegheny County. Business men from Pittsburgh have built their villas there, and its pretty mansions have made it very attractive as a place of residence. It occupies a rank in fashionable society second only to the East End. The Ohio River scenery around Sewickley is magnificent. The population of the town is 2,800. Many gay little villages—Quaker Valley, Osborne, Haysville and Emsworth are also the home of Pittsburghers.[33]

The coming of the new residents marks the beginning of the idea of Sewickley as a town of only very wealthy people. The rich could take the train to a country retreat, leaving the urban poor behind. Railroad suburbs were sprouting all over the country as havens for the rich. As early as 1846 Henry Bowditch, a Harvard Medical School professor who was interested in decent workers' housing, wrote that railroads did not encourage working class passengers because "it might prove annoying to the passengers to have numbers of laborers assembled at the depots. [Such people would] discourage the settlement of a richer class."[34] Sewickley commuters saw the railroad as a way to separate working and upper-class Pittsburghers. This is explained frankly in the book *Sewickley Valley Society* published in 1895.

There are sound and practical reasons why the best class of people are found in Sewickley. That is to say, men who have attained success in life, who represent the professions, and who labor with their heads rather than their hands. Every mile post along a railway leading out of a large city and building to an outskirt or suburban population tributary to the city, may be regarded as a screen or sieve whose mesh is finer in proportion as the distance increases. The railroad fares and the time, consumed in going and coming form the size of the mesh. At, say, two or three miles the screen is a comparatively open one and many pass through it . . . and at 14 miles—the distance of the limit of the Sewickley Valley from the Pittsburgh Court House or Post Office—there are found just such conditions as produce a fine mesh through which the favored class alone can, and care to, pass.

Hence, Sewickley is par excellence a place of lovely homes, a place beyond the admission of trades and the vast industries that darken the sky above the Iron City and fill its vicinity with the eternal din of a million noises. There is no factory in the valley. There are only stores enough in the Village to meet local needs.[35]

The idea of Sewickley as a rich man's suburb persists to this day. As all Pittsburghers know, the perception of a place lives long after changes have occurred. Go to other cities, and the mention of Pittsburgh will bring images of impenetrable smoke. The smoke has been cleared up for over 45 years. The other image is a city of steel mills; now the proper image would be a city of disappearing steel mills.

At least the images of Pittsburgh were valid at one time. In the case of Sewickley, they were not. Despite the influx of the new suburbanites, Sewickley Borough remained a heterogeneous community. Kenneth Jackson says,

Unlike the post-World-War II suburbs, which are relatively homogeneous socioeconomically, those of the tracked city were not restricted to a single economic class. There was diversity behind the posh Main Line stereotype. Even the richest communities were dotted with the small dwellings of those who furnished the support a group of large mansions required. In most railroad suburbs, about 30 percent to 50 percent of the heads of households in the late nineteenth century were affluent businessmen who traveled at least five miles to work and whose families were devoted to the pursuit of culture and recreation in the company of social equals. Similarly, most such towns had a larger and poorer group of citizens whose function was to provide gardening, domestic, and other services for the wealthier class. Only 25% of the population in Brookline Massachusetts were executives or professionals in 1870. Brookline called itself the richest town in the world.[36]

Early in the railroad era, in 1860, Sewickley Borough had 36 heads of household who were managers or professionals; 189 were laborers or craftsmen.

The railroad changed Sewickley from a sleepy country town catering to travelers and neighboring farmers. It became a first class suburb where fortunate Pittsburghers could escape the crowded, dirty city of Pittsburgh.

1 George Ogden, *Letters from the West*. New Bedford, Mass., Melcher and Rogers, 1823, p. 7.

2 Willard Glazier, *Peculiarities of American Cities*. Philadelphia, 1883, p. 334.

3 James Parton, "Pittsburgh." In *Atlantic Monthly*, January 1868, p. 17-18, 21-22.

4 Ibid., p. 7.

5 Lewis Mumford, *The City in History*. New York, Harcourt, Brace, Jovanovich, 1961, p. 485.

6 Ibid., p. 485-487.

7 Frank J. Scott, *The Art of Beautifying Suburban Home Grounds*. N.Y., American Book Exchange, 1881, p. 31.

8 Parton, p. 22.

9 *Sewickley Valley Society*, 1895, p. 15.

10 *Sewickley Herald*, November 28, 1908, p. 6.

11 Catherine E. Beecher and Harriet Beecher Stowe, *The American Woman's Home*. N.Y., Arno, 1869, p. 221-222.

12 Andrew J. Downing, *The Architecture of Country Houses*. N.Y., 1850, p. 38-41 and 276-8 and his *Victorian Cottage Residences*. Dover N.Y. 1981, p. ix.

13 Frank J. Scott, *The Art of Beautifying Suburban Home Grounds*. N.Y., D. Appleton, 1870, p. 51, 215-216, plate 22.

14 David P. Handlin, *The American Home*. Boston, Little Brown, 1979, p. 181.

15 Scott, p. 237.

16 *The Presbyterian Church, Sewickley, Pennsylvania, 1838-1988*, p. 69.

17 S.C. Ritchey, p. 7.

18 Handlin, p. 175.

19 *Presbyterian Church of Sewickley*, 1914, p. 96.

20 E. Douglas Branch, "Success to the Railroad." In *Western Pennsylvania Historical Magazine*, v.20, March 1937, p. 7.

21 Ibid.

22 *Sewickley Valley Time Table*, 1910.

23 *Gleanings of the Harmony Society*. Ambridge, 1960, p. 13.

24 *Sewickley Valley Society*, 1895, p. 15-16.

25 *Pittsburgh Gazette Times*, July 31, 1921.

26 Andrew Jackson Downing, *Rural Essays*, NY, 1853, p. 47.

27 Library of Congress. Manuscript Division. *Olmsted Association Papers*. Shelf 20,112.2. MFL Reel 158. Letter October 26, 1905.

28 Joel A. Tarr, *Transportation Innovation and Changing Spatial Patterns in Pittsburgh, 1850-1934*. Pittsburgh, C.M.U. Transportation Research Institute, 1971, p. 3.

29 Samuel Hays, *City at the Point*. Pittsburgh University Press, 1989, p. 227.

30 Ibid.

31 Branch, p. 10.

32 Hays, p. 279.

33 *Pittsburgh and Allegheny Illustrated Review*. Pittsburgh, J.M. Elstner, 1889, p. 126.

34 Handlin, p. 157.

35 *Sewickley Valley Society*, 1895, p. 14.

36 Kenneth T. Jackson, *Crabgrass Frontier*. N.Y.: Oxford University Press, 1985, p. 99.

60

Chapter 9
Government for a Growing Town

When the railroad came to town, it became clear that Sewickley would become a bustling commuter center. Residents soon realized that some form of local government was needed to deal with community problems, to protect the people, to solve problems beyond the reach of individual action, and to restrict individual actions as necessary if they infringed on the rights of others. As we have seen from looking at the Way family papers, by 1800 there was local government in the form of a justice of the peace to settle local squabbles and a constable to enforce his decisions. Such basic services were inadequate as the town grew. In Pennsylvania, the larger villages were usually incorporated as boroughs. In 1853, the Citizens of Sewickleyville petitioned the Court of Quarter Sessions of Allegheny County to become a borough, an election district, and a school district "under the corporate style and title of the Borough of Sewickley." The petition was signed by 61 freeholders (landowners) and 21 voters who were not freeholders. The Court referred the petition to the Grand Jury which recommended granting the petition "after a full examination of the case, hearing the objections and arguments of the exceptants." It would be interesting to know what these objections were. A simple form of local government was established with a burgess, an assistant burgess, and seven town councilors. This is remarkably similar to the current town government with a mayor corresponding to the burgess, a ten-member town council, and a borough manager.

The early ordinances give a good idea of the concerns of the citizens. Ordinance Number 7, passed in 1853, deals with the width of the sidewalks. Later ordinances in 1867 and 1881 give specific instructions. Council could order homeowners to complete sidewalks within 30 days or be charged for the work. If the sidewalks were to be paved, they had to be three inches above the level of the carriage way, then paved with good hard brick or, if Council ordered, flagstone. Plank sidewalks, too, had to be raised above street level "to afford at all times a dry crossing."

Of all the issues facing a new town, why concentrate on sidewalks? Some urban historians think that sidewalks have two important functions. One is purely utilitarian. Consider the muddy state of the roads in Western Pennsylvania after several days of rain. One visitor to Pittsburgh in 1806 complained that all the streets were so muddy that it was impossible to walk on them without wading over the ankle. A native asked rhetorically in the newspaper if the mud on the corner of Fourth Avenue and Wood Streets had been reduced to two feet. Wooden sidewalks, later replaced by concrete or slate, kept pedestrians clean and dry. Country folk would have to put up with the mud. Having sidewalks at such an early date shows that Sewickley Borough residents thought of themselves as suburbanites, not overcrowded farmers. In 1870, Frank J. Scott advised home seekers to "go no farther in the country than . . . where good sidewalks have been made, or are pretty sure to be made within a short time."[1]

The other function of the sidewalk is less obvious but just as important. Sidewalks give flavor to a town. They encourage walking and standing around to chat with a neighbor without fear of being hit by a vehicle. Lacking sidewalks, a pedestrian must cling precariously to the curb. Vincent Scully, a noted architectural historian, claimed:

> [The sidewalk is] one of the nineteenth century's triumphs . . . . It always manipulated the scale of the town in favor of the individual. It personalizes the street, gives release from traffic flow, and a place for loitering, provides a hierarchy of spaces, and a multiplicity of uses in what would otherwise be a passage. Indeed, once vehicles dominate, individuals on foot are banished from, literally have no place upon, those suburban streets where sidewalks are omitted. Police cars investigate them all.[2]

Two of the ordinances passed in the borough's first year deal with standardizing measurement. Evidently, unscrupulous salesmen were selling underweight or inadequate merchandise. A measurer of stone coal was appointed. The contents of each carriage or cart must be weighed and branded with his seal before it could be sold. Similarly, a measurer and inspector of boards, scantling (timber) and joists was appointed to insure quality and quantity of wood. Both measurers were paid by the users, neatly avoiding tax levies. The stone measurer was compensated by a charge of 50 cents for each carriage and 25 cents for each cart.

Other ordinances were designed to try to make citizens keep the town neat and clean. When the area was sparsely settled, smells and dumps harmed only the individual householder. As settlement increased, others were harmed as well. Ordinance 3 declared,

> Anyone who casts earth, brick, or stone or coal, wood, lumber, ashes, mortar, rubbish, lime, shavings or manure on any street, lane, or alley . . . shall pay for each offense, besides the expense of removing the same, the sum of $2.

A later ordinance outlawed butchering or slaughtering of animals in the Borough in order to prevent smells.

One of the first ordinances discussed in 1853 would have prohibited the running at large of hogs. Hogs were the first sanitation engineers in early American towns. Charles Dickens reported seeing "two portly sows . . . and half a dozen gentlemen hogs" on Broadway in New York City. They were returning home after scavenging all day. Mrs. Frances Trollope visited Cincinnati where,

> The pigs are constantly seen doing Herculean service . . . and though it is not very agreeable to live surrounded by herds of these unsavoury animals, it is well they are so numerous, and so active as scavengers, for without them the streets would soon be choked up with all sorts of substances in every stage of decomposition.[3]

The banning of pigs in Sewickley was very controversial. The "progressive faction," mainly from the city, was in favor. The older residents were not. A letter signed by 46 petitioners to the members of council dated September 13, 1853 gives reasons for their opposition to the proposed law:

1. "It will hurt the poor" because they can harvest the pig without incurring the costs of feeding it.

2. There was not time to think the proposed law through because "the law came upon us unlooked for and unprepared."

3. "Hogs help by eating garbage thrown in the street and, being left to putrefy, must sooner or later be the cause of sickness."[4]

The law banning pigs was not passed until twelve years later, when hogs were included in a more general law to "prevent horses, cattle, sheep, hogs and geese from running at large in the Borough of Sewickley." If caught by the constable, the animal was taken to the pound.

Dogs have been a problem in all American communities. Owners find them irresistibly charming; others find them a public nuisance. One of Sewickley's first laws prohibited "running of dogs known to be troublesome." In 1887 an ordinance required that dogs without a muzzle be killed and buried by the constable for a 50 cent charge to the bereaved owner. An 1889 ordinance directed that any dog running at large be killed.

Protected from wandering dogs, citizens were also saved from speeding traffic in 1877. "If any person shall willfully drive, or ride any horse, mare, gelding, or mule in or through any of the streets or alleys of the borough at a rate of speed exceeding six miles per hour . . . [he will pay a] fine not exceeding $5." The speed limit was raised to 8 miles per hour in 1878.

Sewickley residents tried to have a beautiful town. They were in the forefront of the movement to plant trees. Cities like Philadelphia had tree-lined streets in the eighteenth century. But, according to David P. Handlin,

> [It was not until 1900 that] a few progressive towns took a more active role in trying to create a parklike atmosphere . . . . Massachusetts led the way by passing a law in 1899 that made it mandatory for each town to have a tree warden.[5]

Sewickley had tackled the problem as early as 1867 when an ordinance established a Committee on Shade Trees composed of "three reputable citizens." They were to prepare a plot plan of all the streets, listing the number and kind that homeowners had to plant on their street. As in the case of the measurers, the town did not need to levy taxes for planting trees. The wily councilors assessed property owners for costs. The resulting vistas of tree-lined streets were picturesque but, with no diversity, a blight such as the Dutch Elm diseases could destroy views in a large neighborhood.

As the town grew during its first fifty years, the government became more complicated. In later years, ordinances dealt with the new inventions which now seem like necessities: the telephone, gas, and electricity. Sewickley was right in the swing of the new technology, acquiring the latest techniques with dispatch. The first commercial telephone switchboard was installed in New Haven, Connecticut in 1878. Three years later Sewickley authorized telephone poles and wires. Natural gas was known only as an obscure local phenomenon until the 1880s; not until 1883 was the first natural gas pipe line constructed to the east side of Pittsburgh. In 1885 Sewickley granted a right of way to the Baden Gas Company for laying natural gas pipelines. Thomas Edison invented the electric light in 1879. In 1888 the Sewickley council authorized the Valley Electric Company to erect poles. Within 10 years, 1878-1888, life in Sewickley changed dramatically, at least for those who could afford the new services. Telephones for communication, gas for heat and fuel, and electricity for light changed life forever.

Many ordinances dealt with roads. Between 1853 and 1907, 53 ordinances involved opening, closing, paving, or widening roads. Only 62 dealt with all other matters. After 1892, first the main roads and later smaller roads were sewered and paved with brick at the same time.

Sewickley Borough Council in its first fifty years dealt with many problems common to all times and places: sanitation, roads, safety, and beauty. Readers of *The Sewickley Herald* today will find Council wrestling with the same problems, although the answers differ. Hogs have been replaced by garbage trucks; speed limits have increased; there is no problem with animals running wild on the streets, except for the occasional dog. The success of today's community rests on the its creative answers through time.

[1] F. Scott, p. 29.

[2] Vincent Scully, *American Architecture and Urbanism*. N.Y. Prager 1969, p. 83.

[3] Spiro Kostoff, *America by Design*. New York, Oxford, 1987, p. 157-158.

[4] "Sewickley Borough History." In Library and Archive Division, Historical Society of Western Pennsylvania, Hays File.

[5] Handlin, p. 186.

64

Chapter 10
Well Met: The Development of Social Life

The Sewickley Valley in its early days seemed a lonely place with few entertainments and little organized activity to enliven everyday life. But, in the latter part of the nineteenth century, there were many activities. Increasing wealth and leisure time encouraged people to expand their horizons. In 1852 Frederick Law Olmsted, the landscape architect, noted the importance of clubs in developing communities.

> A man who is not greatly occupied with private business is sure to become interested in social enterprises. School, road, cemetery, asylum, and church corporations, literary, scientific, art, mechanical, agricultural, and benevolent societies; all these things are managed chiefly by the unpaid services of gentlemen during hours which they can spare from their private interests. [Our young men] are members and managers of reading rooms, public libraries, gymnasiums, game clubs, boat clubs, ball clubs, and all kinds of clubs; they are always doing something.[1]

Mr. Olmsted mentioned only the men; in Sewickley the women were also heavily involved.

Numerous clubs for various purposes sprang up in the growing community: some clubs were intellectual; some social; some athletic. Early Sewickley newspapers announced the programs of all the groups, giving a good idea of their variety. Choosing which groups to join must have been a problem. As a practical matter, most activities were available only to the wealthier people. Servants, laborers, farmers, and most merchants worked long hours with little time for social interaction. Churches, of course, were an exception, serving as religious and social centers for their members, rich or poor. A Pittsburgh newspaper of 1870 gives a description of a typical church activity.

> A fair and festival has been open the last three evenings of the past week at the Catholic Church in Sewickley, and the same will be continued two weeks more. A great many articles of value and amusement will be disposed of at the "wheel of fortune." Fine chairs and other articles of furniture are being sold by chances. Two splendid gold-headed canes—one to the most popular clergyman, and the other to the most popular physician of the village—will be voted for, and the contest for either promises to be very lively. An elegant set of silver is to go to the most popular ticket agent, and a silver watch to the most popular policeman. For the most popular young lady, a gold watch is provided.

Intellectual Groups

The organization to mention first is important in its own right and as a necessary foundation for many others: the library. Free public libraries, now taken for granted, were rare in the nineteenth century. The first public library in the country was started in Boston in 1854. Before that, access was limited. Society libraries circulated books to members only. The first such "social library" was established by Benjamin Franklin in 1731. Fifty subscribers paid 40 shillings initiation fee plus 10 shillings a year to pool resources for the purchase of books. Only members could borrow.[2] In Pittsburgh, John Boyd established a short-lived subscription library at the office of the *Gazette* in 1788. In 1847, another library for a special group opened: the Young Men's Mercantile Library and Mechanic's Institute. It had 60 members the first year and, by 1860, it had 446 members and circulated 4,052 volumes. It was not free: members paid $4 a year, or $35 for a life membership.[3] Sometimes philanthropic businessmen opened their libraries to others. The most famous person to do so was John Anderson, who gave Andrew Carnegie access to his collection. Carnegie returned the favor with interest, establishing 2,500 libraries throughout the world.

In Sewickley, the struggle to start a library began in 1873. John Way, Jr., grandson of Squire Way, told the history of the library's beginnings.

> It owes its origin to the arrival of a whiskey boat at Saw Mill Landing Saturday evening 1872-73. Subsequent riot and disorder on succeeding Sabbaths led some interested in the welfare of the young men to think that such things would not be had with a place for proper and rational amusement and self-improvement for that class of our population. I do not think that their expectations have been realized. Very few of those for whom the Reading Room was opened have ever made use of it, and it cannot be expected that they ever will.

Nevertheless, the Reading Room and Library Association, or the Young Men's Library Association opened in May 1873 in a room above McElukin's store. Rent and the librarian's salary were budgeted at $500 a year. The total budget of $1,000 was obtained from gifts, membership dues of $5, and library card fees of $3 a year. Because no taxes supported the library, budgetary problems continued through the early years. John Way, Jr., president, reported various fundraising efforts such as a Minstrel Show, readings, a lecture course, and a festival "organized by the ladies." Rent payments were cut in 1880, when the library moved into the public school building.

The library grew slowly. In 1876 there were 200 books. John Way, Jr. issued a report covering the library's first two years. "The magazines, papers, and reference books in the Reading Room, I regret to say, are very rarely used." Eighty percent of the books circulated were fiction. Mr. Way was disgusted with the "excessive reading of novels to the exclusion of the more solid books which train the mind and strengthen the faculties." A list of the most popular titles in 1873-1875 contains many that are now unknown and a few that have stood the test of time.

Title	Times Borrowed
1. *Barriers Bound Away* by Reverend E. P. Roe	57
2. *The Other Girls* by Mrs. Whitney	52
3. *Under the Cedars* by Alice Hatch	49
4. *John Halifax, Gent.* by Miss Nichols	46
5. *Sam Shirk* by George H. Derereux	37
6. *Uncle Tom's Cabin* by Miss Stowe	32
14. *Journey to the Center of the Earth* by Jules Verne	28
22. *Little Women.* by Miss Alcott	20

One serious group of users must have been pleasing to Mr. Way and his successor, Alexander C. Robinson. The Query Club worked closely with the librarian. Started around 1865 and still active, the club began as the History Class, led by the Reverend Dr. Bittinger. The class met weekly in the Presbyterian Church parlor. Each year members chose a new subject for study. Topics included Shakespeare, Milton, the French Revolution, and the Crusades. The club continued with the same general purpose through several changes of name: the Milton Club; the Shakespeare Club; and the Qui Vive Society. In 1885 it became the Query Club, named after a London periodical *Notes and Queries*. Any member curious about a topic placed a question in a box. Questions were answered by any other member. Later, in addition to queries and answers, each member was required to present two papers each year. Because meetings were held in private houses, membership was limited to 40.[4] To ensure an active membership, the club decreed that "if a member absent himself from three consecutive meetings without giving satisfactory excuse to the secretary, his name shall be dropped."

The club continued its original format, studying a different topic each year. In 1890-1891, for example, the Query Club studied Spain. There were required readings from a textbook. Members had to come to meetings prepared to define Islam, Moslem, Morisco, Arab, Moor and Saracen. In 1895-96, the topic was India. Each member had to read assigned chapters from the textbook, *Hunter's Brief History of the Indian People*. Some papers read at meetings were: "The Eastern Question", by Mr. J. T. Findley; "The Aryans", by Mr. C. M. Robinson; "Caste", by Mrs. E. C. Woods; and "The Monroe Doctrine", by Mr. Charles A. Woods.

Other brave souls sharpened their wits with spelling bees. Noah Webster's *American Spelling Book*, first published in 1789, was very popular. By 1900 it had sold over sixty million copies. Its surprising success rests on the American wish to speak and write "correctly." In England, speech depended on class. Lords and ladies had one form of speech, laborers another. In America, anyone could learn upper-class speech and spelling.[5] Spelling was taught rigorously in schools. John Way, Jr. remembered the method.

The whole school stood in a row and the questioners gave words to spell. [If anyone missed], the next, if the next one spelled correctly, he went up, so there was always an ambition to get "uphead." I think the matter of spelling was better attended to than in modern times.

The best adult spellers entered spelling bees. These attracted great crowds around Pittsburgh in the nineteenth century. They combined the excitement of watching a competition with, sometimes, the smug satisfaction of knowing you could have beaten the contestant. Currently, television game shows like *Jeopardy* have the same appeal. The Sewickley paper in 1871 reported the results of a contest: "Colonel Nevin was stricken with 'pneumonics.' Captain George Cochran got 'palid' and yielded up the ghost. Mrs. Hawes in vain endeavored to preserve her 'tranquility.'"

The Parliamentary Club, which met at the Episcopal Church, studied the rules of governing legislative bodies, according to *The Valley Gossip*.

[It was] one of the most popular organizations in Sewickley. It was conducted according to the Rules of the Pennsylvania House of Representatives. Hon. B. C. Christy was the Speaker. . . . Every member represented some county in the State. . . . Bills properly drawn up were introduced by the various members and went through the several readings to final passage. Debate upon the merits of the different Bills was a nightly occurrence, and some of the finest oratory ever made use of in Sewickley was indulged in by some of the members during these discussions. It was in reality a school of oratory.[6]

Lectures and Entertainments

In addition to these regular club meetings, early papers describe many lectures on a wide variety of topics. Nineteenth century Americans were thirsty for knowledge. Itinerant lecturers made a career of touring the country, enduring dirty trains, bad hotels and boarding houses. The season ran from November through March, when travel was the most difficult.[7] Sewickley newspapers described a number of talks. In 1876, "Reverend Robert S. VanCleve gave a very interesting and instructive lecture on the Indians in the chapel of the Leetsdale Presbyterian Church on Wednesday evening which was listened to with marked attention." In 1881-2, *Valley Gossip* announced "a series of interesting lectures at Way's Academy." The December 15, 1881 issue reported, "Miss Frances Willard lectured to a rather slim audience on last Wednesday. Subject: Temperance." The Young Men's Library Association had three lectures.

The Pleasant Hour Club combined music and discussion. For example, the January 1896 meeting featured singing by Captain and Mrs. J. Sharpe McDonald and discussion of the writing of Robert Burns.

Some entertainments shocked the more staid members of the community. In March 1881 the paper reported,

A one-horse sleight of hand performance given in Choral Hall, the prominent feature being vulgar expression of the ventriloquist and the giving away of considerable cheap prizes. We hardly think these gentlemen will afflict the village again, as Mr. John Way, Jr. gave them notice not to open here, as their entertainment was a species of lottery. . . . The show owners gave vent to considerable profanity.

Charitable Organizations

The Sewickley Lodge of the Knights of Pythias was a group of men organized in 1874 to promote the betterment of mankind by providing benevolent associations, help for aged and infirm members, disaster relief, and camps for underprivileged children. The Knights held meetings in Mozart Hall on the corner of Broad and Beaver Streets. In order to join, men had to be American citizens "of good moral character".

Other secret societies sprang up: the IOOF (International Order of Odd Fellows) in 1879; the K. of H. (abbreviation unknown) in 1879; and the United American Mechanics.[8]

Women, too, were involved in charitable works. The Sewickley Ladies' Relief Committee reported results for 1878-1881.

Proceeds of concert given by the Sewickley Minstrels.	$ 69.34
Proceeds of entertainment, music, tableaus, etc.	78.74
Cash found on street	5.75
Sundry donations	4.50

Balance from old poor fund.	22.49
Proceeds of concerts by Sewickley Mendelssohn Club	100.00
Proceeds of supper, given by young ladies of Presbyterian (Dr. Bittinger's) Church	50.00

Expenditures

Cash paid for shoes	$ 5.50
for nurse	15.00
for rents	25.50
for undertaker	3.75
for physician	15.00
for coal and hauling	11.36
for groceries and dry goods	95.87
for drugs	11.24

The Relief Committee contributed to families as needs arose. If a family were caught short with no money for groceries, for instance, they could get help from the Relief Committee.

A similar organization started in 1898 and continues in 1998, The Union Aid Society. Originally, women from several churches helped the needy with clothes, food, medicines or even rents on an individual basis. Without bureaucratic entanglements, specific needs were addressed on a totally private basis.

Religious Groups

One of Sewickley's longest lasting organizations, the Sewickley Camp Meeting, was one of a whole series of Methodist meetings in Western Pennsylvania dating from 1803. Methodism was characterized by religious fervor and dramatic conversions. Bishop Francis Asbury wrote to Thornton Fleming, his presiding elder in Western Pennsylvania, in 1803,

> I wish you would also hold Campmeetings; they have never been tried without success. To collect such a number of God's people together to pray, and the ministers to preach, and the longer they stay, generally the better—this is field fighting, this is fishing with a large net.

Elder Fleming organized a meeting near Brownsville which produced 15 preachers, over 3,000 people, and 100 conversions. He exulted:

> Oh, my brother, when all our Quarterly Meetings become Campmeetings and one thousand souls shall be converted in each, our American millennium will begin. And when the people in the towns and the country assemble by thousands, and are converted by hundreds, night after night—what times![9]

In Sewickley, blacks and whites held separate camp meetings. Black meetings, started before the Civil War, took place at the Water Works Park and reservoirs.

The white's annual Sewickley Camp Meeting took place at the Mt. Sewickley Camp Meeting Grounds on Camp Meeting Road on the Heights, across from the present D. T. Watson home. Camp meetings combined socializing with religion. Methodist ministers preached on a rigorous religious schedule which could assuage the most delicate conscience that might whisper of wasting time. A typical day included six different religious activities.

7:00 A.M. . . . . . . Sunrise Program
10:00 A.M. . . . . . General Class
11:00 A.M. . . . . . Morning Sermon
3.00 P.M. . . . . . . Afternoon Sermon
7:00 P.M. . . . . . . Young Men's Prayer Meeting
7:30 P.M. . . . . . . Evening Sermon[10]

Singing by soloists and a volunteer choir accompanied many programs.

Campers were called to services by the blowing of a horn during the early days and, later, by ringing bells. Services took place in an auditorium with an organ, minister's pulpit, and chair on one end and seats for 200 at the other. Up to 300 people more could be accommodated on benches set up in front of the auditorium or outside.

Dr. F. K. White remembered the Camp Meeting when he was a youth in the 1880s. The camp grounds were built in 1868 in a beautiful grove on 25 acres, well supplied with spring water. A temporary community sprang up on the hill with chapel, grocery store, and a barber shop. For the first two years, everyone lived in tents. Later, individual families built 73 wooden cottages, each surrounded by a board fence. Each cottage had four rooms and an adjoining building of similar size for the dining room, kitchen and servant's quarters. After a few years, water was piped into the kitchens. Owners came from a wide range of society and included: Judge J. W. F. White, Captain James Porter, B. C. Christy (lawyer), D. R. Miller, John Ague (storekeeper), Baldwin Gray, and George Rudisill.

Many came for the day by horse and wagon. They tied the horse to a tree as they picnicked, socialized, and worshiped. People from farther away could reach the camp grounds by taking special Sunday trains from Allegheny City and Beaver Falls to the Leetsdale station. Four hacks drawn by horses were available to take them up the hill to the gate where each paid ten cents for admission.

The Camp Meetings lasted about ten days but the cottagers often came early and stayed late. Dr. White remembered a boyhood idyll with picnics, taffy pulls, and mumbledy-peg. The boys enjoyed going on squirrel hunting expeditions and eating their quarry. "The memory of those delicious pies makes my mouth water."

Camp Meeting continued well into the twentieth century. The 1929 meeting included services conducted by Methodist Episcopal pastors from Coraopolis, Sewickley, Aspinwall, Mount Lebanon, and Ambridge. The highlight of the year was the screening of Cecil B. DeMille's 12-reel motion picture "King of Kings." As always, there was much to do besides attend religious events, *The Herald* reported.

> The Mount Sewickley services and the pleasant associations of the campground cottage life have attracted an increasing number of people for a number of years past, and more of the cottages are occupied this year than for a long time. The young people find plenty to do, with the tennis courts and other sport facilities, and the older folk enjoy the walks under the magnificent forest trees, and the visiting back and forth among the shaded front porches around the camp ground circle. There can hardly be a pleasanter place to spend a quiet vacation, with spiritual as well as physical benefits.[11]

Musical Groups

Listening to music under the stars was an incentive to attend the camp meetings. With the exception of religious occasions, the only way to hear music before radio and the phonograph was to listen to local groups or to make music yourself. Music and theater groups abounded in the valley. The McDonald orchestra, led by John McDonald, included seven members of his family. The Ladies Vocal Club, under the direction of Mrs. J. Sharp McDonald, gave concerts. The Sewickley Quadrille Band played at special events, such as a reception given by Knights of Pythias in Choral Hall in 1881.[12]

The Mendelssohn Club was a singing society which presented "parlor concerts" for friends of the club with "only those receiving invitations being able to procure cards of admission." The concert in May, 1881, included a wide variety of music, all accompanied by the valley's most celebrated composer, Ethelbert W. Nevin. The program read, in part.

Selection from Mendelssohn's Hymn of Praise.
1. Chorus..."All Men Praise the Lord"
2. Soprano Solo and Ladies' Quartette
    Mrs. J. S. McDonald and Ladies
3. Tenor Solo.."He Claimeth your Sorrows"
Piano Forte Solo
"Minuette ....Moszkowski
"Polinaise" ....Chopin
Finale Chorus—"Hallelujah"..................................from Beethoven's "Mount of Olives"

A combined sport and musical program took place at the Sewickley YMCA in May, 1895. The first part included a Martial Hymn with cornet accompaniment and a Tinker's Song with timpani. Part two featured a Thrust Drill, a Dumb Bell Drill, and a Parallel Bars demonstration.

The Sewickley Valley Club was organized in 1886 "for the advancement of social amusement in the Sewickley Valley." Its objective was the "Giving of Dramatic Musical and Other Entertainments." The first play, *School*, was produced in May 1886. The club was immediately popular, attaining a membership of 129 in its first year. It combined social and theatrical events. There was a lawn fete on July 6 and a picnic on August 9. The annual meeting, held September 11 1888, featured five "entertainments": *She Stoops to Conquer—a Comedy and Farce"; Olla Podrida*; *Love*; *The Minstrels*; and *Married Life*. With such a variety, most of the members must have been involved. Interest faded in 1893; the board resigned due to "lack of enthusiasm and the almost impossible task of casting plays." Things improved, however, during the 1894-95 season, which was "conspicuously successful in every respect."

The 1888-1889 program included tableaux *Taking the Carmelite Veil*, and *Fleeting Time*. An orchestra accompanied a Tableau Vivant *Vintage Festival of Ancient Rome*. Tableaux were a motionless representation of a picture or scene by persons suitably costumed and posed. They gave shy actors a chance to perform without needing to learn any lines or movements.

In 1899 the Sewickley Valley Club produced a full-fledged comic opera, *The Economites*, by Sewickley's own Arthur F. Nevin, brother of Ethelbert. The Sewickley Auditorium was jammed with 1200 people, including 150 who had come from Pittsburgh on a special train. John Duss, trustee of the Harmony Society at the time, might have been the only one who was not amused. He said the the play was "not true."[13]

The 1901 production was a vaudeville show. The paper reported:

It was probably one of the most hugely enjoyed programmes ever presented by the club. An eight-year-old, Elsie Hammerton, introduced the show with acrobatics. She was followed by "The Apple Sisters, Seedie and Corie." "The Bunch Quartette," with their darkey songs, in costume, was one of the best performances. [There followed] "The Sailor's Hornpipe," a tableau in which Miss Gray Emery appeared as the Goddess of Liberty. The band played "The Star Spangled Banner", giving a patriotic finale.[14]

The culmination of all this developing talent came early in 1905 when Sewickley residents proudly produced Arthur Nevin's musical comedy *Candy Man*. There were two performances in the Sewickley Auditorium and one in Wheeling. Both local and Pittsburgh publications described the event.

Social and musical circles of Sewickley Valley are looking forward with great expectation to the production of *The Candy Man*. . . . There are about 70 people in the cast, comprising the young social element of not only the Sewickley Valley but Pittsburg and Allegheny as well. The music is bright, catchy and tuneful, but is a higher average than the usual comic-opera. Special accommodation in the way of train service will be made for Pittsburg and Allegheny people desiring to attend.

Original scenery for every act is being painted under the supervision of Mr. Riddle Haworth, and many beautiful theatrical effects are being planned by Mr. Gilbert Hays with the apparatus brought by him especially from New York. These will include a great waterfall in the last act, the scene of which is laid in California. The most popular of the many tuneful songs in *The Candy Man*, will probably prove to be "Bon Bon," sung by Miss Beardsley and chorus, the kissing song by Miss Beardsley, Mr. Alec Hays and Mr. Edward Dilworth, and the song and dance by the double sextette of art students and candy maids.[15]

Other Activities

Most entertainments are easy to classify. Two fall outside any easy categorization. The first is a performance described in a broadside of 1873.

Mrs. Jarley's Wax-Works!
No Open Air Wagonry. No Tarpaulin and Sawdust

Historical Group
Henry VIII and Catherine Parr
King Charles. Lady Jane Grey

Group of Beauties

Group of Horrors

Boss Tweed. Woman who Poisoned 14 families

Lady Macbeth. Captain Kidd

The other singular entertainment was the excursion of an ad hoc group that went on a trip to Beaver Falls to view Chinese workers. The Chinese had come to America to work on building a railroad to New Orleans. Later, they were hired by the Harmonists to work in their cutlery factory in Beaver Falls. A visit in March 1873 by a party of Sewickley adventurers was reported in a local paper.

We publish below a few items from the "log" of this trip in the hope that revealing as they do what new experiences and sensations, as well a useful bits of knowledge can be obtained by a very short trip down the Fort Wayne railroad "to see the chinies."

Left Sewickley at 9:30 A.M. and arrived at Beaverfalls [sic] at 11:00 without incident on the way. Party consisted of 28 men, women and children, and created quite a sensation when we disembarked from the train and proceeded in double file down the narrow board-walk which leads toward the cutlery establishment. The party was at once ushered into the works. A long room filled with rows of heavy falling hammers, in which the knife blades are beaten into shape, was first visited; to every hammer a workman patiently holding and turning the glowing steel. The ladies got talking to such of the Mongolians as could say yes and no, and as the familiarity grew, it was easy to see that the interest was mutual. The Chinamen were evidently as curious to see our ladies as the ladies were to see and talk to them.

It was a strange and charming sight in the great flashing room. Here a group of blonde ladies surrounds a bright-yellow intelligent boy of twelve, and get him to count one hundred in English. Farther off Miss T., daughter of a missionary to China, is engaged in an earnest and amicable, but exceedingly difficult, conversation with Yang Cheng who "speakee little Inglis." Behind these whirring flywheels Medames I. and K. and the Misses N. have, by signs and gestures, persuaded a compliant Celestial to unwind his long black silk cue [sic]. While on the other side stand a group of little girls in short dresses wondering why the Chinese they are looking at are chattering so volubly and pointing at their natural-sized uncramped feet.[16]

[1] Quoted in *The New Yorker*, March 31, 1997, p. 98.

[2] Daniel Boorstin, *The Americans: The Colonial Experience*. New York, Random House, 1958, p. 311.

[3] Donald M. Goodfellow. "Centenary of a Pittsburgh Library", In *Western Pennsylvania Historical Magazine*, v.31, 1948, p. 21-25.

[4] *Sewickley Herald*, January 24 1990, p. 4.

[5] Boorstin, *The Americans: The Colonial Experience,* p. 284-5.

[6] *Valley Gossip*, May 1 1881, p. 6.

[7] Daniel Boorstin, *The Americans. The National Experience*. N.Y., Random House, 1965, p. 317.

[8] *History of Allegheny County, Pa.* Evansville, Indiana, Unigraphic, n.d., v.2, p. 203.

[9] Wallace Guy Smeltzer, *Methodism in Western Pa.* Little Valley, N.Y. Stright Publishing, 1969, p. 22.

[10] *Sewickley Herald*, July 5, 1935.

[11] Ibid., July 19 1929, p. 5.

[12] *Valley Gossip*, Dec. 15, 1881.

[13] *Pittsburgh Dispatch*, February 2, 1899.

[14] *Pittsburgh Evening Chronicle*. January 31, 1870, p. 3.

[15] Hays File, Sen. John Heinz Regional History Center.

[16] Clipping Sewickley Library dated March 15, 1873.

Chapter 11
Sports in the Valley

Even with so many intellectual and social activities to attend, residents found time for sports of all kinds. For women there was a class in Physical Culture given by Miss M. Emma Kelly every Tuesday morning. If they wanted a more competitive sport, ladies might join a Lawn Tennis Club, organized in 1881 according to *The Valley Gossip*. Its eight young ladies, described as "fair or otherwise" met once a week at Mr. John Irwin's house in Edgeworth. "The club will soon adopt a suitable costume, à la bloomer, a full description of which will appear in time."

Sewickley women prided themselves on their athletic skills. *Sewickley Valley* reported proudly in 1898.

The young woman of today is a healthy young athlete. A college girl is quite as familiar with the golf stick, the bridle or the foils as her brother. Young matrons and maids of Sewickley are surrounded by every advantage in the way of fine golf links, beautiful country roads for riding, driving and cycling, and the broad Ohio for rowing and fishing. For example, Mrs. Alexander C. Robinson is an expert wheelwoman. She plays golf well, and is an enthusiast on physical culture.[1]

Boys could participate in team sports. Football was played on Murray's field, now the site of the United Presbyterian Church. The goals were the Beaver Street fence and the present line of Centennial Avenue, then not a street. An article in the *Weekly Herald* described the game.

There were no rules whatever, the line-up being two opposing sides, embracing as many players as could get on the field, frequently one hundred to one hundred and fifty being engaged at a time, captains alone being selected, no other positions being known in those days. . . . The ball was merely kicked off and then the scrimmage began, one side merely bucking against the other, rough and tumble, the whole affair being always a case of weight and brute force, with frequent fights as the game progressed, so frequent in fact, that ordinarily they were not noticed by the all-absorbed players. Shins were kicked, eyes blacked, legs and arms twisted, few of the players coming out without at least a piece of cuticle missing, which indeed was considered a mark of distinction. There were no scores as we know them today, other than one side kicked the ball against the opponent's fence so many times during the row.[2]

Although called football, this sounds more like a game specific to Eton in England called the Wall Game. After teams are picked, a ball is thrown into the air and everyone scrambles for it. Any means can be used to score by throwing the ball against the opponent's wall.

The Sewickley Bluestockings, members of the Pittsburgh Suburban League, 1889. Courtesy Sewickley Library.

Baseball was the most popular sport for boys. It was fairly new in Sewickley's early days, dating from just 1839. The same article in the *Weekly Herald* that described football tells about an early form of baseball.

> Previous to 1870 a gentleman visiting in the Valley instructed a number of young fellows in the then new game, first playing on the lot adjoining Mr. J. Sharp McDonald's place along the railroad. The rules were few, the game, a very crude affair compared to present day scientific regulations. The batter continued to strike until he got a good ball, the bases were big rocks, with bats of the crudest shape, a limb of a tree, piece of fence or anything that took the player's fancy. The scores were something wonderful, as many as 140 runs being made in a single game, as high as eleven home runs being made in one inning.

> The playing gradually became more scientific, and in 1870 the LaBelles, the first organized team in Sewickley was formed, becoming famous among the teams in Western Pennsylvania. The home grounds were on "Murray's field," where the United Presbyterian Church now stands, and the meadow between the Little Sewickley Creek and the Beaver Road, in front of the old Shields residence. A grand tour of Western Pennsylvania was made one season, playing in Beaver, Rochester, New Brighton, Beaver Falls, New Castle, Sharon, Meadville . . . and Uniontown, winning every game played.

Other teams succeeded the LaBelles: the Crescents; the Sewickleys; the Independents; and two which represented local businesses, the F. A. Myers hardware store, and the C. P. Miles drugstore.

At least one famous Sewickley resident was not fond of baseball. Judge J. W. F. White lectured a boy who stole some clothes and, when questioned by the judge, confessed to a fondness for professional baseball. The judge replied:

> You should never go to a game. A majority of the persons connected with base ball bet on the result of the games, and all betting is gambling. Base ball is one of the evils of the day. It encourages poor devils like you to follow the example of the heavier gamblers, and to bet your last half-dollar, and if you haven't got that, ten cents.[3]

Baseball fever reached its pitch in 1934 when the famous Homestead Grays, the "Colored Champions of the World," came to Sewickley to play the local teams. Four hundred people paid to see the Grays win.

Sewickley Athletic Association, 1885. Clubhouse at center used for storage of racquets, bats, and nets. Courtesy
The Sewickley Valley Historical Society.

The Sewickley Athletic Association was the center for baseball and other sports activity in Sewickley from 1882 until the 1890s. Located on four or five acres leased from R. H. Davis just east of Nevin Avenue and north of Centennial, it contained nine tennis courts equipped with nets, balls, and racquets; a ball field with gloves, masks, balls and bats; an archery field; a croquet ground; and a greased climbing pole. The clubhouse had dressing rooms, bath, lockers and two bowling alleys. All this was available for $4.00 annual dues for men, $3.00 for women. The 200 members included "almost every family of social prominence in the valley," according to an article in "Qui Vive", July 1885.

Not all sports were organized. Residents could roller skate at the Sewickley Roller Rink in the 1880s. In winter, ice skating was popular on Harbaugh's pond, located between present-day Ohio River Boulevard, and Maple, Chestnut and Pine Streets. Edgeworth had another, larger pond, between Edgeworth Lane and Shields Lane. It was made by damming up the stream that ran along Beaver Road. Boys and girls played games there. At night, huge bonfires provided light and warmth for the skaters, "though not enough to prevent much 'spooning' in the shadowy corners and more secluded nooks."

The hills were perfect for sledding, an exhilarating but dangerous activity. *Valley Gossip* reported in 1880:

> All the young people who were used up in the collision, when sled riding on Mrs. Joseph Fleming's hill, are now able to be about, and waiting for another snow to try again. [Sled riding is a] very rare sport but a little dangerous.[4]

Another storm in 1881 engendered an accident.

> During the cold spell Cemetery Hill has been crowded with boys and men coasting, the sleds running down Broadway as far as the Methodist Church, crossing Beaver at railroad speed. It is customary to have a person stationed at the Beaver Street crossing to warn vehicles etc. of approaching sleds, but a young man from Beaver, not heeding the warning, drove a buggy across Linden Avenue at the time a large bobsled, heavily loaded with boys, came flying down the hill. Of course there was a collision which utterly demolished the rear wheels of the buggy. . . . The unfortunate buggy man was forced to put his wrecked vehicle and horse up at Eaton's stable, and take a train for the city.

Girls and women were excluded from sledding, probably because it was indelicate to ride in skirts. They could participate in sleigh rides, which were also popular for all children and teenagers. One extravaganza in February, 1881, included all the schoolchildren. The Economites invited them to Economy for a visit "in return for the courtesies shown them [the Economites] on their recent visit to our village." The children were loaded into 25 large sleds.

> The brass band tooted up, and the procession started, after parading several streets. Had it not been for the disgraceful conduct of some well-known Sewickleyans who, without invitation, accompanied the excursion, the affair would have passed off very pleasantly.[5]

"Uncle Joe" writing in 1890 about his youth "40 years ago," remembered another sleigh ride.

> A great wagon-bed filled with straw was placed on an immense sled and into it were packed from 12 to 20 boys and girls, and away we went, shouting and laughing and sometimes singing a merry song, unmindful of oft-repeated orders to keep our mouths shut in the frosty air. Sometimes a party was gotten up to go to one of the towns a few miles distant, where we rested and had supper, and it sometimes happened that in our reckless driving the sleigh tilted and spilt a few of us out, but except for being cooled off a little we were generally none the worse and went our way rejoicing.[6]

Sewickley was the destination for some sleigh rides. Henry Clay Frick took his wife for an excursion to Sewickley for dinner at the Sewickley Inn in 1892. Mr. Frick drove the horse, sleighbells ringing. Mrs. Frick, protected from the cold by a sealskin coat, warm scarf, gaiters and rubbers, was snuggly tucked into warm robes.

One children's delight discouraged by adults was exploring an "Indian Cave," remembered by "Uncle Joe".

> On a hill back of town was a wonderful Indian cave, which some of the more venturesome explored. A sort of rude ladder was contrived and, descending this to the depth of perhaps ten or twelve feet, a long, narrow passage led to a place something like a gate-way, very narrow, called "the fat man's misery." It was quite an effort for some of us to get through it. I remember the boys from the village Academy were often seen with long ropes and candles in hand going to the cave, which they were supposed to explore to a greater depth than any one else, which fact made us think them very brave.[7]

The Ohio River was often the source of entertainment. Fishing provided double pleasure: catching and eating. John May traveled down the Ohio River to Marietta in 1788, He noted in his diary.

> We catch any quantity of fish, and of a considerable variety of kinds—bass of two sorts, sturgeon, and others. Joseph is our fisherman. There has been a fish caught here which weighed 100 pounds, and the story goes that he drowned the man who caught him. . . . [Later] Two lads brought to my quarters a number of fine fish, just caught. Amongst them were two

perch weighing 24 pounds. They are very handsome, good fish, something resembling a haddock: a little higher in the back, and much better eating.[8]

Neville B. Craig described fishing in the river in 1851.

It is high amusement to those who are fond of fishing to angle in those waters, more especially at the time of a gentle flood. I have seen a canoe half loaded in the morning by some of those most expert in the employment, but you will see in a spring evening the banks of the rivers lined with men fishing at intervals from one another. This with the streams gently gliding, the woods at a distance, green, and the shadows lengthening toward the town, forms a delightful scene.

Dr. Fletcher White remembered fishing in the river when he was a boy in the 1880s.

When the dog-wood and lilac blossoms were in bloom, that was a "true sign" the red tail and mud suckers were waiting to be caught . . . on trot-lines. These lines were about fifty feet long and one end (on the shore) was attached to a peg driven into the ground, or tied to a stone near the water's edge. The other end was tied to a flat stone to be thrown out into the river as far as the line would reach. About eight or ten hooks (bass size) were tied to a string about twelve inches long and it was tied to the main line. It was a firm belief with many of the boys that if you had a bunch of Catnip leaves, or garlic in your bait can of angle worms or grubs (for that was the bait used) you were sure to have good luck in fishing. We seldom had more than two or three of these lines to look after for they were slowly drawn into shore about every half hour, keeping the line near the surface of the water, and when we came to the hooks, or a fish, we walked up stream, keeping the line far enough away from the river so the fish couldn't flop back into the river. The fish we caught were mostly the red tail and mud suckers, but we did catch other fish and never showed any mercy in dispatching the "River Alligator," which always swallowed the hook, and they were a mean reptile to handle and not pleasing to look at. [The River Alligator is probably a salamander called the Hellbender which can be two feet long.] If the river was right and the sport was good, you would see many a boy with ten or fifteen fish on his string as he marched proudly homeward. If the fishing was done at night a big bonfire was built from drift wood, so the light would reflect in the water, attracting the fish.

Rod and line fishing near Sewickley was mostly seen at the Haysville Dam or from some barge or dock rather than from the shore. Judge J. W. F. White and two of his boys went to the dam one delightful Fall morning for jacksalmon, as the law was closed on bass fishing at the time. The boys had gotten two buckets of fine lively minnows from Little Sewickley Creek the day before for the occasion. We reached the dam in good time and the Judge had caught several "jacks" while the boys were looking after the boat, minnows, lunch, etc. Soon he had a vigorous strike and had some fine sport in playing his fish, which we boys felt sure would be a fine big jacksalmon. Sad to relate, it proved to be a small bass, about $1\frac{1}{2}$ pounds. He stood looking at his victim at his feet, not offering to remove it from the hook and moralizing about observing the law regarding bass fishing out of season, etc. One of the boys, not so keen about such laws remarked, "Mr. Bass hadn't any business to get caught," and he roved the fish (which had been crippled from swallowing the hook) and soon hid it on the string with the other fish. The evening papers the next day came out in glaring big head lines, "Judge White came into court this morning, fined himself, and paid his fine for catching bass out of season."[9]

When Dr. White was about 15 years old, he was one of the "River Rats," boys with names like Punch, Dump, and Paddy, who spent most of the summer in and out of the Ohio River. Swimming and jumping on freight trains was their principal amusement. When the river was low, they could swim from bank to bank. Or, they might get a boat and ride the first wave behind the wake of a working boat, like a kayaker on the Youghiogheny. When swimming, they left most of their clothes on the bank, in defiance of an ordinance of 1894 which forbade swimming without a suit between five A.M. and nine P.M. Pranksters would punish the offenders by making the clothes into "green apples," tying them in knots as hard as green apples.[10]

There was at least some rowing on the Ohio River, according to the *Sewickley Valley*.

A boat race rowed Saturday, September 14, 1878 between John Lynch of this place and R. Brown of Pittsburg. The race is to be 3 miles with a turn, and is to be run over the Sewickley course. The race is for $1 a side.

Sixteen lucky young Sewickleyites spent a week on the river in May, 1881, sailing on the steamer *Scotia* to Cincinnati and back.

The days and nights were passed by the party in numerous ways. The mornings generally in reading, and gossiping on the forward deck; at times, when the boat would lay at a point for a few minutes, in creating a sensation in the streets of the several towns by a parade of the entire party in twos, each armed with an immense straw hat and fan. At several places they were mistaken for some kind of circus, and would be followed by admiring crowds of small children. In the evenings, when the sun had sunk into its golden western bed, with the exquisite perfume of the locust blossoms which lined the banks of the river, wafting on the gentle zephyrs (and the fragrance of the colored deck hand on the lower deck ascended), the party would assemble on the hurricane deck and pass an hour or two in singing the familiar songs dear to every young heart, to an appreciative audience of passengers and officers, until the cool night air compelled the singers to retire, the sedate to the cabin, the romantic or 'spoons' to the pilot house. In the cabin trouble began as soon as the party appeared, and was kept up until a late hour, waltzing, quadrilles, and with a Virginia reel to finish.[11]

The river provided entertainment and activity for many. Others preferred to take advantage of the flat bottomland next to the river for horse-related events. There were several livery stables in the neighborhood. The one owned by Thomas C. Little is described in an advertisement in the *Sewickley Valley* in 1895.

During these beautiful evenings every person longs for a drive along our excellent roads and over our picturesque hills. Mr. Thomas C. Little, whose livery establishment is located at the corner of Little Street and Duquesne Way, has in his stable some of the nicest, safest, horses in town, including his beautiful team of blacks, Black Bess and Jersey Lilly, which can be secured on very reasonable terms.

Marlatt & Sons ran a rival livery which advertised in the same paper.

We have large and roomy buggy, surrey, phaeton or
carriage for entertainments.
Safe and easy Saddle Horses.
Broad Street above Post Office.
Funeral Director   Embalmer
Private Chapel

This might seem like an odd combination of services, but the same horses that were "safe and easy" for renting could be used to pull the hearse at funerals.

Dr. Hazzard Schuyler Jackson, a veterinarian, opened a livery stable in Sewickley in 1894. The next year, Dr. Jackson took over a race track and stable in Edgeworth below Edgeworth Lane between Ohio River Boulevard and the river. The *Sewickley Valley* described it.

Jackson's Livery Stable. Courtesy The Sewickley Valley Historical Society.

Dr. Jackson will furnish to order any kind of vehicle for driving, be it buggy, surrey or his unexcelled four-in-hand, so well known in the valley. All vehicles of the latest styles.

A special feature will be that of saddle horses for ladies and gentleman. Any animal turned out from these stables can be relied upon as being safe and easy riders. In fact the reputation of the Doctor as a thorough horseman is such that it seems almost useless to state that any horse or vehicle driven from his stables is of the best.

One of the most important features will be the training and breaking of young horses, which under the personal direction of Dr. Jackson will be correctly and intelligently done. Animals in the least afraid of cars will be quickly trained to be absolutely safe.

It is proposed, in order to accommodate many persons who may wish to use the track, to issue season tickets at a very reasonable figure, which will certainly be appreciated by the horsemen of the valley. In fact, Dr. Jackson expects to cater to the best class in the valley, and with an establishment so well and fully equipped can satisfy the demands of the most fastidious.

The opening of the race track and stables will afford gentlemen from the city an opportunity to have their horses cared for in a very satisfactory manner, and be in a position to afford them, with but little trouble, the splendid driving on the roads in the valley. A gentleman can, on leaving his place of business in the evening, order his horse hooked up, by telephone, and in 25 minutes ride from Allegheny station [now the North Side] can be seated behind his horse on the track or public roads at Edgeworth. This is fully as quick as he can do were he to keep his horse in the East End and have to take the cable or electric cars to reach it. With the opening of the new hotel in Economy, many persons can, after a lively spin of 5 miles, secure an A 1 supper, and in the later evening return, after taking some of the many picturesque drives in the valley, in time to catch a seasonable train for the city, as the track is immediately next to the railroad station.[12]

Dr. Jackson's stable provided a full menu of equine activities. It was the site of a riding academy run by Louis Schuldenburg and Charles Bishop where students learned either to ride or to drive horses. For those already able to ride, the stable provided horses for pleasure riding.

The race track that Dr. Jackson started was somewhat scandalous in conservative circles. Horse racing, which easily leads to betting, was forbidden in Pennsylvania in 1794. "An Act for Prevention of Vice and Immorality" outlawed cockfighting, dice, billiards, and horse racing. At least in the case of horse racing, the law was ineffective. McKeesport and Allegheny City had races as early as 1800. Races were even run in Pittsburgh at the foot of Grant's Hill. Later, around the middle of the century, racing was legal on private tracks which catered mostly to the upper class. Tracks sprang up in Wilkinsburg, East Liberty, and on the South Side.[13]

The Sewickley area's race track and grandstand were next to the Edgeworth railroad station. On opening day, May 30, 1895, a crowd of 500 spectators sat on terraces along the river, while residents sat on their porches. There were both trotting and pacing races and an impromptu race between Joe Graff's gray pony, ridden under saddle by the owner, and Aliquippa, the handsome bay mare of J. P. Bailey. The pony won by three lengths.[14] During the summer of 1895 there were more races and a flat race for ponies. Either the Sewickley Brass Band or the Economy Band furnished the music.

Increasing opportunities for competition encouraged owners to improve the quality of their stock. One trainer, Jim Karr, was in charge of 30 horses at the Edgeworth stables.

[In the fall of 1895, he ventured to Lexington, Kentucky to] select some fine stock for Sewickley gentlemen. One of these horses was a fast, blooded, black stallion, well built, with fine lines, purchased for Mrs. S. F. Cole, costing just $600. These horses came up from Kentucky by way of the Ohio River on the steamer Hudson.[15]

Some horses, like their owners, went south for the winter season, but some remained at Edgeworth. A reporter from the *Sewickley Valley* visited them in December, 1895.

In good weather the trainers exercise horses on level roads that the valley affords, while in bad weather they sit around the barn on feed box, pail or 'soak tub' and talk 'horse,' reading pedigrees and fighting over again many 'close finishes,' while their sleek charges munch sweet timothy, or stand with their heads over the half doors of their comfortable boxes, listening with apparent appreciation to the yarns of their two-legged companions.

When the track closed sometime before 1902, drivers could still exercise their horses on the roads in the Valley.

Almost the only suburb of Pittsburg that has not been cut up by numerous trolley lines and through which one can drive for the genuine pleasure to be derived from speeding a fine horse on good roads (except for the occasional automobile) is found in the Sewickley valley and on the surrounding hills. A number of well-known people come from the city during the summer bringing their horses with them that they may enjoy this privilege and vie with their friends and neighbors in their smart equipages, handsome trappings and blooded stock. A number of these horses have records. . . . There are a number of fine horses on the road. Mr. George E. McCague's pair of handsome bays and drag, in which his family take their daily airing, is a familiar sight. Mr. Henry Buhl's smart drag with his well-matched team is also seen daily on the road. Mr. Mansfield Brown's bay team with the owner may be seen any pleasant afternoon speeding on fine stretches of road in the valley. Many men and women dispense with a coachman and drive natty traps, gay break carts, stanhopes and basket carts, handling whips and ribbons. . . . The children follow in the wake of their elders, the spirited ponies they drive in village carts, miniature traps, runabouts and two wheeled cars are exceedingly pretty.[16]

With many horses and excellent, unspoiled countryside for riding, many horsemen's thoughts turned to fox hunting. Hunting without horses had long been a custom in Western Pennsylvania. Originally, early settlers got together for a circle hunt. All formed a large circle and, using dogs, clubs, pitchforks, and sticks, drove the game toward the center, slaughtering any creature in their path. As early as 1818, 700 men from townships around Ligonier made a 40-mile circle and destroyed five bears, nine wolves, fourteen foxes, and 300 deer. These circular hunts were not sporting events. They were organized to get rid of undesirable animals and to get food.[17]

Sewickley men often hunted locally in the hills. Others went farther afield. "John Way and Dr. Frank McCraedy were among a party that bagged three deer, several wild turkeys and other small game [in Virginia.]"[18]

As time went on, hunting became more elitist. Hunting on horseback limited participants, and only purebred hounds were used. Special clothes were encouraged or required.

The Sewickley Hunt, 1925. Mr. and Mrs. John O. Burgwin. Huntsman Michael Cullinane on right. Courtesy of Richard Smith.

Sewickley was the site of the first live fox hunt in the Pittsburgh area. After several Pittsburghers had enjoyed hunting in Chevy Chase, they tried to induce the huntsman, Joseph Holloway, to start a hunt in Pittsburgh. Mr. Holloway came to Sewickley on October 12, 1897 to demonstrate the joys of hunting. Riders went for eight miles; nonriders followed by road. A Pittsburgh paper described the event.

> The good people of Sewickley were amazed yesterday afternoon to find their quiet little town taking on the appearance of an English sporting village during the hunting season. First through the streets early yesterday morning paraded the Chevy Chase pack of hounds in charge of J. Holloway and his whippers-in, and after that all the rest of the day and until late at night, a constant procession of lithe, nervous hunters, led by English grooms, passed out through the town. The headquarters for the hunters is at Jackson's livery stable and it was impossible to get a stall there last night.

> Those [who] will take part in the drag hunt today will go down on the train leaving Union Station at 1:20. A large number, however, have elected to drive down to Sewickley, and these last made an early start this morning. On Sunday Mr. Holloway, in company with S. W. Taylor and H. N. Van Voorhis, went over the ground and mapped out a run from a point near the McKean Shooting Club, out four miles and return. . . . The course as laid out can be followed on the road, so that those who drive or ride bicycles may witness it from start to finish. The hounds will be thrown promptly at two o'clock as they have the reputation of being the largest and fastest pack in this country, there will be some tough riding to keep them in sight. After the hunt a luncheon will be served to the participants at the McKean Shooting Club. The chase today is to be merely a preliminary, for the real hunt will come on next Saturday afternoon. On Friday night, Mr. Holloway will turn loose a live fox, and the run on Saturday will be for the brush. Every horse and rig in Sewickley has been engaged for the hunt this afternoon and it is estimated that, with the Pittsburg contingent, fully 200 people will follow the chase along the road.[19]

A later article reported that there were 50 in the hunting field and "1,000 turned out to witness the chase."

Perhaps because of the obvious enthusiasm shown for this event, the Pittsburgh Hunt established itself in Sewickley in 1898. It remained only two years when, finding that Sewickley was too far for many members, it moved to the Pittsburgh Country Club grounds on Beechwood Boulevard. Fox hunting did not return until 1921 when Mr. and Mrs. John Burgwin started a private hunt on their farm on Blackburn Road.

An interesting but short-lived equine phenomenon was the Sewickley Cavalry, organized in 1896 by Captain David Shields, chairman, and E. P. Coffin, promoter. The cavalry held several drills and adopted a dashing uniform of white hat, belt, and trousers, blue blouse, and saber. The Cavalry would certainly have made a great addition to the Sewickley parades, but the governor refused its application for permanent status.

Horses had always been part of the Sewickley scene, whether used for work or for transportation. As the area developed, horses became valuable for sports and entertainment. A totally new source of sport and entertainment arose with the development of bicycles that were easy to ride. The earliest prototype of the bicycle in 1690 consisted of two wooden wheels joined by a piece of wood. The rider straddled the backbone and pushed with a backward motion of the feet. In 1860, pedals on the front wheel were invented. As bicycles developed, larger wheels were added to increase speed, but the contraption was unsteady and difficult to steer. Nevertheless, many Sewickley boys braved the dust, ruts, and stones of the streets on the unwieldy devices.

As early as 1894, the Council felt it necessary to regulate the more overzealous riders: bells or gongs were required; no more than three could ride abreast; nobody could ride after eight at night; and nobody could ride on sidewalks.

Sewickley joined the bike craze sweeping the country. There were bike parties, dinners, picnics, and races. Because Sewickley was on the route from Pittsburgh to Cleveland, people saw big league racers. One local race held about 1890 was described in the *Sewickley Herald*. Twenty-five of the Valley's best bikers followed a five mile course to Big Sewickley Creek, looped twice.

> The two rivals, Eugene Murray and Sam Young, ran neck and neck most of the way. The race ended at Walnut Street. Murray won by one length. Young collapsed, fell off, and broke his collar bone.[20]

Enthusiasts formed a club, The Sewickley Valley Wheelmen, in 1895 and built a small clubhouse on Thorn and Little Street.[21] Franklin Nevin described the club when it was new.

> Summer evenings saw the club members on the road. Usually they would meet at the Athletic Grounds, then in groups down Beaver Road they would go, and out Little or Big Sewickley creek. . . . Then towards dusk came the return trip to the

clubhouse porch for a smoke and chat and later, lighting the oil lamps that hung from front wheel hubs inside the spokes, the riders wended their several ways homeward.[22]

Club members joined in long distance rides. In June, 1895, the Sewickley Club joined members of the Associated Cycling Clubs for an excursion back and forth to Pittsburgh, followed by supper at the Park Place Hotel.

In 1879, H. J. Lawson in England geared the pedals to the rear wheel with chain and sprockets, creating the "safety" bicycle. Nevin complained in 1928: "With the passing of the high bicycle, the gymnastic element in the sport was eliminated and the wheel gradually settled down into its present more or less utilitarian character."

Sewickley recreational activities have remained remarkably similar over the last hundred years. Some sports have enjoyed a comeback recently: fishing is now possible again because river pollution has abated; bicycle riding is popular; horses and hunting remain, although limited to the Heights. One activity will probably never return. It is hard to imagine riding sleds down Broad Street.

[1] *Sewickley Valley*, May 28, 1898.

[2] *Weekly Herald*. In Hays File.

[3] *Pittsburgh Commercial Gazette,* October 8, 1887.

[4] *Valley Gossip,* Dec. 1880.

[5] Ibid., Feb. 1881.

[6] Uncle Joe, pp. 17-18.

[7] Ibid., p. 7.

[8] Harpster, pp. 187, 190.

[9] *Sewickley Herald,* June 29, 1929 p. 6.

[10] Ibid., Feb. 21, 1935.

[11] *Valley Gossip*, June 1, 1881.

[12] *The Sewickley Valley,* April 13, 1895, p. 10.

[13] Martin, p. 164.

[14] *Sewickley Valley,* May 30, 1895.

[15] George A. Hays, *Reminiscences of the Sewickley Valley.* Harmony Press of Sewickley Pa., 1968, pp. 17-18.

[16] *The Pittsburg Index,* August 2, 1902, p. 17.

[17] J. Blair van Urk, *The Story of Rolling Rock.* N.Y., Scribners, 1950, p. 50.

[18] *Sewickley Herald,* Sept. 19, 1903, p. 5.

[19] *Pittsburgh Leader,* Oct. 21, 1897.

[20] *Sewickley Herald*, Oct. 23, 1920, p. 3.

[21] *Sewickley Valley,* May 30, 1895.

[22] F.T. Nevin, p. 153.

82

Chapter 12
Development after the Railroad

Sewickley in the 1850s was the right place at the right time. It was an attractive, accessible place to live that offered an excellent alternative to the grimy city. Suddenly a long day's trip to Pittsburgh had become an easy commute. The Borough population tripled between 1850 and 1910.

Year	Population	Increase Number	Percent
1850		500 (estimate)	
1860	1,586	1,086	217%
1870	1,472*	(114)	
1880	2,053	581	39%
1890	2,776	723	36%
1900	3,568	792	28.5%
1910	4,479	911	25.5%
1920	4,955	476	10.6%
1930	5,599	644	13%
1940	5,614	15	.27%
1960	6,157	543	9.67%

(U.S. Census)

*Leet township withdrew from Sewickley in 1869. Its population in 1870 was 629.

As would be expected, building boomed concurrently. The easiest way to get an idea of the swift growth of Sewickley is to look at maps of 1862, 1876 and 1897. For example, the Hopkins lot between Boundary, Peebles, Beaver and the railroad had two houses in 1862. By 1876, there were ten, and in 1897, twenty-one.

As real-estate investments and speculation swelled, prices and transactions increased. Property south of Beaver Street, which was within easy walking distance of the station, was especially popular. Charles and Sophronia Thorn lived in the block between Broad, Beaver and Walnut streets in the center of Sewickley. Their land was part of a large tract of land that ran from Division to Ferry Streets south of Beaver Road. This larger tract was the property that Mrs. Thorn got from her father, Thomas Hoey. The Thorns sold to James Chadwick in 1838. Chadwick divided the land into lots, and part of one of the lots (Number 9) was sold in 1850 to Green by Chadwick's administrator. Green resold to D. E. Nevin the same year. Nevin sold part of the land to John Norris in 1851. Norris sold to Reverend John White in 1856. Nevin sold another part, containing only one quarter acre, to the school district for $100 in 1853. Thus in fourteen years parts of Lot 9 were reshuffled and sold five times. These must have been heady days in the Sewickley real-estate market.

Another division near the Thorn property described above was the Sands and Adair plan of 1873 between Ferry and Walnut Streets, just north of Bank Street. This was a subdivision of 97 lots of prime real estate, easily accessible to the railroad and Beaver Street. On the 1876 map it had one occupant, Reverend C. Thorn. David Sands and James Adair bought the property in 1872. New streets were needed to give access to the new lots. Instead of laying out lots in a grid, without regard to natural contour, Sands and Adair decided to introduce the new techniques in landscape design popularized by Frederick Law Olmsted and incorporated in the planning of Riverside, a suburb of Chicago. Olmsted's Riverside plan included large lots, 100 by 225 feet, with houses set back thirty feet from the street. Olmsted said that a modern suburb should have curved roadways to "suggest and imply leisure, contemplativeness, and happy tranquillity." The grid was "too stiff and formal for such adornment and rusticity as should be combined in a model suburb."[1] A grid system suggested the efficiency of a factory or the economy of city row houses. Undulating streets, on the other hand, suggested a rolling landscape dotted by rural retreats.

James Adair described how he was influenced by the Chicago school of landscaping in a letter written in 1910.

In 1872 David Sands and I purchased the White-Harbaugh farm of 90 acres for $50,000. I had to go to Chicago right after the fire, and took Professor Goff's survey of the property. I looked at the Chicago system of plotting. I was impressed by the curves they were making in their avenues or boulevards and decided to adopt the idea.[2]

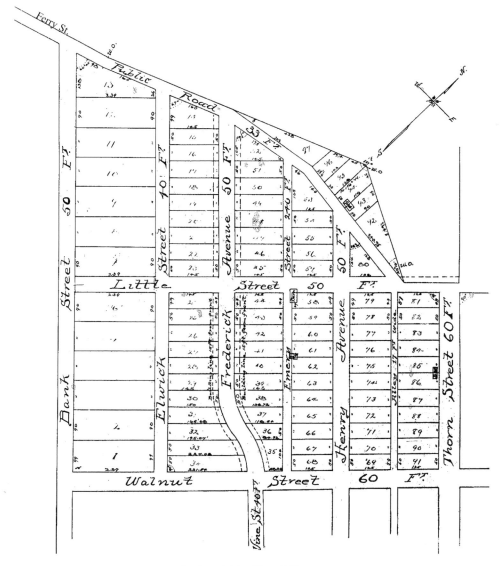

Sands and Adair Plan, 1873.

The streets were named after Mr. Sands' and Adair's own children, Elwick, Frederick, Emery and Henry. This was not uncommon in early Pittsburgh. The streets on the South Side, for example, were named by the man who had laid them out, Nathaniel Bedford. In McKee's Rocks, the streets record members of another early family, the Schoens.

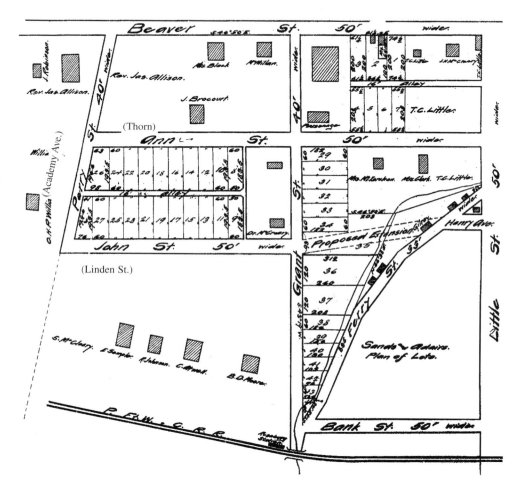

The Sands and Adair plan boomed. By 1897 there were 77 houses on 91 lots. The lots were sold at an auction held on two days in June 1873. Over $60,000 worth of lots were sold.[3] Perhaps the sales were helped by John Pryor, Sewickley Presbyterian Church's black sexton, who passed out free hot coffee and ham sandwiches to all.

To get another idea of the growth of Sewickley, look at the extreme western part of town between Academy Avenue, Ferry Street, Beaver Street, and the Ohio River. In 1862 most of the land belonged to John Little. There were three houses, one church, a grist mill, and a saw mill. By 1897 there were 100 lots with 70 houses. The mills were gone and the only non-residential use was the Ohio Valley Oil Company office on Ferry Street.

The reason for the rapid development of the Little property was a sale by John Little's executors on June 23, 1877. The proposed development called for small lots; most had only 60 feet of frontage on the road. An advertisement for the sale, with lots labeled, describes the plan:

The Executors of John H. Little will offer at Public Sale on the premises, in the Borough of Sewickley, on Saturday, June 23, 1877, at 1½ o'clock P.M., the lots on the above Plan, numbered from 1 to 44. As a whole, they are the finest lots ever offered for sale in the Borough, and this is the most favorable opportunity for securing a first-class building lot at a fair price. They front on Main street, and nearly all have rear alleys. They are most favorably located for Churches, Schools etc. and are very convenient to Railroad Station. Terms of Sale: one-fourth cash, the balance in three equal annual installments, with annual interest.

[Signed] J. W. F. White, Thomas and Samuel Little

The statement that the lots faced Main Street must have been some sort of real-estate hyperbole. There is no Main Street in Sewickley. If it be assumed that Beaver is the Main Street, the statement is still not true. Only three lots were on Beaver.

Some purchasers bought more than one lot: Charles Atwell took three; F. Semple, three for two houses; and George Anderson, two. Some bought single lots, which gave an urban look to the landscape. For example, lots four to seven,

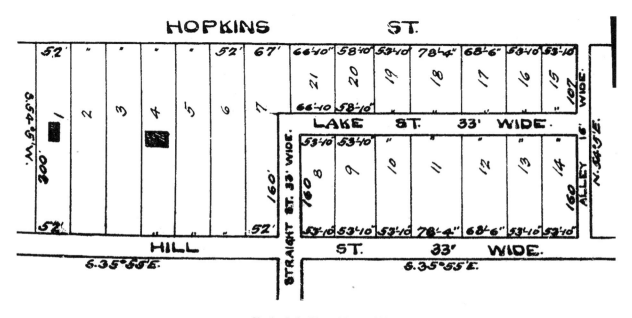

Charles Lake Plan of Lots, 1882.

each with 55½ feet of frontage on Thorn Street, all had houses by 1897. The 20 lots between Thorn and Linden, all with 60 feet frontage, had ten houses by 1897, Looking ahead to 1940, 26 of John Little's original 44 lots had houses. If the original plan had been followed, the area would be more urban than it is.

Not only the wealthy got involved in real estate. Small investors, too, tried their hands. John Ague, for example, was a butcher born in 1822 in Pennsylvania. He had a wife and five children, and, according to the 1860 census, had property valued at $700. He invested in three lots on Fountain Street, one lot on Mechanics Street, and three lots on Mulberry Street.

The commercial section of town developed along with the residential section. Beaver Street between Broad and Blackburn, for example, had 18 structures in 1862, all on rather small lots. By 1876, there were 22, and in 1897, 33.

North of Beaver Street subdivisions blossomed, mostly as large tracts were developed with rather small lots on which small houses were built. One example of this is the Lake Plan of 1882. Note that Straight Street ends half way through the subdivision and turns 90 degrees to form Lake Street. This made it possible to double the number of lots from seven, as there were in the western half, to 14.

Another large subdivision was the Elizabeth Grimes plan. Thomas Hoey sold his land north of Beaver Street and west of Division to John Fife in 1828. Fife divided the property with his daughter, Elizabeth Fife Grimes. She submitted

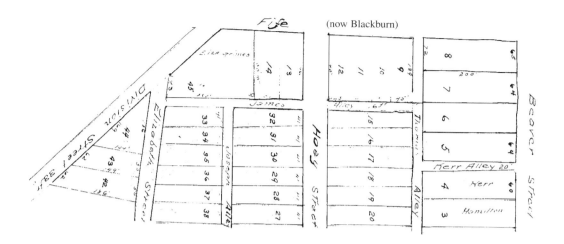

Elizabeth Grimes Plan, 1863.

a subdivision plan in 1863 for 44 lots on her land, which lay between Fife (now Blackburn) and Grove Street north of Beaver. The plan was signed "Elizabeth Grimes, her mark x." Elizabeth might have been illiterate but she was smart. Although she was married to Captain James Grimes, and most married women did not work outside the home, she found time to invest in real estate. The 1897 *Plat Book* shows that her subdivision had been a success. Almost every lot had a house. Mrs. Grimes herself lived in a house on a large lot between Grove and Grimes on Beaver Street.

Some parts of town resisted development. The whole area east of Peebles and south of Beaver had five houses in 1862. By 1897, there were 18. East of Nevin and north of Beaver all the land was owned by the R. H. Davis heirs, L. H. Willard, and the heirs of Mrs. A. J. Miller. There was only one house in 1897.

A Diversified Neighborhood

What kinds of people lived in Sewickley Borough in the early years of the suburban movement? As mentioned above, the population was not all composed of rich commuters. The detailed manuscript report of the census taker in 1860 gives an example of occupations of 147 families. The town was remarkably heterogeneous, with many different nationalities working in numerous occupations. Thirty-six people were employed in managerial or professional occupations, including seven teachers, three lawyers, three druggists, one capitalist, three manufacturers, eight merchants, four doctors, and three clergyman (all Methodists). The occupation of three men is listed as "gentleman." The census shows 189 people employed in non-professional, non-executive jobs. Altogether, there were 49 different occupations listed. Men's occupations were varied: one iron mason, one tinner, one silver plater, three "brickmoulders", and a cooper. Several occupations deal with transportation: five men worked with boats, six with railroads, six men were teamsters and one was a carriage driver. Many were employed building houses for the burgeoning population: there were 31 carpenters; five painters; four plasterers; and five stone masons or cutters. In 1860, only 33 women worked outside the home, all in very traditional women's jobs, including one confectioner, and twenty domestics.

Not only were Sewickley citizens employed in many jobs, they came from many backgrounds. Of the total population found in the manuscript census, 100 were foreign born and 58 were born in states other than Pennsylvania. The largest number of immigrants (46) came from Ireland, probably forced to abandon their country by the potato famine in the 1840s. Language and ethnic differences were not a big factor in this early wave of immigration to Sewickley.

Eighty-one residents had immigrated from English-speaking countries. An exception was the 14 residents who came from Germany, perhaps pushed from their homeland by the wave of revolutions that swept middle Europe in 1848.

Sewickley in the second half of the nineteenth century was becoming a thriving town with a mixed population engaged in various careers. As time passed, different segments of the population tended to settle in specific sections of town and Sewickley began to be more stratified in living spaces. Railroad suburbs developed in this way, according to Kenneth Jackson, an urban historian: land within walking distance of the stations was especially valuable. Farther away from the tracks it was still difficult to commute. Only the very wealthy, who could afford a horse and driver, lived out in the country.[4] The upper-class commuters often lived near the station. The 1860 census, which gives data on wealth, demonstrates this. In 1860 the neighborhood south of Beaver and west of Division Streets had a population that was predominately, but not exclusively, wealthy. John P. Kramer, for example, was a broker with $6,000 worth of real estate and $1,000 personal estate. Living with him was James Gray, 75, from Ireland, who listed his occupation as Gentleman. Gray owned $5,000 worth of real estate and was probably John Kramer's father-in-law. The next person to be listed was another Gentleman, D. N. White, who owned $9,000 in real estate and $6,000 personally. White's son, Albert, aged 17, was a telegraph operator, the high-tech trade of the day. The next listing was George F. Rudisell, master carpenter, with $6,000 real estate and $1,500 personal. Then came Jacob Guy, a lawyer with $8,000 real estate and a $2,300 personal estate. Although this neighborhood was predominately wealthy, it varied. A day laborer, Abraham McCray, lived next to lawyer Guy. Then came Washington Gibb, a gardener. Gibb was probably overly modest in his job description. He was assisted in his gardening by a day laborer, and his wife was assisted by a domestic servant. Next came two master carpenters: Bruce Tracy and Jacob Ringley; then, James Camahan, a tailor. The next dwelling, and probably the most interesting and lively, belonged to Joseph Travelli, aged 51, whose occupation was Principal in Academy. Mr. Travelli had 17 people in his household including: son John, a teacher in the Sewickley Academy who had been born in Singapore; five other children; Abigail Travelli, 71, his mother; George and Joseph Tracy, 18 and 16, from Madeira; three servants, one with a child of 12; and two laborers. The neighborhood continued with William Harbaugh, merchant, with property of $34,900. His father-in-law Charles Thorne, a Methodist clergyman, lived with him. Then came Theodore H. Nevin, a white lead manufacturer. The next few households were less grand: Charles Jones, farmer; an unoccupied dwelling; Mary Smith, widow, and her son, who was a mate on a boat; and three dwellings occupied by day laborers and their families.

Part of the same neighborhood in the 1880 census was solidly white collar. Looking at the area south of the railroad (now Ohio River Boulevard) we find: Fred R. Dippold, boat captain; Professor Robert Patterson, educator, with a daughter who was a schoolteacher and a nephew who was a railroad clerk; J. Sharp McDonald, contractor; T. H. Nevin, banker, with a son who was a bank clerk; A. B. Nevin, bank clerk; Charles Harbaugh, merchant and bank director; J. W. Mills, job painter; J. Murdock, educator, with two daughters and seven sons, one in medical school and one a railroad clerk; B. W. Doyle, railroad clerk; J. H. Davis, steel wire manufacturer, with one boarder who was a music teacher; J. E. Wakeham, schoolteacher; William Harbaugh, retired merchant and bank director; J. P. Kramer, retired bank cashier, with a son also a bank cashier and a son-in-law who was a railroad clerk; S. McKelvy, Burgess. All but two of these households employed from one to three servants.

In other neighborhoods, craftsmen and tradesmen predominated, according to the 1860 census. Many tradesmen and workers lived north of Beaver. Traveling along Beaver Street, for example, the census taker found: Samuel Galton, merchant; Frederick Ringley, master shoemaker; Westbrook Zunsaal, day laborer; Zachariah McPherson, bricklayer; William Lappe, merchant; Alexander McIlwain, merchant; and John White, day laborer.

Sewickley Borough changed rapidly after the coming of the railroad. In other parts of the Sewickley area, change was slow. Sewickley Township in 1860 included the area along the river, now Edgeworth, and much farmland in the hills behind the river. The township contained the wealthiest people of the time, all living in a homogeneous neighborhood near the river. Just west of Camp Meeting Road lived Dr. John Dickson, aged 48, with an estate valued at $16,000. Next to him was David McKinney, 65, a Presbyterian clergyman worth $18,000. Both of these families employed a male laborer and a female servant. The next two households were headed by James and John Woodburn. James was an insurance agent worth $15,000 and John, a boat captain worth $21,000. John lived on the river next to the Edgeworth station.

In addition to private residences, there was some commercial activity in Sewickley Township. According to the 1876 map, there were two brick kilns, one on Leet Street and one near Edgeworth Avenue; a wagon shop; McCormick & Son store on Shousetown Lane; and the Sewickley Gas Works.

In 1860 there were fewer different occupations in the Township (24) than in the Borough (49). In the hills a large majority were farmers. There were 70 farmers in the township, assisted by 35 laborers. The next largest groups were domestics, with a total of 25, and teachers, with six, four of whom were members of the Way family.

A large number of Township residents (74) had been born in Germany. The next largest group was Irish (54), then Scottish (26).

Transportation innovation governed the growth of Sewickley and neighboring areas on the river. Places near the railroad changed rapidly, while the hills remained sparsely populated.

---

[1] Jackson, p. 80.

[2] Hays File. Senator John Heinz Regional History Center.

[3] F. T. Nevin, p. 181.

[4] Jackson, p. 101.

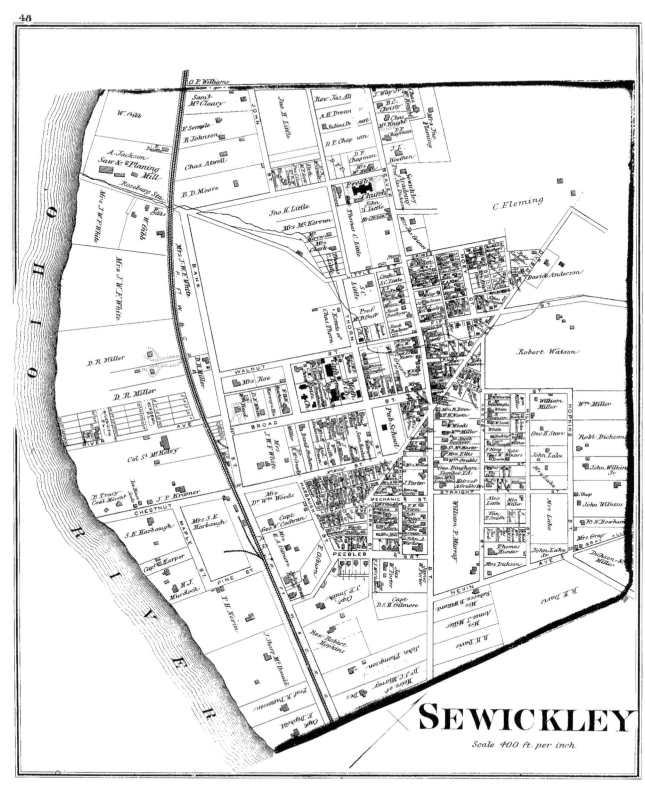

Sewickley Borough, 1876.

Chapter 13
Industry and Commerce 1850-1900

During the second half of the nineteenth century, Pittsburgh industry and population boomed. Population multiplied over sixfold, from 46,601 in 1850 to 321,616 in 1900. Factories grew along the three rivers, turning once pleasant river towns into communities jammed with houses and industrial plants. The same changes that occurred in Hazelwood and Homestead might have happened in Sewickley. Hazelwood became a railroad suburb in the 1850s and 1860s with large houses, many weekend retreats, and a private club. Its convenient location proved its ruin as a suburb when blast furnaces, rolling mills and coke ovens drove the wealthy elsewhere.[1] *The Pittsburgh Leader* described what was happening in Hazelwood in 1901.

Gradually but surely are the manufacturing interests that are now putting on such aggressive airs encroaching on the choice residence parts of the city. Districts that 15 or 20 years ago were beautiful with handsome homes, splendid lawns and fine old shade trees are now mere ghosts of their former selves, sad pictures of decay and neglect. Their former occupants have moved away to avoid the plebian air that inroads of the wage-earner class have given the neighborhood. Such is the fate of Hazelwood, which 20 years ago was perhaps the choicest suburban section around Pittsburgh. In that time a melancholy change has come over the district. Gigantic coke ovens and mills, railroads and other manufacturing enterprises have gradually encroached on the charming rural homesteads, nestling in their green-clad environs, and in a few short years, the wiseacres predict, beautiful, quiet Hazelwood as an aristocratic residence district will be a thing of the past. Old families that gave the place its claim to social precedence are moving out daily.

Many of these old families ended up in Sewickley or Sewickley Heights, perhaps because, at least in the valley, the landscape resembled their old home town. Familiar Sewickley names of families that moved from Hazelwood are Burgwin, Laughlin, McCargo, and Oliver.

Sewickley escaped the embrace of Pittsburgh industry, although nearby towns such as Ambridge, Aliquippa and Leetsdale all had mills. A quote from a 1914 history of Allegheny County tells why:

[Sewickley] is one of the most favorable situations on the Ohio, and has been settled by wealthy families, who have united in making it an elegant suburban place of residence. For this purpose they have strenuously opposed all attempts to introduce manufactories in the place, and have even refused to give their support to such necessary institutions as hotels.[2]

The townspeople of Sewickley fully appreciated avoiding the industrial sprawl, as is reported in *The Village Gossip* in 1881.

Our village is fortunate in the possession of an industry which possesses no unpleasant attributes. There is no firey array of furnaces or clouds of murky smoke to be seen, nor clang and rattle of machinery to make night hideous. Nor does the industry require the services of such a class of operatives that pay day is a term synonymous with disorder and drunkenness.

One industry in Sewickley was the Pittsburgh Boat-Building Company, Ltd. located on the river at the foot of Ferry Street. *Valley Gossip* described it:

The boat-yard is always an attractive place for Sewickley folks. The perfume of the newly cut timber and sawdust and chips is a pleasant one. The click of the caulker's mallet is fully as pleasing a sound as that of the croquet mallet, and long may the trans-Ohio hills give us the echoes of the boat-yard hammers.

The boatyard had developed from a saw and grist mill located on the site in 1862. In 1877 it was the Sewickley Planing Mill owned by E. W. Scott and J. A. Lake, advertising "Sash and Door Factory. Scroll sawing a specialty. Dealers in all kinds of Lumber, Coal and Lime." The next year, three businessmen, Stuart S. Colville, J. Sharp McDonald, and W. F. Speer, bought the mill and started the boatyard with a capital of $10,000. *Valley Gossip* continued,

Thousands of dollars were expended in machinery of the latest pattern. The old single muley saw gave way to a 'gang' saw, and large 'bands' saw and a huge circular saw were added to the wood-shaping machinery. The first boat, launched in 1879, was the sternwheel steamer *Butte*. It was followed by other sternwheelers, sidewheelers, barges, and towboats. The boats were active in trade all over the inland waters of the United States, including Jacksonville, St. Louis, the lower Mississippi River, and Tennessee. A goodly fleet truly! Seventeen proud steamers that must carry the name of Sewickley to the uttermost corners of our land."[3]

Sewickley's other industry, oil and gas wells, was not as environmentally neutral as boat building. Oil wells dotted the landscape of Western Pennsylvania after Colonel Drake's well in 1859 started an oil craze. Environmental hazards in Sewickley were oil leaks ruining the creeks and river, oil rigs despoiling the suburban scene, and noise pollution of incessant pumping. People alive today remember the noise, claiming that they could hear the wells being pumped all night along Little Sewickley Creek. They became so accustomed to the noise that when the wells stopped pumping, sleep was impossible.

Early wells were flops. Around 1861, a well was bored in the Waterworks hollow with a crude spring pole apparatus. After getting down about 100 feet, it was abandoned. Another drilled at the Fair Oaks station about the same time was abandoned after finding mere traces of oil at 500 feet.

Sewickley never became the boom town that some of the promoters wanted, but some wells were successful. A well on Ferry Street between Frederick and Elwick produced some oil. A gas well on River Street near the Park Place Hotel supplied all its needs. An exciting find in the borough was reported in the *Pittsburgh Leader*, July 10, 1886.

> The well is one of the most remarkable in any of the gas fields for two reasons: first, it is a double well, there being two separate and distinct gas sands from which a flow is obtained. At the depth of 1,460 feet a flow was struck sufficient to supply about thirty houses for domestic purposes. At a depth of 1,370 feet a flow of 300 or 400 pounds pressure, very rich in carbon, was struck. The well has been cased down about 1,680 feet, and the heavy flow is piped up above the top of the derrick, burning with a flame sixty or seventy feet high. Many people are attracted by the novelty of the sight.

Other wells succeeded on Sewickley Heights. On March 27, 1886 the Ohio Gas Company found a big gas well on the dairy farm owned by Cochran Fleming. The *Weekly Herald* reported:

> At the first stroke of the drill in the gas sand rock the gas roared out. Mr. Fleming, Mr. E. P. Young and Mr. Standish were present at the time. The gas pressure was so great that the tools could not drill, being suspended in the well. A torch was applied and a blaze flashed up strong enough to light the streets of Sewickley. The pressure was nearly 500 pounds to the square inch. A 60 pound weight in the well was lifted out as if it had been a feather.

The Grubbs farm on Audubon Road was the lucky location of Sewickley's best remembered oil well. It is said to have produced 1,000 barrels a day. In any case, it flowed so quickly that it filled up the valley behind the farm and all the creeks between the well and the Ohio River. The well became a tourist attraction. One livery stable cashed in on the oil craze by meeting Pittsburghers who had taken the train to Sewickley and taking them up the hill to see the great well. The well's success prompted additional drilling in the hills. Shacks sprang up to house the oil drillers. One remains, just before I-79 on Blackburn Road.

The U.S. Geological Survey in 1911 surveyed all the wells in the area. It found that most were slowing up after flowing for 8 to 20 years. Some had been large, "from 1,000 to several thousands barrels a day."[4]

Oil fever reappeared in the 1920s. Entities, probably corporations or partnerships, known as the Hartle Farm Oil and Gas Lease and the Sewickley Farms Oil and Gas Lease planned to drill deeper on the Heights properties, hoping to release more oil. An article in the *Sewickley Herald* sounds like an advertisement.

> The Sewickley Farms Oil and Gas Leases engaged the services of Mr. B.M. Francis, a prominent geologist, [to pick suitable sites] He selected the Wolfe Farm, which gives promise of HEAVY PRODUCTION, the Holzer Farm, within plain view of the largest Grubbs well, and the Minnick Farm, which lies a short distance south of the Grubbs well. . . . The capitalization of this copartnership is $100,000, divided into 1,000 shares, with a par value of $100 each. . . . Remember, the opportunity is knocking at your door to become independent through a small investment in this company, which is backed by successful and enterprising business men. . . . You may see a small investment of a few hundred dollars bring returns of thousands. It is just a question of time before the alottment is sold and shares command a much higher price.[5]

A month later, the *Herald* tried to give a more balanced view.

> Oil may be struck almost any time within the next two weeks by the company whose drilling operation is already under way or by one of those whose subscription lists are rapidly filling to the point where they can begin work. We hope it may be so, and in rich quantities; and the prospects seem hopeful. There is a good deal of interest in oil projects here, although no such universal madness as some of the city-paper advertisements would indicate; but if a good oil-strike comes in and some of the early investors blossom out in sudden wealth, then there will be plenty of excitement. And there will be plenty of promoters ready to play that excitement for all it is worth.[6]

The oil flurry did not produce the desired great wealth for small cost. Wells continued pumping patiently in the area but no roaring gushers disturbed the neighborhoods.

Public Services

If Sewickley turned its back on large industry, it welcomed the broad array of service industries that were required to maintain a comfortable and safe life for its citizens. A family living on a farm or large suburban estate can provide for most of its own needs, such as water, food, and sanitation. A family in town, however, must rely on shops and utilities for these necessities.

In the nineteenth century, the water in both Pittsburgh and Sewickley came directly from rivers. Even drinking water was not treated. This is astonishing, considering the grime and pollution for which the area was famous. Indeed, water for Pittsburgh came straight from the rivers until 1906. As a result, Pittsburgh had the highest death rate from typhoid fever in the nation until the water treatment plant in Aspinwall was built utilizing an up-to-date sand filtering system. Then the typhoid rate plummeted. In 1907 there were 5,652 cases of typhoid, in 1909, only 955.[7]

In Sewickley many citizens relied on the river, others on wells. Probably the safest water came from cisterns. As early as 1853, Mr. James Ellis installed the first cistern for holding filtered rainwater in his new house on Beaver and Chestnut Streets. A more general solution for the whole town seemed necessary. A number of citizens called a public meeting at Mozart Hall in June, 1872. A petition signed by 188 persons recommended that the Town Council appoint a water commission. Accordingly, on June 24, 1872, the Council passed "An Ordinance for Appointing Commissioners for the Erection of Water Works in the Borough of Sewickley." The five commissioners were authorized "to purchase all necessary engines, machines, pipes, materials, etc, to contract for the erection of all buildings and structures, and the doing of all necessary work in the erection and completion of Water Works."[8]

Waterworks Park. Foot bridge and one of trails, 1903. Courtesy The Sewickley Valley Historical Society.

Where should the water come from? The original plan was to use the river but, according to an article written in 1916, "There were strong objections to this plan among some of our citizens, on account of the impurity of the water, resulting from the sewerage poured into it from cities above us." In 1873, the Commissioners decided to use Peebles Run as the source of water. The Run comes into town from high up in the hills near what is now Dickson Road. It could be tapped high enough so that the town's water could flow by gravity. In 1874, the work was completed, resulting in both a dependable water supply and a beautiful park described in a 1916 article:

> From a primitive forest, covered with underbrush, has been evolved a beautiful park embellished with winding paths, shrubbery, inland lakes filled with clear, sparkling water screened from contamination, welcome shade and all the requisites of a wooded park. Years and years of work, and loads of money have been devoted to making the Waterworks Park what it is, a thing of beauty, and something of which the people of Sewickley are proud.[9]

Waterworks Park in Winter. Courtesy Sewickley Valley Historical Society.

The citizens of Sewickley had a right to be proud. Schenley Park, the first in Pittsburgh, was not started until 1889, fifteen years later. Unfortunately, the new water system did not eliminate typhoid from Sewickley. In 1896 there were 9 cases of typhoid, or 3 per thousand.

Although the town council was willing to support a water system, it was not willing to take responsibility for a fire department. Fires had always been fought with the old-fashioned bucket brigade. These might have been valuable in promoting cooperative community spirit, but they were not effective in fighting fires; if there were fires, most buildings burned anyway. Both Travelli's Academy for boys and the Edgeworth Female Academy had serious fires.

With improved water supplies, improved fire fighting was feasible. In 1876, men met at Mozart Hall to organize the Cochran Fire Company, named after Burgess George W. Cochran. Public subscriptions were solicited. Some gave money; some, labor and materials. Thirty-eight men became members. The company purchased a hose and reel mounted on a four-wheel hose cart and drawn by hand. Enthusiastic citizens welcomed the new equipment as a brass band led it through the town. This apparatus survived until 1908 when it was replaced because it had taken almost an hour to drag the old rig up the hill to a fire at Mrs. Henry Rea's house in Sewickley Heights. Mrs. Rea bought the best horse-drawn combination fire wagon available, paying $1,325. In 1917, the colorful horse-drawn engine fell victim to a more modern motor-driven truck.[10]

Another less obvious requirement for the growing town was a cemetery. Rural families could bury their dead in small family or church cemeteries. Sewickley residents who were Presbyterians used the church burying grounds. Others used the town's small graveyard near Division Street. In these early burying grounds the gravestones were lined up in rows with names and dates and perhaps an instructive inscription. Cemetery style changed in the mid-nineteenth century. The latest trend was the carefully landscaped park like Pittsburgh's Allegheny Cemetery, established in 1844. Here people came on weekends to stroll, picnic, and admire the elegant tombstones. Sewickley, wanting to be in style, organized a nondenominational, nonprofit cemetery in 1859 on a twenty-two acre plot just above the town. A cemetery report explains, "In order, so far as possible, to disconnect the cemetery with ghastly connections and to give our grounds an ornamental and park-like appearance, the corporation adopted some years ago what has been termed the 'Landscape Style' of ornamentation."[11]

Shopping

Water supply, fire protection, and burial space were all requirements of suburban life. The suburban housewife expected to enjoy many of the other goods and services that had been available in the city. There were various ways of obtaining these goods and services. If her husband were willing, the housewife could have him bring items home from the city. This sometimes led to complaints, however. One commuter grumbled, "The bundles I have carried! And the bundles I have yet to carry! to tote! to tote!"[12]

Hegner Hardware's two story building. Sign says Hardware, Cutlery and Tools. Practical Harness Maker. Courtesy The Sewickley Valley Historical Society.

If her husband balked, or if she just wanted a day out in the city, our housewife could easily set forth on the railroad to shop in Pittsburgh, returning on an afternoon train. This was a convenient way to shop. In 1910, for instance, there was a train at 9:15, 9:24, and 9:53 in the morning and at 12:46, 1:05, and 2:08 in the afternoon. Next day, the packages arrived at the railroad station and were delivered to her door by the Adams Express Company, which had offices at the Sewickley, Quaker Valley, Edgeworth, and Shields railroad stations.

Shopping in the city was a new delight for suburbanites, according to John R. Stilgoe.

City shopping, for all the problems of crowds and dirty streets, at least partly satisfied the growing need of American women—borderland and urban—for self-determination. In the department store, in the streetfront shop, women decided what to buy. There, along with other women and free of all but the half-forgotten admonitions of absent husbands, women made up their minds, and in that decision-making they enjoyed some taste of the larger independence they craved.[13]

Such a grandiose purpose of shopping must be taken with a grain of salt. Probably women were mostly looking for a day off from ordinary life. City shopping was a treat.

Women were drawn to Pittsburgh by the development of a new and exciting retailing innovation, the department store. Between 1860 and 1900, these consumers' palaces sprang up in all major cities. Such household names as Lord and Taylor's, R.H. Macy's, John Wanamaker, Jordon Marsh, and Hudson's all date from the period. Women who used to shop in markets or small specialty stores could now browse through a cornucopia of goods. Everything from the latest gadget to the latest fashion was available in one enormous building containing as much as forty acres of floor space.

Pittsburgh had its share of the new stores. The Boggs and Buhl department store, started in 1869, was always a favorite of Sewickley shoppers. Other department stores were Kaufmann's, started in 1885, and Horne's, in 1902. Suburban shoppers were important customers, specifically targeted in advertisements. In 1904, for example, Kaufmann's advertised:

Kaufmann's The Big Store.

Free excursion on all Railroads next Tuesday, Thursday and Saturday. Purchase not less than $10 merchandise. Fort Wayne Division of Pennsylvania System. Sewickley. Shields. Edgeworth. Quaker Valley. Glen Osborne.[14]

Many Pittsburgh and Allegheny City stores, department stores, and other retailers advertised in Sewickley publications, evidence that Sewickley customers must have been important to them. A 1912 cookbook, for example, has advertisements for Boggs and Buhl, Elliott and Ulam Florists, Singer Sewing Machines, and R. Taggart & Sons Footware. Joseph Fleming's on 84 Market Street advertised its health products.[15]

Most housewives did their regular shopping in local shops in Sewickley. Stores were a convenience for suburban residents, but the town prided itself on not being a large commercial center. *Sewickley Valley Society* explained:

Hegner's Emporium. Courtesy
The Sewickley Valley Historical Society.

There are only stores enough to meet local needs, and there is nothing more suggestive of trade throughout the valley than the delivery wagon of these stores or the vehicles representing the adjacent dairies and the local butcher.[16]

The shops were centered on Beaver Street, the Main Street of Sewickley. Its importance to the whole valley is described by Spiro Kostoff in his *America By Design*.

The one indispensable element of fledgling towns, the one that has survived as a fundamental American institution, was Main Street. Main Street, of course, is much more than a place name to Americans. It is a state of mind, a set of values. It is what has defined the heartland of the nation for generations. . . . Main Street remains one of the central landscapes of American life. It has even been enjoying something of a comeback recently.[17]

What kinds of shops and services were offered on this main street? Information compiled from listings and advertisements in *Polk's Directory,* 1897, *Hayes Atlas*, 1877, *The Methodist Church Cookbook*, 1912, and early local newspapers when combined, give a picture of the shopping area. Although all these stores were not operating at the same time, the list gives a good idea of the town in the late nineteenth century. Many small stores provided different goods and services. Taken as as a group, they provided almost all necessities and some luxuries.

One of the oldest stores is also the best remembered: Hegner's. It lasted through three generations. George H. Hegner immigrated from Germany about 1865 and opened a small shop near St. Stephens Church. The shop sold shoes and harnesses, an unlikely combination chosen because both involve working with leather. Hegner took out a $500 insurance policy in 1866 for "the stock of shoes, boots, and leather and shoemaker's tools contained in a one-story frame building occupied by assigned situated on Broad Street near Thorn." The policy was issued by the German Fire Insurance Company with all the conditions written in German.

As times changed, so did the location and the goods offered. In 1880 Mr. Hegner purchased a building on 439 Beaver Street. This soon became too small, according to an article written in 1895.

From year to year [he made] improvements in the old buildings then standing until he had covered the entire lot with additions and annexes which, as the business increased, were found too small. He then determined to build a building as would not only be large enough for his large business, but which would be an ornament to the town. . . . This building is a three-story frame, with a mansard roof, well lighted by large windows on each floor, giving an opportunity to display the varied stock, and is occupied wholly by Mr. Hegner for business and residence purposes. The show window on the Beaver Street front is a thing of beauty, and not excelled by many of the large business houses in the city. Here is tastefully displayed a line of goods that would be a credit to any concern in the city, and which attracts every person passing.[18]

Note the emphasis on creating a pleasing appearance for the Sewickley street. Sewickley merchants were interested in maintaining the town's image as a stylish suburban retreat with stores that could compete with the city's.

George Hegner and the foundation for the new emporium about 1885. Courtesy of The Sewickley Valley Historical Society.

As Mr. Hegner's space increased, he could sell a wider variety of products. In 1895 he continued to offer shoes, harness and harness repair. In addition, he provided many items available in today's hardware stores: stepladders, buckets, glass, building supplies, sleds, skates, stoves, trunks, farm implements, and crockery. Hegner's boasted that it supplied "everything you need from a clothes pin to a mowing machine."

Still later, Hegner's did a big business in food for chickens, pigs and horses. Miss Helen Hegner, a member of the third generation to work there, remembered, "We got in two big freight cars full of [animal] food. It was more convenient to buy locally than to take the train all the way to Pittsburgh." Miss Hegner recalled another creative marketing idea of her father's.

Dad used to go out and get crude oil from a working well on Sewickley Creek. He bought a fifty-gallon drum and bottled and labeled the oil as furniture polish. It was Pennsylvania crude—a beautiful olive color, not the dark sticky kind of crude.

No other stores offered the same mix of merchandise, but there were two others that could be called old-fashioned general stores.

McElwain and Company.

Grand display of Holiday Goods, Handkerchiefs. Spool cotton. Fine writing paper. Children's wool socks, leggings, mittens. Lace collars. Lace. Fichus. Kid gloves, Napkins. Our usual stock of Fine Groceries Selling at Hard Pan Prices.

S. Krepley.

Dry Goods, Notions, Gents Furnishing Goods. Positively the Cheapest Store in Town.

More specialized stores:

T. Y. Abercrombie, furniture.
H. I. Jackson, Bicycles and bicycle sundries. Bicycle livery. Electro-plating and enameling.
Frank Schlumpf, bicycles.
Mrs. Kate Schreiber, china.

Seven Shoe and Clothing stores:

Mrs. T. C. Little. "Holiday jewelry, handkerchiefs, collars, fine tidies, yarns, bonnets, hats and ribbons. Little and Beaver Street."
Mrs. G. W. Hagan, Fine millinery.
Jacob Brown, Dealer in Men's, Boys', Women's, Misses', Children's, First Class Boots, Shoes and Gaiters.
J. D. Miller, shoes
R. M. Ellis, Manufacturer and Dealer in Boots and Shoes and Agent for Adams Express.
Valentin Schreiber, shoes
William J. Shull, shoemaker.
Sommer's tailor shop. "Ladies why don't you have your husbands or sons go to Sommer the Tailor. He will always be satisfied."
James S. Gray, tailor.

Grocers:

James C. Grimes & Bro.
S. C. Ritchey. "Our enterprising young friend Mr. R.J. Ritchey has recently opened a stand opposite to the Post Office next to Ellis' shoe store where you can get the nicest, Fresh Fish, Game, Poultry and Oysters at prices not to be beaten in the Village."
Thomas Graham. "Game and Poultry, Oysters, and Produce."

Lake & Baltz McLaren
B. F. Campney
Samuel T. McDonald

Specialty food stores:

Robert Ruttkamp, baker
Joseph Hewler, Confectionery, Ice Cream, Cakes, and Pies. Home-made Bread and Candy a Specialty.
Edward Gray, meats
Thomas Scalise, fruits

Three drug stores:

A. G. Walker. "Purity is Our Motto. Dispensing pharmacist. Walker's Syrup of Tar, Wild Cherry and Horehound for Cough and colds. Walker's Floramel for Chapped Hands and Faces. Sole agent for Economy Boneset Cordial."

P. P. Knapp, "Apothecary. We have everything a good Drug Store should have. Advice, if you want it, costs you nothing; and it isn't forced on you if you don't want it."

C. G. Woods. "Dealer in Drugs and Medicines and Chemical and Perfumery. Pure wines and liquors for medicinal purposes."

Three craftsmen;

Albrecht Sickeler, harnessmaker.
William M. Scott, blacksmith.
William Neely, blacksmith. There were three generations of the Neely family who were blacksmiths in the Valley. The first, William Neely, Sr, worked in the old David Shields shop on Beaver Road. The newer shop in town was described in the *Herald* in 1904.

His present shop is fitted up in modern style. The blast for his drill presses, emery wheels and other appliances is obtained from a six horsepower engine—the engine being in the cellar. The building is equipped with gas and electric lights, and is truly built for handling the large horseshoeing business which Mr. Neely has.[19]

Services

Financial:

The First National Bank of Sewickley, established in 1890 with "Capital $50,000. Surplus and Profits, $26,077.33." The bank building dates from 1894. The bank shared the first floor with the Ohio Valley Gas Company. The YMCA used the second and third.

R. B. Boobyer. Real estate and Insurance Broker.

George Rudisell, real estate.

Personal Services:

Laundry. "Sewickley first-class laundry. Charles Yeng Kee, proprietor. All kinds of Laundry work done in prompt and satisfactory manner."

Funeral services. J. W. Marlatt & Son. "Leading Livery in Town, Funeral director. The best turn-out in the Town."

William Fleming, "Has the only Hot and Cold Baths in Town. Everything clean and comfortable. Single bath 20 cents."

Ice. "Reibert Brothers Ice. Distilled water ice. Our wagons go everywhere."

Barber. Geo. T. Muegge. "Shaving and Hair Dressing Parlor. Ladies' bang trimming, shampooing and children's hair cutting a specialty."

Home Services:

Electrician, Stephen Handy.
Gas. Ohio Valley Gas Company.
Telephone. Central District Party and Telegraph Company, Miss Laura Marquis, operator.

Restaurants:

Mrs. E. B. Gray's restaurant.

The Misses Hood and Mahler's restaurant described in the *Valley Gossip*, 1881.

Sewickley for many years has had no place where strangers could secure meals or even a lunch during the day. Through the enterprise of two young ladies, Misses Hood and Mahler, this annoying feature has been overcome. These ladies now serve a first class lunch or oysters in any style during any hour during the day or evening. So popular have these lunches become that a number of families frequently have their suppers prepared by Misses Hood and Mahler and on all sides we hear of the excellence of these meals praised."[20]

Builders' Supplies:

A. L. Gray, agt. "Slate and Tin Roofing. The Best is always the Cheapest and to get the best, use nothing but Brownsville Maine Slate and Hamilton re-dipped tin."

Bower & Abercrombie, "Tin and slate roofing and plumbing. Remember we are here to stay"

Alden F. Hays, Coal, ice, and building supplies

William Dickson. Masonry and Bridge builder.

John Patton, Jr. "Hot water heating, gas fitting, Favorite hot air furnaces, sewering."

Professionals

Lawyers	Doctors	Dentists
T. M. McCready	Robert McCready	M. Burns
Henry A. Davis	William Johnston	J. Collard White
Clarence Byrnes	J. M. McCready	
	R. J. Murray	
	J. W. Douthett	
	I. B. Chantler	
	Samuel D. Jennings	
	William Nicholson, veterinary surgeon	

Compare this list to a shopping center in the twentieth century. In either case, most of the needs of the surrounding population are met in a small area. The shopping center has many of the same kinds of stores. Just as an example, note the stores in an existing shopping center, Carrolltown Mall, near Baltimore, Maryland and those in Sewickley at the end of the nineteenth century.

Comparable Stores

Carrolltown Mall	Sewickley
KMart	J. McElwain general store
KMart Garden Center	John Lent, Sewickley Green House
A & P	S. T. McDonald, grocer
	Sylvester Ritchey, grocer
	Thomas Scalise, fruits
	Edward Gray, meats
	Robert Ruttkamp, baker
	Joseph Hewler, Confections, Ice Cream
Ace Hardware and Crafts	Albert Gray, roofer
	J. Patton, plumber
	Alden F. Hays, Coal, Ice, Building Supplies

	John McMillen, Dealers in Lumber, Coal and Lime
	Scott & Lake, Sewickley Planing Mill, Lumber, Coal and Lime
	George Thornburg, painter
	Joseph Ague, painter
Fashion Bug	James Gray, merchant tailor
	Eliza Tiffany, dressmaker
Rite Aid (Drug store)	C. G. Woods Sewickley Pharmacy
Katz Jewelers	A. Merz, jewelers, est. 1885
Barber	George R. Muegge, barber
Fava Shoes	William J. Shull, shoemaker
Hess Shoes	John D. Miller shoes
	Valentin Schreiber, shoes
NuLook Cleaners	Charles Yeng Kee Laundry
Five restaurants and four food court merchants	Miss Hood and Miss Mahler's
	Mrs. E. B. Gray, restaurant
Maryland National Bank	First National Bank of Sewickley
The Investment Center	
H & R Block	George Rudisill, Deeds, Bonds, Mortgages
Remax Real Estate	George Rudisill, real estate
Health Maintenance Organization (HMO)	Doctors
Psychiatrists (Group of 4)	
Dentist (1)	Dentists (2)

Stores and services only in Sewickley

Kate Scheiber, china	Fred Albrecht, music teacher
Frank Schlumpf, bicycles	William M. Scott, blacksmith
Albert Sickeler, harnessmaker	Stephen Handy, electrical repair
William Fleming Baths	Reibert Brothers Ice
Lawyers	

Stores and services only in Carrolltown Mall

Movies	Radio Shack	Just a $	Peebles Department Store
Little Professor Books	Hallmark Cards	JoAnne Fabrics	Carrolltown Liquors

Conspicuously absent from Sewickley's list is a liquor store or saloon. *Sewickley Valley Society,* boasted in 1895, "For over forty years no license to sell intoxication liquor has been issued in the village, or in the valley for that matter." The only legal dispensers of liquor were the drug stores, where it was sold only for "medicinal purposes." There were also illegal sources, according to *Valley News,* 1876. "There are several places in this town that deal out intoxicating drink. Do they want us to expose them?"[21]

Many of the stores in a strip shopping center are operated by women. In Sewickley in 1897, there were few. Mrs. Kate Scheiber had a china store; three ladies ran restaurants; and Laura Marquis ran the telephone exchange.

One great advantage enjoyed by early Sewickley housewives was delivery to the door. Department and local stores took it for granted that they were responsible for delivery. Such excellent service was supplemented by vendors, who sold their wares door-to-door by horse and wagon.

The nineteenth century was the high point of Main Street. Earlier towns were plagued by garbage, mud, and transportation problems. In the twentieth century, competition from malls destroyed Main Streets. Sewickley gives an excellent example of Main Street at its peak.

[1] Samuel Hays, pp. 202-3.

[2] J. McKees Boal, *History of the Erection of Allegheny County its Townships, Boroughs, and Cities*. Pittsburgh, Union Fidelity Title Insurance, 1914.

[3] *Valley Gossip*, September 1, 1881.

[4] M. J. Munn, *Geology of the Oil and Gas Fields of Sewickley Quadrangle*. Washington, D.C, U.S. Geological Survey, 1911.

[5] *Sewickley Herald*, February 28, 1920, p. 8.

[6] Ibid., March 13, 1920.

[7] Pittsburgh, Dept. of Public Health *Annual Report, 1909-19*, pp.1003-4.

[8] Ibid., April 1, 1916.

[9] Ibid., April 1, 1916, p. 8-10.

[10] *Sewickley Herald*, January 28, 1976, pp. 14A.

[11] *Sewickley Cemetery Handbook*, 1908.

[12] Dallas Lore Sharp, "The Commuter and the Modern Conveniences." In *Atlantic*, October 1910, pp. 554-564.

[13] John R. Stilgoe, *Borderland*. New Haven, Yale University Press, 1988, pp. 209-210.

[14] *Post Gazette*, May 12, 1904.

[15] *St. Stephens Church Parish Cookbook*, 1912.

[16] *Sewickley Valley Society*, 1895, p. 15.

[17] Kostoff, pp. 164-167.

[18] *Sewickley Valley*, December 21, 1895.

[19] *Sewickley Herald*, May 6, 1904, p. 9.

[20] *Valley Gossip*, December 15, 1881, p. 7.

[21] *Valley News*, November 18, 1876.

Map of Sewickley, 1897.

Chapter 14
Houses for a Railroad Suburb:
Houses and their Inhabitants, 1850-1900

The Sewickley area developed quickly in the second half of the nineteenth century, becoming more populous and more diverse. Luckily, many houses from the period remain today, making it possible to get a good idea of Sewickley as it was over one hundred years ago. A study conducted in 1966 found that approximately half of the houses in Sewickley Borough were constructed between 1850 and 1900.

Houses in Sewickley still standing in 1966:
Built 1800-1850   30
Built 1850-1910   580
Built 1910-1965   440[1]

Because of the variety and endurance of its houses, the Sewickley area has a wider importance for historians than most towns of comparable size. Vincent Scully, an architectural historian from Yale University, studied Newport, Rhode Island and found that it epitomized American life in the 1800s. Sewickley, on a less grand scale, could serve as another excellent example for Mr. Scully. If the mansions of Sewickley Heights, built towards the end of the period, are included, the parallel becomes more obvious. Substitute Sewickley for Newport in the following quote from Vincent Scully.

The importance of Newport for the architectural historian is that, with certain exceptions, the important developments of American domestic architecture can be studied as in a laboratory. . . . It isolates one critically important phase of American nineteenth century architectural creation, namely the cottage and country house. The atmosphere which produced these cottages was typically American, for it was a suburban one, and it was the nineteenth century suburb which continues to evoke, in a rapidly urbanizing society, that sense of necessity for agrarian experience which had been so important in the political philosophy of Thomas Jefferson. Therefore, however inadequately the suburb may function as a social unit—being neither urban nor really agrarian—it nevertheless, in nineteenth century America, assumed an importance as cultural energies continued to operate.[2]

A closer examination of individual houses and their owners in this laboratory of suburbia should give an idea of Sewickley in the Victorian era.

Anyone building a house in the mid-nineteenth century could choose among a variety of styles. If he were of a conservative bent, he might like to build a Greek Revival house. If he considered himself more romantic, he would choose to build a Gothic Revival cottage. If he thought he was a rational, fully civilized and cultured person, he would choose an Italianate villa. Anyone wanting help in selecting a style had only to go a pattern book to see illustrations of possibilities. As new editions of the pattern books came out with examples of new styles, house designs changed accordingly. The same books, available everywhere, account for the parallel development of styles all over the country. Residents of Pittsburgh, Cincinnati, and Savannah might pick a house plan in Greek Revival style. The resulting houses would be similar.

An early example of one style popularized by the pattern books, Greek Revival, is represented by the second Way house which has already been discussed. Another Greek Revival house, the Warden-Clarke house, was built in Sewickley around 1860 on the southwestern corner of Peebles and Beaver Roads. It is fortunate that this house survives, as it is one of the few Greek Revival houses in the Valley. Greek Revival was the dominant architectural style in the early decades of the nineteenth century, before the building boom in Sewickley. Towns all over the country that started a few decades before Sewickley sported many houses resembling Greek temples. By the time Sewickley developed as a suburb, newer styles had taken root.

The Warden-Clarke property was originally lots 25 through 28 of the Hopkins plan. In 1851, William Gray's parents gave the lots to him "for $1 and for the affection they have for the said W. C. Gray, their son." William Gray sold the lots to Edward R. Shankland of Sewickley for $1,600 in 1855. The same year Shankland bought another lot of 2½ acres on the corner of Beaver Road and Hopkins Street for $1,023. He sold both parcels to Margaret Roseburg Black, wife of Reverend Andrew Black, for $4,000 in 1856. It would seem that no house had been erected at this time because there was no significant jump in the price for the property.

The Black-Warden-Clarke House.
From *Illustrated Atlas of the Upper Ohio Valley* by E. L. Hayes, 1877.

By 1860, Mrs. Black had built a house on the lot. According to the 1860 census, Mrs. Margaret Black was, a 48 year-old wealthy widow. She, not her husband, had originally bought the property. The census lists her wealth as $50,000 in real estate and $500 in personal estate. It is fortunate that she was well-to-do because she had eight children, aged 4 to 21, living with her; six were still in school.

It is possible that the rear section of the Blacks' new house was built first, followed by the front section. The Greek Revival style was going out of fashion in the East by the time this house was built, but it took time for newer architectural fashions to reach Western Pennsylvania. A drawing of the house in 1877 shows many characteristics of the Greek Revival style: a low-pitched gable roof; front door surrounded by narrow sidelights with a rectangular line of transom lights above; rectangular window frames and lintels; and porches supported by square columns. Note that although classical Greek structures all had round columns, square columns were popular in America because they were easier to construct.[3] The 1877 drawing clearly shows decorative Italianate brackets under the eaves of the gable end of the house. These give a hint that knowledge of the newer Italianate style was reaching Sewickley.

In 1865, Mrs. Black sold her house to Benjamin Hallowell, Jr. of Philadelphia for $8,600. The next year, Hallowell sold to James A. Hutchison of Allegheny City, Pennsylvania for $11,000. Hutchison did not move to Sewickley. If he bought the house as an investment, he was disappointed because when he sold it in 1873 it was at the beginning of a depression. He received only $6,500 from John Arthur Warden, little more than half what he had paid. Moreover, because he had not paid off the mortgage to the former owner, he received only $2,000 of the purchase price.

The Warden family occupied the house at the time of the 1877 drawing. The sketch gives an idea of true Victorian era ease and comfort. Children and dogs frolic everywhere. An elegant carriage awaits the master and mistress for a drive through town or countryside. A large yard beckons with shade trees, an arbor, and a barn for horses and ponies. There are porches everywhere, some added since the house was first built, for sitting, enjoying the view, watching passers-by and perhaps engaging them in a friendly chat.

Mr. Warden was a partner in the Pittsburgh firm Warden & Oxnard which produced Elaine Oil, an illuminant so good that it was used in lighthouses for beacons along the Ohio and Mississippi rivers. It was advertised in a Pittsburgh paper in 1877.

A positive protection   Safest, cheapest and
from   Best light known
Explosives

Elaine—The Family Safeguard Oil
Warden & Oxnard
Duquesne Way and Seventh Street
Pittsburgh, Pa.

Mr. Warden died in 1878, leaving his wife Catherine in charge of a large household. The 1880 census lists Catherine, 43, Juliet, 20, David, 17, a student at the Pennsylvania Military Academy, four other children, and two servants. Mrs. Warden, like Mrs. Black, was well off. She owned 105 shares of Standard Oil stock, 29 shares of Natural Gas Trust, land in Sewickley, and an interest in her husband's Pittsburgh business. Adelaide Nevin described Mrs. Warden in her book, *The Social Mirror*, which was the Bible of society in 1888.

> Mrs. Warden, widow of John Warden, of the firm of Warden and Oxnard, a branch of Standard Oil Company, is one of the most perfect hostesses. She is a St. Louis lady of good family, and her style of hospitality is fashioned on the Southern plan—free, openhanded, spontaneous. Mrs. Warden is quite wealthy and recently bought a magnificent place at Quaker Valley Station. Miss Juliet, her daughter, has the same candid, generous nature, and is a great favorite in society. Miss Warden returned a month ago from a year's study abroad. She spent last winter in musical study in Dresden. Annie and Betty Warden, the younger daughters, are almost ready to enter into society.[4]

Having moved to her "magnificent place" in Quaker Valley, Mrs. Warden no longer needed the Peebles Road property. She sold it in 1894 to Lenora H. Clarke, wife of Robert P. Clarke of Sewickley, for $8,000. The Clarkes lived in the house for three generations: Mr. and Mrs. Clarke, their son James, and his children.

Today the house stands proudly on its corner, looking remarkably like its picture in 1877. The porches are reduced and changed; the shutters are gone; and the windows are new; but the basic structure and many of the Greek revival characteristics remain.

Greek Revival architecture was followed and largely supplanted by Italianate and Gothic styles. Andrew Jackson Downing, America's first great landscape designer and the arbiter of taste for the early suburbs, was a proponent of the newer styles, which he considered more suitable for domestic architecture. Downing thought that the function of a building should be obvious by looking at its exterior. Thus, anyone looking at a structure resembling a Greek temple would assume it was a religious building, not a house. He wrote in 1873:

> The expression of the house is that of domestic comfort. It is easy of access, has a sheltering porch, and is invitingly connected with the terrace, gardens and piazzas. . . . The roof and chimneys are boldly treated, so as to indicate the purposes for which they are adapted.

> The different styles of architecture have been very aptly compared to different languages. Thus, if we talk pure Greek, and build a Grecian temple for a dwelling, we shall be little understood, or perhaps only laughed at by our neighbors. Let us rather be more sensible, though not less graceful in our architectural utterances, and express a pleasant every-day language in an old English mansion, a Rural Gothic cottage, or an Italian villa.[5]

In the Sewickley valley, the transition from Greek Revival to the later Italianate style, popular in the United States from 1840 to 1885, is exemplified in the house at 1008 Beaver Road, just east of the Sewickley boundary in Osborne. Dr. William Miller built the house sometime between 1860 and 1864 on a nine and a half acre lot that was part of the Samuel Peebles tract. The house turns its back on Beaver Street, facing instead the Ohio River and what used to be the railroad tracks, now Ohio River Boulevard. The original house, pictured in the 1877 Hayes *Atlas*, has some Greek Revival elements: the rectangular windows with no decorative details, the plain columns on the porch, and a general air of simple elegance. The newer Italianate style shows in the house's square shape (Greek Revival houses were usually rectangles); the low-pitched hipped roof; the decorative brackets under the roof; and the taller windows on the first floor. Dr. Miller and his builder must have decided to pick and choose from the older, more traditional style and the innovations being introduced in the more romantic new styles.

If someone were to look for the house today, using only the aid of the 1877 drawing, the search would be fruitless. In 1898, it was completely remodeled by Rutan and Russell, one of Pittsburgh's premier architectural firms. They transformed it into an elegant Colonial Revival mansion with a Greek temple front complete with pediment, dentils, and columns. A gracious entrance hall runs through the house from front to back, leading to three large rooms: the parlor, the sitting room and the dining room. In 1925 a huge wing was added for the owner's mother-in-law. The wing, designed by Sewickley architect William Boyd, contained all the requirements of a separate house including kitchen, living room, bedrooms and baths. It was connected to the older house on one side. After the mother-in-law's death, the wing was moved to 420 Boundary Street, where it remains today, a freestanding house.

Residence of Marshall McDonald,
From E.L. Hayes, *Atlas*, 1877.

Same house with William Boyd addition on the left.
Addition is now separate on 420 Boundary St.

The owner of the house from 1871 until his death in 1896 was Captain Marshall McDonald. He bought the property for $24,300, which seems like a substantial amount for the time. Mrs. Black received only $8,400 when she sold her house in 1865. Captain McDonald represents an important group of Sewickley residents in the nineteenth century, men who worked on the river and did not want to live too far from its banks. Other members of this group are easily identified on an 1876 map. Captain F. Dippold lived on the river just west of the Sewickley borough line. Captain David Gilmore lived in Sewickley three houses from Captain McDonald. Gilmore's lot touched Captain J. P. Smith's. Captain George Cochran and Captain Harper were each two houses away from Captain Smith.

Captain McDonald was a wealthy man with numerous and varied business interests. An inventory upon his death in 1896 records "Goods, chattels, rights and credits" totaling $139,376. He ran a large coal business and owned the following boats, barges and flatboats:

The Hornet #2 towboat	$15,000.
Bertha (towboat)	$ 6,500.
Barges on hand	$20,725.
Coal on hand	$10,326.
Coal boats	$ 6,326.

Captain McDonald held real estate investments on Big Sewickley Creek, in Monongahela City, and in Hopewell Township, Beaver County. Other investments were:

Catsburg Coal Company	$12,000.
5 shares Union National Bank	$ 2,500.
Oil land leases West Economy	$ 25.
Big Sewickley Oil Company stock	$ 50.
2 Insurance policies	$ 8,166.

Household goods, listed in a special inventory, seem remarkably sparse, considering the size of the house and the wealth of its owner. The total value, $280, included 3 beds and bedding; 4 bureaus; 7 lamps; 9 chairs; 2 pairs curtains; 3 tables; 3 stands; and 2 carpets. There are very few hints of luxury: one vase and some pictures. Perhaps because he was a widower with no wife to follow the latest dictates in Victorian era decoration, he eschewed the cluttered look so popular at the time.

Lurking dangerously in all this apparent wealth were two items:

Bills receivable	$25,000.
Book accounts receivable	$18,366.

When the executors settled the estate, they found its debts greater than its ready assets. The Captain's assets had provided income but, upon his death, they were not easily turned into cash. The executors were forced to sell the house to raise cash.

Another captain settled near Captain McDonald. Around 1872, Captain Zehu P. Smith built five Italianate houses on or near Peebles Street, one for himself and four for his children. Captain Smith's house, now gone, was on a large lot bounded by the railroad tracks, Graham Street, and Clark Street. A contemporary advertisement in *The Valley Gossip*, December, 1881 gives a good description of the property.

Handsome two-story frame dwelling of ten large airy and pleasant rooms. . . . Elegant porches surround almost the entire building. The lot contains four acres fronting on R. R. [railroad] and Peebles street with beautifully laid out grounds and lawn. Ornamental shrubbery, fruit and shade trees. Stable for 3 animals and carriage on premises with all necessary outbuildings. This is one of the handsomest and most desirable pieces of property in Sewickley Valley and only one square from the station.

Both the captain's and his children's houses, and even his barn, are in the Italianate style. Identifying characteristics are overhanging eaves with decorative brackets, low-pitched roofs, and tall, narrow windows with arched tops. The Captain's house sports a square tower, often considered the salient feature of real Italian villas. Andrew Jackson Downing himself recommended the Italianate style, along with the Rural Gothic style:

[They] are much the most beautiful modes for our country residences. Their outlines are highly picturesque and harmonious with nature. Their forms are convenient, their accessories elegant, and they are highly expressive of the refined and unostentatious enjoyments of the country.[6]

Captain Smith's house on the bottom. Children's house above. Hayes *Atlas*, 1877.

If Captain Smith tired of swapping tales with his cronies from his riverboat days, he had only to go next door to visit one of his children in one of their four nearly identical houses. The houses still stand, ranged impressively along Peebles Street (Numbers 304-322). All of the Smith houses are charmingly pictured in the *Hayes Atlas* of 1877. The children's houses seem to be lacking yard space, but they and their children would have been able to use their father's large lot.

Captain Smith was a river pilot and captain of a towboat. Like Captain McDonald, Captain Smith did not restrict his activities to his primary profession. He invested in coal lands. In 1878, his estate received $805.29 in royalties. Captain Smith was also a partner in the wholesale drug firm of George A. Kelly, on the corner of Wood Street and First Avenue in Pittsburgh. The firm, which employed 19 people, sold drugs, paints, oils, varnishes, dye-stuffs, and chemicals.[7] Captain Smith's share of the business was estimated to be $23,159.23 at the time of his death.

Despite this impressive list of assets, when Captain Smith died in 1878, his executors found:

[He] had greatly overestimated the value of the assets and underestimated the amount of liabilities. The value of the entire personal estate, apart from the Drug House, would not reach $10,000, while the debts of the estate ranged from $30,000 to $35,000. [The executors were forced to sell the homestead in order to] save the widow's interest in the Drug House, which is a source of revenue.

Next to Captain McDonald, on the eastern boundary of Sewickley, lived Dr. James C. Murray. He, too, had opted for the fashionable Italianate Style, although the outbuildings are strictly utilitarian. It is strange to the modern eye to see such obviously elegant houses for the upper middle class located right on the railroad tracks, where the noise and the cinders, not to mention the danger, would seem to be obvious. These disadvantages must have been overcome by convenience to the stations. At least one of the noises that would have made nearby residents jump out of their skin was outlawed: a Sewickley ordinance banned train whistles in the borough.

An interesting house on Broad Street next to St. Stephen's is no longer there. The *Hayes Atlas*, 1877, shows the Residence and Greenhouse of John Lent, Esq. Florist and Landscape Gardener. Extensive greenhouses surround an attractive house, complete with tower. A horse and cart loaded with flowers and plants stands ready to provide landscaping to one of the many new rural retreats sprouting up in the Valley. John Lent's Sewickley Greenhouse did not last long after the picture in the *Atlas*. The property was auctioned but not sold in 1881, according to an account in the *Valley Gossip*.

Residence and Greenhouse of John Lent.
From E.L. Hayes, *Atlas,* 1877.

Owing to the great heat and the disagreeable, in fact terrible, dust but two bidders were on hand. One was lawyer Johnston and the other General Manager Jackson, of the Interlocking Switch Company, Pittsburgh. Bidding was begun at $5,000 and run up to $7,100—bid by Mr. Jackson. At this point the bottom seemed to fall out of the business, for bidding ceased and the property was withdrawn. It would be too cheap at $8,500 cash. The house is one of the most completely finished in our village and cost about $7,500, and the lot is 246¹/₂ feet deep by 100 feet 10 inches along Broadway.⁸

Neither bidder got the house. The property was sold the same year, 1881, to John Richardson. He remained until at least 1906. Mr. Richardson tore down the Italianate house and replaced it with a building in the more up-to-date Shingle Style.

Another Italianate house is still standing on 335 Chestnut Street on the corner of Thorn Street. It belonged to John and Cecilia McMillen from 1876 to 1906. The McMillen's sons, Edward D. and Frederick J., lived with them. All the men worked at John McMillen's & Sons on the corner of Boundary and Bank Streets. Here they sold lumber, coal and builders' supplies, taking advantage of the boom in house building at the time. A Patron's Business Notice in *Hayes Atlas*, 1877, lists

John McMillen: Contractor and Builder.
Jobbing promptly attended to.
Also Dealers in lumber, lath, and shingle, moldings, etc.
Office and yard corner Mechanic and Division Street.

The McMillen house is less elaborate than Captain Smith's, looking like a basic Pennsylvania farmhouse in fancy dress. Strip off the bay windows, the scrolled brackets under the roof, the carved porch, and the window hoods and you will find a vernacular farmhouse. This is not to denigrate the charming house, but to point out the varying forms that the Italianate style could accommodate. The house itself has been adaptable; in the 1920s, it was Ritchey's funeral home.

A far smaller house with a completely different aspect demonstrates the variety of Sewickley architecture at mid-century. The wooden cottage that is now part of the Laughlin Children's Center on 422 Frederick Avenue dates from about 1845. It is a simple rectangular house, enlivened by a bay window and porch. The house has had a variety of uses over the years, showing the bent in favor of conservation rather than destruction that has served Sewickley well. Originally it

John McMillen House, 335 Chestnut Street,
Photo by John H. Demmler.

Gilkerson-Christy house, now the Laughlin Children's Center.
Built 1845. Frederick Avenue. Photo by John H. Demmler.

Andrew Jackson Downing: "A House with Feeling."

was the Gilkerson house, then the George Christy house, then a doctor's office, and now a children's center.

The house shows the influence of Andrew Jackson Downing and bears quite a resemblance to his picturesque "House with Feeling" illustrated here.⁹ Both are small, wooden houses in the Gothic style, which was popular nationwide for suburban and rural residences in the nineteenth century. The cottage does not have exact Gothic references: there are no castellated turrets, towers or pointed windows. This is a middle class adaptation of the style which takes elements from the Gothic and plays with them. Gothic Revival houses usually had large, decorative chimneys. According to Downing, the chimney was the most important element in domestic architecture, serving to label a building a house.

> Chimney-tops are highly expressive of purpose, as they are associated with all our ideas of warmth, the cheerful fireside, and the social winter circle and they distinguish apartments destined for human beings from those designed for lodging cattle. They also distinguish a dwelling-house from a manufactory or workshop.[10]

The large chimney is based on the large chimneys necessary in medieval houses for cooking and heating. By the middle of the nineteenth century, furnaces and cooking stoves had replaced fireplaces but, according to Downing, "While the furnace gives heat enough for ordinary purposes, the wood fire is used for extra warmth and ventilation."[11]

The bay window in the house is a simplified copy of the oriel windows of a medieval hall. Oriel windows projected from the wall and were supported by braces above and below. The Gothic style emphasized the mysterious, as portrayed in the Gothic novels popular at the time. An air of mystery was produced by the play of light and shadows on the facade. Overhanging eaves produced shadows that varied during the day. The bay window and the verandah produced part shade, part light.

Gothic Revival houses blend with their surroundings. Trellises, eaves, and dormers break up the silhouette, cooperating rather than competing with their surroundings. Downing said that architectural beauty must be considered conjointly with the beauty of landscape.

Like most Gothic revival houses, this is made of wood, a natural material that blends in with its surroundings. The boards were set vertically because, according to Downing,

> We greatly prefer the vertical to the horizontal boarding, not only because it is more durable but because it has an expression of strength and truthfulness which the other has not. The main timbers which enter into the frame of a wooden house and suggest the structure, are vertical, and hence the vertical boarding properly signifies to the eye a wooden house.[12]

The house at 422 Frederick Avenue is an example of very early Gothic Revival. A later example, built by Charles Atwell in 1862, is larger and more fanciful. The house, across the street from the Laughlin Children's Center, is now called the Christy house. Owned by St. Stephen's church, it is used for various church functions. This house shows the growing importance and popularity of the porch in nineteenth century architecture. Porches were for resting, reading, and enjoying the view. The porch was neither indoors or outdoors, but a safe lair that provided a pleasant place to enjoy nature while enjoying protection from wind and sun. Andrew Jackson Downing wrote:

> The porch, the veranda, or the piazza, are highly characteristic features, and no dwelling-house can be considered complete without one or more of them. . . . The veranda, ornamented by brackets between the supports, which shelters the entrance-door, affords an agreeable place both for walking in damp or unpleasant weather, and to enjoy a cool shaded seat in the hotter portion of the season.[13]

The verandah was usually in the front of the house so that the family could view the passing scene.

George Christy purchased the Atwell house in 1869 and added a large kitchen wing in the rear. The former kitchen became the dining room and the former dining room and kitchen became a large living room with fireplace. Downing would have admired the house. It has just enough decoration to express its function.

The aspects of "home" so admired in the Victorian era are exemplified by the Christy family and its house, as Adelaide Nevin explained in the *Social Mirror*, 1888.

> Mrs. George H. Christy has a pleasant home situated in the very heart of Sewickley. She is the mother of an interesting family and evidently takes great pleasure in the company of her sweet young daughters and tall sons. With her husband, Mrs. Christy does a great deal of traveling. They are said to be quite wealthy. Miss Marshall, Mrs. Christy's aunt, makes her home with the Christys.[14]

The grounds around the house were a good example of the landscaping of the time and would have been admired by Frank C. Scott, author of *The Art of Beautifying Suburban Home Grounds*, 1870. There was almost an acre of vegetable and flower gardens in the large lot behind the house. The gardens were supervised for nearly 70 years by Nicholas Geary who had walked westward from New Jersey and found a "temporary" job with the Christy family. Mr. Geary was responsible for planting the fruit trees that provided both beautiful blossoms in spring and fruit in season. Family and guests could lounge on wicker furniture on the side porch or the patio while admiring the immaculate lawn. Later, they could play lawn tennis on the court Mr. Christy had built across the street or croquet on the lawn. These games, imported from England after the Civil War, tested both skill and character, according to an article in *Good Housekeeping* in 1885,

> [The fascination with croquet had] increased in violence and became an epidemic. . . . A half hour on the croquet ground, under adversity, will better display the real disposition of a person than any other acquaintance of years' duration.[15]

One of Frank Scott's landscape plans shows a large expanse of green where "Mr. Smith and his good family enjoy the possession of fine croquet grounds where children, youth, and old people are alike merry in the open summer air with the excitement of the battles of the balls."[16]

Christy House, 1862. 403 Frederick Avenue. Photo by John H. Demmler.

Mr. Christy was a member of the new group of Sewickley residents who earned their livelihood elsewhere. He commuted by train from Sewickley to East Pittsburgh where he was a vice president and attorney for Westinghouse Air Brake. A few years later, tiring of the corporate grind, he retired from business and opened a law office in downtown Pittsburgh. He found that he still required space to have a home office, so he built a separate structure, hoping to find respite from the turmoil of an active family. Soon, however, Mr. Christy's peaceful haunt was invaded. His wife moved the laundry facilities to the new office and the children discovered that the steep steps to the second floor made it a perfect secret hiding place.[17]

A house in the same Gothic style sits at 29 Beaver Street across from the Sewickley Presbyterian Church. It is the epitome of the rural Gothic style that was sweeping small towns all over the country in the mid-nineteenth century. It has the delightful carved vergeboards on the gable ends that are associated in everyone's minds with the Victorian era. Such imaginative flights of fancy were possible because of the newly perfected scroll saw. Gothic cottages like this are asymmetrical, with steep roofs of varying pitches. The lancet windows with their diamond panes are similar to the medieval-inspired House of the Seven Gables in Salem, Massachusetts. The round windows under the gables are borrowed from similar designs in medieval halls. A Gothic cottage like this is designed to blend into the landscape to form a romantic picture which could be framed and titled "Home."

The house at 29 Beaver Street was built around 1828 by Daniel DePetron. It belonged from 1862 until at least 1876 to Charles McKnight. Mr. McKnight owned a pressed brick manufactory near Shousetown, opposite the mouth of Big Sewickley Creek. He was also editor of the *Pittsburgh Evening Chronicle*, later the *Pittsburgh Sun-Telegraph*, and a writer of historical books such as *Captain Jack of Old Fort Duquesne*, *Our Western Border*, and *Simon Girty*.[18] When the family moved to Sewickley from Homewood, Charles McKnight's brother-in-law thought it was a mistake. In a letter of November 1, 1862 to his father The Honorable T. H. Baird, he says,

> You have no doubt heard of Charles' purchase of property at Sewickley. It is none of my business, but I fear he has got an elephant on his hands. The value of the ground consists principally in its high—in fact perfect state of cultivation, and in order to keep it up he must pursue a system with it, which I doubt very much he has the ability to do.

McKnight House, 29 Beaver Street, built about 1828. Photo by John H. Demmler.

Despite such misgivings, the move seems to have been a success. In January 1863, Charles McKnight's wife, Jeanie Baird McKnight, reported to her father:

We are almost fixed in our new home, and although we have had most dreadful weather ever since we moved, which has confined us entirely to the house—yet I think we will like it very much. The place is very prettily situated and we have very fine views from all parts of it, which you know adds very much to a country home.

You ask me if we have a church near us. The new Presbyterian Church which has just been built is only about forty yards from our front entrance. Our Minister, Rev. James Allison, is not very popular with people here, but we have all liked him very much every time we have heard him. Both Bug and I like the people here, much better than we did out at Homewood; they seem to be much more intelligent and sensible, and they do not seem to think half so much of dress and fashion. I do hope we may get to like both place and people more and more for Charlie is so very anxious we should.

The next style to reach Sewickley, Second Empire, was really a variation of the Italianate. All the Italianate features remain: hoods over the windows; brackets under the roof line; and porches supported by carved columns. The significant addition is the mansard roof which has two slopes on each of its four sides, a steep slope on the outside, and a gentle slope on top. The lower slope is broken by dormer windows. The mansard roof, named for François Mansard, a French architect, was used extensively in Paris during the rule of Louis Napoleon (1848-1870). Their advantage lay in making the attic a large usable space.

The Sewickley area has several examples of Second Empire houses. One of the most attractive is the house at 406 Peebles Street, built in 1866 by Captain James Wilson Porter. It has all the characteristics of the Second Empire style except the hoods over the windows on the two lower floors. The 1998 owner, Mark Leavitt, discovered while doing restoration that the hoods and scrollwork had been removed.

The house sat on a 2.25 acre lot, completely surrounded until the 1920s by a wrought iron fence. Lawn and gardens filled the space between the house and Beaver Street. The Porters could stroll in the garden, admiring the marble lions and the fountain, or they could sit on marble benches and view the passing scene. Behind the house were a wash house and a barn for horses and carriages.

Inside, the rooms are large. When buying wallpaper for the front hall, Mr. and Mrs. Leavitt discovered it was the size of five big rooms in an average house today. A walnut and mahogany staircase dominates the hall. Despite its size and elegant appointments, the house had no toilets until after Captain Porter's death in 1901. Family legend explains that the Captain did not approve of using toilets. He believed that was not something one did in the house.

Captain James Wilson Porter's parents immigrated from Scotland to New York City before Captain Porter was born. The family moved to Sewickley in 1837, when James was eight years old. After starting as a clerk on a riverboat when he was 20, James Wilson Porter rose to be captain of a boat. A self-made man, he became rich during the Civil War, according to *The History of Allegheny County* published in 1889.

He has been a successful man and in the space of fifteen years of river life amassed a fortune. He was in the government employ in the civil war, carrying troops, ammunition, transport, etc. He was at the Battle of Pittsburgh Landing, capture of Fort Donelson, Belmont Island Number 10, and other engagements. At one time he carried Gen. Buckner (the present governor of Kentucky), with his staff and two hundred rebel prisoners, from Fort Donelson, where they were captured, to Louisville, Ky., on their way to Fort Delaware, near Philadelphia. With his boat he ran many rebel batteries, and had many narrow escapes.[19]

Another family legend says the army paid Captain Porter to ship Confederate prisoners north to prison camps and to ship guns and alcohol to Union troops. This would explain his sudden wealth.

After the war, Captain Porter started an iron business, J. W. Porter & Co. He became a prominent citizen, a director of banks and insurance companies, and a board member of Western Pennsylvania Hospital. He built the house at 406 Peebles Street for his wife, the former Martha L. Ebbert. The Ebberts, a wealthy family from Pittsburgh, strenuously opposed Martha's marriage to the nouveau riche Captain Porter. They disinherited her.

The Porters had four children: John E.; J. Wilson Jr.; Mary Cree; and Martha A. Mrs. Porter died a few days after bearing her fourth child. Mr. Leavitt thinks that Captain James built a house next door around 1882 for his parents so they could supervise raising his children. He thinks that the two households shared meals and staff because the newer house had no kitchen when it was built.

Porter-Leavitt house, 1866. Courtesy of Pittsburgh History & Landmarks Foundation.

About 1910 John Ebbert Porter, the Captain's son, built a large house on 808 Beaver Street on part of the family lot. The house has been torn down but an idea of how the gardens looked comes from a landscaping plan by J. Wilkinson Elliott, an important landscape architect who lived in Edgeworth but practiced all over the area. Mr. Elliott thought the plan "an unconventional treatment of a corner lot that few people would have the courage to carry out [because] the public cannot see the garden from the street." Masses of shrubs, evergreens, and deciduous small trees shielded the interior garden.[20] The public could enjoy the greenery from the street and the shade provided by pin oaks planted every 40 feet along the sidewalk. The plan was unconventional because it differed from Andrew Jackson Downing's idea of houses and gardens providing a continuous landscape of pleasing scenes as one walked along the sidewalk.

The rest of the Porter family continued living in their Second Empire house even after James' death in 1901. The 1910 *Census* lists as head of household J. Wilson Porter, single, aged 39, occupation, "manufacturer." J. Wilson continued his father's business, but not successfully. The sisters lived with him, according to the *Census*, on their "own income." They traveled to Europe, and rode around Sewickley in one of the town's first electric cars. In the 1920s they started a gift store called the Highway Shop. Mrs. Jane Evans, a granddaughter of Captain Porter, said:

It was started by Martha Nevin, but not called the Highway Shop then. Martha Porter didn't do anything [with the shop]; she served wonderful meals and was responsible for the household. Aunt Mary Cree and she would go to England and buy good china like Wedgewood and it got to be quite a shop for wedding presents.

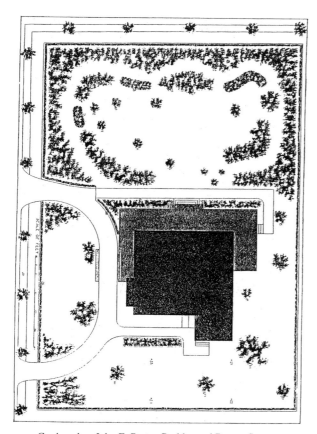

Garden plan, John E. Porter, Peebles and Beaver Streets,
by J. Wilkinson Elliott.

Around 1946 the sisters moved into the house next door at 402 Peebles Street and rented the family homestead. When Martha died in 1949, she left the smaller house to James Wilson Porter. The rest of the estate went three quarters to Mary and one quarter to James. After their deaths, the grandnieces and grandnephews received $500 or $1,000 bequests. The residue went to the First Church of Christ Scientist of Sewickley and Boston. Martha's estate included $81,000 in stocks, $200 in bonds, and $800 cash. Personal items were: Hudson seal coat, three diamond rings, a diamond brooch, and a diamond-platinum bracelet.

Mary Cree Porter's estate inventory is more complete. The total value was $106,759, including $5,909 cash. She had three fur coats and three coats with fur collars. The furniture in the smaller house was quite spare. Dining room: dining table with 6 chairs, $10; sideboard, $10: Living room: one settee; three chairs; Victor radio; small leaf table; and desk. There were kitchens on the first and second floors. Also on the second floor were three bedrooms. An attic above escaped the estate inventory, but contained many valuable objects.

Meanwhile, the original Porter house on 406 Peebles, rented for years, had fallen into disrepair. When Luanne and Mark Leavitt bought it in 1987, it had not been painted in 30 years. Like many large houses, it had been turned into apartments. The elegant staircase had been painted white. Steps were sagging and some pieces of the banister were missing. There were four apartments and three kitchens. Mr. Leavitt remembered:

From its appearance on the outside, we knew the house had suffered terribly, but we were even more disheartened when we walked inside. Where we expected to find treasures from the past, we found cheap renovations and nonexistent maintenance. The house had been stripped of all that it had been 100 years previously.

Rooms that had been large and grand had been divided and divided again into apartments. The only things left in the house to suggest its grand past were the staircase and fireplace mantels. The roof and box gutters leaked; the floors sagged; the plaster was falling and every mechanical system was on the verge of extinction. . . .

Since we purchased the house, we have labored to restore it to its original appearance, committed to reinstalling architectural elements that have been removed over the years. Nothing original is removed from the house unless it is totally rotted and useless. Among other things, we have rebuilt entire windows, sashes and frames and used 100-year-old glass to replace broken panes. We have researched the original exterior paint colors on the house, and we have used those colors.

We have been working on the house about five years now, and I'm sure we've got another five to go. Yet it has been worth it; bringing a grand old lady back to life, and filling her walls with the sounds of laughter and love.[21]

The Porter-Leavitt house is a good example of the vicissitudes that changes in taste and life-style can bring to a dwelling. It is a story repeated often in towns all over America. This story has a happy ending; in many other cases, the story ends in destruction.

Second Empire houses like the Porter-Leavitt's are vaguely French: another style of the same period has English overtones. Sewickley's example is Maple-Hurst on 249 Broad Street between Frederick and Bank. It was the home of the D. C. Herbst family from about 1881 until 1906. The family is described in 1888 in Adelaide Nevin's *Social Mirror*.

Mrs. D. C. Herbst is tall, finely formed and quite a handsome woman always richly dressed and wears big diamonds. The handsome mansion in Sewickley is fully and splendidly furnished, a lovely conservatory opening out from the dining-room. Nowhere is to be found more lavish hospitality or more perfect housekeeping and finer table appointments of china, glass and silver. Mrs. Herbst and her daughters drive a spanking team of spirited black horses, a drag in summer and a close carriage in winter. Mr. Herbst is said to be quite wealthy. Mrs. Percy Rider, one of the married daughters, and Miss Stella Herbst, with their parents and Mr. Rider, comprise the home circle.[22]

Mr. D. C. Herbst was born in Long Island but moved to Pittsburgh about 1837. In 1846, he ran a grocery business on Smithfield Street and First Avenue. Later, he established a steamboat line between Pittsburgh and Wheeling. After this proved unsuccessful, he joined a partnership to develop some West Virginia territory for lubricating oil. At the time of his death in 1907, Mr. Herbst was a partner of John Warden in the firm Warden & Oxnard.

Mr. Herbst's will gives an idea of the standards of elegance of the time. First, he set aside money for a tomb in the Sewickley cemetery. Then, he left $5,000 to each of his three daughters and $2,000 to each of his nine grandchildren. Other designated items were: gilt cabinet and contents; marble bust "Reading Boy"; two embroidered pieces; two diamond pins; and large bracelet with many diamonds.

The "handsome mansion" mentioned by Adelaide Nevin was built between 1876, when the map shows no house on the lot, and 1881. It is in what could be called the Charles Addams style, or, more formally, the High Victorian Gothic. This house would never be confused with a farmhouse. Its mansard roof was copied from Second Empire French styles.

St. James School. Formerly Herbst house, Broad Street.

Heavily Gothic windows strongly accented in contrasting colors and textures denote the style, which was often used in college architecture of the time. This house was not used by a college, but it was a school and a residence for nuns from 1914-1954.

Still another popular house style in the Victorian era was the Queen Anne style, characterized by steeply pitched roofs with many projections in all directions, patterned shingles, an asymmetrical facade, and use of various materials to break up any flat smooth walls. The Queen Anne style can generally be described as the opposite of Greek Revival. Greek Revival houses are strictly symmetrical; Queen Annes delight in being asymmetrical. Greek Revival houses use one material; Queen Annes, several. Walls in Greek Revival are smooth and in one plane; Queen Annes avoid simple, flat walls by employing bays, towers, overhangs and wall projections. If any wall has a large flat surface, several materials of different textures are employed to break it up.

The house on 319 Elwick Street, built near the end of the nineteenth century, is a rather subdued example of the exuberant Queen Anne style. Like several others in the neighborhood, it belonged to a railroad man. River captains liked to settle near the river; railroad executives, near the tracks. Because the town of Sewickley was all within a few blocks of the tracks, it was a convenient place for railroad employees to live. In 1880, for example, 34 men in Sewickley Borough worked for the railroad. There were 381 households at that time; almost one in ten earned their livelihoods from the railroad.

Elwick Street, set high on a bluff with a view of the river and of the railroad tracks, was a perfect location for a railroad buff. Number 319 Elwick belonged to H. L. Howard Blair of the Pennsylvania Railroad. Nearby, on the corner of Walnut, lived J. Morton Hall of the Baltimore and Ohio Railroad.

Mr. Blair was born in Yellow Creek, Ohio, in 1858. He came to Sewickley to go to Sewickley Academy and remained for the rest of his life. After graduating from Western University, now the University of Pittsburgh, in 1877, Mr. Blair joined the Pennsylvania Railroad, becoming assistant general manager of the western lines. He married Annie M. Cunningham, daughter of Captain William Cunningham, symbolically joining two strains of Sewickley society, the river captains and the newer railroad managers.

Blair house, 319 Elwick Street. Photo by John H. Demmler.

The houses discussed so far belonged to well-to-do people. Sewickley residents prided themselves on having an attractive town and congratulated themselves on keeping out undesirable people. *Sewickley Valley Society*, 1895, tried to explain why.

> The homogeneity of the village and of the valley is one of their marked features. Beautiful homes are the uniform rule, and the almost entire absence of small, unslightly residences will be noticed by the most unobservant. Strangers utter no little surprise, yet it is a legitimate effect of a natural and legitimate cause. The workman, and by that term is meant the members of that vast and noble army of toilers that are the basis of Pittsburgh wealth, cannot afford the time it takes to go to and from Sewickley. . . . Hence Sewickley is par excellence, a place of lovely homes; a place beyond the admission of trades and the realm of the vast industries that darken the sky above the Iron City.[23]

There were, however, smaller homes for the "army of toilers." As the number of wealthy commuters increased, so did the number of people required to serve their needs. These people required affordable housing. Shopkeepers and some professional men often lived and worked in the same building. Dr. Robert McCready lived and worked at 335 Beaver Street; George Hegner lived in the same building as his store; Mrs. Kate Schreiber sold china out of her home on 402 Beaver; Valentin Schreiber sold shoes from his; Mrs. Eliza Tiffany lived and worked at 422 Beaver; and James S. Gray, a merchant tailor, worked at home on Broad Street near Beaver. Servants sometimes lived and worked in other people's houses or boarded in one house and worked elsewhere. Other servants acquired housing of their own. Possible houses for a workingman's family were listed in December 1881 in the local paper.

> Two-story Frame Dwelling of 9 rooms divided into two separate apartments of 4 and 5 rooms each. Lot 32 x 200 situate on the corner of Broadway and Thorne street, opposite Methodist church.
> Two-story Frame Dwelling of three rooms. Lot 32 x 200 situate on Thorne street. Fruit trees on lot.
> Small frame dwelling of four rooms. All necessary out-buildings; water convenient, nice large lot, situated on Clark street near Peebles.

None of these houses had heat or water. "Necessary outbuildings" would include outhouses and washhouses.

Not all of the houses in Sewickley were as attractive as the picturesque homes in the *Hayes Atlas*. A newspaper article in 1881 hints of unscrupulous landlords.

> Sewickley needs to pull down barracks that bring 10 or 12 per cent cash and put up neat, pretty homes that may not net them over 7 per cent. . . . There are rookeries in our village that could be more in place in a coal mining community.[24]

Many of the worker's houses were located near the center of town. Others were built as near as possible to Sewickley Heights, which was being developed at the end of the 1800s, because servants and gardeners had to walk up to the Heights to work. The houses on Nevin Road north of Hopkins, Dickson Road, and Blackburn Road were settled by workers, many of them Italian immigrants and blacks.

Between 1850 and 1900 builders of any house faced a common question: how many of the new "modern conveniences" to include. Before 1850 there was little interest in or knowledge of designing houses for comfort and efficiency, but technological inventions improved the quality of life during the second half of the century. In 1850, for example, only individual rooms in houses could be heated. Fireplaces could overheat part of a room, while farther corners remained chilled. James Way reported how he withstood a cold spell in 1835.

> The thermometer for three days successively stood at 20 or 22 degrees below zero. My young blood felt a good deal like congealing, but fortunately I had little to do outdoors, so kept up the biggest fire and roasted my shins whilst my back froze and vice versa.

Franklin stoves could heat a room effectively. In the years after 1850, furnaces in the basement used wood or coal to heat air which flowed through ducts to each room. Some Sewickley households were supplied with oil from their own wells. *Sewickley Valley Society* reported in 1895, "Even the derricks that supply the most superb fuel that ever was for every house are so tree-embowered as to lose their ungainly lines.[25]

Lighting by candles or whale oil lamps had improved by 1850. The Argand lamp, invented in 1783, could throw enough light for card playing or reading within the radius of its light. Further improvements were possible using the gas from the mains laid in the late 1880s.

At midcentury plumbing was rudimentary. Although Downing declared that, "No dwelling can be considered complete which has not a water-closet under its roof," he admitted that "the expense may yet for some time prevent their general introduction into small cottages."[26] Many relied on chamber pots and outhouses. The first American patent for a toilet was issued in 1871. Even as late as 1870, the best of homes had no flush toilets because they require a central water supply. Until 1874, water in Sewickley came from a well or, at best, from a pump in the kitchen. Through the '70s and '80s various sanitary arrangements, including both dry earth commodes and water-closets, were invented.

Electricity, which was available in Sewickley after 1888, was itself a technological invention and supplied power to other inventions such as light bulbs, fans, sewing machines, carpet sweepers, and lawn mowers.

A prospective homeowner in Sewickley was looking for a house with as many of these improvements as possible. Advertisements for houses stress modern conveniences almost to the exclusion of characteristics that seem equally important, such as lot size, landscaping, and location. Compare advertisements in the December, 1881 issue of the *Valley Gossip* with some in the November 18, 1992 *Sewickley Herald*.

Valley Gossip, 1881

A fine two-story brick dwelling of 8 rooms containing all the modern improvements, Gas, Water, Bath Rooms, etc.

[Captain Smith's house, mentioned above, was described.] Handsome two-story frame dwelling of ten large airy and pleasant rooms. Basement washroom with stationary washtubs. Furnace heats entire house, marble mantels, gas, hot and cold water, bathroom and all modern improvements.

Brick dwelling of ten rooms. Bath room, hot and cold water and all modern improvements.

$25 a month will rent an eight-room brick dwelling with bath, hot and cold water, both gases, nice porches.

The Sewickley Herald, 1992

Grand three story brick with front porch. Beautifully landscaped and sited on prime Village street. Modern kitchen and baths.

Gracious brick and cedar contemporary on 1½ private acres overlooking Sewickley Creek. 4 BR's, 3 full baths, log burning fireplace.

On a picturesque table-top lot, graciously proportioned 1½ sty residence, 4 bedrms (ea w/own bath), family room w/frpl overlooking private professionally landscaped grounds, lower lvl gamerm w/frpl, 2 car gar.

Note that fireplaces, which were taken for granted in the older advertisements, in later times were regarded as amenities. Furnaces, taken for granted later, were amenities in earlier times.

Most Sewickley residents lived in single family houses. Some, however, chose to live permanently in hotels. The Park Place Hotel was a popular choice. Originally the home of Samuel McKelvy, it was purchased in 1852 by Joseph Travelli, who added two wings and turned it into the home of Sewickley Academy. The school closed in 1863 and the hotel began shortly after the Civil War.[28] Boarders were able to entertain guests at the hotel, according to the *Pittsburgh Index*, 1912.

Mrs. George Barrett, of the Park Place Hotel, assisted by her daughter, Miss Cora Barrett, entertained last Saturday afternoon at a pretty fancywork party in honor of her sister, Mrs. Elizabeth Lowrie, and her niece, Miss Blanche Lowrie, of Milwaukee. During the afternoon Miss Lowrie, who is quite a musician, rendered service on several instrumental solos and the hostess, who excels at elocution, recited several times.[29]

Park Place Hotel, Chadwick Street. Back view, 1906. Courtesy Sewickley Valley Historical Society.

Elmhurst Inn. A.H. Diehl, Photographer. Courtesy Sewickley Valley Historical Society.

Another hotel was the Elmhurst Inn, located on the former property of James C. Murray. Walter J. Kerr leased the building in 1890, proposing to run a hotel. The newspaper supported his idea, suggesting that a hotel would increase real-estate values and help the economy. The inn had among its boarders Dr. and Mrs. James C. Murray, and Margaret Morgan, justice of the peace.

Sewickley is best known for its gracious old houses carefully tended by wealthy families. But, from its early days, it has had a variety of housing choices for a variety of income levels.

1 Mash, p. 36.

2 Vincent Scully and Antoinette F. Downing, *The Architectural Heritage of Newport, Rhode Island.* 2nd. ed. New York, Clarkson & Potter, 1967, p. 130.

3 E. L. Hayes, *Illustrated Atlas of the Upper Ohio River Valley.* Philadelphia, Simmons & Titus, 1877, p. 60.

4 Adelaide Nevin, *The Social Mirror.* Pittsburgh, T.W. Nevin, 1888, p. 193.

5 Andrew Jackson Downing, *Victorian Cottage Residences.* New York, Dover, 1981, pp. 23-23, 211.

6 Ibid., p. 23.

7 *Industries of Pennsylvania, 1879-1880,* p. 116.

8 *Valley Gossip,* Sept 1, 1881.

9 Handlin, p. 95.

10 Downing, *Victorian Cottage Residences,* p. 211.

11 Ibid., p. 12.

12 Antoinette F. Downing and Vincent J. Scully, *The Architectural Heritage of Newport, R.I.* Cambridge, Harvard Univ. Press, 1952, p. 122.

13 Downing, *Victorian Cottage Residences,* pp. 13, 29.

14 A. Nevin, p. 179.

15 Handlin, p. 181.

16 Scott, p. 226.

17 "Jack O'Neil, *"The Christy Houses."* In *Sewickley Magazine* July/August/Sept. 1988, pp. 10-13.

18 *Sewickley Herald,* Sept. 4, 1974, p. 10.

19 *History of Allegheny County.* A. Warner, 1889, p. 250.

20 J. Wilkinson Elliott, *A Plea for Hardy Plants.* N.Y., 1902, p. 60.

21 *Sewickley Herald,* November 10, 1993, p. A13.

22 A. Nevin, p. 183.

23 *Sewickley Valley Society,* pp. 14-15.

24 *Valley Gossip,* March 1, 1881.

25 *Sewickley Valley Society,* p. 24.

26 Downing, *Victorian Cottage Residences,* p. 5.

27 Capt. Federick Way, Jr. File. Sewickley Library.

28 *Pittsburgh Index,* July 19, 1902, p. 21.

Chapter 15
Health and Home

Housewives in the nineteenth century had to make a great many of the foods, health, and cleaning products that manufacturers thrust upon their counterparts today. On the other hand, the modern housewife might envy the domestic help which many families were able to afford. The 1900 U. S. census defined a lower-middle-class household as one that had fewer than three servants. Nevertheless, the degree of difficulty of the tasks involved in running a household outweighed the advantage of the extra help. A scrapbook kept in the later part of the nineteenth century by Verlinda Means Doyle, Mrs. Henry Chalfant's grandmother, is full of newspaper clippings, recipes, and advice for the housewife. Unless otherwise noted, the information in this section comes from it.

Here, for example, is an 1868 recipe for blackberry wine. Cover blackberries with boiling water. Mash with hands. Let stand three of four days. Strain fluid. To every gallon, add four pounds sugar. Put in cask eight to ten days. Bung it tight. After six to twelve months, bottle.

Or, try elderberry wine. To every quart of berries, add one quart water. Boil one half hour. Run through sieve. Add three-quarters cup sugar to each quart of liquid. Boil one-quarter hour with Jamaica pepper, ginger, and a few cloves. Put in barrel. Add four cups yeast and piece of toast. When it ceases to hiss, add one quart brandy to eight gallons liquor. Close barrel, wait six months and bottle.

Methods of conserving food were interesting to the housewife. To preserve potatoes, a newspaper reader advised putting slaked lime on the floor under the potatoes and sprinkling more over them. To keep cabbages:

Tie two together by the heels, and hang them over a low pole in the cellar, so that the heads will just clear the ground; tuck loose straw around them, and sprinkle twice during the winter with brine. As fresh and crisp in April as when first taken from the ground.

Cider could be preserved by putting the fresh cider in casks for a few weeks.

When it has attained to lively fermentation, add to each gallon three-fourths of a pound of white sugar, and let it ferment again until it possesses the brisk, pleasant taste which it is desirable should be permanent. Pour out a quart of the cider and mix with it one quarter of an ounce of sulphite of lime for every gallon the cask contains. Stir until it is intimately mixed, and pour the emulsion into the liquid. Fermentation will be arrested at once.

Preserving butter involved putting it in the cellar in large stone jars sunk nearly to the tops in sand. The tops were then covered by a thin cloth, a layer of salt, and a weighted board. Lard, obtained by rendering the fat from a year-old pig, could be stored in a cool cellar but "no matter where you store it, if it was not well cooked in the process of rendering, it will not keep sweet."

Many products now available at any hardware or drugstore had to be manufactured at home. Mrs. Doyle's scrapbook has recipes for skin care.

Cold cream. Take one pound oil of almonds, four ounces white wax. Melt together gently. Stir in 12 ounces rose-water.

Pomatum, or perfumed hair ointment. Melt mutton suet, skim and strain. Add three pounds lard and melt together. Add two ounces bergamot.

Lip salve. Take one ounce white wax, two ounces hog's lard, one shilling's worth of balsam of Peru, a few raisins shaved fine, and as much alkanet root as will color it. Dissolve and strain.

To Whiten the Hands. A wine glass each of Cologne and Lemon Juice, into which is scraped two cakes of Brown Windsor Soap, when hard; is excellent for this purpose.

Cleaning products sound equally complicated.

Laundry starch polish: Take equal parts of white wax and spermaceti; melt them together and run them into thin cakes on plates. Gives a luster to the clothes.

Cleaning carpets. Oil can be taken from a carpet by putting one tablespoonful of ammonia and two of beef's gall into a pint of warm water, and sponging the spot very thoroughly. Another method. Eight ounces borax, four ounces sal soda, one pound soap. Shave it fine. Dissolve in two gallons water. Put all in four gallons, a little fuller's earth; then use sponge.

Labor-saving soap. Dissolve a quarter of a pound of lime in a gallon of cold water, then take off the clear; dissolve half a pound of sal-soda in a quart of water, and mix it with the clear lime-water; one pound of brown soap, dissolved in a gallon of water, is then to be added to the clear liquor formed with the sal-soda and lime-water, and this forms the soap. This soap is excellent for boiling white linens.

If a homeowner wanted to whitewash the walls of a house, the whitewash had to be made:

Take half a bushel of nice unslaked lime; slake it with boiling water; cover it, during the process, to keep it in the strainer; and add to it a peck of clean salt previously well dissolved in warm water, three pounds of ground rice boiled to a thin paste, and stirred in boiling hot, half a pound of clean glue which has been previously dissolved by first soaking it well, and then hanging it over a slow fire in a small kettle within a large one filled with water. Add five gallons of hot water to the whole mixture; stir it well, and let it stand a few days covered from the dirt. It should be put on right hot; for this purpose, it can be kept in a kettle on a portable furnace.

Health was a major concern of all households. Borough ordinances dealt with public health problems. An ordinance in 1893-94 decreed:

No sewer drain shall empty into any lake, pond or other source of water used for drinking purposes. No house refuse, offal, garbage, dead animals, decaying vegetable matter or organic waste substance of any kind should be thrown on any road.

Cellars had to be cleaned and whitewashed each year in the month of May. Nothing for human food could be sold that was not "fit and safe for such use, nor any animal or fish that died by disease." All residents had to be vaccinated. Doctors were required to vaccinate anyone unable to pay, their fees to be paid by the borough.

Sewickley did have its share of physicians. The Dickson family provided three generations of doctors. Dr. John Dickson started to practice in Sewickley in 1822, when he was still less than 20 years old. He had studied medicine in Canonsburg, reciting to a Dr. Leatherman, and received a medical degree from the University of New York. In 1837, Dr. Dickson left Sewickley to attend lectures in Britain. After returning to the States, he set up practice in Allegheny, but continued to live in Edgeworth. Dr. Dickson was well-known as a surgeon. A contemporary physician remembered:

He performed the operation of lithotomy [removal of bladder stones], as far as I can learn, more frequently and with better results than any man in Pennsylvania. In 1866 he performed it eleven times, all the subjects recovering. . . . There were few better chemists or botanists in this state. He nodded to the 4,000 plants within our floral region as to familiar friends, and called them by their names. . . . From the absorbing duties of his life he allowed himself but one relaxation. He was an ardent sportsman, a capital shot and a bold rider. It was not uncommon to hear the baying of his hounds, the herald of his approach on his daily rounds.[2]

John Dickson's son, Joseph, born in 1846, followed in his father's footsteps. After graduating from Sewickley Academy, he went to Jefferson College and Jefferson Medical School. He joined his father's practice and opened a private dissecting room in Allegheny where he taught anatomy. Dr. Joseph Dickson organized a group of 50 doctors who took a special train to Johnstown after the flood of 1889. For 13 days he directed the relief effort. Dr. Joseph Dickson's son, Dr. Robert Watson Dickson, continued in the family profession. He practiced in the Sewickley Valley and lived in the house erected by his grandfather.

Another medical dynasty was founded by Dr. Robert McCready, who practiced more than half a century in the Valley. Dr. McCready was the typical general practitioner. He made house calls either by horse and carriage when the roads were passable, or on horseback with his medical supplies in his saddlebags, if they were not. A former patient remembered that, when he had typhoid fever as a boy, Dr. McCready visited him once but did not return for several days. He had been out the whole time, visiting and treating other patients. Dr. R. J. Murray described Dr. McCready:

He came to Sewickley when the village was not large enough to support a physician and his practice covered the country on both sides of the river for a radius of five or six miles. . . . Day and night, regardless of danger or fatigue, he was almost constantly on the road. He was an admirable judge of horses and kept a large stable of fine animals. Owing to bad roads, much of his travel was on horseback. He never neglected a case no matter how much hardship was involved.[3]

Charles Butler remembered Dr. Jennings, another old-fashioned family practitioner.

Dr. Jennings would come to your house, and he wore a derby and he had his little satchel, and he'd get out his little bowl, and he'd get some pills, and he'd take them and pulverize them and put them in a little paper thing and give them to you. He'd pull teeth, too. He pulled my grandfather's teeth. And that was when they didn't have Novocaine.

After 1902 doctors were supplemented by a nurse employed by the Sewickley Union Aid Society. The nurse helped the very poor.[4]

Health care improved with the opening of the Sewickley Hospital in 1907. A committee of twenty solicited subscriptions for $15,000 and obtained a charter in 1902. There was a major problem, however, as nobody wanted a hospital as a neighbor. Mrs. Henry W. Oliver resolved the issue by donating 4½ acres. The hospital became the focus of fund raising events. Mrs. George Phelps Rose founded the Dramatic Club, later called the Sewickley Cot Club, to produce plays benefiting the hospital. Proceeds provided beds, flowers, equipment and toys for the hospital.[5] A fair outside the YMCA netted $5,000 in a real community extravaganza, typical of Sewickley. Local churches organized supper, a local artist produced silhouettes "your picture while you wait." There were Punch and Judy movies in the gymnasium, an opera for boys and girls, and a side show.

Medical professionals lacked the means to perform the miracle cures that modern medicine can sometimes effect. Moreover, the dangers of sickness must have been terrifying to mothers whose only recourse was often folk medicine.

Sewickley Valley Hospital. Courtesy The Sewickley Valley Historical Society.

The worried housewife, therefore, was always concerned with her own preventative and palliative remedies. Some of these might seem silly with the benefit of hindsight but, without knowledge of the causes of disease, logical cures were difficult to find.

At least one Sewickley fortune was based on health. John Fleming went into the drug store business in Pittsburgh with a Mr. Wilcox. When Mr. Wilcox died, he left the business and the right to make Dr. C. McLane's liver and worm pills to Fleming. The business was so successful that when Mr. Fleming died in 1870, he left one million dollars. Two of the sources of his success were a long-standing remedy and and two unlikely nostrums. An advertisement for the former, liquor, promised:

> Fleming's Old Export is alike the drink for buffets,
> sideboards, cupboard and sick trays.
> $1 a quart, 6 full quarts $5. 8 years old. Absolutely pure.
> 410-412 Market Street, Pittsburgh

One of the unlikely nostrums was a worm medicine called Dr. C. McLane's Celebrated American Worm Specific or Vermifuge. It was advertised in *The Valley Gossip* in 1881.

Symptoms of Worms

The countenance is pale and leaden-colored, with occasional flushes, or a circumscribed spot on one or both cheeks; the eyes become dull; the pupils dilate; an azure semicircle runs along the lower eye-lid; the nose is irritated, swells, and sometimes bloods; slimy or furred tongue; breath very foul, particularly in the morning; . . . stools slimy; not unfrequently tinged with blood, &c.

Dr. C. McLane's Vermifuge
will certainly effect a cure.

It does not contain mercury in any form; it is an innocent preparation, not capable of doing the slightest injury to the most tender infant.

The genuine Dr. McLane's Vermifuge bears the signatures of C. McLane and Fleming Bros. on the wrapper.

The other nostrum was:

Dr. C. McLane's Liver Pills are not recommended as a remedy "for all the ills that flesh is heir to," but in affections of the liver, and in all Bilious Complaints, Dyspepsia and Sick Headache, or diseases of that character, they stand without a rival.

Beware of Imitations.

Insist upon having the genuine Dr. C. McLane's Liver Pills, prepared by Fleming Bros. of Pittsburgh, Pa., the market being full of imitations of the name McLane, spelled differently but same pronunciation.[6]

There was fierce competition for liver remedies. Two rival brands touted their efficacy. One was Schenek's Mandrake Pills:

To all, particularly invalids, spring is a trying season. Indications of sickness should at once be attended to. Fatal diseases may be caused by allowing the bowels to become constipated. . . . We advise all who are troubled with the complaints now very prevalent—headache, indigestion, disordered liver, want of appetite, nausea, or feverish skin, to take without delay, Schenek's Mandrake Pills. . . . They will relieve the patient of headache in one or two hours, and will rapidly cleanse the liver of surrounding bile.

Egyptian Liver Pad. Cures by absorption. The best nerve tonic known. Regulates and strengthens the Liver, Kidneys, and Bladder, Stomach, Brain, Nerves and all Vital Organs. Cures Catarrh.

Readers were probably skeptical of the extravagant promises of advertisements. If the housewife had believed the following advertisement for Pond's Extract "the universal pain extractor," she would have been able to dispense with most other medicines. The following advertisement from the Sewickley *Valley News,* 1876, is greatly condensed.

Pond's Extract, The People's remedy.

No family can afford to be without Pond's Extract. Accidents, Bruises, Contusions, Cuts,
Sprains are relieved almost instantly by external application.

Female Weaknesses. It always relieves pain in the back and loins.

Varicose Veins. It is the only sure cure.

Rheumatism Neuralgia, Toothache and Earache are all alike relieved, and often permanently cured.

To Farmers. No stock Breeder, no Livery Man can afford to be without it. It is used by all the
Leading Livery Stables, Street Railroads, and Horsemen in New York City.

Mrs. Chalfant's grandmother clipped a piece from a paper quoting a dentist's good advice for care of the teeth.

Use cold water and a tooth brush and pick teeth after every meal and, before retiring at night, run a piece of soft thread through the teeth. In walking along the street you often see a "fakir," by way of advertising his dentifrice, call a small boy from the crowd and, opening the boy's mouth, rub the dentifrice on his dirty teeth and in a minute take off all the tartar and make the teeth perfectly white. His preparation, composed of a powerful alkali, is eating away at the enamel of the boy's teeth, and in a few months the poor youngster will not have a sound tooth in his head.

Some cures were based on folk medicine or what might be called old wives tales. The cure for rheumatism, for instance, was cooked celery "to avoid the acid blood. If the blood is alkaline, there can be no rheumatism and equally no gout."

[Relief from neuralgia.] As the doctors have not discovered any method or medicine that will permanently cure it, we simply state that for some time past . . . we made the application of horse radish, bruised and applied to the wrist on the side of the body where the disease was seated [which] gave almost instant relief to a severe attack of neuralgia.

Lemon lozenges for sore throat and a mysterious "summer complaint" could be made by beating two whites of eggs with orange flowerwater, then adding pulverized sugar to make a stiff paste. Add raspings of lemon peels and roll into balls the size of a thimble. Put in the oven to bake.

The Methodist Cookbook, 1897, has a recipe for homemade cough medicine that sounds delicious. Put a pinch of hops in one quart water. Boil and strain. Add one pound crushed sugar, three lemons, three figs, and simmer one half hour. Keep cool. Give one tsp. every hour.[7]

An article in the paper gave advice on treating diphtheria.

A gentleman who has administered the following remedy informs us that it has always proved effectual in affording speedy relief. Take common tobacco-pipe, new, place a live coal within the bowl, drop a little tar upon the coal, and let the patient draw smoke into the mouth and discharge it through the nostrils.

A cure for diphtheria advised; "Take bi-chlorate of potash, a teaspoonful, and dissolve in about a tumbler full of water and take a teaspoonful about every hour. It kills the poison and prevents it from spreading."

In 1908 the *Weekly Herald* carried advice on curing the common cold.

Many people have a narrow escape from pneumonia and consumption as a result of a cold that hangs on. Foley's Honey and Tar cures coughs and cold no matter how deep seated and prevents pneumonia and consumption. Refuse substitutes. P. P. Knapp.[8]

A remedy printed in 1869 promises a "certain safe and sure cure for Dysentery." When churning milk or cream, skim off the small particles or globules of butter and let the patient drink. "It never fails to cure if taken in time."

Of course if it failed, it had not been taken in time.

To treat burns, "apply ordinary white lead used by painters. This was used in relieving the sufferers in a late steamboat accident and was effectual in about ten minutes."

The Methodist Cookbook, 1897, has remedies for common problems.

When stung by a bee or wasp, make a paste of common earth and water. Put on the place at once and cover with a cloth.

For Dandruff: One-half teaspoon borax, one teaspoonful sulphur, one pint boiling water. Put on the place at once and cover with a cloth.[9]

Consumption or tuberculosis, was a widespread disease. An advertisement in the *Weekly Herald*, 1907, suggested a remedy.

All nations are endeavoring to check the ravages of consumption, the "white plague" that claims so many victims each year. Foley's Honey and Tar cures coughs and colds perfectly and you are in no danger of consumption. Do not risk your health by taking some unknown preparation when Foley's Honey and Tar is safe and certain in results. The genuine is in a yellow package. Sold by P. P. Knapp.[10]

Some advice circulated in newspapers was harmless. Other recommendations seem to be not only useless but apt to prevent more useful known treatment. Persons bitten by a snake were advised; "The bite of a viper, when left to its course, is death; but by the speedy application of a little olive-oil, the bite of a viper is rendered as harmless as the sting of a wasp."

Quassia, a tropical hardwood used to cure worms and as an insecticide, was one of the remedies for alcoholism.

To prevent an uncontrollable thirst that attacks and never gives up until they give way, take a decoction of ground quassia, a half ounce steeped in a pint of vinegar, and put about a small teaspoonful of it in a little water and drink it down every time the liquor thirst comes.

Another remedy was even more drastic, bichloride of gold and atropine. It was recommended by a Dr. Keeley who had founded 344 Keeley Leagues throughout the country. He claimed that he had cured 200,000 alcoholics. An urgent dispatch from San Francisco, however, warned of its dangers. Several young men had died of atropine poisoning.

Some folk remedies, like this one for insomnia, were pseudoscientific.

It has been found in most cases that insomnia is caused by disordered stomach. Worry will unsettle the stomach, as indigestion will inflate the blood vessels of the brain. Before going to bed the person afflicted should bathe the lower limbs in hot water—as hot as possible. This is for the purpose of drawing the blood from the head, for when the blood vessels are inflated, they press against the skull and fears, apprehensions and dread of going to sleep result.

One of the most effective ways to promote health is scarcely used today: quarantine. Although the cause of many diseases was not known, contagion was a possibility. An 1894 ordinance introduced the idea of separating the sick. If any household member suffered from a contagious disease, no member could go to any public place or, "as far as possible," visit private houses. If the patient died, there could be no public funeral.

More stringent rules followed in 1909. The Board of Health posted a sign on any house where a contagious disease was present. There were two categories of quarantine. Under absolute quarantine, nobody except health officials could go in or out of the house. No object could be handed out of the house. "Necessaries of life," however, could be sent in. Modified quarantine was somewhat less stringent.

The wage earner only is allowed under modified quarantine to continue work, provided he at no time comes in contact with the patient and that he has an outer room set apart where he can change his outer clothing and disinfect exposed surfaces.

What diseases were considered contagious? The 1894 ordinance stated.

The following named diseases are declared to be communicable and dangerous to public health, viz: Small-pox, Cholera, Scarlet Fever, Measles, Diphtheria, Typhoid Fever, Typhus Fever, Yellow Fever, Spotted Fever [any of several fevers with spots on skin, especially cerbro-spinal meningitis,] Relapsing Fever, Epidemic Dysentery, Hydrophobia [rabies], Glanders [a highly infectious bacterial disease usually confined to animals but transmittable to man,] and Leprosy.

Additional diseases were included in 1909: anthrax (a malignant infectious disease of cattle, sheep, and man,) bubonic plague, chicken pox, erysipelas (infectious streptococcus disease,) and German measles.

In most of these diseases, quarantine was a useful method of limiting contagion. With the great benefit of hindsight, sometimes it was not: typhus fever and relapsing fever are transmitted by lice and fleas; yellow fever, by mosquito bite; hydrophobia, by animal bites; cholera comes from a polluted water supply; and dysentery comes from contaminated food or water.

Several people remembered being quarantined. Margaret Halpin said,

Every little thing you were quarantined for—a good thing. My dad wasn't bothered when I had measles because he was separate. Mother was very careful. She had a big basin outside my bedroom with Lysol. All the dishes went in there. No one else got it.

Charles Stinson remembered,

The fire chief tacked up a sign on the house: Measles, Mumps, Scarlet Fever. Dad was not allowed in the house. He came around with goods and groceries and checked up on us.

Mrs. Josephine Sybo remembered the scarlet fever epidemic after the 1936 flood.

The doctor wouldn't even come to the house. He was too busy. In those days, they quarantined. You were not allowed out in the yard or off the property. One person in the family got it [scarlet fever], then another. My younger brother had it the worst. He was delirious. The quarantine lasted for two months. They burned all the toys. The young boy and girl who lived up the street would stop every day and Mother would tell them what she needed at the grocery store. My dad was the only one allowed to leave the house, and he wasn't allowed in the rooms where we were.

Most diseases and sickness struck on an individual level. Epidemics of measles, mumps, or scarlet fever hit families, but usually some family member had already had the diseases and was immune. This was not true of the Spanish Influenza epidemic which hit in October, 1918. By November 2, 728 cases and 15 deaths were reported in Sewickley;

in Edgeworth there were 83 cases and three deaths. When the epidemic had abated in December, 1918, there had been eight deaths in Edgeworth.

There was much advice on ways to avoid contagion. The most common advice was to get plenty of fresh air and sunshine, called "the greatest curative force in the present epidemic." John Walter, president of the Sewickley Board of Health, said, "The sunshine of the past few days has been a great aid in combating the disease."[11] *The Herald* gave other advice.

Don't cough or sneeze except in your handkerchief.

Avoid meetings and gatherings of any kind.

Keep the temperature of rooms below 68 degrees F.

Eat light, wholesome, easily digested food.

Keep the bowels open.

Avoid great fatigue.

Rinse the throat and nose frequently with solutions such as Glycothymalin, Hydrogen peroxide, Tannic Acid, etc.

Drastic quarantine restrictions were enacted to contain the disease. In the past, restrictions were on the family level, involving only those in contact with a contagious person. Now the whole area faced restrictions. The Pennsylvania Department of Health led the effort, ordering the immediate closing of "all places of amusement, including theaters, moving picture houses, dance halls, pool rooms and saloons, until further notice." The Sewickley and Edgeworth boards of health closed all churches, Sunday schools and public gatherings. Even the Halloween parade and the parade to honor war workers were canceled. There were no complaints about these stringent regulations, according to *The Herald*.

Two recent deaths in the Valley from the new scourge made it very easy for people to take the precautionary order very seriously. And beside, Sewickley people have come to really welcome a government order that will inconvenience them, the very deprivation seem to them a way of helping the big cause.[12]

The Edgeworth Board of Health kept constant track of new cases.

Certain sections of the Borough were kept under constant supervision during this time; daily house to house canvasses were made to ascertain sickness. It was the hope of the Board to locate any case of sickness in these crowded localities even before they were reported, that they might be properly isolated. . . . Throughout the course of the epidemic, all physicians were called by telephone every morning so that a careful record might be studied.[13]

Emergency hospital facilities for flu patients supplemented the crowded Sewickley Hospital. The Presbyterian Church House, staffed by four Red Cross nurses, had 17 beds. The Edgeworth Board of Health requisitioned the Edgeworth Public School building for a temporary hospital. Within two days, the school was transformed into a fifty-bed hospital. Carnegie Institute of Technology loaned a complete medical laboratory for testing blood, urine, and sputum samples. The Edgeworth facility admitted patients from any community not equipped to hands the epidemic. No case was ever refused. Total hospital days from various places were:

Ambridge	21	Neville Island	59
Coraopolis	19	Pittsburgh	32
Edgeworth	217	Sewickley	77
Glenfield	38	Woodlawn	1
Leetsdale	35		

Frank Vescio remembered that his father was one of the flu victims who died at the Edgeworth school-hospital.

Most everybody was sick. We had to stay in and didn't visit anyone. They said if you drank good whiskey, you would survive the flu. But where were you going to get it? You had to get a prescription from the drug store. We all had the flu light, but my father had it pretty bad—he died. He was only 28 years old. I was 6 or 7, Jerry was born two months after. My mother had four kids.

Jerry Vescio, Frank's brother said. "My dad died October 23, 1918. My uncle was 31 and he died three weeks later."

Charles Butler remembered that Dr. Jennings fought the flu with asafetida, a soft, brown, gum resin which smells so bad that it was used as an animal repellent.

Only one doctor could do anything with the flu: Dr. Jennings. You ask any old-timer about Dr. Jennings. He used asafetida. You got asafetida and put it in a bag and leave it hanging around your neck. You inhaled those fumes—it was like inhaling something—smelled worse than garlic but something like. Everyone was wearing it. People were dying like flies but no one of my family got it. It was the asafetida.

The flu epidemic provides a good example of how Sewickley Valley residents rally together in times of crisis to solve or alleviate problems. The next chapter, on Sewickley's response to several wars, will further illustrate this trait.

[1] *Practical Receipt Book by Experienced House-Keepers.* Sewickley. Published by the Young Ladies Aid Society of the Methodist Episcopal Church, Sewickley, 1897, p. 121.

[2] John W. Jordan, *Genealogical and Personal History of Western Pennsylvania.* N.Y. Lewis Historical Co., 1915, v.1, p. 420.

[3] *Weekly Herald,* January 21, 1911, p. 8.

[4] Philip Klein, *Social Study of Pittsburgh.* 1938, p. 82.

[5] *Sewickley Herald,* March 21, 1997, p. 11.

[6] *The Valley Gossip,* June 1, 1881.

[7] *Practical Receipt Book,* 1897.

[8] *Weekly Herald,* April 4, 1908, p. 2.

[9] *Methodist Cookbook,* 1897, p. 121.

[10] *Weekly Herald,* August 24, 1907, p. 12.

[11] *The Sewickley Herald,* October 12, 1918.

[12] Ibid., Oct. 12, 1918.

[13] Ibid., December 14, 1918.

Chapter 16
Unbounded Patriotism

During wartime Sewickley erupted in a wave of patriotism. Organizations strove to support America's and, more specifically, Sewickley's own soldiers.

Civil War memorial "Fame." In Sewickley Cemetery. Monument 1866. Photograph 1906. Courtesy The Sewickley Valley Historical Society.

The Civil War

At the outbreak of the Civil War, 99 Sewickley young men formed the Sewickley Rifles. Spectators thronged to watch the new company drill at the Presbyterian Church building, which had just been roofed and floored. Citizens furnished stylish uniforms for all in light gray material trimmed with green braid. On the Sunday before they left, the soldiers went to services at the Presbyterian Church in the morning and the Methodist Church in the afternoon, walking two by two to special reserved seats.

On July 6, 1861, the morning of the troops' departure, there was a large gathering where each man received a New Testament, and Captain Conrad Mayers, Lieutenant William C. Shields, and Lieutenant John I. Nevin were presented with swords.

The company was mustered into service July 11 as Company G of the 28th Regiment of Pennsylvania Volunteers. The first casualties were not on the battlefield. A. Jackson Gray died of disease. A notice in a Pittsburgh paper quoted a resolution by his fellow soldiers.

> Resolved, That we his fellow-soldiers, tender our sincere sympathies to his family in their bereavement; for as they have lost an affectionate son and brother, so have we lost a kind and cheerful comrade, and our country a good man and true.
>
> Resolved, That although he was denied the death that a soldier covets—that of the battle-field—and suffered that which alone he shrinks from—a death by disease, far from home,—yet he did his duty.[1]

The second death, too, was not in battle. Joseph Moore died of typhoid fever. Typhoid struck again, attacking several soldiers and killing William I. Nevin, who had recently left college to join the Company. A newspaper report said the outbreak was caused by camping in an "unwholesome spot."

At the battle of Antietam three Sewickley soldiers were killed, John D. Travelli, John Dickson Tracy, and William C. Richey. Memorial services at the Presbyterian Church were filled to overflowing. The regiment lost Lieutenant William Shields at Chancellorsville. Shields was within four feet of Sergeant Nicholas Way when he was shot through the breast. Twelve men were killed in battle during the war; 16 died of wounds and diseases. This was not unusual. Disease was the major cause of death in the Civil War. It killed two soldiers for every one that died in battle.

Sewickley citizens did all they could to support the war effort. In the early days, they even visited the troops. A letter from Dick Tracy dated October 17, 1861 reported that Reverend Allison, Mrs. Dickson and Mrs. Rhodes had been to the camp. Mr. Allison, pastor of the Presbyterian Church of Sewickley, preached twice on Sunday.

Closer to home, Miss Rebecca Way organized a group of girls who met weekly at the Presbyterian Church to sew flannel shirts for the soldiers. Each month Mrs. Gazzam and a friend walked from Sewickley to the far end of Edgeworth collecting money to buy them food and clothing.[2]

Ladies supported the Sanitary and Subsistence Commission, a group appointed by Secretary of War Simon Cameron that used private funds to provide relief for sick and wounded soldiers. Commissioners visited camps to promote sanitation and decent nutrition. The Sanitary Commission, chaired by landscape architect Frederick Law Olmsted, was headquartered in Washington but had associate members in the larger cities. In 1864 the Pittsburgh Sanitary Commission decided to hold a Sanitary Fair at Allegheny City near the present Carnegie Library branch on the North Side. They bought the buildings of the recently closed Cleveland Sanitary Fair and draymen brought them to Pittsburgh free. Carpenters also donated their time to put the buildings back together.

The Fair was like a county fair, but far more elaborate. Florists and nurseries contributed plants to create Floral Hall with a special exhibit of the Garden of Eden. There was an exhibit of cannons and cannonballs fabricated in Pittsburgh. The Old Curiosity Shop sold 1,100 "collectibles" including two cottage houses made of shells by a woman from Ohio. One exhibit featured a small replica of the "Monitor" which chugged around a small lake. Mrs. B.F. Jones, wife of one of the founders of Jones and Laughlin Steel Corporation, was in charge of the dining hall, serving food donated by farmers. The Fair at Allegheny City opened on June 1, 1864 and ran 18 days. It raised $322,000, including $84,000 contributed by businesses.[3] The purpose of the fair was at least partially to promote the fight for freedom from slavery. Ironically, no ticket was knowingly sold to a black person.[4]

Neighborhoods and suburbs of Pittsburgh had their own booths. Of course, Sewickley had one. An article in a Pittsburgh paper described it.

> Numbers 9 and 10 are the booths in which are displayed Sewickley's offering, and a highly creditable one it is, too. It will be remembered that the children and ladies of the Sewickley Valley lately gave a local fair, which realized the handsome sum of $480 for the Sanitary and Subsistence committees; but the ladies have been working like beavers since, and . . . they have gotten up a very beautiful display of all sorts of useful and fancy articles. [Fifteen young ladies] together with a number of married ladies, attended at this table by turns, and are doing everything possible to exhibit the merits of their wares.[5]

On the Fourth of July after the war's end, Sewickley held a grand celebration and memorial service that illustrates both the love of panoply of the nineteenth century citizens and their willingness to volunteer for duties both grand and menial. The day started with a bang at dawn as a three-gun salute boomed. Any attempt at sleep was foiled because the first salute was followed at sunrise by a four-gun salute and a national salute at 8:00 A.M. Captain David Shields led a parade of Sunday school students to join citizens and visitors for a special program of speeches and songs by a choir directed by Mrs. J. Sharpe McDonald. Following a large dinner and a few hours of rest, the program continued with more of the same. Of course fireworks rewarded the patient participants at dark.

Mrs. McDonald continued to direct the musical part of the Memorial Day services for at least 21 years. In recognition, the Sewickley post of the Grand Army of the Republic elected her an honorary member and presented her with a special badge.[6]

The Spanish-American War

More than thirty years separated the Civil War and the Spanish-American War of 1898, but the new generation of ladies was just as supportive of the latest war, even though it was fought far away. They organized the Sewickley Emergency Society "for the purpose of being useful to the soldiers in camp and at the front and to their families."[7] The Society had several committees. One sent hospital supplies including towels, sponges, and mosquito netting. The Sewing Committee made sheets, pillow cases, and pajamas. The chairman reported that on one day, June 7, 1898, "the hum of sewing machines filled the air and before we went home, 56 sheets and six pillow cases were finished." A Literature Committee supplied boxes of books and magazines "to keep at least a number of the men supplied with good reading to counteract the temptations of camp life." Another committee assembled 131 kits called "housewives." The kits, containing writing paper with stamped envelopes, needles and thread, shoe laces, safety pins, combs, and rolls of linen for bandages, were welcomed. One soldier serving in Cuba wrote, "It is good to know the people at home are working and thinking of us and we appreciate the fact to the fullest extent."

Parade before men from Sewickley went off to fight in the Spanish-American War, 1898. Broad and Centennial.
Courtesy The Sewickley Valley Historical Society.

For Thanksgiving the ladies sent dinner "worthy of their Sewickley homes" to the troops. "Quantities of turkey, chicken, mince pies, dozens and dozens of doughnuts and home biscuits, the best and sweetest of home-made bread, and all kinds and descriptions of cakes. . . . The Express Company, even at a reduction, charged 25 dollars."[8]

World War I

World War I rekindled the fires of patriotism. The Valley contributed 400 troops, over 100 more than its quota. Thirty-one were black and five were female nurses.[9] Several of the earliest volunteers worked for the American Ambulance Service in the French Army. Tingle W. Culbertson, for example, drove one of the 200 vehicles of the Ambulance Corps in 1917. He received a citation for bravery for rescuing wounded under fire. John J. Way joined the Ambulance Service, receiving the Croix de Guerre three times "for driving under perilous circumstances with complete disregard of danger." Probably because of Mr. Way and Mr. Culbertson, Sewickley residents provided money to purchase two vehicles for the Corps.[10]

Many in the Valley volunteered for service. Clarence Kaelin joined the Canadian Army in 1915, before our entry into the War. He was declared missing May 2, 1915. James M. Shannon joined the army as a private. He was killed by a stray shell in May, 1918. Thomas Kinsley of 123 Challis Street, Edgeworth, died from a shrapnel wound. Edward Harrison, also from Edgeworth, enlisted in 1917 and fought in France in the trenches. He was wounded on June 6, 1918 and hospitalized until August 21. Returning to the trenches, he was wounded again November 10. Mr. Harrison received a citation for heroism and devotion to duty before sailing for home July 19, 1919. Spencer Banks of 10 School Street, Sewickley, claimed to be the "only colored boy who volunteered from this vicinity." Tingle Culbertson survived both his service in the Ambulance Corps and being torpedoed on the steamer "Sussex". After going to officers' training camp, Mr. Culbertson became a first lieutenant in the infantry. A letter from his commanding officer to Mr. Culbertson's parents told of his death in battle.

October 4th, at 5:45 a. m., your son led his company's advance platoon against the enemy. As the battalion jumped off— 781 men, 16 officers—the counter-barrage fell upon us, literally tearing the forward platoons to shreds. . . . Passing over a gentle crest, we came under a heavy machine-gun barrage. Those who entered the wood were met by a tremendous barrage and were unable to hold their ground, falling back to the crest short of the wood. Somewhere between the crest and the wood your son was last seen advancing. A sergeant who was with him declares he was blown to pieces by a high-explosive shell. Of my sixteen officers, four were killed and nine wounded.[11]

Men leaving for World War I, Broad and Beaver Streets. Those departing are standing with flowers in their lapels.
Courtesy The Sewickley Valley Historical Society.

At home the troops were encouraged and supported. Numerous organizations strove to do all possible for the war effort. The help started with the stirring sendoff for the departing troops which was reported in the *Herald*, October 6, 1917.

> The public school turned out en masse, forming about the central corner of Sewickley; the Red Cross Girl Cadets lined up on one side of the square, the Sewickley School Cadets on the other. "America" was sung by all in unison, the crowd joining in heartily. The Sewickley band formed and played a number of martial selections for the benefit of the embarrassed draftees, who were having much ado to pose for the photographs that were taken. Then the boys, each with a Red Cross comfort kit, boarded the brilliantly decorated autos which took them up to the district headquarters at Avalon.

It seems that almost everyone belonged to some unit ready to defend the Valley. Even before the United States joined the war effort, the Sewickley School Cadets were organized, 61 strong. Mrs. Alexander Laughlin ordered uniforms, to be paid for by private donations. Rifles were to be supplied without expense by the United States Army. The physical education director of the YMCA offered his services to teach the cadets U. S. Army setting-up exercises.[12]

The YMCA. organized the Young Minute Men, boys 10-15 years old trained in home defense, home duties, first aid, Bible study and military drills.

High School girls could sign up for military units to learn close order military drills, including the intricacies of squads right and squads left. Girls also learned wall scaling and target shooting in addition to the more usual female duties with the Red Cross.

Men joined the Sewickley Valley Guards, trained in military drills and physical fitness, ready for any home guard duties. Men over 45 might elect to serve in the platoon of men who did not "care to go through the more strenuous features of the training, such as cross-country work and setting-up exercises."[13]

Sewickley women, too, received instruction in shooting.

> Mrs. Todd's Home Defense Class will take up the pistol practice at 4:00 o'clock. Anyone desiring to join the class may register at the Red Cross house or at the shooting grounds at the side of Mr. Frank Richardsons's hill.[14]

Many women volunteered for Red Cross work. Some put together "comfort kits," similar to the Spanish-American War "housewives," for shipment to soldiers overseas. In one month in 1916, the ladies made 1,100 kits, the *Herald* reported:

This phenomenal effort represented a little good-bye gift from the women of the Auxiliary to the defenders of their homes. Comfort bags were provided for all the boys who left the Valley for training camps during the past week.[15]

One hundred Red Cross Christmas packages went out crammed full of socks, handkerchiefs, Chiclets, fruit cake, instant coffee and chocolate, insect powder to destroy lice, note paper, the New Testament, peanut butter, cigarettes, and tobacco.

The Red Cross had many opportunities for volunteers to learn and serve. There were classes in beginners and advanced first aid in case of an invasion by the Germans, although it is difficult understand how the Germans could have mounted such an invasion. The class in Elementary Hygiene and Care of the Sick required 15 lectures and a textbook. Women could spend all day Friday at St. Stephen's making surgical supplies and all day Wednesday at the Presbyterian Church sewing for hospitals. Then, there was a Wednesday Knitting Unit, 100 strong, with others on the waiting list. Any member absent for three meetings without excuse was dropped.

Fear of a food shortage had risen with the nation's entry into the War. Residents were urged to "sell your golf stick and buy a hoe." *The Herald* reported in early Spring, 1917:

The information has been widely circulated within the past few weeks that a food shortage of serious import faces the nation, in common with the other great nations of the earth, and that, unless an unusually large crop is planted this year, the peoples of the world will suffer the consequences. . . . Many a vacant lot, garden and pasture will have its subsoil turned to the sunshine and put in shape for rearing the indispensable tuber or some other form of edible.[16]

Another article in *The Sewickley Herald* recommended planting gardens for several reasons.

Gardening affords a quality and quantity of exercise that has golf beaten to a 'frazzle,' ensures a continuous supply of fresh edibles at a moderate price, adds that much to the general store of the nations, and has an automatic bearing on the high cost of living.[17]

The Young Minute Men planted corn at the YMCA on the tract of land which Mrs. Henry Oliver had given for a golf course.[18] The Sewickley School Cadets grew vegetables on land near the Allegheny Country Club. Captain Frederick Way, Jr., a member of the troop, remembered his experiences.

The thing to do was to raise vegetables but none of us had done any farming. Mrs. Henry Rea gave us a tract of land on the Heights. It was all over brambles (no wonder she donated it to us.) First thing we were going to have to do was clear it. So I said, "That's easy. Let's burn it. The wind is blowing right up the hill and all we have to do is set fire to it." It burned merrily and the embers got flying around. There was a barn right at the top of the hill. The roof caught fire and we couldn't get to it. It burned to the ground. My friends said, "All right, you bright guy, you thought this up. Now go ahead and tell Mrs. Rea what happened." I went over and knocked on the front door. The butler came and took one look at me and all my dirt and said, "Help to the rear!" I said, "I want to tell Mrs. Rea." She was standing there and came over to see what this was all about. I said, "Mrs. Rea, I'm sorry but we burned your barn down." "What barn?" "The one over there on the farm." She said, "I didn't know we had one." She sent the overseer over with me but all he could do was say his blessings over the wreck. That was all that was ever said about it. So I met Mrs. Rea. I was in the Rea house.

After this inauspicious start, the boys continued to raise corn and tomatoes. Captain Way remembered that he made $32 for the whole summer. "We even had farmerettes. Girls put on bloomers and they tilled farms down here in town. People donated land."

Some of the crops went to Mrs. Rea and her Canning Class who preserved, dried, and canned fruits and vegetables for the Pennsylvania House in Paris where Sewickley soldiers spent their furloughs. An anonymous poet praised their work:

Those that eat your fruit shall be happy; they shall say, "Well boys how fair
That whilst we are saving our country, the women are working there
To save our country's produce, fruits, vegetables and all,
And sending it to us, now fighting, in cans big size and small."[19]

Tingle Woods Culbertson and nephew John Dickey Culbertson III
taken around 1916 or 1917 when Tingle Culbertson was in the Ambulance Corps in France.
Courtesy of Tingle Culbertson Barnes.

Among the more unusual donations to the war effort was the "Edorea," formerly the yacht of Henry Oliver Rea. Refitted as a coastal defense patrol boat, its thirty-man crew wore knitted sets made by the Sewickley women for the Navy League.

Anti-German feelings were the obverse of the patriotic coin all over the country. Captain Frederick Way, Jr. remembered how it affected him personally. He had learned German in his early years at Miss Jane McDonald's school and continued it at Sewickley High School until the coming of the War. "Then German was verboten. I had to take French, so I have a salad of German and French."

World War II

As always, Sewickley responded promptly and patriotically to the national crisis of the Second World War. Citizens joined armed forces or became volunteers on the home front. Victory Gardens sprouted. This conflict was different, in two major ways: there was an elaborate rationing system for gasoline and many foods; and air raid protection was a new problem.

Registration of volunteers began on a daily basis in December, 1941, the first month of the war. By December 18, the *Sewickley Herald* reported:

> With but 250 workers registered, compared with a goal of 2,500, there is urgent need for more volunteers. We need hundreds of other citizens to come down to the Borough Building, talk to the registrars, tell them what they can do, what hours are free, and be found a place in the defense of America.[20]

Sewickley sought volunteers in many fields including: practical and professional hunters, air raid wardens, electrical repair units, emergency medical forces, nurses aids, demolition and clearing squads (strong, husky men), road repair units (strong, husky men), car owners to perform driving chores, stenographers and clerks, radio operators, and messengers. One patriotic woman volunteered her home and services in caring for small children in order to release their mothers for defense work.

An interesting volunteer project was the War Cafeteria Committee to provide supper for defense workers and servicemen and their families who were stationed in the area but had no cooking facilities. This was a joint project of six churches and the YMCA, each institution providing six captains and 24 volunteers for its assigned week. Mrs. Bradley, Sewickley's well-known caterer, cooked and set the tables.

Any unused plot of land was a potential site for a Victory Garden. The Victory Garden Committee assigned plots, did the initial plowing, and provided expert advice. The gardener, in turn, agreed to sow seed, keep the weeds down, and clean up his own garden. In Sewickley Borough alone there were 11 properties given for Victory Garden plots. The golf course at the YMCA became many small Victory Gardens. It never returned to being a golf course. The Tener property on Centennial Avenue had 45 individual garden plots and 31 school gardens. Here there grew 110 varieties of vegetables and flowers. Thirty-six baskets of produce were donated to the hospital in one year.

An early form of voluntary recycling appeared during World War II in the scrap collection drive. The Sewickley Salvage Committee, Mrs. Margaret Morgan, Chairman, issued a broadside to all residents.

Do you want to Win the War?
Throw your scrap into the fight!
Metal Scrap—Old stoves, radiators, plumbing, tools, toys,
beds, cooking utensils, rods, compacts, etc.
Rubber Scrap—Old automobile tires and tubes, rubbers,
boots, garden hose, bathing caps, crepe rubber soles.
Keys—please give your keys to the pupils.
Give Scrap that is needed for Fighting Weapons for the Boys at the Front
Show your Patriotism

Mrs. Morgan asked the air raid wardens to visit each home to ask for scrap metal and rubber. One donation deprived Sewickley of one of its historical mementos. The Sewickley Cemetery Association donated the four cannons around the Soldiers' and Sailors' monument.

In all earlier wars, there had been no substantial threat of direct action by a foreign power, but in 1941 people believed that there was. The fear of an enemy air raid is the biggest difference apparent when reading government notices or newspaper articles of the time. The *Sewickley Herald* put it well in December, 1941.

> Danger of local bombing seems remote, and is probably well in the future; yet we all know that Germany, Japan, and other Axis forces would surely center their attention on Pittsburgh and its sprawling industrial districts along its three rivers if ever such an attack became practicable. And in these days of unexpected war developments, who can say what may or may not be practicable now or soon?

Leaflets issued by the Civil Defense were designed to be reassuring but seem quite scary.

> The enemy wants you to run out on the streets, create a mob, start a panic. Don't do it. The chance you will be hit is small. It is part of the risk we must take to win the war. Don't scream. Don't start disorder or panic. Be strong, be calm, be order-ly. Lick the aggressors. Put out all lights you cannot closely screen, so no light reaches the street—the light that's out or covered tight will never guide a Jap!

The Sewickley Defense Council set up an auxiliary field hospital with a 22-bed ward in the basement of the pub-lic grade school. A map of the area with colored pins showed the location of trouble. A mobile first aid unit could speed to the scene. The *Pittsburgh Post-Gazette* reported:

> The moment an emergency alarm is sound, hundreds of Sewickley citizens will move into action. . . . The hospital was set up not only in preparation for air raids on this vital center, but in the fear of more probable industrial disasters. Miss Helen Pratt, superintendent of Sewickley Valley Memorial Hospital explains that in event of a sudden large scale catastrophe, convalescent patients will be removed from the main hospital to the emergency hospital to make way for the critically injured. The hospital is more than a wartime necessity. It is a symbol of community unity and co-operation.[21]

The Sewickley Defense Council issued posters to hang in every house on "What to do in preparation for an Air Raid and What to do in an Air Raid." Families should select a shelter room on the first floor with inside walls and stout tables. In case of an air raid, the whole family was to assemble in this room. "If an incendiary bomb falls, do not wait for the Fire Department, but fight it with a spray (not a stream or splash) from garden hose—switch to stream to put out any fire started from bomb."

A demonstration of handling incendiary bombs had a surprise ending. The plan was to build three shanties on the high school field to be "bombed." "A phosphorous bomb, placed out in the football field, but not far enough away, show-ered a section of the crowded bleachers with white-hot foul-smelling bits of phosphorous." Fortunately, it just burned the clothes.[22]

Sewickley Borough was divided into 11 air raid warden posts. Each post was manned by a senior warden and from five to ten wardens, all with first aid and other special training.

By early January, 1942, a month after Pearl Harbor, there was an observation post on the top of the bank building, manned 24 hours a day by two people to watch for enemy aircraft. World War I veterans from the American Legion sup-plied many of the observers.

Another new development in World War II, rationing, was not frightening, but it was time-consuming. Some items were rationed because they were needed for the war. A consumer instruction sheet explained.

> Every week we are sending shiploads of canned goods to feed our fighting men and our fighting allies in Africa, Britain, and the Pacific Islands. We must see they get the food they need. We at home will share all that is left.

Other items were rationed because the war restricted or ended imports. Rationing provided a fair share for all. Each household had to contend with four different ration books for buying scarce foods: sugar, coffee, meat, and canned goods. Take the canned goods as an example. Each family member received a ration book with stamps of different num-bers and letters. Stamps marked with specific letters could only be used during a given period. Newspapers carried charts of points needed for each item. Scarce foods required more points. Housewives had to calculate how to utilize their stamps to provide the best menus, while making sure not to use up their stamps too soon. Once a family's stamps were gone, they had no more until the next period. They could, however, use fresh produce if it was available. On going to the store, the stamps had to be detached in front of the grocer, probably to avoid a black market.

The same process with different ration books pertained to coffee, sugar and meat. An editorial in the *Pittsburgh Post-Gazette* was sympathetic:

> This is the time of year when, ordinarily, children tiptoe fearfully through the halls, and the household clatter is stilled, and the brooding silence of the domicile is shattered only by the occasional expletive that escapes from the room where the lord of the manor wrestles with his income tax blank.
>
> But in 1943 something new has been added. While father studies his receipts and his exemptions and searches through the check stubs for another elusive deduction, mother's brow is furrowed too. Point rationing has begun. From now on each meal must be calculated with an accountant's accuracy; else the number of points in the monthly allowance will not balance with the number of meals on the table.
>
> Plenty of concentration will be required to add a can of beans to a can of asparagus, subtract a can of spiced apricots, and come out with a balanced ration for the month. But with full confidence in the virtues of American womanhood we state, firmly, confidently and without fear of successful contradiction, that mother will work out this problem if it is workable. She has performed miracles before; and she, if anyone, can perform this one.

Cans and jars were rationed because large supplies were needed for sending to troops overseas; sugar and coffee, because the country depended on foreign supplies no longer available. Gasoline was rationed for a less obvious reason. There was an adequate domestic supply of gasoline in the United States, but no domestic supply of rubber. The best way to make sure existing rubber supplies lasted through the duration was to reduce wear on tires by limiting gasoline consumption. Each ration book provided stamps for 12 gallons of gasoline per month.

Cars had to be registered at the local school. At that time, all tires had to be declared, and any extra tires had to be disposed of before any gas ration card was issued. One unfortunate result of the "mileage rationing," as it was officially called, was a new form of thievery. The *Herald* warned, "Those who leave autos on the streets all night are apt to lose their tire to thieves."[23]

Sewickley's patriotic support of the national war effort was unflagging. It seems that the slogan "My country right or wrong" was not strong enough to describe the popular view. My country being wrong was unthinkable. The only question asked, at least in newspapers and public documents, was how can we best help the country and, especially, the fighting troops. All this patriotic fervor might seem extreme to modern eyes but it is refreshing to look back on wars supported so unswervingly by the populace.

[1] Ellis, p. 254.

[2] Ibid.

[3] Dorothy Daniel, "The Sanitary Fair." In *Western Pennsylvania Historical Magazine*, v.41, 1958, pp. 153-158.

[4] Charles W. Dahlinger, "The Pittsburgh Sanitary Fair." In *Western Pennsylvania Historical Magazine*, v.12, 1929, p. 101.

[5] Ellis, pp. 258-259.

[6] Ibid., pp. 262-267.

[7] Sewickley Valley Emergency Society, *Minute Book*, mss. at Sewickley Valley Historical Society.

[8] Clipping from *The Sewickley Herald*, no date. Hay File.

[9] *Sewickley Herald*, July 14, 1917, p. 1.

[10] Ibid., Jan. 20, 1917, p. 3.

[11] St. Stephen's *Messenger*.

[12] *Sewickley Herald*, March 17, 1917, p. 14.

[13] Ibid., Oct. 6, 1917, p. 5.

[14] Ibid., Sept. 15, 1917, p. 15.

[15] Ibid., October 6, 1917.

[16] Ibid., Ap 14, 1917, p. 6.

[17] Ibid.

[18] Ibid., May 5, 1917, p. 11.

[19] Ibid., October 6, 1917.

[20] Ibid., Dec. 24, 1941, p. 7.

[21] *Pittsburgh Post-Gazette*, May 16, 1942.

[22] *Sewickley Herald*, Dec. 31, 1941, p. 11.

[23] Ibid., October 29, 1942, p. 11.

Chapter 17
Schools

Education in Sewickley and the rest of Western Pennsylvania was rather hit or miss in the early days. Many schools and teachers came and went, leaving students to find other means of education, either public or private. When Pennsylvania passed an act to provide free public schools in 1834, there were no school buildings. In Pittsburgh, four empty buildings, two former factories, and two empty warehouses became improvised schools. There were no desks or chairs; students sat on the floor or on window sills. Classes were crowded, averaging 44 students per teacher. If there was not enough room, students were sent home.

Sewickley, too, adapted an existing building for a schoolhouse before building a proper school. Sewickley's public school operated in an old log house in Addy Beer's Grove near the present YMCA. Other small, one room schools, either public or private, were scattered around the countryside. Most public schools were small, often with one room and one teacher. An article probably written by Gilbert Hays, a Sewickley historian, describes the trials and tribulations of teachers around 1865-1870 in a one room school midway between Fair Oaks and Leetsdale on the Beaver Road.

The population being widely separated, naturally the attendance was small, but what it lacked in number was made up by the pernicious activity of the boys enrolled, a set of young barbarians, whose time apparently was more given to deviltry than to their lessons, and whose ingenuity in devising schemes to annoy the teacher was surpassed [only] by that of the Inquisition.

The school term ran for six or seven months of the year, but one teacher being in charge of the pupils, whose ages ranged from six to twenty, the teacher generally being a very young girl. The change in teachers was frequent and sudden, as might be expected from the tales below narrated.

Broad Street Public School.
Courtesy The Sewickley Valley Historical Society.

There were many diversions from the monotony of the studies. Snakes, ranging from the harmless garter, water, black and house snakes, to the more venomous copperheads, were in abundance in the vicinity, many of the boys being adepts in the capture alive of these terrifying creatures, which served a useful purpose, when the school hours seemed long and irksome. At recess a number of the snake hunters would scour the woods . . . and quickly secure half a dozen reptiles, ranging from two foot garter snakes to a five foot blacksnake, all alive. In cans or jars, and often under their coats, the snakes would be taken into the school, and just when all seemed serene, with lessons progressing finely, there would be a shriek from some girl, who would jump on top of her desk or run out of the building. Snakes travel quickly, and it took but a moment to have the school in an uproar, with all hands outside. School would be dismissed. It was generally understood that the snakes crawled into the building unaided.

Once the boys found a hornet's nest almost as big as a bushel basket in McCormick's orchard, just below the school. As several hard frosts had occurred, the occupants of the nest had apparently vacated for the winter. Cutting down the limb from which it was suspended, the trophy was taken into the school room, affording much curiosity to teacher and scholars alike, and hung over the blackboard back of the teacher's chair. The warmth of the room soon developed a buzz in the nest, and in a short time hundreds of mad hornets were seeking the disturbers of their winter's sleep, breaking up any further exercises for that day.

The old trick of throwing red pepper on the stove and scattering it over the floor, was frequently tried, the entire school fair sneezing their heads off.[1]

John Way, Jr. attended classes in the schoolhouse built by the Shields family in Edgeworth. He remembered his school days in a short memoir dated May 26, 1894.

My first school recollections at the little brick house at Shield's. Samuel Shannon, teacher. Pay school, about 1828 to 1831. After Shannon the Public School System with different teachers from year to year, among them William Reno. All the boys and girls from Squire Anderson's to Hays on the river, up Little Sewickley . . . attended the school from time to time. Text books [were] U.S. Spellingbook, English Reader and Bible, Western Calculator. Geography and grammar were not taught. I taught one term, about 1841, at $15 per month, boarded myself among the pupils David, John and Mary Anderson, Kate Wilson, George and Harvey Scott, James and Elias Reno etc. Mine was the first school report in detail the Directors had ever received.

[Later] I went to school at the old log house, I think about 1835 or 1836: pay school before Nevin and Champ's school began. Don't remember what the teacher's name was, but he was a cross Irishman who kept a long rod in the house, as thick as your thumb, and used it too. We barred him out Christmas and kept him out nearly a week. . . . After this I attended Nevin & Champ's school, and then six years at Mr. Travelli's.

Teachers found it hard to deal with their charges. Special training for teaching was not available. John Way, Jr. remembered how he got his first job.

In the early days of the public schools, [they] did not have all the red tape about examinations of teachers as they do now [1894]. When I applied [to teach] for the school, D. E. Nevin and William Reno were the examining committee. I went before them with fear and trembling. Mr. Reno said to Mr. Nevin that he would vouch for my reading and spelling if he (Mr. Nevin) would vouch for my writing and arithmetic, which was assented to, and there ended the examination.

The brick [school]house in the borough was built by Ohio Township . . . . After the borough was organized, from time to time, there were two or three annexes to it. The old brick and annexes got too small and the directors concluded to build a new [school]house and the present [in 1894] lot was leased with the privilege of buying for $1,400 whenever it could be paid. This was in 1861. The war threatening frightened the people and a petition signed by two thirds of the property holders was sent to the directors asking them not to build the [school]house. But the old house was so full and running over, and in a mean muddy place, notwithstanding the petition, the directors went on and built the [school]house.

The new school Mr. Way mentions, on the corner of Broad and Thorn Streets, was the first building specifically designed to be a school. As population grew, so did the building, adding four rooms in 1878 and four more in 1882. A picture shows a graceful brick structure topped by a decorative tower. The building burned down in 1893. The next year it was replaced by a new building designed by Elmer E. Miller, an architect who lived in Sewickley and had his office in Pittsburgh. The new school building was in the Richardson Romanesque style made popular nationwide by Henry Hobson Richardson. The style was particularly available for imitation in Pittsburgh, where Richardson himself had designed one of his most famous buildings, the Allegheny County Courthouse. Like the Courthouse, the Sewickley school had a tower with Romanesque arches, Romanesque windows in the facade, and half-cylinders incorporated into the design.

The Sewickley school was the only one large enough to offer high school. After finishing eight grades at one of the small schools, students who wanted further education had to get to the Sewickley school, an impossible feat for many children who lived beyond walking distance. They had to get to school by foot or by horse and buggy. This explains why the Sewickley High School had only 22 students in 1899, with a graduating class of four.

Despite its small student body, the high school offered a wide curriculum, according to a brochure from 1912. There were four "Courses of Study": (1) English Latin, for those intending to go to college and for all students who were undecided; (2) the General Course, for "those who wish to go out from High School with a broad and directly useful fund of information"; (3) the Scientific Course, for "all who intend to take up work in Carnegie Tech" or other scientific study; and (4) the Commercial Course, only two years, "to prepare students for office work." The English Latin course required four years of English and Latin, three years of German, one and a half years of history, three years of math, and either physics or chemistry. The Commercial Course was practical, with courses in bookkeeping, stenography, and commercial arithmetic. The only courses not job-related were Ancient history and Medieval and Modern History.[2]

Public schools were supplemented by private schools. A Pittsburgh city directory in 1841 lists 33 "Select Private Schools and Seminaries."[3] Many came and went quickly. All that was needed to start a school was a room and a teacher. Advertisements in newspapers between 1800 and 1825 described 43 different private schools. Schools were often located in private homes. One was held at the Nicholas Way house in the 1830s, according to Agnes Way. She said that Nicholas had a little house built in his garden for the children. There they learned spelling, geography, U.S. history, the Psalms, Proverbs, and the three R's. Girls learned sewing, knitting and crocheting.[4]

Because most schools did not last very long, one person's education could be disjointed. A letter from T. H. B. McKnight, who grew up in Edgeworth in the 1860s and 1870s, records a surprising number of changes.

> I was entered in Sewickley in the school at seven years old. [The teachers were] Reverend Samuel G. Norcross, a delightful New Englander, with a long black beard, and his wife, a plump little person with brown hair and eyes. I remember when Mrs. Norcross had the Mental Arithmetic class line up before her. The first question that came to me was too much. I made a diversion by calling attention to a disagreement between two of the Norcross cats (the family lived in the upper story of the building) and left the line to separate the combatants. Mrs. Norcross sternly called me back, and I was obliged to confess with shame that I could not answer.

> In 1869-70 I was a pupil at Episcopal School conducted by Reverend Samuel Earp, Rector of Saint Stephen's, in the old wooden church building. Then I remember Mr. Wakeham's school in the old Academy building. I attended 1870-71. The first day of the new term Professor Wakeham explained that he found it necessary to discontinue school. Restrained until he was out of hearing, [were] our shouts of joy at the unexpectedly long vacation.

> Back to Episcopal School under the quite scholarly Mr. Moore, Rector. The assistant was a burly middle aged Englishman who tried to rule by fear and threats. During his temporary absence from the room one morning, Ethelbert Nevin and I broke into pieces and threw out the window a large watch he had bought to enforce his ideas of discipline. When he returned, he blamed me and advanced toward me angrily, upon which I made good my retreat. Expelled. I did not mind much, especially as Miss Agnes Hays, the charming teacher of the younger children, invited me to a party she was having for her part of the school that afternoon!

> My last school in Sewickley was run by Professor Dickson in the old Presbyterian Church building as a day school and as a normal school for older scholars who boarded with the Principal. He was assisted by his wife.

> It certainly was a precarious and uncertain education the youth received in Sewickley in my younger days![5]

The most ambitious schools were the academies, private schools modeled on Benjamin Franklin's Academy, opened in 1751 in Philadelphia. By 1800 there were 13 academies in Pennsylvania. At the peak of the academies' popularity in 1850, there were 263,000 students in 6,085 academies in the United States.[6] Academies provided secondary education for anyone wanting to go to college, to enter a profession, or just to get more general education before leaving school.

The Pittsburgh Academy, organized in 1789, offered courses in "English, French, and Latin languages, writing the different hands, arithmetic, book-keeping, surveying, trigonometry, geography, the use of globes, chronology, and algebra."[7] Other academies followed in Western Pennsylvania: English and Classical Academy at Fourth and Liberty Avenues; Washington Academy in Washington, Pennsylvania; and Beaver Academy in Beaver.

Sewickley was fortunate in having two academies: Sewickley Academy, which was sometimes co-educational and sometimes for boys only; and the Edgeworth Ladies Academy (sometimes called Edgeworth Female Seminary.) Both made the area attractive to commuters because they could be assured that their children could receive an adequate education.

Edgeworth Seminary in 1908 after being rebuilt as a residence.
Courtesy Sewickley Valley Historical Society.

What is now Sewickley Academy had a checkered career in its first century. Started as a school for boys, it opened in 1838 in the older of the two Way houses on Beaver Road. An advertisement in 1839 announced, "Nevin & Champs Classical and Commercial school for Boys: on the Ohio River, fourteen miles below Pittsburgh. Term, $75 per season of five months; half paid in Advance."[8] The building was partially destroyed by fire on December 8, 1839, according to David Shields' diary.

A fire occurred this day P.M. in the house occupied by Nevin and Champ as a boarding school, which destroyed the northern or old end. The day was calm, and the atmosphere damp and heavy, and the people active and zealous. On the ninth, the rubbish was removed, and on the tenth carpenters began to rebuild and repair.[9]

Champ and Nevin both moved away. Mr. Joseph Travelli, a former missionary to China, reopened the school as a boarding school in the rented Fife house on Beaver Road and Grove Street in 1843. After this house too burned in 1851, Mr. Travelli bought a house near the river and added two wings. This structure later became the Park Place Hotel. By 1860, Mr. Travelli had attracted 75 day and boarding students. An advertisement in the *Presbyterian Banner* in 1862 describes the school:

Sewickley Academy: A Classical and Commercial
Boarding School for Boys
On the Fort Wayne and Chicago Railroad
12 Miles from Pittsburgh
Reverend Joseph S. Travelli A.M. Principal
40th Session will Commence Monday, May 5, 1862
Inquiries contact Principal. Sewickleyville P.O. Allegheny County, Pennsylvania.[10]

At the outset of the Civil War, southern pupils left and some teachers and older boys enlisted in the army. The school closed in 1863. Sewickley Academy reopened in 1865 in the old church building opposite the present Presbyterian Church. In 1866 there were 83 students. It was here that T. H. B. McKnight finished his "precarious and uncertain" education in Sewickley.[11]

In 1874, Professor Dickson and his wife operated the school from their house on the corner of Chestnut Street and Beaver Avenue. They boarded the students, boys downstairs, girls, upstairs. Suspended in 1875, the Academy reopened in 1877 on the northwest corner of Academy and Beaver Avenues.

John Way, Jr. took over Sewickley Academy in 1878. He explains the reasons in a memo written the same year.

> I am now giving my leisure time to the superintendence of an Academy which, in a moment of desperation, I started a few months ago for my own boys, as we have no good schools here, although our population is over 3,000. I am now erecting a large and expensive building for the purpose, on my own farm, and have every encouragement for success (not financially however.)

John Way, Jr. had a firm hand and strong ideas on education. His personality and principles are apparent in a handbook for 1886.

> The School in all its departments is subject to the oversight of the Superintendent, who desires to do all that can be done to promote the mental, moral and physical health of the pupils. Bright pupils are encouraged to press on; dull ones are cared for.
>
> It is our conviction, based upon a school experience of many years, that education does not mean so many pages of so many books in some given time, but rather that cultivation of the mind by which a pupil is enabled to seek information for himself and to make practical use of it.
>
> Please do not allow society duties (!) [sic] during the school term. All such pre-occupations of mind retard the pupil, discourage and disable him from work, cause damage to the class and permanent injury to the school.
>
> *English.* It is a crime to teach a child to read and not at the same time to teach him what to read. It is desired in the English Course to cultivate a taste for pure and good reading.
>
> *German and French.* The method pursued in the school in teaching German and French differs from that usually followed, in that the pupil learns the language without aid of grammar or dictionary, purely as a spoken language, and much in the same way that a child would learn it. English is banished from the class-room; the time is used in conversation.[12]

Edgeworth Seminary, or Edgeworth Ladies' Seminary, run by Mrs. Mary Olver with help from her husband, James, was an important educational institution, drawing students from far away. Part of the original building remains today, remodeled into a house on 420 Oliver Avenue. The two wings, which housed the dormitories and classrooms, burned in 1865.

The academy, originally located in Braddock, moved to land purchased from David Shields in the Sewickley valley. David Shields was a reluctant seller, according to a letter in 1834. "I have not any desire to sell, yet for the purpose of a female Seminary such as yours, I would do it." He agreed to sell 40 acres of prime bottomland for $30 an acre and, if needed, additional uplands for $20 an acre. Mr. Olver reported in May 1835 that he had met with his architect, John Chislett, one of Pittsburgh's most famous architects of the time. Mr. and Mrs. Olver's choice of such an accomplished architect to design their Academy shows that they planned a first class establishment equal to the finest schools in the east. The original building was a large stone structure with long porches supported by pillars on the front and back. Wooden wings extended from either end of the main structure.

A notice sent potential clients shortly after the move stated:

> This institution has lately been removed from Braddock's Field to Sewickley, an eligible situation on the north Side of the Ohio River, and near the village of Economy. The site is fine, overlooking the Beaver Road, and a handsome landscape that falls irregularly beyond, toward the stream of the Ohio, the distance of about one quarter of a mile. A situation more favorable to health is not to be found in this entire region.

The school was a success. By July, 1838, there were 50 pupils. The Edgeworth Seminary patterned itself on the English public school portrayed in *Tom Jones School Days* where, faced with a tough curriculum, frequent canings, and primitive living conditions, school boys were supposed to become men. It is unusual that the Female Academy applied the same formula to women's education, fortunately without the canings. The curriculum was ambitious and far-ranging, including subjects now rare.

Science and Math: Nature study; Astronomy; Botany; Arithmetic.

Language studies: Elocution; Rhetoric; Analogy; Logic; "Telemachus," [the first four books of Homer's *Odyssey*]; French;

Social Sciences: Philosophy; Intellectual philosophy; Outlines of history; Political economy.

Religion: Ecclesiastical history; Natural theology; Evidences of Christianity.

Home economics: Sewing.

Basic fees were $80.00 for each of two 22-week terms; music, singing, French, drawing and washing were extra.[13] A bill to David Shields for 1840-41 shows extra charges of $15 for French and $24 for drawing.

Eliza Leet Shields described the Seminary as it was in 1850 when she was a pupil.

In the neighborhood of Pittsburgh was a large and fashionable Seminary known as Edgeworth Ladies Seminary. It was first established in Braddock's Field, that historic spot, by an English woman, Mrs. Olver, or, as she was affectionately called, Mother Olver. . . . This school prospered and remained at Braddock's for many years when its growing demands forced Mother Olver to purchase land, and build a more commodious house in the beautiful Sewickley Valley. . . . She died shortly after its establishment there, and it passed into the hands of the Reverend Daniel Nevin. . . . There the grandmothers and mothers of most of the prominent families of Western Pennsylvania and Ohio received their education, indeed such was its reputation that many from Eastern Pennsylvania and New York were sent there.

It was situated some hundred yards from the river—which was not visible—and fronted the public road [Beaver Road]. The very extensive grounds were beautifully laid out and kept. They sloped gradually to a little stream over which was a rustic bridge and along the banks of which grew very closely, willow trees. The carriage drive and foot paths wound in graceful curves down to this bridge and over it to the road, over which passed the stages and wagons on their way between Pittsburgh and the West. For it was not for some years after that a rail road was built west of Pittsburgh. The only transportation was by means of private carriage, stage once a day, or steam boat, which while being the most delightful, was uncertain owing to the stage of the water.

Stretching out to back and side, was a large apple orchard, a favorite resort of the girls, where ensconced in the branches of a tree, with a lap full of apples either green or ripe, and a book in her hand, she would study her lessons or perhaps read and weep over one of Grace Anguillar's novels.

In contrast to the beautiful grounds, and the imposing exterior of the building, the interior was crude, bare, and uninviting. . . . The Study or Principal's private room, was the "Blue Beard's Chamber" of the establishment, dreaded by all.

The lower floors of the wings were devoted, one to the kitchen, dining room and private sitting room of the family, and the other to the class rooms. There were three large rooms separated by folding doors, which were thrown open every morning for prayers and twice a year for public examinations.

Every morning at nine o'clock a large bell called to prayers. When the hundred or more pupils assembled, a chapter of the Bible was read and a short prayer offered, or if it was necessary a lecture or reproof delivered, after which the doors were closed and each room devoted to a class. (There were smaller class rooms in other parts of the house.)

The rising bell rang at half past five or six in the morning and breakfast was at half past six; from half past seven till half past eight all assembled in the large rooms for study, where one or more teachers kept order. At nine, school began and continued until twelve, when we had dinner and perhaps a breathing spell in the open air. At one o'clock in winter and two o'clock in summer, back again to classes until four or five; then an hour or so for recreation. . . . At six o'clock we had supper, and from seven till eight or half past study again. At nine the great bell rang for bedtime.

The pupils sat around the large tables. The teacher then put questions to each one; we knew nothing of writing our lessons; each question must be answered immediately and if not correct, a mark was given. There were black boards for classes in mathematics and each one had to take turns at it.

In grammar, the parts of speech, the rules, the adverbs, adjectives, etc., etc., were committed to memory, and then we began parsing, which was done by taking first some easy sentence and each pupil parsing a word. Then something more difficult, until we were considered sufficiently advanced to take up "Milton's Paradise Lost" which was the acme of our ambition, and the end of our lessons in grammar. [Parsing is breaking a sentence down into its component parts of speech with an explanation of the form, function, and relationship of each part.]

The Saturday morning session was devoted to the reading of "compositions". I should say that one half the pupils read one Saturday, the others next. The poor girl trembling and scared stood up and read her trite little essay.

The rooms were the most bare, uncomfortable, unhomelike looking places imaginable. Two beds, two girls to each bed, a strip of carpet beside each bed, four straight wooden chairs, a high mantle piece with a solitary candle on it—no bureaus, no wash stand. There was plenty of running water, towels, and all necessary arrangements for the toilet But Oh! it was so cold going down the cold stairs through unheated halls. No wonder we jumped about and clapped our hands to get warm afterwards. In each room there was one delight, and that was a grate for a soft coal fire, and plenty of taffy was made on that coal fire, smoked and scorched most likely, but so delicious. Most of our nights were spent in this way.

At the close of each session, Spring and Fall, there was a public examination. The examinations began by the calisthenics class coming in robed in white muslin, with wreaths of ivy on the heads meandering in and out in some intricate figure, after which a class was called.

We took our position on the stage facing the audience. The Principal informed the assembly how far we had progressed and, taking a book, held it out asking "if any one in the audience would be kind enough to take the book and question the young ladies." There was never wanting some clergyman or Professor of some rival school to take advantage of this, and try, and generally succeed in confusing us, so that really bright girls appeared like dunces.

Then the Principal stepped forward with a handful of diplomas, each rolled up and tied with blue ribbon. One was delivered to each graduate with some good advice, and touching remarks.[14]

Such public examinations, terrifying for the student, were common in the academies. Outsiders were invited to attend to hear oral examinations and to view exhibits of Latin and English compositions of the students.

Agnes Way was a pupil at the Seminary shortly after Eliza Shields. She remembered when the Mexican War veterans passed the school on their way home in 1845 or 1846.

The household from the Seminary and families near assembled in the grove of large maple trees on the bank of the river below the Seminary, all undergrowth and rubbish having been removed. All farmers and farm hands from the Way and Shields estates and their friends from the farms on the Heights were assembled below as far down as I could see; it was an assembly of 200 or more.

It was a large boat, having over 2,000 officers and men; as they rounded Dead Man's Island they came near shore and very slow, almost stopping. The party from the Seminary arose, went close to the bank, waved hats and handkerchiefs—but not a sound. The cheers from those along the bank below, the farmers and farm hands, though, was a mighty roar like a prolonged wave of sound, with an echo. It was an "event" in the lives of the people.

Miss Agnes Way had fond memories of excursions for picnics all around the Seminary. Because there was no long summer vacation, there was plenty of opportunity for outdoor picnics. On the Fourth of July in 1858, the girls went to the same riverbank where they had greeted the Mexican War soldiers.

The younger girls were allowed to go up and down the beach; they gathered mussel shells and pebbles; the older ones skipped shells. When the down train from Pittsburgh came, there were ten boys got off—"brothers", cousins and boy friends of the Pittsburgh girls, bringing their own lunch and a lot of goodies for their sisters. All had a grand time and no one was reprimanded.

[Another picnic site was Little Sewickley Creek.] It was a sunshiny day in September: all were cheery. Most of the Art students came prepared to sketch; quite a number with a chaperon went around the bend of the creek to wade—some looked as though they might have had a dip. They came back bringing bunches of white daisies and Black-eyed Susans, quite outshining the Botany class in color, who had three kinds of small fern, some mosses and quite a number of rare fungi.[15]

There was a succession of other private schools in the Sewickley area. One school operating in 1911 was the Sewickley Preparatory School on 20 Thorn Street. It offered education for grades K-12 and, upon graduation, its "certificate admits pupils without examination to Cornell, Smith, Wellesley, and other colleges."

In 1913 St. James Parish opened a school on 249 Broad Street in the former D. C. Herbst house, purchased for $21,000. The bishop of Pittsburgh donated a bell and tower for the old house. Rooms were named for the saints corresponding to the names of donors of $100 to $500. In its first year, the school enrolled 80 students. Josephine Herbst Sybo remembered the school when she was a student in the 1930s. Enrollment was not restricted, but there was tuition.

The school was run by four teachers and a principal, all nuns, who worked for very little and lived in the same building as the school. Mrs. Sybo remembered that there were no uniforms because:

It was the Depression, children were lucky to have clothes. Sometimes the nuns outfitted the children. [Each classroom had two grades.] You got a double education. You heard everything twice. Many children came out of St. James that were valedictorians of Sewickley High School. [Most walked home for lunch.] You had to be a special case to take lunch to school. Children needed the exercise. They worked off energy walking and were ready to sit still.

Running schools was an acceptable occupation for women at a time when few women worked. Sewickley had many such female entrepreneurs. Mrs. E. L. Mudie took over the school in St. Stephen's parish house in 1876. Miss Stevenson advertised in *Sewickley Valley*, September 17, 1898.

Miss Stevenson's kindergarten and primary school will reopen Monday, October 3 at her house on Frederick Avenue. The primary class will be conducted by a competent teacher.

Miss Ella Gordon Stuart conducted two schools, one in Oakland and one in Sewickley. The Sewickley school advertised in 1899.

Miss Stuart
College Preparatory School
126 Thorne Street
Sewickley, Pennsylvania.
A Suburban School. Boys and Girls prepared for the Leading Colleges
Academic Course for those not intending to enter college
Music and Art Departments
A few girls received into the house.
Miss Ella Gordon Stuart
City Address Fifth Avenue and Craig Street.[16]

The school remembered fondly by long-time Sewickley residents was Miss Jane's or, more formally, the Maple Cottage School on 334 Little Street. Mrs. Harriet Orndorff remembered, "It was a simply enchanting school. All kinds of flowers were on the blackboard. Miss Jane painted them with colored chalk." Miss Jane McDonald ran the school from 1892 to 1923, when she retired at age 84. The private school had only grades one through three, named the Dewdrops, the Sunbeams, and the Golden Sunbeams. Miss Jane was remembered as a kind but strict teacher. Her sister, Miss Margaret, was intimidating. Mariana Chapin remembered that Miss Margaret was very strict about spelling and arithmetic, and was always shouting, "But she gave us a good background." Others remembered her as being mean. Mrs. Nancy Chalfant: "Miss Jane was very nice, tall and skinny. Miss Margaret was awful. She was so mean, we all hated her." Captain Frederick Way, Jr. said,

She was loud, and to children that always sounds mean. She scared the daylights out of you. I think it was because she had been Sewickley's first telephone operator and had had to shout into the mouthpiece so she could be heard on the early equipment.[17]

Captain Way remembered Miss Jane's:

The first three grades were all in one room—delightful. You could listen to the other two classes, of course, so by the time you got to third grade, you knew pretty much what third graders should know. It didn't seem distracting to us. That's the way you went to school.

Miss Jane taught German at that age. That is the time to plant it in kids. We learned German songs; she spoke to us in German during German classes.

At a slightly later date, there were the two arch rivals, Miss Munson's and Miss Dickinson's. Mrs. Harriet Orndorff, who went to Miss Dickinson's, remembered how the rivalry developed.

Miss Munson's was very well established and a very fine school. Miss Munson hired Miss Dickinson to teach English. At the last minute, Miss Munson said she had to teach math. Miss Dickinson said she couldn't. She had never been any good at numbers. Miss Munson said your contract is canceled. Miss Dickinson started tutoring people.

In 1909, Miss Bertha Dickinson started a class in English and science in connection with the Sewickley Valley School of Music. In 1917, after becoming independent and moving several times, Miss Dickinson bought the house on

246 Broad Street that is the American Legion in 1998 and converted it into a school. An advertisement in the *Sewickley Herald,* 1920 explained the school's philosophy.

> At Miss Dickinson's children learn by doing. Education must arouse the interest of the child. At Miss Dickinson's, a child will learn through actually living through situations . . . in a happy atmosphere devoid of suppression.[18]

Mrs. Adelaide Ritchey went to Miss Dickinson's.

> Miss Dickinson's had mostly girls. There were only four boys. There were all women teachers. Madame Douteau taught us French. She was really French. She got us into college. Not too many of the ones I went to school with went to college. It was a "finishing school", literally.

Both Miss Dickinson's and Miss Munson's merged into Sewickley Academy in 1925.

Despite this wide choice of local schools, many students from wealthy families went to boarding school. Sewickley Academy only went through eighth grade because, after that, most students went away to school in the East. James Higgins, who went to Groton in 1929 when he was 13, remembered that all of his friends went away. "Your parents decided where to go to school. You had no say. I didn't know anyone at the high school. I had a group of 20 or so that I palled around with. Then later, when I could drive, with more [friends] from in town and Fox Chapel." Sending children to boarding schools was part of a more general trend among the Pittsburgh social elite studied by John Ingham in his "Steel City Aristocrats."

> The Pittsburgh social elite became less provincial and at least somewhat more cosmopolitan. . . . Families [sent] their children to eastern prep schools and colleges. Among the Pittsburgh iron and steel elite there was a decided shift away from local academies such as Sewickley and Shadyside, toward schools like the Episcopalian St. Paul's in Concord, New Hampshire.[19]

Sewickley offered a cornucopia of schools over the years, everything from the school that occupied extra rooms in a home to the grand curriculum of The Edgeworth Female Academy. Today only Sewickley Academy and the public schools remain.

---

[1] *Hays file.*

[2] *Revised Course of Study for the Sewickley Public School,* 1899 and *High School Course of Study,* 1912.

[3] Charles F. C. Arensberg, "The Pittsburgh Fire of 1845." In *Western Pennsylvania Historical Magazine,* March, 1945, v.28, p. 12.

[4] *Way file,* Agnes Way mss. "Three Edgeworth Schools," 1927.

[5] *Hays file.*

[6] Stanton C. Crawford and John A. Nietz, "Old Schools of the Ohio Valley." In *Western Pennsylvania Historical Magazine,* v.23, pp. 250-251.

[7] Edward Park Anderson, "The Intellectual Life of Pittsburgh, 1785-1836." In *Western Pennsylvania Historical Society Magazine,* v.14, 1931, pp. 18-19.

[8] F. Nevin, p. 27.

[9] Quoted by B. G. Shields in the *Sewickley Herald.*

[10] *Presbyterian Banner,* March 29, 1862.

[11] Brochure of Sewickley Academy, 1928.

[12] *First Catalogue of the Academy,* Year ending Jan. 29, 1866.

[13] Annie Clark Miller, *Chronicles of Pittsburgh and its Environs.* Pittsburgh, 1927 and letters in Sewickley Library from Mr. Olver to D. Shields.

[14] Eliza Leet Shields, "School Girls of 1850." In *Western Pennsylvania Historical Magazine,* v.13, Number 3, July 1930, pp. 182-188.

[15] Clipping from the *Sewickley Herald,* undated.

[16] *Blue Book.* Pittsburg, Kelly, 1899, p. xxiii.

[17] *Sewickley Magazine,* January, 1985, p. 12.

[18] *Sewickley Herald,* September 18, 1920, p. 18.

[19] John N. Ingham, "Steel City Aristocrats." In Samuel B. Hays, *City at the Point,* Pittsburgh, University Press, 1989, p. 281.

Chapter 18
The Sewickley Valley in the Early Twentieth Century

Changes in Government

The Sewickley area has been gradually divided into townships and boroughs as the different characters of its neighborhoods became established. The first was, of course, Sewickley Borough. Next came the borough of Osborne just up the river from Sewickley. When Osborne separated from Ohio Township in 1883, it was a different kind of neighborhood from the farming community in the hills. Osborne was a purely residential railroad suburb with comfortable homes set on large well-landscaped lots. It had no commercial center and only one through road, Beaver Road. It did have a railroad station from which many Osborne citizens commuted to work in Pittsburgh.

Osborne citizens petitioned the Court of Quarter Session to separate from Ohio Township in 1881. The Court directed that a grand jury look into the matter. Despite opposition from several large landowners, the grand jury recommended granting the petition. Osborne had only 30 residents and landowners in 1881. By 1900, the population was 500. It remains a tiny borough. Anyone driving west from Haysville on Beaver Road would not realize that he or she was passing through a separate borough.

The next neighborhood to form its own government was Edgeworth which separated in 1897. Like Osborne, it wanted to separate because its suburban character differed from its neighbor. An article in *The Pittsburgh Leader* July 31, 1904, states the problem.

> Edgeworth, the latest aspirant for borough honors, forms what is in all respects the western part of Sewickley. Together with Glen Osborne on the east, the three form one continuous residence center that for beauty, taste and desirability has not an equal in the Pittsburg district.

> For many months the people of the town debated and considered the question of forming a borough which will take in Quaker Valley, Edgeworth and Shields—from Sewickley to the Little Sewickley creek. From all accounts the majority seemed to be of the opinion that to incorporate was the proper thing. This, however, was not advocated for the main purpose of getting improvements, as is the case with most boroughs formed, for Edgeworth has already nearly all the improvements it could wish for. It was proposed simply because Leet township, of which Edgeworth forms a part, is becoming too diversified in its interests to be under a township government. In the township are two towns, Leetsdale and Edgeworth, both of very opposite character, one a high-class residence place and the other an industrial center. Leetsdale is demanding jails, police, and other things which Edgeworth does not need and does not feel called upon to pay for. Edgeworth citizens do not see why their taxes should be increased to pay for Leetsdale improvements. Police are not needed in Edgeworth and neither is a jail or lockup. There is a justice of the peace there, but he has little to do in trying cases of infractions of the law. . . . The feeling among businessmen in Edgeworth seems to be that the taxes will not be raised by incorporating as a borough for the good reason that there is nothing to increase the taxes for. The rate is now four mills. The town is completely provided with sewers, lights, macadamized streets, good sidewalks, and has water of a very pure quality. There is no need for police service. While there are no arc lamps on the streets there are plenty of gas lights. Many private places are illuminated by arcs, however, which tend to further dissipate the shade of the town.

The next important split from an existing township was Sewickley Heights Borough which separated from Sewickley Heights Township in 1935. Before the formal separation the large property owners which comprised the new borough already had formed the Sewickley Heights Protective Association. The Association hired its own police force of a dozen men, mostly former policemen. The petition to form a new borough was signed by 58 of the 78 residents. The petition to the Court of Quarter Sessions stated that the split was necessary to protect existing properties through zoning laws.

All of this centrifugal force that seemed to be affecting suburban communities was resisted by a centripetal force that made it necessary to work together. One issue requiring concerted effort was prevention of industrial development along the Ohio River. Residents feared that the river bottoms would become the site for large industry. In 1900 a group of wealthy citizens, Henry W. Oliver, James B. Oliver, and Richard R. Quay, attempted to buy riverfront property to preclude unsuitable development. They abandoned the project, thinking the asking price too high.

In 1912 the *Weekly Herald* published an article "Save the Sewickley Valley."

A narrow strip of land along the river front of the Sewickley district is a menace to twelve million dollars worth of homes. Are we so blind, narrow and inert that we will allow this evident damage to become a real injury to property? The greater part of this territory is occupied by attractive residences, trees and shrubbery. This beautiful country is menaced alone by the one strip of land along the river side of the district. . . . Regulation or control of the low-lying unoccupied land on the Sewickley side could be made the means of protection [for] all the residential property now extending northeastwardly from the river.[1]

Concerned citizens of Leetsdale, Edgeworth, Sewickley and Osborne formed the River Front Protection Committee to collect subscriptions from individuals to either buy the land along river or have it condemned for parks "in order to prevent the use of such lands for any purposes or in any manner detrimental to the surrounding neighborhood as a residential district." The *Herald* supported the Committee. "Everyone should contribute liberally. The success of the project will preserve forever Sewickley Valley as a beautiful home district; its failure will be ruinous, as the mills and factories are creeping closer and closer."[2] By March, 1913, the committee had received $200,000.

The Borough of Sewickley and The Committee of the Riverfront Protective Association contracted with the railroad to relocate the railroad tracks along the edge of the river and give up the current right of way for a new boulevard, now Ohio River Boulevard. The stated purpose was:

To provide for such control of lands along and near the Ohio River in the Boroughs of Edgeworth, Sewickley and Osborne as will be beneficial to the surrounding neighborhood as a residential district and as will prevent the use of such lands for purposes detrimental to the surrounding neighborhood as a residential district.[3]

The Committee is an interesting example both of communities working together and of individuals contributing money to effect a project normally undertaken by government.

Another force for pulling disparate communities together came from outside the Sewickley area: the attempts to form a metropolitan government. Sewickley managed to foil the first attempt in the 1890s, *Sewickley Valley Society* reported.

[To Sewickley] can truthfully be applied the term Queen of Suburbs, and certainly the most delightful residence spot in Western Pennsylvania. Its claims are such that a desperate effort has been quite recently made to include Sewickley in the ambitious scheme of a Greater Pittsburgh. This has been wisely abandoned. The village and the valley of Sewickley are too far from the city to be incorporated therein by the most pretentious (and grasping) scheme, and yet near enough to enable every Sewickleyan to reach his city office in from thirty to forty-five minutes after leaving his or her own door.[4]

Pressure for cooperation resurfaced 25 years later with the Metropolitan Plan promoted by the Greater Pittsburgh Movement which strove in the 1920s to form a federation of Allegheny County's 122 municipalities. There were two reasons to favor the plan. Pittsburgh promoters, led by the Chamber of Commerce, were incensed that their city was ranked eleventh in the nation by the U. S. Census Bureau although it would be ranked fourth if the entire metropolitan area were counted. In 1920 the population of Pittsburgh was 600,000; the population of the County was 1,185,000. A Chamber of Commerce official stated,

It is absolutely ridiculous that Pittsburgh, with so many boroughs closely connected to it, should be a city of the eleventh or twelfth rank. Here is an unbroken, continuous chain of connecting streets, a stretch of eight miles of built-up city and it is only right and proper that the boroughs should become a part of one big Pittsburgh. Our position as the fourth city in the United States will attract industry and create increased employment.[5]

Proponents argued that a greater Pittsburgh was needed to tackle problems common to the whole area such as city planning, transportation, sewage, recreation, and health. This type of problem could be handled better by one regional government than by 122 local governments. It was always emphasized that the local governments would continue to handle local affairs and that the metropolitan government would handle only expressly delegated matters. All residual powers remained on the local level.

One of the major arguments in favor of a limited federation was protection against outright annexation by Pittsburgh. This might seem far-fetched today, but in the early 1900s it was a real threat. Pittsburgh had absorbed what is now the South Side in 1872 through political chicanery. The state legislature had enacted a law in 1871 stating that a majority of the inhabitants of both jurisdictions involved must vote in favor of a merger. But in 1872 the legislators enacted a supplement to the law which was read three times without debate and swiftly enacted. The supplement stated simply that the South Side was annexed to Pittsburgh and made a part thereof. Similarly, in 1906 Pittsburgh had swallowed the City of Allegheny, now the North Side, despite Allegheny's strong opposition. In this case, the 1871 law was changed. Instead of requiring a majority in both jurisdictions, only a majority of the total vote was needed. Pittsburgh was a far larger city than Allegheny. The voters of Pittsburgh, who were largely in favor of aggrandizement, carried the day.

Since then the League of Boroughs and Townships had consistently defeated Pittsburgh's proposals to the state legislature to facilitate annexation. The League did favor the federated city authorized by the Metropolitan Plan because it guaranteed each local unit continued existence with its current boundaries.

In 1923, the mayor of Pittsburgh and the League of Boroughs and Townships agreed to establish a Metropolitan Commission. The Commission drafted an amendment to the state constitution authorizing consolidation. Supported by the Republican, Democratic, and Independent organization, the League of Women Voters, and the Chamber of Commerce, the amendment was ratified in November 1928. Having received authorization by this amendment, the Commission drafted a specific Metropolitan Charter which was submitted to the voters of Allegheny County in June 1929.

Sewickley, historically so anxious to preserve its individuality, was surprisingly receptive to a regional plan. A Sewickley resident, Charles A. Woods, was on the state commission to study consolidation. Most articles in the *Sewickley Herald* favored the Charter. "Throughout the conference the safeguarding of borough and township rights was a paramount consideration. The Metropolitan Commission is able to report that in the Charter now submitted not one particle of protection . . . was eliminated."[6]

Of course the guarantee against annexation was popular in Sewickley. The Metropolitan Commission took an advertisement in the *Herald* urging Sewickley to vote for the Charter.

> The fear of forcible annexation is forever allayed. . . . Not only are the rights of municipalities retained now under the charter but, by constitutional amendment effective only upon adoption of the charter, they are guaranteed for all time, and for the future. Forcible Annexation is Prevented.[7]

The Metropolitan Plan came very close to passing. Although the County as a whole voted two to one in favor, the Plan did not receive the required two-thirds vote in a majority of the governmental units. It did achieve a two-thirds majority in 47 municipalities, but not the 62 that were necessary. The vote was sufficiently close, however, that one political pundit observed that 374 additional votes, strategically distributed in key municipalities, would have reversed the result.[8]

Locally, only one district in Sewickley voted two-thirds in favor of federation. The *Herald* seemed disappointed in its readers:

> For the rest, it looks as if the stay-at-home vote, which might have been expected to show a broader knowledge and sympathy with the charter proposal than the voters who always take an interest in elections, had defeated the proposal through sheer indifference and failure to study the plan and record their conclusions at the polls.[9]

Some form of metropolitan government has been promoted often in Pittsburgh history. Never has it come so close to fruition. Had it been adopted in the 1920s, the fate of the region would certainly be different, whether better or worse is a matter for conjecture.

Sewickley Borough

The town of Sewickley was the focus for the whole area including the Heights, Osborne, and Edgeworth. Even common ways to refer to Sewickley Borough show its centrality. The town was not named in ordinary conversation. Instead, when going to the shopping district, you said, "I'm going up street," if you lived east of town. If you lived to the west, you said, "I'm going down street." People from the Heights merely said they were going to the village.

Of course the town was the site of the Sewickley Borough Municipal Building. This delightful structure, built in 1911, reflects the spirit of the time. Sewickley considered itself an important town, Pittsburgh's finest suburb. It needed an important town hall to express this pride. The building is a mixture of styles, its plain Georgian facade enlivened by a monumental staircase and a 55-foot ornate tower that was used for drying fire department hoses. The second floor had an apartment for the superintendent and a council room. The jail was in the basement. The fire department had a club room, a stable with four stalls and hay loft, and a wagon room. In it rested the "fine new chemical engine, a present from Mrs. Henry R. Rea in appreciation of services in saving her home." A *Sewickley Herald* reporter attended the opening.

Municipal Building. Post Card, 1910.
Courtesy The Sewickley Valley Historical Society.

Hauling cannon up Broad Street to Sewickley Cemetery, 1905.
Courtesy of The Sewickley Valley Historical Society.

[People] admired and praised everything. Burgess W. Kennedy Brown and Council members made everyone feel at home. . . . This tastefully modeled edifice will, in the simplicity of its dignity and beauty, grace the landscape and become a permanent feature of which the people of this town may well be proud.[10]

The village was the religious center where the great majority of worshippers gathered on Sunday. It was the center for education: the Sewickley High School and several private schools drew students from the whole area. The town was the employment center as well. Workers living in town supplied labor to the wealthy on their estates in Edgeworth, Osborne, and, especially, Sewickley Heights. Organizations like the YMCA, the American Legion, and the library drew people from the whole area.

Shopping

The town was the shopping center during the week. On Saturday night, if the weather was warm, Sewickley was the social center for many. The stores stayed open until 9:00 and people promenaded up and down the streets. "You met a lot of people on Saturday night," Joe Reiser said. The street as a place for socializing is an old Spanish custom. Small towns in Spain celebrate Saturday night with a paseo. Young and old dress up and walk back and forth along the main street, greeting acquaintances and chatting with friends. In Sewickley and the Spanish towns the street became an outdoor room with storefronts as walls. These walls were not bare, however, but were embellished with attractive window displays and doors welcoming shoppers. This is the antithesis of the suburban mall, where only car fanciers would want to wander down the rows of parked cars which inevitably sit in front of the stores.

Many stores and services were similar to the ones in the nineteenth century. Others catered to new needs. Sewickley stores and businesses were remarkably diverse. The merchants prided themselves on providing for most needs, and urged residents to buy locally. An article in the *Herald* in 1935 asked,

What will they do for you? If you buy wearing apparel, furniture, hardware, drugs, meats or groceries from out-of-town dealers do you think these out-of-town merchants will help pave the streets of your town or contribute money towards making your town a better place to live? You know they will not. When you buy your needs here, your money stays here.[11]

There were grocery stores scattered all over the town, within walking distance of all residents. Before World War II many households had only one car, so it was convenient to be able to walk to the store. The neighborhood grocers provided more than food. The shopper got a chance to visit with neighbors and chat with the store owner. This pleasant experience is rare in the modern super stores. Three generations of the Morgan family have managed Select Market as it grew from a fruit and vegetable store to a full service grocery. They knew the customers. Marshall Morgan, manager in 1997, said his father Israel "enjoyed every day of his business career, made many friends and cherished them all."[12]

Beaver St. looking east from Blackburn and Walnut, 1906. Note hitching posts instead of parking meters.

The *Sewickley Directory*, 1910 lists 11 grocers and four meat markets in Sewickley. Some of these were three A & P stores, Campney's, Mooney's, Select, Stevenson's, Rogroff's, Kramer's meat market, and Valenti's fruit and vegetable store. Eight groceries were clustered around Beaver Street. Small mom and pop stores served people who lived a few blocks away: Ague's on Straight Street near Hill Street and Grimes' on Blackburn Avenue.

The town was well supplied with other kinds of shops: three druggists, three dry goods stores, four cleaners and dyers, three florists, four hardware stores, three Chinese laundries, two shoe stores, and two ice plants. Allburgh's candy store was situated close to the school. Handy's Bicycles and Electric Store on 432 Beaver Street was where Joe Reiser and his friends stopped off every day after school to see what new train catalogs had come in.

Newspapers were delivered to an office across from Safran's. Boys picked them up and sold them on the street. Joe Reiser remembered, "You got a penny profit for the daily paper, two cents for Sunday. Sometimes you had a little cart, especially if you had a route. The *Press* furnished it."

Most of the stores in town supplied useful goods and services. Some sold a strange mixture of goods. In 1915, Miss Martha Nevin ran a shop on Broad and Beaver that sold valentines, linoleum, and curtains. In addition, Miss Nevin would cater cakes and sandwiches "served by an experienced maid." A few stores dealt in luxuries. Miss Nevin's business later became The Highway Shop on 504 Beaver Road, owned by the Misses Porter, who lived on Peebles Street. The Highway Shop had china, fancy yard goods, silk stockings, and gift items. Merchandise varied by the season. At Christmas, it carried French dolls, games and mechanical toys. For the Sewickley Horse Show, it offered place cards, ribbons, crops, and stocks. Another luxury store, The Specialty Shop on 502 Broad Street, sold "Everything to please the feminine taste, dainty negligees and lingeries, neckwear." The Bandbox sold dresses, hats and wraps. The Little Shop on 431 Broad Street sold hats for ladies.

Sloan's Pharmacy, 1938. Corner of Broad and Beaver Streets.
Courtesy Sewickley Library.

Broad and Beaver Streets 1998. Compare with previous photo.
Photo by John H. Demmler.

One luxury item was the New Victor Radio sold by W. J. Mullan on 420 Beaver Street. In 1929, he advertised the "Micro-synchronous radio" from $155 to $275.

The stores and services in town reflected changes in taste and technology. This is best shown in transportation innovations. In the early 1900s, horses were useful both for transport and for pleasure. In 1915 Sewickley had many businesses that were horse-related. There were three carriage shops, five livery and boarding stables and two blacksmith shops. Mr. Adam's blacksmith shop was near the corner of Division and Locust streets. Horses were boarded at Mr. Malone's stable on Blackburn Road. On McCready Way, across from the stable, Mr. Cannon had a riding school and livery stable. J. F. Malone had a feed store on 527 Blackburn Road. P. J. Monroney sold harnesses, whips, robes, and blankets.

Horse-related businesses were more prevalent than garages and automobiles in 1915, but the tables were turning. Cars had an increasing impact on retail sales growth both in Sewickley and Allegheny County. By 1929, there were 292 automobile dealers, 382 garages, and 527 filling stations in Allegheny County. These provided 14.6 percent of total retail sales in the county.[13] Sewickley participated fully in the boom. Some foresighted merchants shifted from horse- to car-related businesses as demand changed. After Birney Strange came to Sewickley in 1891, he opened a livery stable on Pine Street. About 1901, he gave up horses and carriages, moved to 439 Division Street, bought a Ford, and started a taxi service. Mrs. Hettie Anderson Richmond remembered that her father bought a stable on Broad and Centennial that had horses and carriages. He turned it into an automobile salesroom, Anderson Automobile Company. By 1929 car businesses included Sewickley Automobile (605 Beaver Road), the Bower Auto Company, Raymond Connelly, Valley Chevrolet, Witherspoon Brothers, John Herbst (batteries), Highway Service Station, and J. R. Jackson's garage.

Sewickley had seven contractors, taking advantage of the building boom in the early twentieth century. The largest was D.W. Challis. Richard McPherson, who worked for Challis from 1926 until his retirement, remembered:

> Steam was the most powerful thing you could get. Challis had a steam shovel, steam roller, steam paver. He had a water wagon to follow behind because steam [equipment] would run out of water. You had to fill up the boiler. Challis brought in blacks from Mississippi. They came to the railroad station and walked up to Challis' office. They were in [the] charge of Bruro Jones, an old colored preacher. They stayed in tents and went South in winter. Pay was four or five dollars a day. On payday he [Bruro Jones] got his cut. If anyone didn't do what he said, he would either send them home or not bring them up anymore.

Challis did work for Mrs. Rea. One year he had close to one hundred men working on her roads. We used to cover them with limestone chips every year. She had close to four miles of roads through her place.

Mr. Challis bought a steam roller in 1906. Its first big job was macadamizing the roads and making sidewalks, sewers, and curbs on the Oliver property on Meadow Lane and Beaver Road.

Challis Building.
Courtesy Sewickley Library.

Restaurants

There were several places to eat in town. Mr. Curcio had a restaurant between Safran's and the corner. The Butlers, a black family, owned Valley Catering, a successful soda fountain and catering service on the corner of Beaver and Division Streets.

There was a tea room on the second floor of the building on the corner of Beaver and Broad Streets (438 Beaver). Mrs. Halpin recalled, "It was run by two English women who served plain good home cooking. We called them the Hippity Hops because they were so slow."

Mrs. Andrew Black, a well-to-do woman, ran the Community Kitchen on Beaver Street and Little Street. It

Corner Broad and Beaver Streets.
Courtesy Sewickley Library.

Broad and Beaver Streets 1998. Compare with previous photo.
Photo by John H. Demmler.

might seem strange that a society lady would start a restaurant in 1920, well before the era of career wives. But it had a higher purpose. The Community Kitchen, as the name implies, was first organized to provide dinners for families in their homes to make the housewives' lives easier, according to an article in the *Sewickley Herald* when the Kitchen opened in 1920:

Cooked dishes will be delivered to the door in special returnable containers providing the main dish of the meal which the busy mother can easily supplement by a salad and a dessert also purchasable at the Kitchen. The quality of the food is the best that can be procured; and the price commensurate with the most modest income. This does not seem at first glance to be true; but if a prospective customer takes a pencil and paper and honestly calculates the saving in wages, gas, electric light, waste, board and lodging [for the cook], then adds costs of materials, the price of a cooked dinner becomes a positive economy.[14]

The Community Kitchen was a success. Mrs. Charles Butler worked there after she finished school. She remembered that it served lunch and tea and ran a flourishing catering service. Its original high purpose had faded, but the store thrived.

Liquor

In addition to restaurants for the hungry there were places to quench a thirst, legally or not. Even before the start of Prohibition in 1920, liquor sales were banned. Speakeasies in Sewickley, however, operated outside the law and are not well documented. The official police report for 1925 recorded 17 speakeasy arrests, 21 gambling arrests, and 6 for disorderly houses.[15] In addition, hearsay abounds. There was one speakeasy on Broad Street, where a parking lot is now; one near Sickler's across from the Pittsburgh National Bank parking lot; two on McCready Way; and two on Dickson Road. Often a restaurant had a speakeasy in back. Miss Mattie's Tea Room, 515 Pryor Way, served more than plain tea. Miss Mattie was charged with operating a disorderly house when police found "three men engaged in a card game with 25 cents in the pot and . . . a gallon of grain alcohol gurgling out under the bed."[16]

Some of liquor sold in the speakeasies came from stills in the hills behind town. *The Herald* reported on January 29, 1928 that several stills were confiscated and large quantities of mash destroyed in a raid. At times, the product of the stills did not make it down the hill. Mrs. Jane Evans remembered going to a speakeasy almost at the top of Camp Meeting Road. An article in 1919 reports:

Complaints [have been made] for some time of a good many hilarious and irresponsible gentlemen, mostly of the colored persuasion, enlivening the Blackburn Road with their presence in the evening hours. Last Sunday raids were made on two residences on Quarry Hill, high above the Blackburn auto-artery. Two householders and a dozen or so customers [were arrested] for selling liquor without a license and selling on Sunday.[17]

Some whiskey, on the other hand, came from far away. Bert Miller ran a grocery store in Haysville. He supplemented his income by taking "fishing trips" to Canada in his 1925 red Buick touring car. It turned out that Mr. Miller was fishing for good Canadian whiskey, which fetched high prices in Sewickley Heights.[18]

Beaver Street, Sewickley 1909. Note the unpaved street.
First National Bank is next to striped awnings.
Courtesy The Sewickley Valley Historical Society.

Jane Evans remembered another bootlegger. "He sold kegs of grape juice, then he sent his serviceman around and added something to make it turn hard. They would come and doctor it."

The bootleggers and speakeasies seem like amusing anecdotes, but they had serious consequences because they were sources of income and power for the Mafia. Bruno Toia recalled:

They had the Mafia in those days, 1931, '32, and '33. It was terrible here in Sewickley. You would never believe that this went on in a nice town like Sewickley. Things like that just didn't happen—but they did happen.

I had two older brothers. One was killed by the Mafia here in Sewickley. My brother was 24 years old, married six months. They ambushed him up on Division Street. It was Prohibition, and he had a restaurant. He was selling moonshine and he wasn't buying it off the right people. So they got rid of him. That's what happened to a lot of families here in Sewickley. Mr. Sgro was killed in front of Tucci's store on Nevin Avenue in broad daylight. Mr. Sacco was killed in '31 up at the cemetery.

The police wouldn't do anything about it. As long as the Italians were killing each other, why worry about it? The police department was bought. On Dickson Road the cops used to come up and get their booze. Free. Two or three times a day they came up on their motorcycles. They knew where to go—which houses. If there was a raid, they would get tipped off before. We knew this; we saw it every day.

It was so bad. When they [the Mafia] wanted money, they came up and said to you, "I want five dollars." And you gave it to them or else—even if you weren't involved. It was a collection. Now, there were always some like my father-in-law. They came up to him up at the house and asked him for five dollars. They came part way up the steps. He got a shotgun and he says, "You get down off my steps and don't come back because I don't have money to give you!" Now, he was brave; everybody wouldn't do a thing like that.

Of course there was support for Prohibition. The Reverend Alleyne Howell of St. Stephen's Church noted in his diary on March 19, 1912. "Miss Dippold, teetotaler, called and scolded me for calling on Gundelfinger's [wine merchants]." Reverend Howell did promote sobriety. His church sponsored a temperance speaker on February 8, 1920:

Reverend Jarvis of Church Temperance Society said at St. Stephen's, "The efficiency of workmen has been increased 200 per cent now that liquor cannot be bought."

In 1932, Miss Norma Brown and Mr. James Crain of the Flying Squadron Foundation landed in Sewickley to fan the movement. They spoke to members of the Baptist, Methodist, Presbyterian, and Episcopal churches, urging them to vote for dry candidates to all public offices.[19]

Services

In addition to shops for buying goods and restaurants for food and drink, the 1910 *Sewickley Directory* lists many useful services. Often these came from people working at home. There were five music teachers and four plumbers. Health services came from two veterinarians, (including an X-ray specialist,) three osteopaths, and 16 doctors. Midwives often delivered babies at home. Two sisters, Miss Brown and Mrs. Jackson, delivered almost all the babies of the Italian community.

Many services were delivered to the door. Miss Anne Stolzenbach remembered:

Farmers came every Saturday door to door. Large department stores such as Kaufmann's and Boggs and Buhl delivered. They kept beautiful horses in Sewickley. They shipped the stuff by train and delivered all around the town with a horse and van. They delivered all around the hills, too; they would deliver a handkerchief. And they didn't charge for delivery.

Most of the local stores let their customers charge. Mrs. Josephine Herbst Sybo stopped every day after school at Mooney's store on Beaver between Broad and Division Streets. She telephoned her mother to see what groceries she needed. She charged the purchases. "We didn't carry cash. If a store didn't have charge accounts, it didn't stay in business." Charge accounts were convenient for the customer but a headache for merchants. They could not just refuse to sell to people who did not pay because they wanted to keep the business. Mrs. Sybo remembered her father's problems at his gas station.

> People would charge and not pay for six months. He [her father] had to pay for the gas before they put it in the ground. I remember my dad coming home and saying, "If we don't get some money soon, I don't know what we will do." Mother said, "You better get on the phone." The little guy in Sewickley was at the bottom of the list [to be paid].

First National Bank. Broad and Beaver.

Most shopping could be conveniently accomplished in Sewickley. Some people, however went to Pittsburgh. Mrs. Margaret Halpin's father was the stationmaster at Osborne. She remembered:

> People in Osborne did shopping in Pittsburgh. I remember the horses took the women to the station—most of the men walked. The women went to the Allegheny Market—it was a wonderful market—and had things sent down on the train in the baggage in big high-topped baskets. Each woman had her own basket. The horses came to pick them up. I remember when the first car came to pick up the groceries!

The corner of Beaver and Broad Streets in 1938.
Photo by Harry Reno.

Mrs. Orndorff recalled that her mother ordered groceries at the Allegheny Market, just across from the old Fort Wayne Station on the North Side.

> Mother went to Campney's for most things but there was this idea that you got more choice up there. People would order baskets of food and it would come down on the train. People could send their horses and buggies down to pick up the baskets at the railroad station. Mother used to get 12 pounds of butter every week from one market in Allegheny. She called on the phone. The clerks in all the stores knew just what she liked. The clerks at the department stores, Boggs and Buhl and Horne's, would call Mother and tell her they were having special sales.

Until about 1900 most women and children had their clothes sewn at home. The 1910 *Directory* lists 25 dressmakers in Sewickley and Sewickley Heights. This seems like a large number, but most clothes for women and children were made by dressmakers who came to the house. Mrs. Orndorff recalled: "We had our clothes sewed here. You didn't buy ready-made clothes." A couple of decades later, many went to Pittsburgh to buy ready-made clothes. Mrs. Richmond said, "There were no dress stores in Sewickley. It was so easy to get back and forth to Pittsburgh. Boggs and Buhl was a wonderful store, right up the street from the station. We went mostly just to Boggs and Buhl." Oliver Ward looked forward to expeditions to Pittsburgh. "We usually caught the train. Mother bought her clothes at Boggs and Buhl, then, walked across the river to Gimbel's and Kaufmann's; those are the three stores she used to go to. Then we went to the movies at the Stanley Theater."

Post Office and Sewickley Valley Trust Building, 1907.
Courtesy Sewickley Valley Historical Society.

Post Office. Built 1910.
Courtesy Sewickley Valley Historical Society.

Mrs. Susan Maze, a Sewickley resident, worked at Joseph Horne's for 30 years. Sewickley customers asked for her personally when they came to buy suits or dresses. She offered extraordinary service. "I would walk up to Sewickley Heights with my samples and Mrs. B.F. Jones was always the nicest. She'd tell me to sit and rest before showing her my dresses."[20]

Nancy Chalfant remembered shopping even farther afield:

Mother didn't particularly like the Pittsburgh department stores. I don't know why. Best's, dePinna's, Lord and Taylor's and a couple of shoe companies came to the William Penn. We went to Pittsburgh and went to one of the bedrooms of the hotel and they had all the clothes laid out. It was kind of fun. I did the same with Henry and Ann [her children.] We used to go to New York quite often on the "Pittsburgher," the overnight train. We shopped and went to the theater. Coming home, we always had to leave the theater a little bit early to catch the "Pittsburgher."

Sewickley in the first half of the twentieth century offered most necessities, many luxuries, and all services to its residents. Someone living near the town would have seldom needed to venture farther to buy anything desired. Stores were owned and operated by local people, not divisions of larger companies. Long-term customer satisfaction was required to stay in business.

[1] *Weekly Herald*, Nov. 2, 1912, p. 5.

[2] Ibid.

[3] Borough of Sewickley. Ordinance No. 461.

[4] *Sewickley Valley Society*, 1895, p. 13.

[5] *Sun*, July 21, 1920.

[6] *Sewickley Herald*, May 31, 1929, p. 14.

[7] Ibid., June 21, 1929, p. 14.

[8] Joseph T. Miller. "Pittsburgh Consolidation Charter." In *National Municipal Review*, October 1929, p. 604.

[9] *Sewickley Herald*, June 28, 1929, p. 4.

[10] Ibid., March 21, and 26, 1910, p. 2.

[11] *Herald*, July 5, 1935, p. 2.

[12] Ibid., Sept. 25, 1996, p. 1.

[13] Tarr, p. 40.

[14] *Sewickley Herald*, April 3, 1920, p. 5.

[15] *Sewickley Municipal Review*, 1926.

[16] *Sewickley Herald*, February 1, 1935, p. 12.

[17] Ibid., January 25, 1919, p. 14.

[18] Unpublished mss. by James Shaughnessy, 1985.

[19] *Sewickley Herald*, Oct. 21, 1932.

[20] Ibid., June 17, 1992, p. A12.

Chapter 19
New Transportation for a New Century:
Trolleys, Airplanes, and Automobiles

Sewickley's success was based on its connection with transportation: first, its access to the river and the Beaver Road and, later, its access to the railroad. In the years around 1900 new forms of transportation developed. Two were welcomed: the airplane and the automobile. The other, the streetcar, provoked controversy. Why did Sewickley, which had heretofore been in the forefront of changes in transportation, resist one of the latest developments?

Sewickley prided itself on being a railroad suburb. Railroads had an advantage over streetcars. According to a quote from *Sewickley Valley Society* in 1895, a passenger on the railroad did not get "tramped on, sworn at, abused in every way possible besides being made to pay for a seat he never obtains." Moreover, the railroad fares were sufficiently high to enable only well-to-do members of society to live in suburbs like Sewickley. Streetcars were less acceptable to the upper classes. Fares were low, enabling the lower middle class and even members of the working class to aspire to life in the suburbs. Railroad suburbs like Sewickley and Oakmont grew piecemeal as individuals decided to develop their property. Streetcar suburbs were often developed all at once as real-estate investments, with small lots and small houses to maximize profits. Such suburbs, it seems, were suitable for less affluent residents.

Imagine the chagrin when on two separate occasions streetcars were proposed for Sewickley. In 1895, two groups sought a franchise for the trolley. Neither route would have traversed the main streets of town, Beaver and Broad. The Ohio Valley Electric Company proposed a single track from Haysville up Beaver to Boundary, to Centennial, and down Centennial to Academy. The Coraopolis, Sewickley and Economy Electric Railway route would have gone from Beaver to Boundary to Thorn, down Thorn to Academy, and then on to Economy via the Beaver Road.

Not everyone was opposed to streetcars. They appealed to local working men, faced with unemployment as the building boom temporarily faded in the valley. When the streetcar proposal came before the borough council, according to an eyewitness, "several attorneys sprang up with remonstrances and our fellow townsman, William Dickson, fought the objectors [to the streetcar] and their attorneys single-handed. But how could one person withstand well-trained lawyers: and so some could ride undisturbed [on the train] while others took a ride on foot."[1] After much controversy, the streetcar was rejected in 1897.

Some citizens retained a sense of humor about the battle. One resident of Academy Avenue bought a streetcar for his children's playhouse. He took it to the end of the line in Bellevue, then had it hauled down Beaver Road when the surface was hard and dry. A team of four big black horses provided the power. The Sewickley Brass Band played inside the car while, on top, 12 young men fired rockets. Signs on the side lampooned local businesses. "Don't go elsewhere to be robbed. Go to Kreps." "Why is Walker's store like home? Because it is the dearest place on earth."

Alden P. Hayes Ice Wagon, 1900.
Courtesy The Sewickley Valley Historical Society.

The streetcar question resurfaced in 1904, just in time for reports in the first issue of the *Sewickley Herald* on September 19, 1903. This serendipitous juxtaposition gave to the *Herald* a burning issue to boost sales and, to the historian, a wonderful sample of public opinion. The problem was stated in the first issue.

An issue of the greatest importance awaits the decision of the people of Sewickley. The question is whether the tradition and usages of two or three generations shall give way to the onward march of progress. Whether the hand of the iconoclast shall shatter the idols of a century past. The mere thought is enough to cause a feeling of horror to enter the hearts of some of our staid and peaceloving citizens.

As we have stated elsewhere, Sewickley is a beautiful rural retreat, free from the dust and smoke and din of the mill and factory, with naught to disturb its peace and serenity save the rattle of the cart-wheel, the chug-chug of the automobile or the whistle of the passing train.

But the scene changes. The evermoving car of progress has stopped at our door demanding admittance. In other words, the right to run electric trolley cars through this place has been asked of our people through their representatives in council. Having the charter in their possession, the owners are desirous of securing the right of way and arranging for the opening of traffic.

Interviews with citizens on both sides followed over a period of months. Some were in favor of the streetcar. Workingmen said, "There ain't enough work for us in Sewickley. We need to go other places." "I would favor streetcars on Beaver Street rather than debar them for women's and children's sake, or put a wire fence around Sewickley" Another vote in favor came from "a tradesman, whose work was scattered throughout the different towns near here, [who] complained that he was under the necessity of rising very early in order to get a train that would stop at the smaller station where his work is located; and also that he had to stop work early in the afternoon so that he could get a train home."[2]

Still another opinion came from "a gentleman who is a property owner and business man, and who is usually well versed in municipal matters."

While I am personally not greatly in favor of the incoming of a street car line, yet I believe it is inevitable. In the first place, this town is growing rapidly; and in the second place, in a year or so there will be a town of ten or fifteen thousand inhabitants between Leetsdale and Ambridge. These places will become overcrowded and the surplus will have to come eastward and a demand will be made for a more rapid and convenient mode of transportation. Already some of the citizens from the valley below us are clamoring for rapid transit service. We must look at the interest of all the people. If I believed the people here really wanted a trolley line I would certainly favor it.[3]

Others argued that progress was inevitable. "I have always been in favor of streetcars here. They are a necessity. The progress of events will soon compel their admission. Look at the way in which Ambridge and the country surrounding it are growing. The people who are connected with it cannot all live there; there will not be room for them. Some of them will have to come this way. The streetcar is bound to come."

Some were not violently opposed, but thought the proposal would not pass. "The streetcar is no more inevitable than it was ten years ago. Why, the question had been agitated for years, and I don't believe it is nearer a solution now than when it started. Some years ago Richard Quay and some others got a charter and tried to get a franchise through Sewickley and failed. If they could not get one, how do you suppose any one else could?"[4]

Opponents offered various opinions:

Yes, I am much opposed to the streetcar in Sewickley. This is a residential town. We want it left so. . . . Beaver Street is too narrow for street cars along with automobiles and carriages. I would not feel my children were safe.

No, I do not want the street cars. What do we want them for anyhow? They would be of no use to us at this distance from the city. Even if they run a through service it could not compete with the railroad lines. And if they sold tickets as low as three for twenty-five cents, the difference would not be worth wasting time on. . . . As I said before, I am against its coming into this place. I have lived here a good many years, am owner of considerable property, and do not desire to have anything come in here that will be a detriment to the town. We have several good streets and driveways and why do we want street cars to spoil all this?

Would you like to have your rest disturbed by [street]cars passing any hour of the night? Another feature of the matter is this: Sewickley has been a quiet and orderly town. It is a pleasant place to retire from the cares of business and the heat and rush of the city. If we allow the [street]cars to come here we will have undesirable elements here from the manufacturing centers below this, which we do not want; we will also have an influx of Sabbath desecration.[5]

One resident feared that if the streetcar came, "Sewickley will not be the restful homelike place of yore but just like other towns—sans comfort, sans quiet, sans rest. There is nothing that a rich man hates as much as a trolley line near his house."

The opponents won. In June 1904, Sewickley council voted against the trolley, unanimously.

The Great Trolley Battle shows two opposing views of what kind of town Sewickley should be. One faction, composed of the working class and the small businessmen, sought growth. Ambridge was growing mightily; why should Sewickley stagnate? The other group, especially the commuters, wanted Sewickley to remain a quiet, residential suburb. The battle would rage in other towns again and again as suburbanites fought developers they feared would destroy their special retreats. Edgeworth, just west of Sewickley is a case in point, according to The *Pittsburgh Leader* July 31, 1904:

> Many newcomers are seeking homes in Edgeworth and Sewickley, people who wish to get away from the dust and turmoil of the city and from street cars and enjoy a little idyllic peace that is so hard to find in this rushing world. Like Sewickley, Edgeworth is firm in its determination to keep street cars out, for the people say the cars interfere with the fine driving and are dangerous for children. This may be all right for people who are in their coaches and carriages or their autos, but to pedestrians with children the idea gains ground that autos and carriages discount trolley cars every time as danger-producers.

The railroad emerged as the only form of public transportation until the advent of buses.

Airplanes

A proposal for an airport near Sewickley today would provoke immediate wrath. The noise pollution of airplanes landing and taking off is well known. Around 1920, however, two communities around Pittsburgh were delighted to have airports: in Fox Chapel there was Rodgers Field and, near Sewickley, the Pittsburgh Landing Field. The Sewickley airport was actually in Leetsdale, just below Little Sewickley Creek between the river and the railroad. Here was a level area 2,000 feet square, easily accessible to the railroad. The property was controlled by the River Front Protection Association, which leased it for ten years to the Johnston Aviation Company because they considered an air field "unobjectionable." The Aviation Company was founded by two men who met in France during World War I, where they had a chance to see the potential of airplanes. Captain Archibald Johnston, president, had flown with the Lafayette Escadrille. His friend, W. C. Stevenson, vice president and treasurer, from Lark Inn, Beaver Road, was in the ambulance corps.

Captain Johnston arranged for six former instructors of the American service to be pilots at the new field. He started negotiations to make the field a stop on the transcontinental air route and the airmail route. He planned to sell planes for business or pleasure. Because airplanes were a novelty in 1920, the airfield would have planes and pilots ready to take passengers for short flights.

The Pittsburgh Landing Field opened to great hoopla April 24, 1920, according to the *Sewickley Herald*.

> It has a cinder road for the entrance of automobiles and about 50 cars were parked there on Saturday afternoon at a time, those that departed being quickly replaced by late arrivals. The landing field was roped off and hundreds of people massed back of the rope, straining forward for a better view.

> George A. Hays of Sewickley had been the first passenger to go up, having taken the ride to Pittsburgh and back Saturday morning. George Snowden was the first passenger in the afternoon, staying up about 15 minutes and going through a "retournement" or "turning on the wing" that looked rather exciting from the ground.[6]

The same day the airport opened, it closed. A railroad strike held up delivery of necessary supplies and equipment. The field was back in operation by October 1920. The Company's aerial photographer, W. L. Scott, was employed to make a complete map of Sewickley. On October 9 it celebrated Air Stunt Day. Two celebrated fliers, J. C. (Loop King) Hall and A. J. (Fearless) Bohanon performed.[7]

The airport, fortunately for residents of the valley, was not successful. In 1930 there were three small airfields in the Pittsburgh area: Bettis in McKeesport; Mayer in Bridgeville; and Rodgers in Fox Chapel. There is no mention of the Leetsdale field.

The Sewickley Bridge

The next transportation innovation was not a means, such as airplane, car, or trolley, but a facilitator. The Beaver Road had provided roughly east-west access from Sewickley to Pittsburgh since the Revolution. But north-south routes were interrupted by the Ohio River. There was no bridge across the river between Pittsburgh and Wheeling, West Virginia. Trade with towns on the other side of the Ohio was difficult. Two ferries alleviated the problem, but they were seasonal. In winter, the ice stopped service and in rainy periods, the river was too high for safe service. Jacob Lashell

168

and William Stoops owned 3,000 feet of river front on the opposite side of the river from Sewickley. Lashell started a ferry service from the foot of Chestnut Street in Sewickley sometime after 1847, when he bought his land. He was followed by Stoops, whose service from Ferry Street began after his purchase of the land in 1869. *Hayes Atlas* of 1877 has an advertisement for Stoops.

> Proprietor of Steam Ferry Boat.
> W. Stoops. Proprietor and owner of steam ferry "Jefferson."
> Also dealer in family groceries.
> Narrows Run. Opposite Sewickley.

Both men ran the ferry service as a sideline to other river careers. Jacob Lashell was a mate on steamboats and had a flatboat business, loading his flatboats with farm products from Neville Island. He floated down the Ohio and Mississippi Rivers to New Orleans where he sold the produce and the lumber from the dismantled flatboats. William Stoops was a river captain and owned the sawmill on the river at Ferry Street.[8]

A bridge would be a better way to cross the river in all seasons. Gilbert Hays called a meeting to consider a bridge in 1894. Committees were formed and meetings held that winter. The group petitioned the Court of Common Pleas, Sewickley's own J. W. F. White presiding. A board of viewers came to inspect the proposed bridge site, but decided against the bridge because, "only a small section of the county would benefit."

The issue was reopened in 1906, when a new committee presented a new petition. The members of the Bridge Committee agreed to contribute towards a

SEWICKLEY-CORAOPOLIS BRIDGE CELEBRATION

SEPT. 19-20 1911

Audley Nicols

Sewickley Bridge. Artist's conception by Audley Dean Nicols.
Courtesy of The Sewickley Valley Historical Society.

bond for the county to use to settle suits of disgruntled expropriated property owners. Joseph Craig signed up for $2,800; George Hegner, $50; James Gray, $25; J. J. Brooks, $300; and Dr. R. J. Murray, $100.

The old stagecoach in the Sewickley Bridge Parade. The two Misses Dippold representing Sewickley.
Courtesy The Sewickley Valley Historical Society.

This time the viewers gave a favorable report. The Grand Jury appointed to hear the case agreed. On July 21, 1909, the first sod was turned. The opening of the bridge on September 18-23, 1911, was a grand occasion, remembered fondly by all who attended, and widely reported in the Pittsburgh papers. It even inspired an anonymous poet:

Straight across the old Ohio
We have stretched a band of steel
And it needs a lot of racket
To express just how we feel.
Let the halls take up the echo.
Let the day reflect the light
Of the rockets and the fire-play
For at last we've won the fight.
Roll ye muddy, muddy river.
Your supremacy is gone.
Bank to bank our hands are joined
And our thriving towns are one.

The celebration continued for three days, with fireworks every night. There were various sports activities: a baseball game between Sewickley and Coraopolis, a pony show, and aquatic events in the Ohio River. Other events included a twelve-mile parade through the streets of Sewickley, over the bridge, and through Coraopolis. The streets of both towns were decorated with bunting and illuminated by 5,000 electric lights. Six bands furnished the music. Leading the parade was one of the town's oldest and favorite citizens, Captain John Anderson, riding in a carriage, and followed by a Conestoga wagon pulled by a six-horse team and a four-horse stagecoach. There were several historical floats; one depicted Queen Aliquippa seated at the opening of her tent with Sewickley's mascot Indian, Scarouady, in a canoe beside her. Indians appeared also in a performance of "Hiawatha" and in the wonderfully anachronistic Audley Nichols picture of the bridge opening, where Chief Scarroyaddy and two of his scouts gaze at Sewickley from the hill on the Coraopolis side of the bridge.

The Amusement Committee organized a side show and carnival with balloonists and high divers. In a high-wire act on Broad and Beaver Street a performer did head stands and pretended to go to bed on a high wire. Perhaps the most astonishing act was one Mlle. Oneida who, while hanging by her teeth, performed a one thousand foot "slide for life" from the tower of the bridge 300 feet above the river. Captain Frederick Way, Jr. remembered: "I was ten years old. They had a wire cable stretched from the pinnacle. A girl with gauze wings held onto a pulley with her teeth. She spread out her arms and sailed from the pinnacle clear down. Everyone cheered."

Automobiles

The trolley, the airport, and the new bridge lent temporary excitement to the Sewickley scene. More lasting changes were effected by the automobile. Starting as a toy for the rich, it quickly swept the country. The 1901 volume of the magazine *Index of Pittsburgh Life* featured a column called "Automobilia." One issue had a picture of two young men chatting. "I hear there's a new disease in Pittsburgh." "Is that so? What is it called?" "Automobilemania." The disease produced a fever of poetry in at least one case.

Daimler
Owned by H.C. Frick

Oh, I am an Auto-mobil-ist,
 And I sail the bounding pike.
I give my high-geared wheel a twist
 And I go wherever I like.
I bound along o'er the country roads,
 Past fresh green fields and farms.
And with what joy my heart explodes
As I breast the thank-you-marms!

So its Ho for my trusty Automobile,
 And Hi for the bounding pike.
Let others rave over the horse and wheel—
 The tame and the arduous bike.
Let others rave over the brigantine
 That plies through the realm of the conch,
It's I for the car of gasoline
 With its glorious Honk-honk-honk!

By John Kendrick Bangs

Columbia Electric
Sketches from "Automobiliousness."
See footnote 10.

The first cars were used for fun and adventure. The *Brooklyn Eagle* described automobiling as "the last call of the wild" and the "world's most exciting sport."[9] Serious travel for business was still by public transportation. In Pittsburgh the opening of Grant Boulevard, now Bigelow Boulevard, in 1901 gave owners the chance to show off their vehicles. Intrepid drivers completed daring tours around town. Mr. George Banker, for example, with two passengers took his De Dion runabout on an all night expedition which was described in the "Automobilia" column.

> He left Centre and Highland Avenues at eleven thirty when the streets were clear of traffic. Without once stopping the motor, he drove west on Grant Boulevard, crossed the bridge to Allegheny, climbed the Perrysville Avenue Hill, returned to Pittsburgh, drove to Wilmerding over rough roads and high hills, came back to the East End by McKeesport, and was back in his theater [garage] by seven thirty Tuesday morning. During his eight-hour run his average speed was thirty-nine miles an hour."[10]

Sewickley residents, always up-to-date, soon caught the automobile bug. By 1899, there were three cars in the valley: Percy Stowe and Charles McVay had White Steamers and G. H. Sipe, a Winton Steamer. Cars were shipped by steamboat, and put off at the Sewickley landing where admiring eyes could inspect them. Captain Way said: "If you heard an automobile coming, you would run out to see it. This was an event." People remember clearly who owned what kind of car. Mrs. Adelaide Ritchey recalled: "Mr. Semple bought a beautiful yellow Marmion and that was so exciting. We all were thrilled to get a ride in it." Anne Stolzenbach said:

I remember when cars first came to Sewickley. The horses used to rear up; it was very exciting. Father used to look down from our porch at the intersection of Thorn and Little [and exclaim], "They're going 20 miles per hour!" They were speeding.

A car buyer had to decide what kind of car to buy: not Ford or Chevrolet, but electric, steam, or "explosive motor" (internal combustion.) The latter soon became the most popular. By 1905, there were 53 cars in the Valley, 39 were explosive motor, three were steam, and 11 were electric. The problem with internal combustion was its noise, as reported in *The Herald*:

> The first automobile of this type in the Valley was a DeDion & Bewton Motorette owned by Mr. Percy V. Stowe of Edgeworth. It was built quite low, with a single-cylinder, horizontal, high speed motor. A great storm of angry remarks and strong language was showered on the owner on account of the noise the machine made (it was quiet in comparison to some that run the streets now) and he reluctantly disposed of it to purchase a steamer.[11]

Locomobile

Many of the early cars were electric, considered especially suitable for ladies. The "Automobilia" column advised:

> The women who drive find the gas machine too noisy and fear the the steam machine might blow up. Both are too hard to handle and take considerable strength in cranking. But they are quick to grasp the principles involved in the operation of the electric and consider it the perfect automobile for shopping, paying social calls, sightseeing in the park and on the Boulevard and for an occasional venturous drive through the suburbs.[12]

The *Herald*, too, advised electric for ladies in its column, "Automobiling in the Sewickley Valley."

> The electric is now beginning to receive some of the attention it deserves and will no doubt be extremely popular with the ladies on account of its easy operation, simplicity, and freedom from noise and dirt. It should be stated very clearly, however, that the electric machine in its present state of development will never displace or even supplement the explosive motor machine in touring. The capacity of storage batteries limits the trips to some fifty miles after which it becomes a "dead horse." Power stations on a country road are hard to find, and, as the newsboy says, "Git a horse, mister" is the only thing to do when the power becomes exhausted.[13]

Early advertisements and newspaper articles show a striking variety of automobiles. The 53 machines in the Valley in 1905 represented 20 different makes. By 1950, 2,000 different models of cars had been put on the market in the United States.

The first automobile dealer in the Valley was the Edgeworth Machine Company, run by D. C. and R. L. Anderson. In 1899 it was located on the Edgeworth Water property near the river. Gasoline was stored nearby on the Gibbs property. The Andersons handled several makes over the years: the Waverly Electric; the Babcock Electric; the Franklin Olds; and the Packard Pope-Toledo. The garage moved in 1905 to a new facility on Meadow Lane, behind the Anderson's house. After a fire in 1910 which destroyed 11 cars and 2 motorcycles, the Andersons bought property for a new building on Centennial and Broad Street in Sewickley.[14] Here they established a complete automobile service, according to a 1912 advertisement.

> Automobile Painting, Repairing, Trimming, Upholstering, Slip Covers, etc. Storage, Supplies, etc.
> Open day and night. Cars for hire by the hour only.[15]

Other automobile dealers soon opened. The Sewickley Auto Company, on the corner of Beaver and Chestnut Streets, sold White, Hupmobile, Mitchell, Ford and Waverly Electric cars. The Auto Service Company on Green Street offered Packards and Oaklands.

New car buyers often had to learn to drive. Raymond Connelly, who sold Dodges and Packards, said he did not have to worry about trade-ins because his customers often had no car to trade.

> But we had to teach them how to drive, and we did that. I would send to Harrisburg for them to get them a license. I delivered a Jordan to a wealthy man in Edgeworth. I took him around the park—it wasn't developed then. It had sharp corners, round corners. I took him the easy way at first. It was the first car he ever had.

Drivers were responsible for minor repairs. Captain Way recalled:

Herbst Tire and Battery Service, 1922. "Dependable Service 2U." Courtesy The Sewickley Valley Historical Society.

Uncle Will had a Packard. When the tire blew out, you thought the end of the world had come. It had six or eight pounds of air and when one [tire] let go, it sounded like a revolver. Trucks and delivery wagons had solid tires, but most passenger cars had pneumatic tires. Each car was furnished with a hand pump. You had to make many repairs. Every car had a box of patches to fix your own inner tube.

Lieutenant Masters of the Sewickley Heights Police Force remembered, "One time, we did have a flat tire. My mother gets out, jacks the car up, takes the tire off, gets the tube out, patches the tube, puts the tire back on, and off we go. If you had a problem, you took care of it yourself."

Repairs beyond the do-it-yourself skills of many motorists were handled by a new kind of commercial establishment, the service station. In 1922, John Herbst opened the first gasoline service station in Sewickley on 410 Walnut Street. Mrs. Josephine Herbst Sybo, his daughter, remembered:

He came from out of town. He was a farm boy, but his older brother got the farm. He looked around for service stations, which were very rare in those days, and found one in Sewickley.

He [my father] went to Westinghouse to battery school. In those days, you didn't get a battery off the shelf. It had to be made. We still have some of the original molds. He knew how to make a tire, but we didn't have the molds. He did recapping. They take most of the rubber off, put cement on, put new rubber on, and put it back in the mold. My father prepared them and took them to another shop, and put them in their molds.

The first pumps sat right on the curb. Mr. Herbst pumped gas by hand up into a glass ball on top of the pump. It flowed by gravity into the tank.

A new car owner now had a place to take his car for service. But where to store it between uses? At first, car owners were wealthy people who already owned a horse and carriage. The new contraptions could go in the stable. After World War I, architects began to include garages in their house plans. The 1928 *Home Builders* book contained designs for 50 garages in wood, railroad brick, or Tudor (stucco with wood beams.) *The Herald* carried an advertisement in 1908 for an "Economy Garage all ready to set up and no cutting to do. It is so made in the factory that it is easily put together."[16]

Cars and speed are inextricably intertwined. Articles in "Automobiling" often recorded miles per hour. A 1906 advertisement for a Pope Hartford boasted of a maximum speed of 50 miles per hour. Interest in racing started with the early cars. In 1901, Mr. W. N. Murray, driving his Winter Semiracer, outran a team of trotting horses, going from Pittsburgh to Beaver in two hours and fifteen minutes.[17] *The Herald* in 1916 registered complaints by citizens who were arrested for driving too fast in Edgeworth Borough. They requested that the police officer submit names of violators to the Burgess before arresting them. Officers were not to arrest "nice people."[18]

In 1928 the "Social Items" column of the *Herald* reported the continuing problem. "The Sewickley police have resolved to see that motorists shall enjoy the smooth Beaver Street pavement in moderation. Frank Sperando was in too much of a hurry when he was caught doing 38 m.p.h. He was fined $10 and costs. Theodore N. Booth also came to grief on Friday when Officer Stemmler caught him traveling at 37 m.p.h."

Cars, first considered luxuries, became "necessities" as their usefulness increased. Many Sewickleyites lived part of the year in Allegheny, where they found cars helpful in their daily lives. They could go to Pittsburgh for evening entertainments. An article in the *Index* in 1911 explained the effects.

When a few mad inventors began tinkering with the horseless carriage they did not realize they were about to change the face of society. But this speedy (20 m.p.h.) and comfortable (hoods, air-filled tires) vehicle has cured the aloofness with which Allegheny and Sewickley Valley folk regarded Pittsburgh during the winter. A few years ago they balked at crossing the long, windswept bridge which spanned the river between Pittsburgh and their homes, stayed close to their hearths on wintry nights, despite the attractiveness of theaters and other sophisticated diversion. Sponsors of the late Pittsburgh Orchestra lamented that few Caesars dared cross their Rubicon (the Allegheny); thus lack of attendance caused abandonment of the orchestra. Pittsburgh Golf Club functions suffered because of its distance from the social sets.

But the automobile has changed all that. Tomorrow many a trans-Allegheny socialite will be driven over to the Nixon to snuggle back in her seat as the floodlights dim for the opening of the Chansons et Crinolins—an importation from Paris.

People who stayed in Sewickley for the winter seldom braved the trip to town just for the evening because the roads were too bad. The first state highways started in 1911, but even they were not smooth. In 1913, although 8,835 miles of roads were designated state highways, only 3,000 were paved.[19] Most roads were the responsibility of the community. Property owners along the route often took care of their stretch of road to work off their road taxes. Long distance travel by car was difficult to impossible. In the winter of 1917, for example, the Army Motor Transport Corps decided to attempt to drive a convoy of motor trucks from Detroit to Baltimore for shipment to France. The press described the trip as a "daring adventure, accomplished by process of shovel, tug, push and good luck." All but one of the 30 trucks got through.

Long distance travel ordinarily requires road maps and route numbers. Neither was available. The *Automobile Blue Book* put out small books that described the routes from place to place by detailing landmarks, turns, bridges, and forks in the road. These handbooks were similar to the oral directions still given by helpful citizens to lost drivers. This explains the odd directions to go from Sewickley to Beaver Falls in a 1913 tour book.

Sewickley, bank on left. Turn right on Beaver St.
Fork, small pond in angle; bear right, following trolley on Beaver Road, using Caution for sharp turn with trolley across stone bridge, [mile] 20.3 [from Pittsburgh], Curve left with double trolley into Merchant St. [mile] 20.5, going straight thru Ambridge 20.8.

Economy, Merchant & 14th Sts. turn right with branch trolley on 14th St.—trolley leaves 21.9. End of road; turn left, following heavy poles on poor dirt road, avoiding road to right upgrade 22.6.

Cross trolley 23.1, curving right along same on very poor dirt road.

Just after recrossing trolley bear left on brick across long viaduct. Follow trolley past Baden Sta. 25.0, winding along R.R. on pavement. Cross branch R.R. 27.2 straight thru Freedom 28.4.

Turn left over R.R., turning right in center of bridge. Downgrade along trolley, running between R.R. and river on Sycamore St.

Rochester. Turn right with trolley across R.R.

At iron water-trough bear left with trolley on Brighton Ave. end of street; turn left with trolley downgrade. Do not cross Bridge, but turn right with branch trolley on Delaware Ave., using Extreme Caution for sharp turn under R.R. with trolley 31.0. Follow trolley straight ahead on 3d Ave, going thru New Brighton 33.3; cross long viaduct 33.6 (10 cents) curving right just beyond. Avoid road to left at station 33.8, continuing ahead under R.R. 33.9. Same thorofare becomes 7th Ave; follow trolley on same upgrade to center of Beaver Falls.[20]

In 1913, officials tried to plan a route for the Lincoln Highway from Baltimore to San Francisco. They had to use railroad maps and timetables to pick the route.[21]

Country roads were made for horses and wagons, but cars created ruts that could make them impassable. People remembered the difficulties in the early part of the century. Blasius Kaelin, interviewed in 1935 when he was 79, said that the mud was sometimes three feet deep on Beaver Road. In 1906, signs on Little Sewickley Creek Road requested all automobile owners "to refrain from using this road with their machines, owing to it being a narrow thorofare and quite dangerous for those who drive there."[22] Lieutenant Masters recalled the roads when he was young:

Gasmobile

> The roads were all dirt when I was a kid. In 1936, they got a lot of roads paved. Little Sewickley Road at one time was impassable for part of the year. They paved it in '36 and straightened it out. When I rode out with my mother, I sat in the back with my sister, who was a baby. My job was to keep my sister from falling out.

The roads were better for horses and wagons. They came with teams of horses to pull cars out if they were stuck in the mud.

The Reverend Alleyne Howell of St. Stephen's Church records his experiences with early cars.

April 2, 1909. Towed Ford runabout to Richfield Springs to have it repaired.

April 9, 1909. Charles and Packard towed me in Ford from Richfield Springs to Utica. Clouds of dust made driving uncomfortable. Arrived 4 P.M. Left 11 A.M.

May 9, 1910. Hear we are to have smokeless engines. Excellent for Sewickley.

August 21, 1910. Reverend Quick and self started for Saratoga Springs. At Mud Lake front spring and main spring snapped. Returned home to laughter of whole village.

August 25, 1910. Mr Quick, his son Harry and I left for Saratoga 8 A.M. Ford runs finely, weather and roads excellent.

August 26. Started our for Boston Spa where Harry had gone, via a road that took us down a steep hill, mile long with railroad at bottom. Brakes burned out. Would not hold and I steered car for the bank side of road. Harry jumped and car overturned at Hoffman's with Mr. Quick and myself in it. All of us uninjured save some minor scratches. Car towed in on stone boat to Amsterdam. Took train as I could get no transportation home. Repair on our car $110.

Cars were often retired for the winter. Mrs. Richmond remembered: "Centennial was dirt when we got here: most were. That's why people didn't run their cars in winter. The mud was too deep." Mrs. Josephine Herbst Sybo agreed: "Starting Thanksgiving, people put their cars away and didn't use them until spring. They put them up on blocks and used their horse and buggy."

Commuters relied on the train. Sewickley work crews concentrated on providing access to the station in the winter. Charles Stinson remembered:

> The Borough used horses to get the roads clear so people could get to the railroad. At 4:00 A.M. they were out with a skid as wide as the sidewalk, dragged by horse. They went over every street clearing the sidewalks. Didn't bother with streets. A man could walk or ride on the skid.

Road improvement was a major interest of the Sewickley Borough Council. Of a total of 115 ordinances adopted between 1853 and 1907, 62 concerned roads. As early as 1892, Broad Street was paved with vitrified fire brick. Beaver Road dust was attacked by a combination of public and private enterprise, as described in *The Bulletin* in 1901.

> Mrs. James B. Oliver, Mr. D. Leet Wilson, and a number of other prominent residents of the Sewickley Valley, were the prime movers in an effort to have the Beaver Road sprinkled twice daily from now until November 1, also the Meadow Road. . . . Since the road was improved, which was done under the Flinn Road Improvement Act, it has been so dusty as to make driving anything but a pleasure. The only remedy was the sprinkling cart [which cost $700]. County Commissioners agreed to give one third of the sum, the township commissioners another one third, leaving one third to be raised by citizens of the Valley. As soon as this is accomplished, dirty drives for Sewickleyites will be no more, and the Valley will rejoice. There are some of the finest turnouts in the State in and about Sewickley, and their owners will find a good deal more pleasure in their possession if they can come in from a drive without being choked with dirt.[23]

The Sewickley area was a favorite destination for driving tours. The "Automobilia" column reported on May 3, 1902:

> The country roads are still in very bad condition but Mr. A. M. Byers of Allegheny braved their horror and made the opening run of the season from his home on Ridge Avenue, Allegheny, to the hills back of Sewickley. The Beaver Road, over which the run was made, is in very bad condition so that no records were broken, but the run was made without any accidents.

By May 31 roads were better.

> Country roads are now in good condition and many runs were made by Pittsburg and Allegheny motorists into the surrounding country. Runs were made up the Butler Plank Road. . . . But the majority of runs were made down the Beaver road; some only as far as the Allegheny Country Club, at Sewickley, and some as far as Beaver Falls. On Sunday, May 18th, runs were made by Mr. Charles and Mr. W. C. Arbuthnot and Mr. Reuben Miller, all of Pittsburg, to Beaver Falls and return. . . . These gentleman report the road to be in fairly good condition, though very sandy in places. No attempt at speed was made on these runs, which were made for pleasure alone. The road from Sewickley to the Allegheny Country Club's new home is still in very bad condition, so that few runs have been made out from the city yet, though the members of the Club who own automobiles are anxiously waiting the time when runs can be made out to the club house. Mr. Harry McCandless ran out to the residence of B. F. Jones near the Country Club, on Wednesday of last week to attend the Laughlin-Robinson wedding, and did not make very bad time on the trip, though the roads are very sandy and there were many steep grades to climb.[24]

In 1907, William Way hired a famous Boston landscape architect, Warren H. Manning, to examine the roads and advise how they could be improved. Manning found the roads inadequate.

> Ninety-foot Broad Street runs into fifty-five foot Beaver Street and then is narrowed to a sixty-foot street, and ends in fifty-foot Hopkins Street toward the North. Toward the South, it runs into fifty-foot Bank Street and River Street, which ought to have been its continuation, fails to be so by one hundred feet. . . . Division Street is made up of two short, disconnected thirty-foot alleys and a forty-foot street. . . . Even now [1907] Beaver Street is seriously congested at times by carriages and automobiles. This congestion will increase with the growth of the region.[25]

In order to relieve traffic on Sewickley roads and to make a new route for recreational driving, Mr. Manning proposed a "pleasure drive" along the banks of the river. At this time, similar parkways were being built all over the country. In Pittsburgh, Schenley Park was designed partly to provide a pleasant place for Sunday excursions on its parkways. A drive on Beechwood Boulevard was another popular outing. Mr. Manning proposed a parkway for Sewickley because:

At no point outside of Pittsburgh is there an opportunity to establish a pleasure drive with such a fine outlook up and down the river and to the high wooded bluffs on the opposite sides. You should consider the river is your most important landscape feature and that it has by its erosion made the bluffs and ravines that make your river valley as beautiful as that of the Rhine.[26]

Mr. Manning's plan was never adopted. Sewickley had to wait 28 more years to get a boulevard, and then it was not along the river banks.

One of the more troublesome roads has been Blackburn, supposed to follow the route of an Indian trail called the Kittanning Path. Its hills and curve are difficult in any vehicle. Mrs. Richmond remembered that her great-grandfather was killed there. "My great-grandfather got land out in Sewickley Heights—all forest. He was clearing it off and was coming down the Blackburn Road with a team of oxen. He came to the big curve. Something frightened them, they upset the cart, he was under it and was killed."

The curve, nicknamed "Deadman's Curve," continued to threaten until 1915, when the county decided to make it less abrupt by widening the bridge. Mrs. Henry R. Rea owned the neighboring property. Seeing that the County plans were utilitarian but not attractive, Mrs. Rea negotiated an agreement to have her estate manager, Henry Davidson, plan and supervise the construction. Mrs. Rea paid for it all.[27] Later, in the early 1920s, she paid for the stone wall along the edge of Blackburn Road. Jerry Tignanelli and Jerry Vescio both remembered:

The County wanted to get a straight shot into Sewickley without crazy turns. Mrs. Rea said, "No, that's my property and I'm going to do what I please. I'm going to build a wall." Then Mrs. B. F. Jones [her neighbor] got a little jealous and she built her wall, but she made it higher. When she died, they stopped it.

Richard McPherson said:

They quarried stone from Quarry Road, brought it down on horses and wagons. Stonemasons cut the stone and built the wall—one mile a year. Every morning I went down to the railroad station and picked up four or five stonemasons from Pittsburgh: Gabriel Torquata, Jimmy Rizzo.

The Beaver Road was once part of the Lincoln Highway, originally conceived in 1912 by Carl G. Fisher. He convinced automobile makers to contribute four million dollars to build a coast-to-coast highway between New York and San Francisco. The highway was to be cement concrete, forty feet wide, with four lanes of traffic, allowing a maximum speed of 35 miles per hour. West of Pittsburgh, the Lincoln Highway followed the Ohio River through the towns and boroughs, including Sewickley. Residents of Sewickley balked when asked to rename the historic Beaver Road. When a proposed ordinance to rename came to Borough Council in March 1916, 61 residents signed a petition opposing the change. Council agreed, however, to make new signs for Sewickley using the old name, with Lincoln Highway underneath. This proved to be a wise decision. The Ohio River route had too much traffic on too narrow streets to accommodate the Lincoln Highway. In 1928 it was moved to the present Route 30, on the other side of the river.

A car trip to Pittsburgh from Sewickley was something of an adventure before the Ohio River Boulevard opened in 1934. Captain Way put it most succinctly: "There was no use trying to drive to Pittsburgh. You got covered with mud or dirt, depending on the day." Mrs. Orndorff said:

It was not until the Boulevard was put through that we could go to Pittsburgh [by car.] Glen Mitchell wasn't a good road. We had to go by the YMCA and then up and down the valleys to town. We had to go over the Heights, came out of the Heights at Glenfield. There were two railroad crossings, so that you never knew whether you were going to be held up by a long freight train. There were gullies where the bridges are now. You usually had a couple of punctures along the way. You thought about it before you drove to town.

James Higgins remembered roads in the 1920s: "You didn't drive to Pittsburgh until the Ohio River Boulevard. Mother dragged us to the dentist. It took two hours one way to the East End."

Problems getting to Pittsburgh by car were solved, at least temporarily, by the opening of the Ohio River Boulevard in 1934. Traffic had become a problem because cars had to go through the Borough on Beaver Road. As early as 1910, the Borough Council tried to get the railroad to eliminate all grade crossings. In 1916 the railroad agreed to move the tracks close to the river's edge. John Alexander watched the operation. "The tracks were moved from Haysville on.

Railroad cars brought in slag from the mills. They dumped it and squirted it with water. They had big hoses and they washed it right in. They kept running water through, washing the slag through."

The Boulevard was laid on the old bed of the railroad tracks, which provided a level foundation. On opening day, *The Sewickley Herald* hailed it:

> Sewickley's Biggest Christmas Present. Its board cratings and straw wrappings removed, and its clean, smooth, concrete surface brought to light and turned over to us for our use and pleasure. The Ohio River Boulevard—ready to carry us swiftly and easily from the city, ready to relieve our crowded Beaver Road of much of the hampering and dangerous congestion of cars and huge trucks that have become so burdensome.[28]

The celebration nearly equaled the opening of the Sewickley Bridge fourteen years earlier. A parade through town was followed by a speech by County Commissioner Chris McGovern, who promised that the new highway would "take at least 90 per cent of the traffic off the old Beaver Road." Mrs. James Pontrefact spoke in favor of keeping billboards out in order to avoid looking like Bigelow Boulevard, "of which Pittsburgh ought to be ashamed."[29] There was a special appearance by Robert Wardrop, "Sewickley's oldest commuter, who had traveled on the railroad since 1868, 425,000 miles, or seventeen times around the world."

All the road improvements had one unfortunate result: the ultimate loss of the commuter railroad. Like suburbanites all over the country, residents deserted the trains for the comfort and convenience of their own cars.

---

[1] *Sewickley Herald*, September 26, 1903, p. 6.

[2] Ibid., September 19, 1903, p. 2.

[3] Ibid., September 1 1903, p. 1.

[4] Ibid., Oct. 3, 1903, p. 1.

[5] Ibid., September 19, 1903, p. 2.

[6] Ibid., May 1, 1920, p. 2.

[7] Ibid., October 9, 1920, p. 16.

[8] George A. Hays, pp. 10-11.

[9] Jackson, p. 159.

[10] Mary Stuhldreher, "Automobiliousness." In *Western Pennsylvania Historical Magazine*, v.57, July 1974, p. 278.

[11] *Sewickley Herald*, August 12, 1905, p. 6.

[12] Stuhldreher, p. 280.

[13] *Weekly Herald*, August 12, 1905, p. 6.

[14] *Way file*. Sewickley Library.

[15] *St. Stephen's Parish Cookbook 1912-13*.

[16] *Sewickley Herald*, December 26, 1908, p. 9.

[17] *Index*, June 29, 1901.

[18] *Sewickley Herald*, January 2, 1916.

[19] Tarr, p. 28.

[20] *The Automobile Blue Book*, Chicago, 1913, v.3., pp. 489-490.

[21] Frederic L. Paxson, "The Highway Movement, 1916-1935". In *American Historical Review*, January 1946, pp. 241-244.

[22] *Sewickley Herald*, Sept. 29, 1906, p. 2.

[23] *The Bulletin*, June 1, 1901, p. 17.

[24] Ibid., May 31, 1902, p. 190.

[25] *Weekly Herald*, March 17, 1907, p. 10.

[26] Ibid., March 2, 1907, p. 10.

[27] Ibid., March 11, 1916, p. 2.

[28] *Sewickley Herald,* Dec. 14, 1934, p. 11.

[29] Ibid., December 21, 1934, pp. 1-3.

Chapter 20
Houses and Gardens for the Twentieth Century

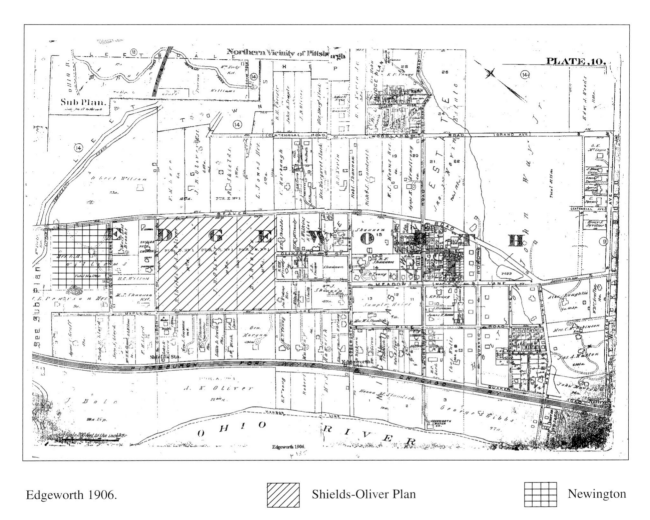

Edgeworth 1906. ⟋⟋⟋ Shields-Oliver Plan ▦ Newington

Around the turn of the century, Pittsburgh and Sewickley were thriving. The nation's best architects designed office buildings downtown and substantial houses for corporate executives and other wealthy citizens in Shadyside, Oakland, and Sewickley. Houses for the well-to-do in all these areas were similar. Montgomery Schuyler wrote a complimentary article on Pittsburgh domestic architecture in 1911:

> The belief is forced upon you that there are an enormous number of people in this country who are very, very comfortable. . . . Only a very few mansions in all this myriad of comfortable homes rise to palatial pretensions. . . . It is not in costliness altogether that the difference lies between the palatial and the domestic. It is in the ostentation and inflation which denote that money has been spent for the sake of spending it, or rather showing that it has been spent, that palatiality consists. Domesticity consists, for example, in renouncing the "state apartments" which evidently have nothing to do with the comfort of the owner or his family. [Rooms] were, to be sure, large as well as rich, but not large or rich enough to give the impression that they were not in constant use and habitation.[1]

This interest in comfort and convenience to the resident explains why Sewickley houses have remained while many of the larger, more palatial mansions on the Heights have been torn down.

Mr. Schuyler goes on to praise Pittsburghers for using architects. "It seems that nobody who can afford to build a house for himself ventures to do so without the advice of an architect." This is true in Sewickley. Several well-known architects settled in the Sewickley area, where their work contributed much towards maintaining the pleasant suburban atmosphere.

Most twentieth-century houses in Sewickley take advantage of the natural beauty of their sites. Contemporary magazines urged homeowners to go outdoors as much as possible. Strict division between outside and inside was softened. To encourage this, comfortable places to sit outside, either pergolas, piazzas, or porches, were incorporated into designs. Picturesque gardens lured strollers outside. Gardens were an important part of architectural design.

Site design played a large part in the development of a key thirty-acre plot in Edgeworth bounded by Beaver, Maple, and Neville Roads and Church Lane. Part of Eliza and David Shields estate, the property was easily accessible to the Shields railroad station on Church and Maple Streets. The land had never left the Shields family. Thomas Leet Shields, a descendant of the original David, had used it to grow plants for his nursery business. In 1905, it was still a farm, owned by Amelia Shields Oliver and her husband, James B. Oliver. Mrs. Oliver had inherited some of the property and had bought her sister's share. Mr. Oliver bought some more.

If this property in the heart of Edgeworth had been laid out in standard fifty-foot lots on a strict rectilinear grid, the neighborhood would have been set up for development similar to, say, the side streets in Shadyside. The James B. Olivers, especially Mrs. Oliver, had definite ideas about how they wanted their land developed. They hired the Olmsted Brothers of Brookline, Massachusetts, the most famous landscape architects in the country, to realize these ideas, which can be studied today both by visiting the area and by reading the correspondence between Mr. Oliver and the Olmsteds.[2]

The Shields family had an impeccable pedigree and a secure place in the landed aristocracy of Sewickley society. This position was enhanced by Amelia Shields' marriage to James B. Oliver, an immensely wealthy Pittsburgh industrialist. Mr. Oliver, born in 1844, joined his brothers in the firm that became the Oliver Iron and Steel Company, with large mills on the South Side which manufactured many kinds of industrial hardware including: bolts for railroad tracks, carriages and bridges; rivets for boilers; and hardware for telegraph and telephone poles. Like many other industrial magnates, the Olivers lived on Ridge Avenue in Allegheny City. They summered in Mrs. Oliver's old neighborhood in Shields, now part of Edgeworth. Their summer house was across the street from the proposed development. The Olivers, then, had both the money and the interest to develop their land in a responsible and innovative way.

By choosing the Olmsteds to plan the project, the Olivers placed themselves in the vanguard of landscape design. The Olmsteds were famous for their opposition to the grid which developers forced upon the American landscape regardless of topography. Olmsted streets curved gracefully, producing sweeping, natural-looking views. Frederick Law Olmsted, later joined by his son and stepson, had designed Central Park in New York City and several towns such as Riverside, Illinois. Locally, the Olmsteds did a master plan for Pittsburgh, a plan for Vandergrift (a model workers' town), and a landscape plan for Henry J. Heinz in Point Breeze, and for "As You Like It," Mrs. William Thaw, Jr.'s estate on Blackburn Road, Sewickley Heights.

The correspondence began June 13, 1905 when Mr. Oliver described his purpose in a letter to the Olmsteds.

We would like to make an appointment [to] look at a piece of land—either of you Messrs. Olmsted, with a view toward laying it out to get the best possibly [sic] artistic results. It is a piece of land susceptible of better development than is usually accorded country building. We want to lay it off in lots 100-foot frontage or thereabouts.

Three days later, the Olmsteds replied that John C. Olmsted would be coming in the next few weeks. A fee of $200 plus expenses was proposed for two visits and a plan.

Mr. Oliver clarified his wishes in succeeding letters.

I want your John C. Olmsted's best skill in laying out [the property] to best advantage artistically and at the same time getting the best results in the way of building lots. Mrs. Oliver is going away August 5th and I am anxious that we go over it together before she leaves. The property is part of her inheritance, and as our house fronts right on it, we are very anxious to get the best results.

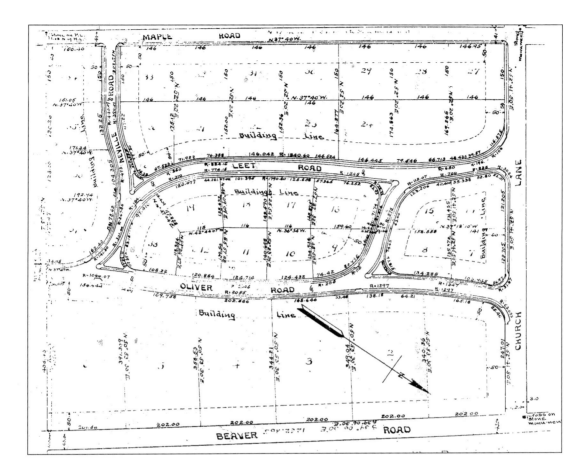

Amelia Oliver Plan

Mr. J.C. Olmsted visited on July 21 and walked around the property. He advised the Olivers to "hold back from sale all the Beaver Road lots, except perhaps that at the southeast, as a matter of their own enjoyment, as their own house is on the northeast side of this street."

Following this visit J.C. Olmsted sent a plan showing the signature curvilinear streets together with a warning:

The adoption of a curvilinear system necessarily involves a less economical utilization of the land than the rectilinear system. . . and could not be expected to enhance the value of the land in any degree proportionally to the probable cost of the improvements. At the same time we are inclined to agree with Mrs. Oliver's idea that there would be a certain picturesqueness and gracefulness characteristic of the curvilinear plan of streets and of the location of some of the houses a little off the square which, if supplemented by suitable tree-planting, ought to be attractive to many people who have thought about such matters enough to appreciate the desirability of occasionally escaping from the strictly rectangular subdivision so universally adopted in the suburbs of Pittsburgh.

At this point, Mr. Oliver evidently had second thoughts about the innovative methods of his landscape architects.

The plans have been studied out by Mrs. Oliver and myself with a great deal of interest. I have also shown them to some of my real estate friends to get their opinion in regard to the adoption of such a plan of lots. Mrs. Oliver and I like them, and we feel that such a lay-out whilst it is expensive, yet the lots might command higher prices. But our real estate friends are doubtful. One who has just looked over them thinks we will be disappointed. I had a long talk with Mr. Samuel W. Black, who is not only our leading real estate man, but he is personally interested in the successful improvement of our property, as his home faces it. He objects strongly to the improvement according to the plans now under consideration. He says that the curvilinear plan looks beautiful on paper, but it will not do in practice. Whilst we would lay out the roads in strict accordance with the plans, the village organization would not keep them up, and it would not be long until all the curves would be gone, and crooked lines would soon be the rule.

The Olmsteds replied on September 1: "We have prepared a rectilinear subdivision and send you a print of it. . . . If you must have a rectangular system of the subdivision, we think this plan will prove decidedly more profitable."

In a note on September 4, Mr. Oliver said he liked the new plan, but would show it to Mrs. Oliver who "still adheres to the curvilinear." This remark offered the Olmsteds hope for their original plan.

As you mention that Mrs. Oliver still prefers the curvilinear system of subdivision, we venture to say that we sympathize with her in this and believe that you would, in the long run, derive a certain mental satisfaction from your connection with the property if you should not only adopt the curvilinear system but carry out a moderate and conservative amount of planting on each of the lots. . . .

Of course it would hardly be sensible for you to carry your appreciation of picturesque beauty to the point of sacrificing the commercial value of the land, but, as to this, you and your advisers are in a better position to form a judgment than we are. We do know that hereabout and in various suburbs of New York, Philadelphia and other large cities a departure from the commonplace rectangular system of land subdivision in the direction of picturesqueness would be a reasonably good commercial proposition. In fact, there are plenty of instances of the curvilinear system of land subdivision which have been just as profitable as the rectangular. . . . We judge, however, that in the vicinity of Pittsburgh a departure from the commonplace rectangular system of subdivision is much more of a novelty, and therefore much less likely to be appreciated. . . . There may be a sufficient number of possible purchasers who would be attracted to the novelty and beauty of the scheme.

This last comment seems to show a touch of Boston snobbery toward the "uncultured" west.

Mr. Oliver gave up:

Mrs. Oliver has converted me to her views on the curvilinear system of subdivision and we have decided to adopt it. Make plans complete in every detail. Mrs. Oliver tells me you sent a man from your Boston house to do planting and superintend the grading and making of roads for Mrs. Thaw. How much would you charge for sending one to us?

The development still lacked a name. Mr. Oliver referred to the development as a whole as the Nursery Property in the early part of the correspondence. On September 20 he wondered about a permanent name.

Would you advise calling it Shields Place or Shields Park: It seems to me the word "Place" is used too much in connection with the cheap lay-outs, and this one is going to be anything but cheap.

Mr. Oliver decided finally on Oliver Place, as reported by J. C. Olmsted.

He wants the property marked on plans as belonging to Mrs. Oliver, as he wishes her to have all the credit (?) for the curvilinear system.

The planting plan arrived October 26, with instructions for preparing the beds.

Have the planting beds staked out, the areas prepared for planting, etc. This can be done by removing turf and weeds from the surface and digging the ground fully one spade deep, incorporating into the ground at the time of spading well-rotted barnyard manure at the rate of 10 cords to the acre. It is extremely essential that the manure should be well-rotted.

Mr. Oliver had suggested cutting costs by getting some of the plants from the woods on his property. The Olmsteds demurred because collected stock "would not be nearly as desirable as properly transplanted, nursery grown material."

It is unknown if the Olivers followed this advice but it as understandable that they thought of ways to cut back. The plan proposed planting 4,658 trees and shrubs, including:

467 roses of various kinds

157 lilacs of 5 kinds

210 dogwood

90 spirea

100 mock orange

Plants were grouped in complementary clusters. Group 25, for example, was a plan for 13 beds with 293 plants four feet apart, namely: 60 flowering dogwood, 65 smoke trees, 100 mock orange and 68 white kerria. Group 26 was a plan for 6 beds with 130 plants 3½ feet apart: 50 hydrangea, 50 rose of sharon, and 30 wild hydrangea. Group 21 was for 5 beds, 110 plants of lilac, all four feet apart.[3]

Mr. Oliver liked the plan.

The shrubbery plan looks beautiful, but there is one thing we must take out, and that is all small plants, flowers, and such like, as they would all be dug up and taken away. All we should plant are trees and bushes, and they should be of such size as would not be stolen.

Who, one wonders, would these flower-loving thieves be? Perhaps Sewickley and Edgeworth ladies or their gardeners, anxious to shine in local horticultural circles. In any case, the Olmsteds said it was no problem.

While it is not quite clear in our minds just what you refer to as "the small plants, flowers and such like", we presume that you had in mind herbaceous plants and annuals. . . . We have not used any herbaceous plants nor any small, fine flowering plants, but have used rather larger and coarser growing shrubbery, having in mind the obstacles which would be likely to appear, such as stealing of the plants.

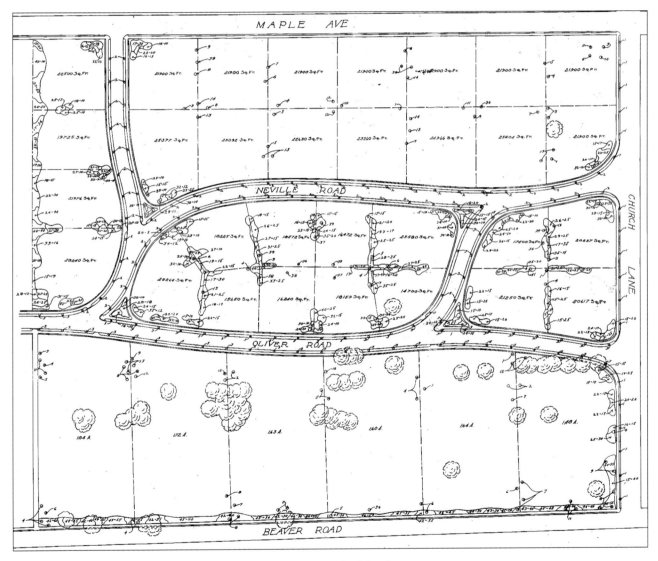

Olmsted Planting Plan for Oliver Property

This delightful correspondence in the Olmsted file ended abruptly November 29, 1905 with an obituary in the *Post-Gazette*.

> Died. James B. Oliver. One of the last of the individual iron masters who have done so much to make Pittsburgh the industrial metropolis of the world.

Mrs. Olivers' representative, A. J. Miller, said she planned to continue the project, but it must have been difficult when the planning had been so much a joint project with her husband.

The last major issue to be decided was what restrictions to put on the deeds to ensure that the plan would be protected in the future. The Olmsteds proposed many restrictions, some more vigorously than others, in a letter dated January 31, 1906:

> Our experience is that lawyers and real estate agents, especially in places where comparatively little attention has been paid to the development of high-class suburban neighborhood, are inclined to object very strongly to such elaborate restrictions. We believe that you will take satisfaction in developing a high-class neighborhood.

Fifteen restrictions were adopted by Mrs. Oliver, all to last until 1965 unless otherwise stated. Some of the more interesting follow. In cases where reasons are not obvious, the Olmsted's reasons are included:

> 1. Not more than one dwelling house, one servant's cottage, and one stable per lot until 1940.
>
> 2. No flat roofs in order to "prevent a distinctly city form of house; that is, those having flat, tin roofs, from being put up in what is intended to be a pleasing suburban neighborhood."
>
> 3. No building more than two stories tall.
>
> 4. No stable, pig pens, or public garage. No horses, pigs, or cattle to be pastured. "Some people like to raise poultry in their back-yard but a great many more people are annoyed by having poultry raised in their neighborhood, especially those who find difficulty sleeping early in the morning, and who are easily awakened by the crowing of a cock."
>
> 5. No house to cost less than $10,000
>
> 6. Buildings to be 50 feet from the street; side and rear walls to be five feet from the property line. However, porches, terraces, eaves and cornices could project as much as 14 feet beyond that line. "The effect in looking along the length of a street lined on both sides by houses built to a line is more agreeable in a suburban neighborhood if such projections are allowed, because the general effect depends rather upon the main front walls of the home than upon bay windows and verandahs."
>
> 7. "No intoxicating liquor shall be sold upon said land, and no mechanical, manufacturing or commercial business shall be conducted on said land, and no hospital, asylum, school or public or charitable institution. . . . But this restriction shall not prevent doctors, lawyers, writers, artists and other professional men or women from having their offices."
>
> 8. No fences or hedges nearer any street than 50 feet until 1940. "It is such a general custom now for front fences to be omitted that we are inclined to think that the majority of land owners will prefer to have no front fences, and if a majority so prefer it would be ruinous in appearance to have here and there a lot fenced in."[4]

The restrictions are interesting because they are precursors of similar restrictions in contemporary suburban zoning ordinances. The restrictive covenants, which ran until 1965, acted as a kind of mini-zoning for the area before the arrival of municipal zoning. They show what kind of development the Olivers had in mind: an upscale suburb with large houses (over $10,000) set well back from the road, with commodious verandahs and sloping roofs with overhanging eaves. It was to be a suburban, not a rural, development with no stables and certainly no pigpens. The development shows the continuing influence in Edgeworth of one its founding families.

The sale of lots proceeded slowly. Captain Frederick Way, Jr. remembered that Mrs. Oliver found few people she considered suitable for her development. In 1916, Lot 6 was sold to Sidney Ligett for $6,000, which must have been a large sum at the time.

The correspondence leaves us hanging and unsure if all of the planting in the plan was completed. The Olmsteds often remarked that the final plan was on the ground. Nevertheless, by driving through the streets today, it is possible to see what the Olmsteds and the Olivers had in mind for their venture into a real-estate development that would be both profitable and beneficial to the community. This planned development of a large area in what is now Edgeworth in large lots with expensive houses influenced future development. Later residents did not hesitate to build in such a prestigious area.

Upper-Class Houses

Such attention to details of landscape design was unusual, even for the Sewickley area. More attention was understandably lavished on the details of designing houses. Sewickley area houses, like those in the previous century, were built in the latest, most fashionable, styles. Just as the nineteenth-century suburbanite could choose a house in the Italianate, Second Empire, or Queen Anne style, so could his twentieth century counterpart choose Classical Revival, Prairie, or Shingle. The same architect could design houses in any of these styles. The houses have fared well; most remain in good condition. A selection of houses from the period gives an idea of their quality and variety.

Quay house, 59 Beaver Street. Photo by John H. Demmler.

A house on 59 Beaver Street, just past the Presbyterian church is an example of the Shingle style. This house was owned at the turn of the century by Richard R. Quay, the son of Matthew S. Quay, political boss of the Pennsylvania legislature. Richard Quay had a part interest, with H. W. Oliver, in the Monongahela Tin Plate Company until the company sold out to U. S. Steel Corporation. Richard followed his father into the Pennsylvania legislature, but never attained his power. He did attain respectability, becoming a member of the Duquesne Club and the Allegheny Country Club.

In keeping with his wealth and respectability, Richard Quay picked the Shingle style, popular in fashionable seaside resorts in the East. His is a large house with a charming carriage house behind it. There is a steeply pitched shingled roof with dormers. The second floor has shingled walls which continue around corners without interruption. The tower is partly incorporated into the main body of the house, and the porch is completely tucked in. This house, in keeping with the Shingle style, is asymmetrical. This results in a comfortable, informal, homey feeling unusual for such a large house.

The house built by George Hubbard Clapp on 425 Woodland Road in Edgeworth is interesting for two reasons. First, it is an example of the houses going up at the time and, second, Mr. Clapp was an example of the new wave of Pittsburgh industrialists moving to the Valley. Mr. Clapp was born in Allegheny City in 1858 and attended public school, the Ayres Latin School, Pittsburgh, and the college that is now the University of Pittsburgh. After working in a cotton mill and a steel mill, Mr. Clapp joined Alfred E. Hunt in forming the Pittsburgh Testing Laboratory, which later became the Aluminum Company of America.

The Clapp House, from the *Bulletin,* Dec. 7, 1929.

Mr. Clapp had numerous other interests. He was chairman of the board of trustees of the University of Pittsburgh, a trustee of Carnegie Institute, and a board member of numerous industrial companies. A devoted collector, he donated 8,000 land shells and 140,000 insect specimens to the Carnegie Museum.

The Clapp house was designed by Charles Barton Keene of Philadelphia. Mr. Keene also did the Pittsburgh Center for the Arts and a mansion for the Reynolds family in Winston-Salem, North Carolina. For the Clapps he designed a low, rambling house. The long, horizontal shingled roof makes the building blend into the landscape. A bay window with a southern exposure lets in ample sunlight and gives a view of a large garden. *The Bulletin* described the garden in 1929.

This estate cannot boast a distant view. It is shut in by high walls of shrubbery on every side, and the house also is shut in similar high walls of evergreens and rhododendron except at the back, and there the house commands a fine view of the broad, well kept lawn. . . . Wide stone steps lead down from the terrace of stone to the lawn and the fountain. At intervals in this reposeful garden, box-woods, brought from the southland, are grouped and the continuity of the oval flower border carries the eye to the shady pergola opposite the house. . . . The pergola is most attractive in spring, when it is loaded with lavender sprays of wisteria bloom. It is also attractive in fall, when the blooms have been turned into long, graceful seed pods which hang in festoons from the archways and, in making a study through the arches, one gets the effect of a Japanese print.[5]

Pergolas are trellises covered with vines, providing shade for sitting. They were popular around the turn of the century as one means of blurring the difference between the outside and the inside. *Craftsman,* a magazine which both created and recorded the suburban movement, explained.

Whatever connects a house with the out of doors, whether vines or flowers, piazza or pergola, is to be welcomed in the scheme of modern home-making. . . . Pergolas can be made to add much to the beauty of a house even when they are not actual living rooms. They can be a continuation of the house, as an arm extending into the garden, gathering it close to its heart, inseparable. . . . Our garden, which should be our outdoor home, must surely have a pergola, a living place outdoors that is beautiful in construction, that is draped in vines, that gives us green walls to live within, that has a ceiling of tangled leaves and flowers blowing in the wind, a glimpse of blue sky through open spaces and sunshine pouring over us when leaves move. With a pergola in the garden you can no more escape living out of doors than you can avoid swimming in the sea if you happily chance to be living on the edge of the ocean.[6]

Two architectural firms, Rutan & Russell and Alden & Harlow, designed many of the Sewickley valley houses. The named partners in both firms came from Boston and settled in Sewickley. All came to work for Henry Hobson Richardson on the Allegheny County Courthouse, remaining in Pittsburgh to pursue successful careers. Alden & Harlow designed The Carnegie, the Duquesne Club, and many mansions, including the Byers-Lyon house on Ridge Avenue in the North Side, and the Richard Beatty Mellon house where the Pittsburgh Garden Center is today. Rutan & Russell designed St. Augustine's Church in Lawrenceville, the Schenley Hotel (now the Pitt Student Union), and the B. F. Jones house on Ridge Avenue, now part of the Community College of Allegheny County.

Frank Rutan and Frederick Russell settled easily into Sewickley life. Mr. Rutan married Martha Fleming, a member of an old Sewickley family. He became president of the Monday Musical Club and was chairman of the music committee at the Presbyterian Church. Frederick Russell was Edgeworth's first burgess, president of the Edgeworth Country Club and was a leader in the Edgeworth Village Improvement Society.[7]

The Rutan & Russell architectural firm designed many area houses in various styles: the Shingle style of the former building of the Edgeworth Club; the Colonial Revival Edward O'Neil house; the Prairie style James Todd house; and, probably, the Queen Anne style Crutchfield house. A contemporary article in *The Architectural Record* explained the variety.

> The demands made upon a busy architect by the exigencies of modern practice are so varied that except in a few occasional instances it is impossible to look for uniformity of idea and methods in the work of any one man or group of men. This is especially true of domestic architecture, which is largely influenced by the taste and predilections of the owner and by the necessarily varying conditions of cost and site. . . . The utmost variety exists in domestic architecture.[8]

The article pointed out Rutan & Russell's good fortune in designing suburban houses for wealthy clients.

> No house is easy to design, easy in the sense of being told off by the thumb: but the designing of suburban houses is hedged in by none of the rigid requirements that surround the designing of a city house. The suburban house has at least air and space, and offers many more opportunities for individual treatment than the city house.[9]

The unifying characteristic of building by the firm is simplicity. After the delightfully ornamented structures of the Queen Anne and Second Empire, taste became more subdued. All the flounces and furbelows thought of as Victorian are missing in the Rutan & Russell houses, which concentrate on materials and craftsmanship.

Cottage of J.M. Tate, Jr., 525 Pine Street, Sewickley.
From *American Architect and Building News,* Oct. 19, 1907.

Excellence of workmanship is perhaps the most notable characteristic of all these designs. Sobriety of treatment is another point in their favor. The building of buildings as buildings, of obtaining effects of form and shade through constructive materials, is clearly their most individual point. This in itself is so rare and unusual and the results obtained are so generally satisfactory, that special importance should be attached to it.[10]

Rutan & Russell created several houses in the Shingle style, plainer and quieter than the Queen Anne style with fewer variations of color and materials. One example is the house Frederick Russell built for his bride on Newbury Lane. The shingled exterior, gambrel roof, and open porch suggest an informal summer cottage. Flowers and vines crowd the exterior.

A similar work is the cottage of John M. Tate, Jr. on 525 Pine Road in Sewickley. The large front porch which runs the length of the building is supported by four Tuscan columns. These columns, with swelling in the middle, were popular in the early twentieth century. The roof sweeps down from the ridge in a continuous line to include the porch. Large chimneys on either end denote domesticity and coziness. The house looks like a summer cottage that Vincent Scully included in his book *Architecture of the American Summer.*

It was not a summer cottage, however, but the home of Mr. Tate, a resident of Sewickley for more than 70 years. He worked for Westinghouse Electric in his early years, later becoming president of Tate-Jones Company of Leetsdale, a crematory in 1912. His most important contribution to Sewickley was his idea to plant sycamore trees along several streets. The Borough approved the plan and appointed Mr. Tate president of the Tree Commission.[11]

Several Rutan & Russell houses were in the Colonial Revival style, popular all over Pittsburgh around the turn of the century. Similar houses can be found in Friendship, Squirrel Hill, and Highland Park. Colonial Revival houses are characterized by wide porches along the entire length of the facade, accentuated front doors, symmetrically spaced windows, and, particularly in Pittsburgh, Palladian windows on the second story just over the front door.

As the name explains, Colonial Revival houses are recapitulations of Georgian houses of a century or more earlier. It is better to say Georgian recapitulation than Georgian revival because the style has never really died out. Houses in the Georgian style have been consistently popular. In a book listing 200 English country houses since 1950, all but a handful are neo-Georgian.[12] Mr. Schuyler noted its popularity around Pittsburgh in the early 1900s.

> One version of the Georgian manor, a more or less accurate copy of the old Hancock house in Boston, is very frequent and conspicuous. A local man remarked, "If a Pittsburgh man were let alone, that is the kind of house he would have."[13]

Colonial Revival architecture reflects the wave of patriotic nostalgia for Colonial days fostered by the Centennial of 1876. It expresses nostalgia for permanence at the time when the United States in general and Pittsburgh in particular were in the throes of social and economic upheaval. Pittsburgh's population was booming with the arrival of immigrants to work in the steel mills. Older residents feared they would be engulfed by a wave of foreigners. The leader of the Daughters of the American Revolution warned of the "danger in our being absorbed by the different nationalities among us."[14] Moreover, upper-class Pittsburghers were afraid of civil unrest. The Homestead Strike of 1892, closely followed by the attempted assassination of Henry Clay Frick, demonstrated how

Residence of Henry A. Davis, Beaver Street, Sewickley, PA.
From *Palmer's Pictorial Pittsburgh and Prominent Pittsburghers,* 1905.

unstable their highly stratified society had become. In such times, houses tended to reflect the styles of the more secure past. Even if a new business tycoon had no roots, he could build a house to look like an old family homestead. *Craftsman* magazine explained in 1908:

> Of course, the most desirable thing one can have in the way of a home is an old house built by one's grandfather or great-grandfather and modified by each successive generation until it comes into one's own possession as an embodied history of the life and nature of one's forebearers, possessing a ripeness and sense of permanence that are eloquent of long years of comfort and usefulness.[15]

The next best thing after a real Colonial family homestead was a re-created version.

An early project of Rutan & Russell's involved changing a house from the outmoded Italianate to the newer Colonial Revival style. In 1898, Henry Davis, a wealthy Pittsburgh lawyer and partner of Mayor Christopher Magee, bought the house on the corner of Boundary Street and Beaver Road. He wanted to modernize the house, which had been built around 1860 by William Miller and later lived in by Captain McDonald. A picture and description of the original house is in the chapter on nineteenth century buildings. Rutan & Russell, architects for the remodeling, added a two story Doric porch, a porte-cochère, and a widow's walk.

Edward O'Neil's residence, 963 Beaver St. Sewickley, PA.
From *The Builder,* February, 1904.

Edward O'Neil commissioned the firm to do a new Colonial Revival house on 963 Beaver Street in Sewickley. The house was featured in *The Builder*, February 1904. Mr. O'Neil, a graduate of Phillip Andover Academy and Princeton University, was an insurance agent. The house, set on a large lot on Sewickley's principal thoroughfare, exudes a sense of dependability and permanence, an entirely suitable image for an insurance executive.

Rutan & Russell also designed the James Todd house on 2 Beaver Street at the opposite end of Sewickley from the O'Neil house. It is also opposite in style. Both houses might reflect their owners professions: Mr. O'Neil as the staid insurance executive; Mr. Todd as the president of the Sterling Varnish Company in Haysville. Instead of the restrained brick walls of the O'Neil house, the Todd house has walls of rusticated stone, reminders of the architects' work on the Allegheny County Courthouse. The heavy stone was lightened by a gracefully curved Spanish tile roof and decorative dormer windows. The O'Neil house looked to the Colonial past. The Todd house, which shows the influence of the Prairie style popularized by Frank Lloyd Wright, looked to the future, as every good executive should. Frank Lloyd Wright introduced Prairie style houses around 1900. They were supposed to complement the midwestern prairie, blending with its gently rolling terrain. The Todd house incorporates some of the features of the Prairie style. The hipped roof with widely overhanging eaves stresses the horizontal. The gently sloping roofs of the dormers and the entrance porch also accent the horizontal. The foursquare footprint, symmetrical facade, and natural stone walls

James Todd's residence, 2 Beaver St. Sewickley, PA.
From *The Builde*r. February, 1904.

accord with the surroundings. *The Architectural Record*, 1904, explained: "The home of Mr. James Todd is built of stone. A stone wall encloses the terrace and porch and again there is dependence on materials alone for effect, for of ornament there is none at all."[16] The outside of the houses is plain, but, like Wright houses, the inside is exuberantly decorated wood. Mary Beth Pastorius described it.

> The architect placed stained glass windows in the stairwell and the dining room, hinting at the visual delights within. No part of the grand hall, staircase, library, living or dining rooms are without ornamentation, the perfect showcase for a manufacturer of varnishes. Rutan plans were crafted in six different woods, by Italian carvers who lived and worked at the house for several years.[17]

House of Frank E. Rutan, Esq., on the corner of Academy and Centennial avenues from *American Architect and Building News,* Sept. 7, 1907.

The Todd house was similar to Frank Rutan's own house on the corner of Academy Ave. and Woodland Rd. The Rutan house is less severe; its low, asymmetrical, rambling outlines, soften the silhouette, relating it to the less formal Shingle style. Like the Todd house, the interior was lavishly ornamented.

The firm of Alden & Harlow designed many houses in Sewickley. Because Margaret Henderson Floyd has studied them in her recently published book *Architecture After Richardson*, only one will be discussed here.

Samuel Black was the real estate developer who discouraged Mrs. James P. Oliver from using the "radical" Olmsted plans. He was a leader in the real-estate field and the organizer of the Pittsburgh Real Estate Board. Mr. Black's firm in the Farmer's Bank Building, Pittsburgh, advertised in 1917: "The Samuel W. Black Company. For 40 years, specializes in Sewickley Real estate." In 1890, Mr. Black bought land from Amelia Shields and engaged Alden & Harlow to build a house on 433 Maple Lane. The house is a smaller version of one in Cambridge, Massachusetts built for J. G. Thorpe. Margaret Henderson Floyd says that the Black house was the first of Alden & Harlow's colonial designs in Pittsburgh. It was followed by many other Colonial Revival houses by Alden & Harlow. Colonial characteristics include Palladian window, Adamesque detailing on the porch, dentils, columns, and symmetry.

Ingham & Boyd was another architectural firm with roots in Boston. Charles Ingham worked for the Boston firm Peabody & Stearns around 1900. William Boyd joined the Alden & Harlow office near the beginning of his career. After graduating from the University of Pennsylvania in 1907, Boyd continued his studies at the École des Beaux Arts in Paris, supplementing his studies with field trips through Europe. After moving to Pittsburgh, Boyd worked for noted architects Frederick Osterling and Rutan & Russell. In 1911, he joined Ingham to form Ingham & Boyd.

The firm designed many well-known buildings in Pittsburgh especially Chatham Village, the former Historical Society of Western Pennsylvania, and the Buhl Planetarium. Houses in the Sewickley area include four on Woodland Road, Edgeworth. The firm, like Rutan & Russell, worked in various styles, putting Mr. Boyd's knowledge of European architecture to good use. Walter Kidney stated:

> Ingham & Boyd was an intelligent office, not creative but tasteful. The Historical Society of Western Pennsylvania, built in Schenley Farms in 1916, was delicate Italianate Renaissance, the nearby Board of Education building, gracious High Renaissance, and the Buhl Planetarium of 1939 on the North Side, a work in the compromise Classicism of the time that attempted to combine tradition and modernity. Chatham Village on Mount Washington shows Ingham & Boyd using a quasi Georgian style.[18]

Samuel Black House, 433 Maple Lane, Edgeworth. Designed by Alden & Harlow, 1890-92. Photo by John H. Demmler.

In 1911, the same year the firm was founded, William Boyd built a house for his brother Marcus on 426 Woodland Road in Edgeworth. Located high up on the hill, the Marcus Boyd house has a view over the valley. The Boyds paid a price for the view, however, because there was no driveway up the hill. Visitors, delivery men, and family had to climb 27 wide stone steps to reach the front door.

Marcus Boyd-Davis House, 426 Woodland Road. Built 1911. Photo by John H. Demmler.

The house has the look of a country manor in England or France. It is a large, fourteen-room structure of stucco with a tile roof. Architects of country houses at the time tried to blur the distinction between rooms and between outside and inside. Rooms were opened up. The Boyd house has no doors between the large hall and the dining and living rooms. Views of the outside are unobstructed. Transitions to the outside are blurred also. A pergola on the west end is neither out nor in; it provides fresh air and shelter from summer sun.

A distinctive outdoor room is the large sleeping porch off the master bedroom, added about 1915 and, according to one of the children, "used by the whole family even in the dead of winter." Outdoor sleeping was popular in suburban houses throughout the country. The magazine *Suburban Life* explained the reason in 1904.

> Why the sleeping-porch? is frequently asked. Why not open bedroom windows? So many think the sleeping-porch merely a fad; that fresh air is just as plentiful in a well-ventillated bedroom, and the expense of building a sleeping-porch can be saved. Open windows are beneficial, it is true, but they do not produce the same result as a wide-open sleeping-porch. In the first place, there is apt to be a draft in bedrooms where air entering the window blows through another. In such a system, unequally warmed, the current of air has frequently been found conducive to colds. . . . Sleeping on a wide-open sleeping-porch is practically like sleeping out-of-doors, and anyone who has slept outside knows how different it is from sleeping in a bedroom, no matter how wide the windows in the room are opened.[19]

Craftsman magazine, the arbiter of suburban taste, supported the outdoor sleeping regimen.

> Now that people are finding that there is a charm, a healthfulness in sleeping out of doors not to be experienced in any indoor bedroom, the sleeping porch has come to be a part of almost every country home. . . . A short trial of sleeping where the air has free circulation will convince even the skeptic of the wholesomeness and delight attendant upon such. . . . The more oxygen we breathe, the less we are affected by heat or cold. It is the oxygen permeating our lungs that keeps us warm.[20]

Many believed that there were two benefits from fresh air. First, a constant flow of fresh air got rid of the carbon dioxide that humans exhale. Fifty cubic feet of fresh air per person per minute was recommended. This is five times current standards. Second, the same fresh air would replace the "foul air" that caused such diseases as malaria, cholera, dysentery, diarrhea, and typhoid.[21]

Because they were used year-round, sleeping porches had to have protection from the elements: special beds and bedding in winter and bug protection in summer. The *Suburban Life* article recommended ten layers of bedding: a waterproof spread, a comforter, three pairs wool and cotton blankets, and a pair of cotton blankets. In summer sleepers needed

Marcus Boyd-Davis House, Pergola. Photo by John H. Demmler.

access to breezes without mosquitoes having access to them. Some people relied on individual netting to deter mosquitoes, but the Boyd house had a full set of screens.

Marcus and Elsie Boyd filled their house with five children. Sister Pauline Boyd, one of the children, remembered her life there.

> Formal parties were few, but informal ones, with full mixture of generations, were many. We played ball in the lower lot, where the men batted left-handed to equalize things. There were Gypsy picnics in full costume in the summer and pirate indoor picnics in winter. On the Fourth of July the men set off fireworks on the hill and we were allowed to stay up until TEN O'CLOCK to enjoy them.[22]

The Sewickley area can boast of a house designed by Benno Janssen, who also designed some of Pittsburgh's favorite buildings. James van Trump, architectural historian, called Janssen's "probably the most important architectural firm of its time in Pittsburgh, and it took over the priority of place which Alden & Harlow had so long enjoyed."[23]

Benno Janssen was born and received some architectural training in St. Louis. Then he worked for the Boston firm of Shepley, Rutan & Coolidge. Like many other architects of the time, he continued his studies in Paris, where he was able to learn firsthand the styles of the past. Following his European studies, Janssen joined the Pittsburgh firm, McClure & Spahr, but soon launched his own practice, first as Janssen & Abbott and later as Janssen & Cocken.

Janssen is the best example of architects who could do work in the multiple styles he had encountered in Europe. Janssen created several well-known buildings on Fifth Avenue in Oakland: the Pittsburgh Athletic Association in the style of a Venetian Renaissance palace; and Mellon Institute and the Masonic Temple, based loosely on Grecian temples. Janssen's domestic architecture is less formal. His Longue Vue Golf Club with its rusticated walls and rough tiled roof achieves a country look that would be admired by Ralph Lauren. La Tourelle, the house in Fox Chapel designed for Edgar Kaufmann, has a similar irregular slate roof with the added rusticity of fieldstone walls.

The house of local interest in the Sewickley area was built in 1929 for Harry B. Higgins on 420 Woodland Road, Edgeworth. Is a romantic, picturesque house that, according to van Trump, "might more appropriately adorn the landscape of a fairy tale or a dream."[24] Several steeply pitched roofs seem to create a space far from the real world. The importance of the roof in Janssen's design can be seen by imagining the same house with an asphalt or flat roof.

The Janssen house on Woodland Road shares characteristics with the Kaufmann house and Longue Vue. All have roofs clad in rough slate shingles; tall, massive chimneys, the symbol of home, contrast with the generally horizontal outline; the rambling footprint suggests that rooms were added for reasons of comfort. Altogether, Janssen houses give an impression opposite to the carefully orchestrated, symmetrical precision of the O'Neil house.

Higgins House, 420 Woodland Road, designed by Benno Janssen, 1929.

Harry B. Higgins spent his working life with Pittsburgh Plate Glass Company, now PPG Industries. After graduating from Harvard in 1904, he started as a stenographer, and in 1944 became president and chief executive officer. Strangely, glass is not a big item in his house. Janssen's contemporaries, Frank Lloyd Wright and Walter Gropius, were using large expanses of glass to bring the outside in. Janssen, on the other hand, seemed to want to keep the outside out. Possibly it is because of Janssen that Pittsburgh has few houses in the styles of Gropius or Wright. Van Trump said he was "perhaps the most facile and talented of Pittsburgh's Eclectic architects of the earlier twentieth century, who had very abundantly and enormously helped to form the architectural image of the city between 1905 and 1940."[25]

Harry B. Higgins son, James H. Higgins, became chairman and chief executive officer of Mellon Bank. He grew up in the house. James Higgins remembered that his mother had wanted a rambling farmhouse. The outside does ramble, but the inside resembles a country gentleman's home more than a farmhouse. There is a formal entry, a pine-paneled living room with exquisitely carved wainscoting and bookcases with reverse scalloped carving. The Higgins family spent most of their time in the smaller oak-paneled library with carved linen-fold doors. Across the hall was the dining room, with "fancy wallpaper with handpainted trees and birds." All the main rooms had buzzers to call the maids. A broad staircase led to the upstairs and its four bedrooms, all with baths. James Higgins remembered that his bedroom had a sleeping alcove with many windows so that he could get enough fresh air. "There was a pediatrician around here who believed in sleeping out, no matter how cold the weather." A wing for the three servants ran off to the left from the stair landing. The third floor had built-in cedar closets and a large recreation room for Ping-Pong.

The gardens were designed by Ralph Griswold, a noted landscape architect known for his work at Chatham Village and Point State Park. James H. Higgins remembered the gardens when he was a child. Off the living room was a covered porch and a terrace with a garden pool and fountain. "A vegetable garden extended from the pantry through the length of the kitchen, the garage, and the turn-around court." Because the house is built into a steep hill, it had a series of terraces separated by sandstone borders and walls. The three lowest terraces had flowers and the highest, grass which extended to the woods. James Higgins remembered: "My father kept the lawn as if it were an English tennis court. He had people on their knees, cutting out the weeds."

Higgins House Roof. Photo by John H. Demmler.

Fred Okie lived in the house after the Higgins family. He said it was built like a fortress. He had to get a commercial telephone installation because the residential company could not get through the reinforced concrete floors. Only the finest materials were used. The concrete floors were covered with wood. Because the house was built before air conditioning, the walls had cork insulation between the plaster and the outside, making it amazingly cool in the summer and warm in winter.

Middle-Class Houses

The houses discussed so far have been large, elegant structures designed by architects for wealthy clients. Most middle-class families in Sewickley Borough lived in smaller houses set on lots about 50' x 100'. How these streets developed can be seen by looking at the history of a typical section, Centennial Avenue between Straight Street and Nevin Avenue. This had been part of a larger 25-lot plan recorded by Samuel Peebles in 1849. The Peebles plan covered the area bounded by Nevin, Broad, Beaver, and Centennial. At that time, the portion between Straight Street and Nevin Avenue had five large lots, most 132 feet by 365 feet, extending from Beaver to Centennial Avenues. William P. Murray acquired the property in various ways. He bought about two-thirds of the Peebles property in 1864 from the estate of Dr. John C. Murray for $10,000; In 1865, he bought the rest from Levi Wilson.

William P. Murray sold three lots in 1889 for $600 each. One went to Mattie M. Ritchey, widow. He sold another to Elmer E. Miller, an architect with offices in Pittsburgh, who designed the old Sewickley Public School on the corner of Thorne and Broad Streets. Mr. Miller was a pillar of the United Presbyterian Church and superintendent of its Sunday school from 1880-1890. He built two houses on his lot. The third lot went to to Nancy W. Little. The Little house was occupied until 1995 by her grandson, Richard McPherson, who remembered its history.

Grandfather Little was a salesman for the L. H. Smith glass company in Pittsburgh. He drowned in the Johnstown Flood [1889]. He had left the hotel and was on his way to the railroad station to come back to Pittsburgh when he remembered he had not paid his bill. He returned to the hotel to pay, and was swept away by the flood. The only thing my grandmother got was the house the company built for her. It was built as a duplex. She and her nine children lived on one side and rented the other for income.

After William P. Murray's death in 1891, his heirs registered a plan for the remaining lots. This plan shows how Murray had reconfigured the Peebles plan to make 15 lots, instead of five. These lots, mostly 50' by 170', were narrower on Centennial and half as deep. An alley inserted between Centennial and Beaver divided the Peebles lots in half, doubling the total number. (See the W.P. Murray heirs plan on Sewickley map, 1897.)

Little-McPherson House. 706 and 708 Centennial. Photo by John H. Demmler.

By 1897, there were seven houses on the south side of Centennial. In 1905, there were 14 structures on the 15 Murray lots, including an oddly shaped building near Nevin Avenue that jutted into the street and was labeled "old" in the insurance map. Most of the houses remain. They are comfortable, mostly frame buildings with porches facing the tree-lined street. Although they are close together, being on fifty-foot lots, they have small front yards and ample back yards. James Shaughnessy remembered his family's house at 718 Centennial when he was growing up in the 1920s.

> The first floor consisted of a large living room, a good size dining room and a large kitchen. The stairway to the second floor was to the right of the entry part of the hall. On the second floor was a bathroom and three bedrooms. The master bedroom and adjacent alcove took up the entire width at the front of the house. The third floor was a large, unpartitioned room with double windows at three of the sides. The house didn't have electricity. I recall there was a gas fixture on the wall of the upstairs hall. The gas had to be lit and the flame burned inside a fragile white mantle. [The back bedroom and the master bedroom had fireplaces with gas heaters.] My father installed a new Boomer gravity, coal-burning furnace in the house as soon as he bought it, so the fireplaces were seldom used. . . . Furnishings in the home were sparse in relation to today's standard. The master bedroom had a double bed, a dresser, a cedar chest, and a rocking chair. The living room was furnished with a black stained oak table, a leather-covered sofa, a chair set, a ladder-backed chair, and a large rocking chair.

Houses in the 700 block of Centennial are typical of small towns across the continent. Most are wooden structures of "balloon framed" construction. They have light frames supported entirely by closely spaced 2 by 4 boards. Principal structural members are made from two or more boards nailed together. Because massive hand-hewn beams were no longer necessary, two skilled carpenters or talented amateurs could assemble a house frame in a day.

Folk Greek Revival. 702 Centennial.
Photo by John H. Demmler.

This kind of construction was used for all sorts of so-called folk or vernacular houses built without architects, but using architectural styles. The two-family McPherson house, 706-708 Centennial, is folk Gothic Revival. Its steep twin peaks both delineate its two-family function and give a taste of the Gothic Revival gables in the Charles McKnight house on 29 Beaver Street that was mentioned in the chapter on nineteenth century architecture.

A folk Greek Revival example is the house on 702 Centennial. The front gable suggests the pediments found in Greek temples; the pediment on the porch reinforces this idea. Folk Greek Revival was popular in towns because the front gable end presents a narrow face to the street, fitting neatly into a small lot.

James Shaughnessy gave a good idea of life on this part of Centennial Avenue in his monograph "The Street Where I Lived." Combining his recollections with data from the 1920 Census gives a picture of middle-class life in Sewickley in the early twentieth century. Occupations ranged widely including:

Newspaper publisher	Ice company owner
Appliance store owner	Dentist
Plumber (3)	Boarding house keeper
Grocery store manager (2)	Victrola agent
Road worker	Train depot manager

James Shaughnessy gave details on some of the more interesting occupations.

[Frank J. S. Patton of 710 Centennial was the full-time resident plumber for the Henry Rea estate on Sewickley Heights.] He spent a lot of time gardening in his back yard. He was usually the one that had the first ripe tomatoes in late June. Of course it didn't hurt that the plants already had tomatoes on them when they were transplanted from Rea's greenhouse to his garden.

[Mr. Metz boarded at 713 Centennial.] He was a night watchman at a plant in Coraopolis. He would leave about 10 o'clock in the evening with an old-fashioned lunch pail for the walk down to the Sewickley Bridge, where he would catch the trolley for Coraopolis. Back he would come about 9 o'clock in the morning.

[In 1920 Mr. Shaughnessy's father, Patrick, built a tin shop in the rear of his house at 718 Centennial.] He had been operating out of a rental building in Coraopolis from 1914 until that time. By 1920 much of my father's roofing and heating business was coming from the Sewickley area, and it was very convenient to have his shop so near his home.

[Mr. and Mrs. Buck Crouse and their family of five children rented 715 Centennial Avenue.] Buck was a retired prize fighter. . . . When he came to Sewickley he had plans of opening a school of physical training to aid some wealthy Pittsburgh businessmen that had employed him to keep them in proper physical condition. His plans never materialized and he became employed as the personal bodyguard for Lewis A. Parks, one of the wealthier men on Sewickley Heights. His job was to protect Mr. Parks when he became inebriated. The disease must have been catching, as many evenings Buck had to crawl up the steps to the house after being let out of a taxi at the curb. Later Buck became associated with Father James R. Cox in operating a soup kitchen at Old St. Patrick's church in the Strip District.

[Mrs. Emma Hite of 720 Centennial ran a successful baking business out of her house.] She baked cakes which were displayed and sold in the prestigious grocery stores of the times, Campneys and Stevensons. My [Mr. Shaughnessy's] first job was to take the cakes down to the stores and put them in the cases. I got five cents a trip. Many were also picked up at her home by chauffeurs of the elite of Sewickley Valley.

[Charles F. Becker lived at 613 Centennial in 1920. His father, Captain Henry Becker, came to Sewickley around 1870 and started an express service, transporting packages and trunks from the railroad station to houses all over the area. The Beckers first used horses and wagons lodged in a large shed right beside his house. Later, they used trucks. When Henry Becker retired in 1898, he turned the business and the house over to his son.][26]

Multi-person Dwellings

Although most people lived in their own houses, there were other choices. In 1940 only 62 percent of dwelling units in Sewickley Borough were occupied by one family. Many Sewickley residents rented. In 1934, 707 dwelling units were occupied by owners; 607, by tenants. For example, on the 700 block of Centennial, Numbers 715 and 719 were rentals. Half of the Little-McPherson house was rented. Number 709 was a rental house until the late twenties when it was remodeled into a two-family house. Number 714 was a rental property that Mr. Shaugnessy's parents bought in 1924 for $5,000. After Patrick Shaughnessy's death, the rent was an important source of income.

Others lived in apartments in houses. Looking again at Centennial Avenue, across Straight Street from Church Way was a large three-story house, remodeled into three apartments by a widow. Number 705 Centennial had a furnished apartment on the third floor, rented in 1940 for $22.50 per month.

The nearest approach to multi-family housing was a strange building nicknamed "The Boathouse" because it had a pointed corner shaped like a ship's prow. Located on 672 Blackburn Road, it was one of the oldest structures in town when it was torn down in 1924. It was originally a log cabin where Joseph Marlatt lived and worked there from 1839 to 1848, pursuing his dual career as carpenter and an undertaker. In 1849 the pointed section which gave the building its name was added. In the early twentieth century, it became housing. Charles Butler remembered: "Four or five colored families lived there. Some worked for Challis, some for Jim Scott. It was there when I was a youngster. It was all attached together, like a row house." Virginia Hailstock said. "My mother's great aunts lived in the old boathouse, across from the YMCA."[27]

The Boathouse, so named because the corner looked like a prow. Multiple family housing on 672 Blackburn Road. Courtesy The Sewickley Valley Historical Society.

Many who would live in apartments today lived in hotels. There were two around the turn of the century, the Park Place Hotel and the Elmhurst Inn. The Elmhurst Inn had been Elmwood, a house owned by Dr. and Mrs. J. C. Murray in 1877. In 1890, the *Sewickley Valley* newspaper hailed Walter J. Kerr's plans to lease it for a hotel because, "It will help the economy. Purchasers will buy places and increase real estate." James Renwick Smith bought the property in 1894 but only kept it a short time. Around

1900 he sold it to Charles Cornelius, who renamed it the Elmhurst Inn and added wings, porches, and a cupola. Another wing, added in 1930, resulted in what George Swetnam described as "an architectural monstrosity, part brick and part frame and obviously the result of adding onto a building for utility rather than beauty."[28]

Nevertheless, the Elmhurst Inn became a fashionable place, boasting good china, linens, silver and even fresh produce from Neville Island. It was a convenient place for widows to live. Margaret Morgan, the first female justice of the peace in Western Pennsylvania, lived there. Gossip columns of the time attest to its stylishness. "Miss Alice G. Wood of Titusville is visiting Mrs. Samuel D. Robinson of the Elmhyrst [sic] Inn, Sewickley." "Eleanor Dravo of the Elmhurst Inn has returned to the Valley from New York, Philadelphia, and Atlantic City." "Management of Elmhyrst Inn, Sewickley, has arranged a series of Saturday evening dances for the entertainment of guests of the house and their guests."[29]

Even in 1932, the Elmhurst Inn was a well-known destination. S. Lee Kann described it in his chatty book *Show Places, Know Places, Go Places.*

> Because Sewickley is one of the most beautiful spots in the entire state, and because when we've needed a little pepping up and the desired rest from our arduous labors, we've always found it here. And we can stop at the beautiful Elmhurst Inn, where the food is delicious, the rooms spacious, and the atmosphere just what we were looking for. And we know of no better ways of spending an enjoyable week end. For your information one can secure a room here for as little as $75 a month which includes breakfast and dinner with three meals on Sundays.[30]

The other hotel in Sewickley, the Park Place, on River and Chadwick Avenues was mentioned in Chapter 14. The Park Place served as a transient and residential hotel and as a summer resort where people came to escape the heat of Pittsburgh. Mary Roberts Rinehart and her family spent the summer there in 1906 before buying a house in Osborne.

In 1920, the Park Place Hotel was rented by Andrew E. Hager and his wife, Bertha. The Hagers had immigrated from Switzerland in 1915. Boarders listed in the 1920 census were:

Alfred Pearson, salesman for a coal company, his wife, son, and daughter.
Arthur Howe, manufacturer, and his wife.
Emma Wallace, widow.
Francis B. Runyon, 28, insurance sales manager, and his wife.
Mary E. Gilmore, widow.
James R. Gilmore, stock broker.
William Satterlee, manager of a steel plant, and his wife.
William Goldin, insurance manager, and his wife and son.
George Wing, salesman, and his wife and son.
Brad and Donald Somerville, both railroad civil engineers.
Louis Ostrander, accountant, and his wife.
Edward McKinstry, stock broker, his wife and son.
Vincent Lewis, engineer in the gas works.
William Higgins, purchasing agent for the gas and electric company.
John Duro, salesman.
Hotel staff consisted of a cook, a porter, a housekeeper, a caterer, a waiter, and two chambermaids.

Captain Way remembered the Park Place Hotel in the 1920s. It was a three-story brick building with full length porches front and back. The hotel had its own gas well between the hotel and the river. The gas ran a generator that made electricity. The dining room could be turned into a large ballroom where Captain Way went to high school dances around 1920.

The hotel was abandoned in 1932 and torn down in 1938. Captain Way said the last occupant was Slim, who "arrived in a houseboat in 1935 and moved into the vacant Park Place Hotel where he raised chickens on the second floor."

Hotels such as the Park Place were convenient because housekeeping was unnecessary and because they were usually near the train station. Similar convenience came from boarding in private homes or boarding houses. Boarding benefited both parties. Owners received extra money. The boarders received a room, meals, and companionship. Families with a bit of extra space took in a boarder or two. For example, in 1920 Ira Gorsung, 709 Centennial Avenue, had a wife, two sons, and one daughter. He took in one roomer, the janitor of the public school. Mr. and Mrs. Hoffmon, 715

Centennial, had four daughters, 16-23, and one roomer, a seamstress. Mr. and Mrs. Charles Becker, 613 Centennial, had two daughters, one son, and one roomer, a worker in a steel mill. The 300 and 700 blocks of Centennial Avenue had a total of 23 boarders.

Others lived in a regular boarding house. Mary L. Green, 713 Centennial, ran a boarding house in a large, three-story brick house she rented from Charles Becker. In 1920, she had 8 boarders. Nearby, on 702 Centennial, Mrs. Charles H. Gordon, widow, ran a boarding house in the 1930s. Mr. Shaughnessy remembered, "Mother Gordon, as she was known in the neighborhood, had a number of boarders who would come every day for their evening meal. She had the reputation of being one of the finer cooks in the town."

Some boarding houses catered to young, single men. Frank Darlington was a well-to-do young man whose grandfather was among the founders of the McBeth Evans Glass Company and the Follansbee Steel Company. Before his marriage, he had a room and ate his meals in Mrs. Chantler's boarding house on 521 Beaver Street.

Although most buildings in the Sewickley valley were well kept, others were not. The *Weekly Herald* reported on housing in 1917.

> [Housing conditions] have been getting worse from year to year. . . . Tumble down shacks and hovels are permitted to occupy prominent locations and unsanitary conditions prevail. These barnacles depreciate the beauty and value of contiguous properties, and allow breeding places of disease and death. . . . Shacks clutter the vicinity of the school grounds, unsavory odors of the manure piles waft the spices of Araby into the school rooms. There is a market for 300 medium-sized dwellings.[31]

Even in 1940 there was no private bath in 12.5 percent of the Borough houses and no private flush toilet in 10 percent.

This chapter has given examples of the variety of houses and housing units which existed in the area in the first part of the twentieth century. Just as houses in the previous century varied by style and size, so did housing still vary in the Sewickley area. Accommodations were available for all income levels, from the president of a major corporation to the laborer in its mills.

[1] Montgomery Schuyler, "The Building of Pittsburgh." In *Architectural Record*, October 1911, p. 265.

[2] Library of Congress Manuscript Division. *Olmsted Associates Papers*. MFL Reel 158, Job File #3055.

[3] National Park Service, Frederick Law Olmsted National Historic Site, Brookline Mass. Archives.

[4] Library of Congress. Olmsted Papers.

[5] *Bulletin*, December 7, 1929, p. 16.

[6] *Craftsman*, v.20, 1911, p. 33 and pp. 575-576.

[7] Mary Beth Pastorius, "Rutan Designs: a Local Legacy." In *Sewickley Herald*, October 23, 1985, p. 5 and November 13, 1985, p. 21.

[8] "The Work of Rutan and Russell in Pittsburgh." In *The Architectural Record*, August 1904, v.18, p. 103.

[9] Ibid., p. 103.

[10] Ibid., pp. 112-113.

[11] *Sewickley Herald*, February 18, 1954, p. 3.

[12] Witold Rybczynski. *Home: a Short History of an Idea*. N.Y., Viking, 1986, p. 104.

[13] Schuyler, p. 265.

[14] E. Digby Baltzell. *The Protestant Establishment*, N.Y., Random House, 1964, p. 15.

[15] *Craftsman*, v.14, No. 4, p. 388.

[16] "Work of Rutan and Russell in Pittsburgh," p. 111.

[17] Pastorius, p. 5.

[18] Kidney, p. 81.

[19] *Suburban Life*, v.18, 1904, p. 303.

[20] *Craftsman*, v.20, 1911, p. 509.

[21] Witold Rybczynski. *Home,* p. 130 and p. 135.

[22] *426 Woodland Road Its History*, unpublished, 1986, p. 11.

[23] James D. Van Trump, *Life and Architecture in Pittsburgh*. Pittsburgh: Pittsburgh History & Landmarks Foundation, 1983, p. 114.

[24] Ibid., p. 116.

[25] Ibid., p. 111.

[26] *Way File.*

[27] *Sewickley Herald*, February 4 and 11, 1954.

[28] *Pittsburgh Press*, Nov. 15, 1959.

[29] *Pittsburg Bulletin*, June 21, May 3, 1902.

[30] S. Lee Kann, *Show Places, Know Places, Go Places*. Lee & Art Publishing Company, Pittsburgh, 1932, p. 85.

[31] *Weekly Herald,* Feb. 17 and March 24, 1917.

Chapter 21
Summering in Sewickley

The Sewickley area at the turn of the century was a thriving community that was remarkably self-sufficient. It had its own churches, stores, clubs, sports, social organizations, schools, and public utilities. In one respect, it was far from self-sufficient. Much of the income came from Pittsburgh via the men who lived in Sewickley but worked in the city. Because of this extra income, life was far grander than it would have been in a small town beyond the reach of commuter trains. Compare Sewickley with Zelienople. Both had wealthy citizens living in large, comfortable houses. But Zelienople's old-money group was not swelled by a new group of well-to-do commuters. The book *Sewickley Valley Society* described the results of this prosperity in 1895.

> The village is not like other villages. Its broad streets are splendidly paved, its public buildings are handsome and artistic in architecture. There are flourishing trees everywhere, and if there exists anything unsightly in Sewickley it keeps in the background most effectually. Added to these traits is the purity and abundance of its water supply, its sewerage system, its superb public school, its churches, and its many excellent stores.[1]

Around 1900 the wealthy class in the Sewickley area grew again as a new group entered the scene. Sewickley and Sewickley Heights became summer retreats for people from Pittsburgh and Allegheny. Summer resorts were sprouting all over America from 1880-1917. Such places as Bar Harbor and Northeast Harbor in Maine, Watch Hill in Rhode Island, and Lenox, Massachusetts became resorts for the wealthy. The same factors that drove people to retreat from the cities, dirt and smoke, drove them to leave for the summer.

The Sewickley valley had been discovered as a pleasant summer resort shortly after the coming of the railroad. By 1898, the *Sewickley Valley* could boast that the area "will have large accessions of the best classes to the population of Sewickley this coming summer." Most rented houses, but some stayed in the Park Place Hotel or in boarding houses. A list of people who rented houses for the summer of 1898 included many prominent Pittsburghers: James Pontrefact of Lincoln Avenue in Allegheny was an iron and steel magnate; William Thaw had steamboat and coal companies; Joseph Horne and Henry Buhl ran their eponymous department stores; and Frank Nicola was the first developer of Oakland. The reasons given for Sewickley's popularity were great natural scenery, pure air, the best society with "good wholesome gentle refined people," fine streets and roads, electric lights, and good railroads.[2]

The Pittsburg Index in 1902 described the town.

> Sewickley was until recently one of the many quiet country towns to be seen from the car windows as one speeds out of Pittsburg westward through Pennsylvania and Ohio. But on account of its natural beauties, its nearness to the city, its many advantages, not the least being no trolley lines, it has become a summer resort, a place of summer home[s], and has risen to prominence as such in spite of itself and the disgust of the "natives," as they are termed by the army of "summer people," who settled in the valley and the surrounding hills. . . . A number of people of the social set in the two cities, [Pittsburgh and Allegheny] who do not own homes in Sewickley attach themselves to the summer colony by renting desirable places in the valley. Among them are Mr. and Mrs. Moses Atwood and family, who occupy Mr. Lawrence Pearson's home at Shields; Mr. and Mrs. Frank F. Nicola have taken Mr. Charles T. Nevin's residence at Quaker Valley, Mr. and Mrs. Henry Buhl have the Shannon home at Edgeworth; Mr. James A. Chambers and family are spending the summer in the old home of Mrs. L. Halsey Williams, at Leetsdale; Mr. and Mrs. W. M. Scaife and family have taken the Sands homestead at Osborne for the summer.

The list continued through eight more names.[3]

Of course as some moved to the valley for the summer, others moved out. The *Bulletin*, which kept track of comings and goings in 1928, noted that Mrs. William Murdock of Thorn Street was leaving for Walloon Lake, Michigan and Mr. Albert Burchfield Craig of Graham Street, for Chatauqua. *The Pittsburgh Index* reported in August 1902,

> Sewickley, which was very gay during June and in a social rush through July, has in August quieted down to such an extent that it seems dead. Most of the visitors have returned home, and many of the social set have left for the mountains, Canada, or the sea shore or gone on an extensive outing in Europe.

Many who came to Sewickley to rent later bought summer houses. *The Bulletin* reported,

Mr. and Mrs. James Pontrefact have opened their country residence at Shields Station (Edgeworth) and will be there from now until fall. Mr. William Witherow gave one of the handsomest receptions of the year at the Witherow family house at Quaker Valley, the event being intended as a housewarming as well as a reception occasion. The Witherow town house is on Sherman Avenue, Allegheny, but for several seasons the family has spent the summer in Sewickley. Last fall Mr. and Mrs. Witherow bought Rokohl Place. . . which they have remodeled and made one of the most beautiful and comfortable residence properties in the Valley of beautiful homes.[4]

The 1904 *Social Directory for Greater Pittsburgh* lists many from Pittsburgh or Allegheny with summer places in Sewickley.

Mr. and Mrs. James B. Oliver
Winter Home, 701 Ridge Avenue, Allegheny
Summer Home, Shields, Pa.

Mr. and Mrs. James G. Pontrefact
1014 Lincoln Avenue, Allegheny
Summer Home, "Bagatelle," Shields, Pa.

Mr. and Mrs. W. H. Singer
934 Western Avenue, Allegheny
Summer Home, Edgeworth

Mr. and Mrs. John Walker
1231 Western Avenue, Allegheny
Summer Homes, Leetsdale, Pa., Beaumaris, Canada

Mr. and Mrs. William Walker
828 Lincoln Avenue, Allegheny
Summer Home, Shields

Some summer residents later moved permanently to Sewickley. General George Cass, president of the Ohio and Pennsylvania Railroad, first summered at the Park Place Hotel before renting a house in the valley where his family enjoyed the healthful waters of the town. Later, General Cass built a large house in Osborne.

Sewickley Heights

Sewickley did not change character with the influx of summer visitors. Sewickley Heights did. From a rural area with scattered single-family farms it became a "rookery of millionaires," a haven for some of Pittsburgh and Allegheny's richest industrialists. The wealth and power of this group is hard to comprehend. Six of the Heights industrialists controlled 25 banks and at least 50 corporations in Pittsburgh.[5] By 1907, the Heights' continuing reputation was established.

Highest of all the Pittsburgh heavens is Sewickley Heights. Twelve miles down the Ohio River lies the select village of Sewickley, in which all vulgar street cars are forbidden; and along the slope behind it, looking as though they were boxes of a vast opera house, stands an array of stately homes. Most of the owners of these mansions are steel millionaires.[6]

Where did the birds in this rookery of millionaires come from? Of the group that moved there between 1900 and 1915, 33 percent came from Allegheny, 25 percent from the East End and 40 percent from Sewickley. They formed a social group of impeccable standing. In 1921, 96 percent of the 47 iron and steel magnates living in the Heights were listed in the Social Register. By 1943, it was 100 percent.

A full 40 percent of the same group were in the iron and steel industry. Seventeen percent were in other manufacturing industries and the remaining 43 percent in banking, investments, or professions.[7]

By 1904, the owners included:

Mrs. Elisabeth M. J. Horne
838 Lincoln Avenue, Allegheny
Summer Home, "Ridgeview Farm," Sewickley Heights.

Mrs. Benjamin Franklin Jones (Jones & Laughlin Steel)
801 Irwin Avenue, Allegheny
Summer Home, "Franklin Farm," Sewickley Heights

Mr. and Mrs. Benjamin F. Jones, Jr.
701 Irwin Avenue, Allegheny
Summer Home, "Fairacres," Sewickley Heights

Mr. and Mrs. Henry W. Oliver (Oliver Iron and Steel)
845 Ridge Avenue, Allegheny
Summer Home, Sewickley Heights

Mrs. William Thaw, Jr. (Father-in-law was railroad executive)
930 Lincoln Avenue, Allegheny
Summer Home, "As You Like It," Sewickley Heights

Mr. and Mrs. Charles Scaife (President of William
Scaife and Sons, steel tank manufacturers)
1136 Western Avenue, Allegheny
Summer Home, Sewickley Heights

Mr. and Mrs. James Wood Scully (Investments)
845 Lincoln Avenue, Allegheny
Summer Home, "Oak Ledge," Sewickley Heights

Mr. and Mrs. William P. Snyder (President, Clairton Steel)
Colonial Place, East End
Summer Home, "Wilpen Hall," Sewickley Heights

Mr. and Mrs. Willard W. Willock (General Manager,
Monongahela Connecting Railroad)
705 Irwin Avenue, Allegheny
Summer Home, "Gladmore Farm," Sewickley Heights

Why was Sewickley Heights' development so far behind the valley and what spurred the rush to the Heights around 1900? One factor was transportation. The Heights were relatively inaccessible before the automobile because the trip from house to train station by horse and carriage was time-consuming. Another factor was entertainment. What was there to do perched on a hill in no matter how grand a house? Again, as with the Valley, there were two reasons for the popularity of the Heights: the push from the problems of the city, especially Allegheny, and the pull of lovely country-side made accessible by new modes of transportation, not the railroad this time, but the automobile.

The push towards the Heights came from the decline of Allegheny. Most of the first summer residents to come to the Heights came from Allegheny. The area around Ridge Avenue had been among the most fashionable in Pittsburgh. Just looking at the few remaining houses will give an idea of its splendid past. The A. M. Byers house, now part of the Community College of Allegheny County, had 90 rooms and 14 baths. Across the road is the former William P. Snyder house, a stylish brownstone complete with ballroom. Down the street lived B. F. Jones in an enormous 44-room Tudor mansion, now used by the Community College of Allegheny County. Between the Civil War and World War I Allegheny was a prime center for industrial magnates. In 1874, 29 percent of iron and steel magnates lived in Allegheny.[8] When Allegheny City was unwillingly annexed to Pittsburgh in 1906, the decline of the area accelerated. By the 1950s, the grand houses had been abandoned.

The pull to the Heights was composed of several factors. One was the beautiful, unspoiled countryside with rolling hills and spectacular views. The railroad had done little for the development of the Heights. A horse and carriage would take at least half an hour to reach the Heights from the station. By car it takes as little as ten minutes.

One man, Benjamin Franklin Jones, is often credited with attracting the rich to the Heights. He built a house for himself and each of his three daughters, forming a ready-made group of compatible companions for others seeking a suburban retreat.

An important force drawing people toward the Heights was the Allegheny Country Club, opened in 1902. It became the social and athletic center of the Heights. When people tired of the long commute from Allegheny to play golf, they were inspired to build houses close by.

Country clubs were the nucleus of the rural retreats for wealthy businessman, springing up nationwide in the early 1900s. Club membership was a prerequisite for living in Tuxedo Park, an outer suburb of New York City. An article in the *Bulletin* suggests that Sewickley Heights was patterned on Tuxedo Park. "The families who would like to make it [the Heights] Pittsburgh's Tuxedo Park lived in suburban Allegheny."[9]

Other similar retreats in the suburbs were:

New York City—Greenwich, Connecticut.
Philadelphia—Chestnut Hill and Radnor.
Cleveland—Shaker Heights.
Chicago—Winnetka.

The development of Sewickley Heights had obvious effects on the Sewickley Valley. The influx of wealth improved sales and services for businesses. The new Sewickley Heights group had enormous estates with houses so large that most of them have been torn down. They had large gardens, dairies, farms, and entertained mightily. Such establishments required huge staffs. According to the 1940 census, 35 percent of the employed population of Sewickley Heights Borough were domestic workers. This includes only those who stayed on the place; others lived in the valley and commuted up the hill to work. This group was made up of Italian immigrants and many more blacks than had been there before.

The Heights gave the whole Sewickley area a far grander image than it had before 1900. The name Sewickley came to denote an exclusive suburb with enormous, almost unbelievable wealth.

---

[1] *Sewickley Valley Society*, 1895, p. 25.

[2] *The Sewickley Valley*, February 26, 1898.

[3] *The Pittsburg Index*, July 19, 1902, p. 21.

[4] *The Bulletin*, June 21, 1902, p. 11 and May 17, 1902, p. 15.

[5] Michael P. Weber, "Community and Mobility." In *City at the Point*, pp. 373-74.

[6] H. N. Casson, *The Romance of Steel; the Story of a Thousand Millionaires*. N. Y., A.S. Barnes, 1907, p. 275.

[7] John N. Ingham, "Steel City Aristocrats." In *City at the Point*. Pittsburgh, The University Press, 1989, pp. 280-281.

[8] Ingham, pp. 274-5.

[9] *Bulletin*, August 22, 1935.

Chapter 22
Sports in the Twentieth Century

YMCA Activities

Active sports continued to flourish in Sewickley as they had in the nineteenth century. Many were centered at the Young Men's Christian Association. Originally housed on the second floor of the bank building on the corner of Broad and Beaver, the YMCA offered a 300-volume library and reading room, a gymnasium with classes for boys and businessmen, and a glee club. Henry W. Oliver donated about five acres at the junction of Backbone and Blackburn for a new facility that opened in 1904. The new building was in the Colonial Revival style popular in many Sewickley houses at the time. It looked like a house, not an institution. The YMCA property was enlarged in 1917, when Mrs. Henry Oliver Rea and Mrs. Henry Oliver donated land for a golf links. The development of the course was postponed during World War I because the land was used to grow corn to support the war effort. After the war, Jack Hutchinson, the professional at the Allegheny Country Club, laid out a nine-hole course. Golf continued until 1945 when the YMCA donated the course to Sewickley Borough for the War Memorial Park.

The YMCA had a mission beyond athletics and entertainment, according to the *Weekly Herald*, 1903:

> If the parents of this community have a right conception of the terrible temptations daily assailing their boys, and the necessity of safeguarding them as far as possible by moral and Christian influences, especially in their hours of recreation, the YMCA of Sewickley will never lack for support. . . . It is to secure from [men and boys] decisions for life which will result in a change of habits, sincere repentance of heart, and a new ambition for service in the Kingdom of God.[1]

High moral purpose aside, there was plenty of fun to be had. Bob Ingram remembered, "Back in the '30s, there was little else to do other than be a member of the Y. If we weren't playing baseball, we were shooting pool, playing Ping Pong, swimming, or playing tennis." The YMCA also offered basketball. Boys went on all-day hiking picnics. The Young Men's Club had gym classes with dumb bells and parallel bars. There was bowling for boys and businessmen. Businessmen were urged to join the volleyball club. "Get into the game a couple of times each week. You can afford the time because it will be time well spent and the added physical welfare will make you feel like a new man."[2]

Harry S. Day was the physical director in the 1930s and 1940s. His daughter, Phyllis Day Goble, remembered:

> He brought roller skating to the gym and froze water on the tennis courts for ice skating in winter. He had a circus every spring in the gym, and he'd always be the clown and perform on the rings and trapeze. Every Easter, there was a gigantic Easter Egg hunt up on the golf course.

The YMCA provided a limited number of sedentary activities. Radios were the high technology fad of the day, so the YMCA sponsored a Radio Club to build radios and learn to use Morse Code. Later, in the 1940s, there were courses in arts and crafts.

The Harvest Fair was sponsored by the Y. The Fair grew out of the Victory Gardens grown during World War II. The first, in 1943, attracted 4,000 people. The next year, attendance doubled. The Fair was similar to a county fair, with a wide mixture of events: competitions in horticulture, canning, flowers, and needlework; selection of a festival queen; a midway; fortune telling; and fireworks.

Later, around the 1950s, Mary Ann Baldridge remembered a "canteen" in the YMCA every Saturday night with dancing in the gym to records. In summer, the canteen moved outside to the black-topped tennis courts.

The YMCA changed gradually with the times. Until 1928, it held only religious services on Sunday. Sewickley's young people welcomed a new policy, however, according to the *Pittsburgh Sun-Telegraph.*

> More than 350 young men, boys and girls swarmed to the Sewickley Young Men's Christian Association yesterday and, for the first time in the history of the organization, were able to abandon themselves to a Sunday afternoon of wholesome sports and amusements. . . . The religious meeting, which was held in the course of the afternoon, was attended by at least twice as many members as a direct sequence of the sports features.[3]

At first, the Y admitted only white men and boys. In 1919, a group of young women met to organize a Young Women's Christian Association, quickly gaining 350 members. The next year, the groups merged. The women got exclusive use of the pool two days a week, the men the other days. Bowling alleys, tennis courts, and playing fields were used by both sexes.

Blacks were not admitted until 1970. They did have their own YMCA after 1913 when they remodeled the St. Matthew's A.M.E. Zion church building on Walnut Street. The ground floor had a library, game room, reception room, and office. The basement contained a 25' x 26' gymnasium and a dressing room. Despite such limited facilities, the Colored YMCA offered many of the same activities as the Sewickley Y. The Round Table Club for Men met every Sunday to study Great Events in the Life of Christ. The Boys' Bible Class studied Men who Dared. A Lyceum sponsored debates. Then there was lighter fare, basketball, social games, luncheons and receptions. The New Year's reception in 1920 attracted 200 people.

Walnut Street YMCA, formerly AME Zion Church. 409 Walnut Street.
Courtesy The Sewickley Valley Historical Society.

The *Sewickley Herald* in January, 1919 lists one week's activities held at the black YMCA or at the school pavilion. There was a basketball game between the Y Tigers against the Scholastic Juniors of Pittsburgh; a pool match between the Walnut Street Y and the Center Avenue Y of Pittsburgh; the Men's Forum had a concert; there was a Sunday evening religious service; the Young Men's Culture Club "gave a reception to their lady friends in their newly furnished club room."[4]

There was also a Young Women's Christian Association for blacks. Miss Hailstock went there. "There was no pool, but we had games like basketball. We knitted for the soldiers in World War I." One week's activities in 1919 give an idea of its programs: an evening speech by the pastor of the A.M.E. Zion Church; an Adult Bible Class meeting; musical and literary programs; French and English classes; and a Leper Mission meeting at the residence of Mrs. Elizabeth Thompson.[5]

Sports on the Ohio River

It was not until the early twentieth century that the Ohio River became a focus of sports activities. This contrasts with Pittsburgh where boating clubs had flourished between 1865 and 1885. Around 1870, the Pittsburgh area had nearly twenty clubs competing in rowing races on the rivers. Why was Sewickley not involved until after 1900? Very practically, boating requires a fairly constant water level. As we have seen, the Ohio River before being dammed fluctuated widely, making boating impossible much of the year. This did not deter rowing on the Allegheny River, however, where the sport flourished despite similar fluctuations in the water level. Excessive rains made the river dangerous in the spring and the river was too low during the summer months. Thrifty farmers often waded across the Allegheny to avoid paying tolls.

Dams improved river flow on both rivers at about the same time. A sandbag wing dam just above Herr's Island, now Washington Landing, was built in 1878 to permit boat access to the Allegheny Arsenal during low water.[6] This also created a pool suitable for rowing. The first attempt to provide for year-round use of the Ohio River came in 1874 with the construction of the Davis Island dam 1.6 miles below Sewickley. This was a wicket dam, utilizing a number of large folding boards, called wickets, which were hinged to a concrete base at the bottom of the river. When the wickets were raised, a pool formed behind them. During high water, wickets were lowered to allow free transportation. The Davis Island dam, completed in 1885, was 1,223 feet long with 305 separate wickets. On opening day, thousands lined the lock walls as twelve steamboats tooted and whistled their way through.[7] Another wicket dam, the predecessor of the present Dashields dam in Edgeworth, was finished around 1907. The dam created a nice pool right on the Sewickley/Edgeworth waterfront. Boats could pass all year long and, luckily, the same pools created for the steamboats could be used for water sports in Sewickley and other river towns.

Strangely, when dams were first proposed to tame the Ohio, coal shippers were violently opposed unless arrangements could be made to pass their fleets through without stopping and separating for the passage through locks. They threatened to blow up any dams. Coal shippers feared that locks and dams would slow traffic. As dam technology improved, they changed their minds.[8] Locks did take valuable time; Captain Way said that in the 1930s it took 17 or 18 hours a trip to negotiate the 70 locks between Pittsburgh and Cincinnati. This disadvantage was outweighed, however, by having the river open to traffic almost all year.

Towboat "Valiant" laid up for low water and ice. Cakes of ice could gouge wooden hulls. Foot of Chestnut Street, about 1904.
Courtesy of The Sewickley Valley Historical Society.

Another reason for lack of river use in Sewickley around the turn of the century was more convoluted. The members of the early Pittsburgh rowing clubs were almost all industrial craftsmen, laborers, or clerks. By 1890 the popularity of the old workingmen's clubs declined and boating became a pastime of the college-educated middle class.[9] The Sewickley Canoe and Boat Club, which was solidly middle class, fit neatly into the new group. Its president pro tem., Gilbert Hays, started soliciting members in April 1907. By July he had 100 members to help celebrate the opening of the clubhouse. The event was recorded in the Society column of *The Pittsburgh Post* which reported that "a number of society women of the valley were in attendance." Gilbert Hays, declared "If enthusiasm counts for anything, the new canoe and boat club is an assured success." The clubhouse, a houseboat moored at the foot of Chestnut Street, contained a dance hall, reception area, and dressing rooms. The opening celebration included canoe and rowboat races and a lantern parade of 50 boats led by the Misses Dippold in their motorboat "Driftwood." The festivities ended with a dance.

It was entirely fitting that the Dippold sisters were chosen to lead the parade because they were Sewickley institutions, famous for their river knowledge. They lived with their father, Captain Fred Dippold, near the river. The Dippolds were river buffs. Captain Fred Dippold conducted a life-long search along the river banks, amassing a collection of ancient relics for a museum in his house.[10] The sisters were two of the first three women to hold first class pilot's licenses on the river. The Misses Dippold used their boat, the "Driftwood," for jaunts on the rivers. In 1899 they took a trip up the Monongahela to its headwaters.[11] Although they refused several offers for jobs as pilots, wanting mainly to be able to ride in the pilot house while taking river tours, Miss Louise Dippold put her skill to good use in effecting a rescue in 1907, according to *The Pittsburgh Post*:

A number of people in a launch became bewildered, not knowing how to navigate their craft in the low water so as to get to Pittsburgh, there being but one foot of water on the sill at dam No. 2. The boat appeared to be surrounded by sand bars. From a window in her house, Miss Louise Dippold observed the predicament of the strangers and started out in a yawl to help them. Much to the surprise of the pilot and others in the party, Miss Dippold guided the launch through channels unseen except to a trained eye.

Steamboat passing Sewickley. Courtesy The Sewickley Valley Historical Society.

Dashields Dam and Locks. Steamboat "Saint Pearl" in the Locks, 1937. *Sewickley Herald.*

While members of Sewickley society enjoyed dancing and regattas at the Canoe and Boat Club, others took advantage of a very popular but less stylish facility that opened on the Ohio River at the end of Ferry Street in 1915. Walnut Beach was the brainchild of Jimmy Gray, a civic-minded tailor and promoter deluxe. It was not a sandy beach but a place where the river was shallow with a stony bottom. It had a pavilion and a tent for bathing facilities. *The Herald* called it "a miniature Atlantic City." There were tables and benches for 1,000 or more, a coffee house, refreshment stands, swings, a new float with high dive and springboard, and a slide like a roller coaster that went out over the water. Electric

Walnut Beach, Sewickley.

lights burned all night. *The Herald* reported that by the end of July 1920, 15 large church groups had already spent the day. Walnut Beach was the site of many company picnics, including a huge event for 5,000 people hosted by the Duff Manufacturing Company.

In 1920, there were 80 camps on the grounds at Walnut Beach and there were 50 on the waiting list. John Alexander remembered, "There were little cottages owned by Pittsburgh people. Families stayed there for the summer and men commuted weekends." The *Pittsburgh Post* sponsored volunteer lifeguards. Mr. Alexander said, "You got a jersey with 'Pittsburgh Post' on it. Some men worked on the Allegheny River and some on Walnut Beach. My brother and I were life guards."

Crowds at Walnut Beach swelled when steamboats brought people down from Pittsburgh. The ship "Islam Grotto" came with 1500 passengers, orchestra, and brass band on the Wednesday after Labor Day in 1920. Another ship, the "Homer Smith" made two trips a day, one up and one down. Sewickley people took the boat to Pittsburgh for the day, while Pittsburgh people came down to enjoy the beach. At night the tide reversed.

It is surprising that Sewickley put up with the noise and commotion of Walnut Beach. On holidays Walnut Beach had as many people as the whole Borough. It had an unsavory reputation among some Sewickley residents. Mrs. Jane Evans, who was brought up on Peebles Street, remembered: "Some nice people from Sewickley had a beach there and then it became Walnut Beach. We didn't go; it was just a tramp place." Mary Louise Johnson said that she never went there. "It was absolutely horrendous. We were never allowed to go near the river. People from all over the area [went there]—all kinds." A letter from Edward Woods to Sewickley Council deplored the conduct on the beach "that if true should be prohibited and if untrue Sewickley people should be able to absolutely deny."[12]

The problem was solved in 1927 when the lease was suspended to enable slag to be dumped in preparation for moving the railroad tracks.

Boating and swimming in the river were not limited to Walnut Beach. Most women remembered that they were not allowed to swim in the river when they were girls. Boys swam whether they were allowed or not. Charles Stinson recalled:

Ohio River, Sewickley. Courtesy Sewickley Valley Historical Society.

I wasn't allowed to play around the river. I went down one day and played around all afternoon. When I got home, my mother knew about it. A few weeks later, I did it again and she knew again. "A little bird told me," she said. Actually, it was a lady who lived on Chestnut Street on the railroad tracks—the way I went down.

John Alexander said:

Mostly boys were involved in escapades on the river. We used to sneak off and go down to the river almost every day. We weren't allowed and we'd get a whipping every time. There was an old fellow who ran the grocery store. He would tell my parents. They would say, "You are going to drown!" As long as I can remember, we never had anyone drown along the Edgeworth area of the river. In Sewickley, they did.

Richard McPherson remembered swimming at Captain Dippold's pilot house, which had been presented to the Captain by the coal combine in appreciation for his years of service. Mr. McPherson said, "As kids if we behaved ourselves, he would allow us to jump off the pilot house into the river to swim. Of course we weren't allowed to do that, but he would let us."

Some boys had their own boats. Charles Stinson remembered his first boat.

A man offered us a barge-like thing three feet long made of very heavy timbers. He was taking his houseboat down the river, and had used this to pole in from the houseboat. We had to make our own oars. Made a sail out of old curtain or drapery. The first time we went down river. We really had to work to get that thing back up. After that, all trips started against the current. Later on, we spent $15 each for a homemade skiff. It was a rowing boat. We got an outboard motor for $75 from Sears. Later, we got a canoe. There was very little water traffic and not much commercial traffic on Sunday.

The "Homer Smith" picking up passengers on Monongahela Wharf to spend the day at Walnut Beach.

Canoes were popular. John Alexander canoed on the river with his friends.

We were on the river all the time. Our favorite thing was to [paddle our canoe] and ride the waves behind the paddle wheels. We tried to catch the biggest one. We tried to get in close.

A group of young canoeists from the Manchester district of the North Side spent summer weekends in two big tents pitched on the river bank. One person would stay all week to watch the canoes. Mr. Alexander and his friends ran errands for him.

Captain Fred Way, Jr. of the "Betsy Ann," a packet steamer on the Pittsburgh to Cincinnati line, promoted the river with annual races. *The Sewickley Herald*, July 5, 1929 reported that the "Betsy Ann" would race the steamer "Tom Greene," flagship of the Chris Greene Lines. "The 'Betsy Ann' was vanquished last year and forced to give up the antlers, symbol of river supremacy. Captain and crew of the 'Betsy Ann' are preparing."

Captain Fred Way's "Lady Grace" continued the boating tradition.

I had a little boat here, built in the back yard. She looked like a little river boat. I took her up to Kinzua Dam. Had a lot of fun out of that boat. I advertised in *The Herald* that I would take people out on the river. We went on picnics up behind Neville Island. There was a nice sandbar up there and we could get out and romp around. I built her in 1955 and tore her up in 1965. She got the infirmities of old age. I was afraid I was going to go down to the dock and see the smokestacks sticking up.

The river was far from clean. Dr. Fletcher K. White complained in 1928:

The Ohio River of today is a disgrace to civilization. All sorts of oils, acids, and sewers pour into the river every hour and, in a few years, if some method is not used to stop this pollution, the river will be worse than at present, if that is possible. It may then be a stench to the nostrils of mankind and a menace to the health of the Valley.[13]

Many boys fished nevertheless. Charles Butler said,

We started catching catfish in the river. At that time that's all you would get. It used to be if you got a fish out of there it tasted oily. They cleaned up the river. Now you catch everything in there.

"Lady Grace," built by Capt. Frederick Way, Jr. Courtesy Sewickley Valley Historical Society.

Richard McPherson remembered, "We used to catch a lot of catfish. Used to catch muskrats as a business. We sold them for muskrat gloves."

Hunting

Men enjoyed hunting, especially in undeveloped places in the Heights. The most organized hunting was on Sewickley Heights at the McKean Shooting Club on the tract formerly owned by Governor Thomas McKean. Organized in the 1880s by Westinghouse Air Brake officials, the club had shooting rights over 2,300 acres. They sowed fields with millet and buckwheat to provide food for quail. Quail had been plentiful in Sewickley near the river in the mid-nine-teenth century. Captain Anderson remembered seeing lots of them in cleared fields and Robert Wardrop found them at Shields and Wardrop nursery in Edgeworth in the 1860s. But hunters shot them for food and for sale at Pittsburgh markets and they were disappearing in the wild.

Party of Successful Deer Hunters. *Weekly Herald, Sept. 19, 1903.*

The McKean Shooting Club imported 1,000 quail in both spring and fall to improve the hunting. Later, the State Game Commission imported a total of 60,000 quail between 1915 and 1925. Unfortunately, the only birds available were the Mexican species. These interbred with the hardier native species and eventually the weaker hybrid died out.

Interestingly, in the same period, 1915-1925, the Game Commission imported 150,000 cottontail rabbits with the idea that if the hunters had rabbits available, they would shoot fewer quail.[14] Many Sewickley men went hunting all over the area. Richard McPherson remembered: "Justin Lees lived in a house that used to be called Groundhog Inn, up the hill towards the Burgwin place. Dad used to take me up there to hunt rabbits and pheasants." Lieutenant Masters: "I hunted up here. The rich people didn't mind a poor man shooting rabbits, but not quail or pheasants. That was *their* sport." John Alexander: "We used to hang out on Spanish Tract coon hunting. We shot them out of the tree."

The *Weekly Herald* described a hunt in 1903:

Every Saturday a merry party of coon hunters, with their guns and dogs, mount a six-horse rig and hie themselves to the shadows of Link's Bridge on Nigger Hollow, Beaver County, where grows the festive raccoon or the luscious possum. . . . During the evening, McMaster spied a juicy possum and just then the possum saw him coming, and the race began. McMaster is a good sprinter, and soon had his victim up a tree, and then went up after him. Whether he secured the prize or the prize got him, we have not learned, as he has not been since seen.[15]

What is now Raccoon State Park was an excellent place to hunt. Richard McPherson remembered,

About 30 businessmen in Sewickley formed the Big Travis Lodge. Each put in $50 and they bought 200 or 300 acres in the middle of what is now Raccoon Park. They hunted raccoons.

All agree that there was no deer hunting in the Heights because there were no deer in the 1920s and 1930s. John Alexander, for instance, said: "There weren't any deer when I was young. They had been killed off." The deer population of Sewickley had fluctuated wildly since the arrival of the first settlers. In the time of the Indians, the deer population was controlled by wolves, mountain lions, and arrows. Later, the hunter's rifle almost exterminated the deer. Most people thought they would disappear from Western Pennsylvania, like the elk, the buffalo, and the wolf. Captain Anderson remembered that when he was a boy in the 1830s there were deer only in Sewickley Heights but, "that was a great place for deer." In 1897, new laws prohibited selling deer meat, shooting at salt licks, and hunting with dogs. In 1907 shooting deer without antlers was prohibited. The population exploded. In 1907, there were 200 deer killed in Pennsylvania; in 1915, 1200; in 1935, 70,000.[16]

When the deer returned to the Heights in 1922 there was great excitement. The *Herald* reported:

Not more than one person in a hundred knows that, after fifty years, wild deer have come back to the hills about Sewickley. For the past year a small herd of deer has made its home in the woods on Sewickley Heights. . . . The Wild Life League reports that dogs are likely to run the deer to death or to drive them out of our hills if some drastic step is not taken to protect the herd. The League says that all dogs not accompanied by their owners and unlicensed dogs are to be shot. After a number of these Airedales and other dogs have been shot, dog owners, the League thinks, will begin to take notice.[17]

Other Sports

Ice skating, another sport popular in the early decades of the twentieth century, was sometimes possible on the river. At other times, if there were sidewalks, people could roller skate. Mrs. Orndorff remembered her first chance to skate.

When we came down [to Osborne in 1908], there were no sidewalks. The road was not paved, just dirt. I can remember when the sidewalks were put in. It was a wonderful place for us to roller skate. We had to take care of our younger sister and brother all the time. I was in charge of my sister Alice; she was just a baby. I loved to roller skate. I held her in my arms and skated on the sidewalk up and down Beaver Road. A neighbor called [my mother] and said, "Do you know that you daughter is skating with the baby in her arms?" I was a very good skater, and Alice loved it.

Roller skaters could take advantage of the town's level ground. *The Herald* reported in 1915:

The roller skate craze has come back. It never really went out as far as children were concerned. Now however, young ladies have taken it up—not on skating rinks by the way, but in the open air for exercise and fun on the sidewalks and smooth pavements of the city streets. . . .

The fad has struck this town along with many others in this country and already the village kill-joys are protesting and calling for laws to prohibit skating on the sidewalks. It was ever thus. No sooner does youth find a new way of amusing itself, no matter how innocent—than some long-faced, vinegar-blooded reformer is out with a protest. . . . There can be no just objection to the young girls bringing the bloom of health to their cheeks by such beneficial exercise as roller skating on the sidewalks of their home town. Let the reformer purchase a pair of skates and use them. It will work off some of the bile and give him a brighter outlook on life.[18]

Helen Hegner said, "We used to skate all over Sewickley. We had skates that clamped on your shoes, not shoe skates. They had steel wheels." Miss Hailstock remembered roller skating in a rink in an old pavilion where the school playground was.

Perhaps the sport most fondly remembered in interviews is sled riding. Here was a sport that all able-bodied citizens could enjoy: blacks and whites, adults and children, males and females. Girls appreciated having an excuse to wear pants because skirts got caught under the runners. Miss Hailstock said, "My brother had a bobsled. Different boys would come—rich, poor, black and white—and borrow that bobsled." Helen Hegner: "If you wanted a good sled, you had to have a Flexible Flyer. Years ago, they had wooden rails. You used to sit higher."

Sewickley is an ideal place for riding sleds because it has hills ending on a flat plain. Sledding on the flat sounds impossible but Miss Hailstock said kids hitched their sleds to cars and rode all around. Dangerous as this sounds, Helen Hegner's description of riding on the hills sounds worse.

The Davis-Baker house [on the corner of Beaver and Boundary streets] was a sledding place for a long time. We also sledded on Hopkins Street and Dickson Road. They weren't paved. It was icy on the intersection of Hopkins and Dickson going down to Beaver. You got in the rut and couldn't get out of it. You couldn't stop. When you came to a curve, you started yelling. To change direction, you heaved.

Charles Butler, a black man, went sledding on Broad Street.

You could go from the top of Broad clear down to the Sewickley station. We took turns riding and guarding. The girl who played the piano for the high school hit the clock by Herzburn's; it almost killed her. You were *moving*. One time I was coming down on a bobsled. The guy on the back was called Swinging Tails. If he saw an accident coming, he was to turn the sled over. We crossed Centennial, and started toward a telephone pole. He turned that thing over. At the Sewickley station, we had a coal fire. Took potatoes and roasted them and heated coffee. One time I got my feet frostbitten. I went to Miss Moorhead's house. She put my feet in cold water. She was the closest colored person.

John Alexander rode sleds in Edgeworth.

Chestnut Street goes up over the Heights. We came down, crossed Beaver. We built a fire and one of us had a lantern. He watched for cars. There weren't that many cars out at night when I was young.

Everyone had a favorite route. Josephine Sybo said, "The best road was Blackburn. You could only do it about twice a night because it was so long." Miss Hailstock described her brother's bobsled run: "They started on the Heights, came down Blackburn, turned on Walnut and went down to the river."

Probably the safest place to ride was the Baker's property on Boundary and Beaver. Francis Torrance Baker remembered,

This has been a public sledriding area as long as anyone can remember. It was already a custom when we came here 60 years ago [in 1930.] It is rather nice. It is safe down there; you are not going to get run over. It's a steep little slope.

The Men's Committee of the YMCA organized community coasting parties. The route went down Cemetery Hill, across Beaver and Thorn, across Chestnut and half way to Pine Street. The *Herald* reported: "Jimmy Gray and his pals were on hand waving red and green lights. For once autoists showed some consideration for the runners."[19] After the exhilarating ride, participants warmed up with hot coffee around a bonfire.

Clubs

Most sports were available to everyone: anyone with a sled could ride; anyone with a rod could fish. Around the turn of the century, however, elite sports clubs developed in Sewickley and many other wealthy suburbs all over the country. Almost as soon as country clubs began, they were disparaged. Lewis Mumford decried the retreat of the best educated and wealthiest citizens from public duties to private play.

As leisure generally increased, play became the serious business of life; and the golf course, the country club, the swimming pool and the cocktail party became the frivolous counterfeits of a more varied and significant life. . . . Compulsive play became the acceptable alternative to compulsive work.

Supreme Court Justice Louis Brandeis recalled the time, at the turn of the century, when wealthy citizens of Boston told their sons,

Boston holds nothing for you except heavy taxes and political misrule. When you marry, pick a suburb to build a house in, join the Country Club, and make your life center around your club, your home, and your children.[20]

A Boston wag described the Country Club of Brookline: "They played with each other, not with others; they competed with each other, not with others: above all, they married each other only." Thorstein Veblen in his *Theory of the Leisure Class,* 1899, described country clubs as private preserves where the rich "engaged in unproductive games and sports purely to define themselves as superior to the working class." For Veblen, golf was the ultimate example of conspicuous consumption, being time-consuming, expensive and nonproductive.[21]

The earliest elitist clubs were downtown men's clubs such as the Knickerbocker Club in New York City, (1871), the Somerset Club in Boston (1851), and, in Pittsburgh, the Duquesne Club (1873) and the Pittsburgh Club (1879). As the population moved to the suburbs, new clubs with sports facilities followed. The Brookline Country Club (1882), six miles from Boston, was the first real country club. Similar institutions sprang up near major cities. By 1895, the Westchester Country Club, the Meadowbrook Country Club on Long Island, the Essex Country Club near Newark, and the Philadelphia Country Club had been established.

In Pittsburgh, the Pittsburgh Field Club was founded in 1882 as the Pittsburgh Cricket Club, with a field on Braddock Avenue in Regent Square. Later, after adding tennis courts, a track, and a few holes of golf, it changed its name to the Pittsburgh Field Club. As golf became increasingly popular, the course became inadequate, according to *The Pittsburg Index*, 1902. "The usual golf scenery is entirely eliminated. Picket fences form bunkers, the Monongahela Traction company's [trolley] tracks for hazards, while otherwise the nine-hole course traverses a rather uninteresting open field."[22] An 18-hole course was required, but there was not enough land on the old club grounds. In 1915, the club moved to a new site with 171 acres in Fox Chapel, then a rural area.

The Country Club, located on Nine-Mile Run near Schenley Park, started in 1896. Its course did not need tracks and picket fences to make it difficult. "Nature laid out the course and natural hazards abound to the elimination of the manmade bunker. Nine-Mile Run crosses and recrosses the domain, which is well wooded, and add still further to the interest of the golfer."[23]

The Pittsburgh Golf Club, founded the same year on the north edge of Schenley Park, had one of the first eighteen-hole courses. The city took over the course in 1910. Some of the members later formed the Fox Chapel Golf Club.

The Sewickley area joined the trend with two country clubs: The Allegheny Country Club and the Edgeworth Club. The Allegheny Country Club was founded in 1895 to "promote and encourage athletic sports and exercises, and to establish and maintain a club house for the use and entertainment of its members." It did not start in Sewickley Heights. The first club house was a remodeled farmhouse on California Avenue near Brighton Avenue on the North Side. This was a convenient location for residents of the fashionable parts of Allegheny City. The club house was surrounded by bicycle trails and bridle paths and had two tennis courts. A six-hole golf course, later increased to nine, was increasingly popular. In 1899 the 129 members decided to move the club to Sewickley Heights. They were attracted both by the wealthy people already settled around Sewickley and the growing society in the Heights. After its move, the Allegheny Country Club itself became a powerful force drawing people to the Sewickley area, particularly the Heights. The new course, opened in 1902, was the first 18-hole golf course in Western Pennsylvania.[24]

The Pittsburg Index chronicled the club's opening in several articles.

The Allegheny Country Club's housewarming occasion . . . will be *the* occasion of permanent interest this month in Country Club circles.

Preparations are going nicely for the opening of the Allegheny Country Club's new links in Sewickley on May 17. The road from Sewickley station to Sewickley Heights is being macadamized and will be completed by June 1. The present arrangement of conveying members from the station on that day is by automobile, and there will be plenty on hand to meet the demand. The event will be notable in every way and will make the entrance of a golf club in Pittsburg into national importance. The new Allegheny Country Club and the beautiful golf links added this year are great attractions and the informal dinners, dances, music, and golf tournaments contribute much to the gayety of this congenial coterie, not to speak of the many well-known bachelors of this set who are domiciled at the clubhouse for the summer. Another year a number of well-known people will build picturesque cottages convenient to the club house. . . . Every train that stops at the pretty station at Sewickley on Saturday brings gay parties to spend Sunday at the "Heights." and the smart vehicles, traps, tallyhos, carts, opera busses, road wagons, run-a-bouts, etc., with their liveried coachmen and fine horses, who meet them, give the modest town an air of elegance of which in its earlier days it never dreamed.

Architecturally the new home fits into the sylvan scene which it dominates. As to the appointment and finish, the latest thought has been developed and the Country Club stands second to none in the United States. The house consists of three stories with sleeping quarters for men and for women, toilet and bath rooms, lockers and a cafe, in addition to the large dining-room; for everything is to be managed on the basis of a hotel that members driving down from the city may spend days or weeks, while every wish is anticipated by the service on the grounds.[25]

The Allegheny Country Club had four grass tennis courts and, more unusually, a horse show ring. By 1906, the Sewickley Horse Show moved to the club grounds. The horse show became an event of national importance as part of the Ideal Spring Horse Show Circuit, with shows in Cleveland, Philadelphia, and Chicago. The Sewickley show soon became both a social and an equestrian occasion.

Dame Fashion will share honors with Sir Horse at the show . . . as she always does at these annual shows. The fashionables of the entire district are usually present, in up-to-the-minute sport costumes, whether they are there as riders or as spectators.[26]

The Sewickley Horse Show grounds at the Allegheny Country Club, 1932. Courtesy Richard Smith.

Activities started with the annual riding and driving party given by William C. Robinson, club president for two decades, and his wife. The *Herald* described a typical parade in June, 1929.

Indians, Roman emperors, farmers, Breton peasants, Spanish grandees in sedan chairs, Tom Sawyer, Belgian flower girls with their dog cart, covered wagons filled with gypsies, Peter Pan on horseback and many other old costumes were worn. All sorts of odd vehicles from a twenty year old Buick to a tandem bicycle were in the parade which wound around the show ring at the Allegheny Country Club and then made its way to the Robinson estate.

In 1921, the club built stables, managed for 33 years by George Chubb. Mr. Chubb came from England and worked for William K. Vanderbilt of Newport, Rhode Island, before coming to Sewickley. He and his family lived above the stables, which accommodated more than 60 horses.

The other club in the Sewickley area, founded in 1893, is the Edgeworth Club. Its members were principally local. In 1903, 226 came from the Sewickley area, 20 from Allegheny, and 23 from Pittsburgh. *The Pittsburg Index* described the club in 1902. "Everybody who is anybody in the Sewickley Valley belongs to the Edgeworth Club which, from the first, became a factor in the social life of the gay little suburb."[27]

The Club was "formed for the purpose of promoting intercourse and friendship among its members and their social enjoyment, and for the purpose of furnishing facilities for bowling, athletic and other innocent sports." The exact nature of innocent sports is not defined, but it might have something to do with the club's injunction against gambling, a non-innocent sport. Other rules prohibited "the use of intoxicating liquor upon the Club premises," and decreed that "the Club house and golf links shall be closed on Sunday."[28]

Riding and Driving Party at W. C. Robinson's Franklin Farm, June 1926. Courtesy The Sewickley Valley Historical Society.

After spending its first five years in a rented house on Meadow Lane, the Edgeworth Club needed a permanent home. Many members were building large, architect-designed houses in Sewickley and Edgeworth. They wanted a club to reflect their community. Pittsburgh clubs have a history of using fine architects for their buildings. Clubhouses were not just a convenient place to change clothes, but a building to express the style of its members. There are many examples of clubs designed by well-known architects. The Edgeworth Club's first building, designed by Rutan & Russell, and finished in 1898, was among the earliest and served as one model for later clubs. Other clubs and architects were in the same tradition. Alden & Harlow, who designed the Carnegie Museum and Library in Oakland, did the Duquesne Club (1889) and the Pittsburgh Golf Club (1905). Rutan & Russell did the Pittsburgh Country Club. Edward Stotz, architect of the Schenley and Fifth Avenue High Schools, did the Oakmont Country Club (1904). Janssen & Cocken, designer of Mellon Institute and the Masonic Temple, designed the Pittsburgh Athletic Association (1911) and the Longue Vue Club (1925). Brandon Smith, who did the B. F. Jones Library in Aliquippa, designed the Fox Chapel Golf Club (1931) and the present Edgeworth Club (1931).

In 1898, the Edgeworth Club had four prominent architects as members: Frank E. Alden, Alfred B. Harlow, Frank E. Rutan, and Frederick Russell. The choice went to Rutan & Russell, who had both worked for Alden & Harlow before forming their own firm. The building they designed burned down in 1928, but many photographs remain. Located on the corner of Academy and Centennial Avenues in Sewickley, it was a large, comfortable structure that looked like a house, or a home away from home, where members could relax among friends. An article in *Architectural Record* described it in 1904.

> The Edgeworth Club of Sewickley is a building that, in some aspects, might be mistaken for a comfortable country house. This, of course, is exactly what a country club is intended to be, and very successful and good this present example is.[29]

Rutan & Russell picked the Shingle style to express this homelike quality. This style, popular in the late 1880s to early 1900s, contrasts with the flamboyance of the contemporaneous Queen Anne style. Like houses in the Shingle style, the Edgeworth Club minimized ornament. Exterior walls were continuous planes, with no interruptions at the corners. Windows and doors were not ornamented. The porch and dormers, common at the period, did not protrude from the structure, but followed the spreading angle of the hipped roof. Even the columns, which were masterpieces of woodworkers' art in Italianate and Queen Anne buildings, were simple, functional supports.

Pictures of the interior of the clubhouse show unadorned furnishings with wicker chairs and a few simple upholstered pieces. The ballroom was more elegant. *The Index* called it "one of the most commodious and beautifully appointed ballrooms in the State." It was a large room, 35 by 70 feet, with French doors opening to a veranda and terrace.

After the first clubhouse burned down in December 1928, The members decided to build anew on the corner of Academy Avenue and Beaver Road in Edgeworth. They selected Brandon Smith, a well-known architect of many large houses in Sewickley and Fox Chapel. Architectural tastes had changed by 1929. The more grandiose Tudor style based on English country houses was

Edgeworth Club, Sewickley, PA. Rutan & Russell, Architects.
From *Architectural Record*, Aug. 1904.

popular in many wealthy suburbs. Brandon Smith, like Rutan & Russell, chose to follow the trend of domestic architecture. Because of the Depression, the new building is smaller than Brandon Smith's original plans. Style and quality of what was built, however, remain. Typical Tudor characteristics are: parapets on the gable ends; oriel windows; tall, narrow windows in multiple groups; steep roofs with massive chimneys; and an elaborate porte-cochere. The stone carving of the Edgeworth coat of arms over the front entrance is a Tudor touch, but is more likely to be found in England than in the United States.

Originally the Edgeworth Club was to be similar to the Duquesne Club, but it soon followed the trend toward country club activities, especially golf. *The Pittsburgh Index* reported:

> The earliest promoters put forward their plan for an indoor club, but the progress of the day has made the out-door life a not insignificant feature at any time but a dominant feature when the men in charge of affairs decided to lease a golf course.[30]

The first course, built in 1897, was on the Shields property off Meadow Lane in Edgeworth. This soon proved to be inadequate so, in 1900, the club built a nine-hole course on the Way estate, between Academy Avenue and Chestnut Road and Beaver Road and Woodland Road. John E. Porter, of the Porter family on Peebles Street, was the prime mover, according to the *Pittsburg Index*, 1902:

> Through his untiring energy the beautiful links, known as the Edgeworth Links, of Sewickley, for the benefit of the members of the Edgeworth Club and their families, was planned and laid out and is considered one of the finest in Western Pennsylvania.[31]

He also served as the amateur architect of the course.[32] Golf at Edgeworth, however, was short-lived. As residential values increased, the Ways wished to cash in. Competition from the new Allegheny Country Club with its 18 holes drew many members from the smaller Edgeworth course. *The Sewickley Valley* reported in 1911, "Golf will probably be abandoned this year. . . . The golf deficit grows each year and the (golf) membership shows but small increase. Enthusiasm

The Edgeworth Club, Brandon Smith, architect. Drawing by Susan Gaca.

tends to tennis rather than golf."[33] Tennis and bowling were the remaining innocent sports. Tennis soon became the more important. In 1957 and 1959, the Club received national attention as host of the Wightman Cup Tournament.

If critics of country clubs like Thorstein Veblen and Lewis Mumford had visited the Edgeworth Club they might have been less critical. The Edgeworth Club had more intellectual ambitions than other country clubs. The Allegheny Country Club was devoted to sports and entertainment. The Edgeworth Club included lectures and musical events as well. In March 1905, for instance, a joint meeting of the Edgeworth Club, the Woman's Club, and the Village Improvement Society heard a lecture on "Slums of New York." The Edgeworth Club sponsored a piano and song recital of compositions of Arthur Nevin in 1906, and a concert series in the winter of 1919-1920. Following in the tradition of the Sewickley Valley Club, Edgeworth gave theatrical performances. In the early days, these were simple tableaux. Later, the Club produced such ambitious plays as "The Man Who Came to Dinner," "South Pacific," and "Plaza Suite."

Most of the intellectual fare and social service provided at the club building, however, came from the Woman's Club, which used the Edgeworth clubhouse for a fee. Members of the Woman's Club did not have to be members of Edgeworth, although many were. In 1897, 55 of the 68 founding members of the Woman's Club belonged to Edgeworth. Founded in 1892 as the Wheel Club, the Woman's Club had 325 members by 1916. It was a worthy continuation of the many uplifting Sewickley groups formed earlier in the nineteenth century: the Query Club, the Tuesday Club, and the Parliamentary Club. In 1907, for example, the Woman's Club held a French class every Monday 9:00 to 12:00 noon; a German class Thursday 1:00 to 3:45 P.M., a literature class Monday 12:30 to 2:00 P. M., and a current events class. Special Artists Days featured recitals. Social work included traveling libraries, teaching children to sew, giving flower seeds to the poor, and giving English lessons to foreign girls.[34]

The surprising variety of sports available in Sewickley in the nineteenth century continued in the twentieth. Boating in summer, sled riding in winter, and walking any time gave residents little excuse for being inactive. Although the country clubs emphasized the difference between richer and poorer citizens, the less affluent could still enjoy robust outdoor pleasures in abundance.

[1] *Weekly Herald,* September 19, 1903, p. 5 and February 27, 1915, p. 8.

[2] "YMCA Today" Brochure. Spring 1994.

[3] *Pittsburgh Sun-Telegraph*, December 31, 1928.

[4] *Sewickley Herald,* January 4, 1919.

[5] Ibid., January 11, 1919.

[6] Jim Schafer and Mike Sajina, *The Allegheny River.* University Park, Pennsylvania State University Press, 1992, p. 50.

[7] *Atlantic Monthly*, v.20, 1887, p. 256.

[8] *Weekly Herald*, August 24, 1907, p. 1.

[9] Francis Couvares, *The Remaking of Pittsburgh*. Albany, State University of N Y Press, 1984, pp. 44-45, 123.

[10] *Sewickley Herald*, September 11, 1926.

[11] *The Sewickley Valley,* April 22, 1899.

[12] *Herald*, Feb. 24, 1923.

[13] *The Sewickley Herald*, June 29, 1928, p. 2.

[14] Bayard Christy, "Bob-White in Pennsylvania." In *The Cardinal*, Audubon Society of the Sewickley Valley, Jan. 1926, p.7-18.

[15] *Weekly Herald*, September 19, 1903, p. 5.

[16] Edwin Peterson, *Penn's Woods West*. Pittsburgh, University Press, 1958, pp. 61-62.

[17] *The Sewickley Herald*, April 8, 1922, p. 9.

[18] *The Weekly Herald*, May 8, 1915.

[19] *The Sewickley Herald*, January 24, 1920.

[20] Mumford, p. 495.

[21] Jackson, pp. 98-99.

[22] *Pittsburg Index,* Jan. 7, 1902, p. 12.

[23] Ibid., June 7, 1902, p. 13.

[24] William M. Kelly, *Edgeworth Club, 1893-1993*. Edgeworth, Pa. 1993, pp. 58-60.

[25] *The Pittsburg Index*, May 3, 1902, p. 6, 10: July 19, 1902.

[26] *Bulletin,* June 2, 1928, p. 9.

[27] *The Pittsburg Index*, June 7, 1902, p. 12.

[28] *The Edgeworth Club*. Pamphlet. 1903.

[29] *Architectural Record*, August, 1904, p. 111.

[30] *Pittsburg Index*, June 7, 1902, p. 12.

[31] July 19, 1902, p. 22.

[32] Kelly, p. 59.

[33] Ibid., p. 67.

[34] *The Pittsburg Bulletin,* November 9, 1907, p. 11.

Chapter 23
Leisure Activities

As we have seen, entertainment in Sewickley in the nineteenth century was self-generated, with plays, music, and lectures largely provided by local talent. But this changed when the movies came to town in the early part of the twentieth century. Movies are passive entertainment; all the consumer must do is choose and pay. The first motion pictures played in the nickelodeons that mushroomed all over the country around 1900. Pittsburgh is thought to be the home of the first true nickelodeon, which showed only movies. It was started in 1905 by Henry Davis and J. P. Harris in a vacant storeroom at 433-435 Smithfield Street. Within a year, eight to ten other nickelodeons opened in Pittsburgh.[1] Several films were shown, each lasting five to fifteen minutes. Subjects included comedy, travel, melodrama, and documentaries.

Sewickley soon got its own nickelodeons. The exact date is uncertain but an advertisement for a nickelodeon, the Casino, appeared in *The Herald* in 1907. "Open daily 3:00-10:30. Saturday 2:00-11:00. Vaudeville in the evening." The Casino, located in a building now the parking lot for Mellon Bank, changed its name first to the Hippodrome and later to the Gypsy Queen. Advertisements described its offerings. One from 1910 promised: "High-class refined Vaudeville down to the minute motion pictures. Admission 10 cents."[2] Another advertisement from 1913 described The Casino.

> The best, safest, and best-ventilated house
> in Sewickley.
> Five large exits. Seven windows.
>
> Well when's the show. By Heck I'll go!!
> To Tuesday, 25th of March,
> The Gypsy Queen. The House with the Arch.

Ventilation must have been a problem, according to an advertisement for another theater.

> The Pastime. Sewickley's Up-To-Date Nickelodeum [sic] Beaver near Broad. Breathe easy, old Colonel Ozone has installed an entirely new ventilating system which will change the air in the theatorium completely every three minutes.[3]

Other early theaters were The Lyric and, most importantly, the Sewickley Theatre which opened in 1915 and lasted until 1979. It was in the building still called the Nickelodeon Mall.

Because nickelodeons cost only a nickel, they were accessible to the working class and were considered vaguely disreputable. A show at the Lyric in 1912 provoked a call for stricter censorship because it illustrated "the grosser details of the white slave trade." Captain Frederick Way, Jr. remembered that the screening of Dante's *Inferno* at the Gypsy Queen shocked some because, "there were all these naked people running around on the screen. You had to be accompanied by an adult to get in."[4] An article in 1910 described the Sewickley response to the continuing question: does seeing violence promote violence?

> The influence the moving picture exerts upon the masses is a subject of general controversy at the moment. Various critics claim that the influence is unwholesome, and that the presentation of pictures showing the holding up of trains in the west, robberies, etc., suggest crime to the weak members of society in whom the criminal instinct is ready for development. In fact, one of the youthful bandits who attempted to hold up a street car in Pittsburgh announced the idea was suggested to him by a moving picture. . . . The condemnation of this popular form of entertainment would not be fair. . . . A middle.ground is the proper position to take in censoring and censuring the nickelodeon with its moving picture show. It is absurd to plead that all incidents that might afford a bad example to children be prohibited. . . . The Bible recites deeds that we would not have the children imitate, yet we put the Bible in their hands. History as taught in public schools makes heroes of men whose actions, if attempted by the boy who reads, would get him a whipping. . . . The moving picture fills a long felt want in the life of the poor man and his family. It provides them wholesome entertainment at a price never before set for amusement of equal interest and value. Many of the shows have educational scenes and incidents.[5]

Until the 1930s both nickelodeon films and regular films were "silent." They were not really silent, however. An organist, pianist, or small orchestra interpreted the plot. In Sewickley, this was an organist, Miss Elsie Kinney. She arrived ten minutes early at the theater to arrange her music and played throughout the performance. At the beginning of the silent film era, music was needed to mask the sound of the projector. Later, it enhanced the plot. Miss Kinney could not rehearse her program for the movies because they changed too frequently to give her time to practice for each one. She had to keep her eyes on the screen to ensure that her choice of music fit the plot. If the actors were dancing, she had to follow the tempo of the dance. As the plot turned tragic, heroic, or martial, she had to change in turn. Miss Kinney had to have a library of music at hand and in her head to draw on as the plot required. In addition, she had to be able to improvise transitions from one melody and mood to the next. Stories abound in the early days of film of musicians, not astute enough to follow the plot, who fell into ludicrous situations. For example, in a World War I film, an army of soldiers was marching in the distance. Immediately the organist played "Three Cheers for the Red White and Blue." He was among the last to realize that the marchers were German soldiers. One critic heard the organist play "I'm Always Chasing Rainbows" in a Biblical film when Salome was condemning John the Baptist.

Books and articles of the time give an idea of the repertoire expected of a silent film accompanist. Edith Lang's *Musical Accompaniment of Moving Pictures*, 1920 has extensive lists of selections suitable for many situations. The following sample contains several references to Edgeworth composer, Ethelbert Nevin (1862-1901). Although his music has gone out of style, Nevin at one time was a popular composer. His most famous composition, "The Rosary," sold two and a half million copies.

Nature themes:
    Nevin. "Country Dances"
    Nevin. "Song of the Brook"
Religious themes.
    Handel. "Largo"
    Sullivan. "Onward Christian Soldiers"
Love themes.
    Nevin. "Love Song"
    Liszt. "Love Dreams"
Festive mood
    Nevin. "Tournament"
    Verdi. "March from 'Aida'"
    Chopin. "Polonaise militaire"
Exotic moods
    Saint-Saens. "Ballet from 'Samson and Delilah'"
    Tschaikowsky. "Danse Arabe"
    Tschaikowsky. "March Slav"
    Rimsky-Korsakof. "Chant Hindou"
Speed
    Chopin. "Minute Waltz"
    Wagner. "Ride of the Valkyries"
Tragedy
    Tchaikowsky. First movement from "Symphonie Pathetique"
    Beethoven. First movement from "Sonata Pathetique"
Death
    Chopin. "Funeral March"[6]

Some sound film experiments had succeeded as early as 1923, but sound was a novelty item, suitable for vaudevillian short subjects and newsreels. The main feature was silent. In 1927, "The Jazz Singer" with Al Jolson revolutionized the industry. Although mostly silent, it had four singing and speaking sequences. On July 5, 1929 the first "talking pictures" came to Sewickley.

Monday Matinee to Mark Opening of
First Talking Picture
"The Rainbow Man" an all talking and

singing screen romance plentifully supplied
with instrumental music, which contains not
one note of "blues" or "vo-de-do"[7]

People who grew up in Sewickley in the 1920s and 1930s remembered that movies were a big treat. The cost had risen to 30 cents for adults; 10 cents for children. A different film came every two or three nights, so varying tastes were served. The Sewickley Theatre published a small magazine, "Movie News", in the 1920s. It carried articles on movie stars, the movie industry, breaking into the movies and, of course, advertisements for specific films. A typical program at the Sewickley Theatre in 1928 featured:

Thursday and Friday. Lon Chaney "While the City Sleeps"
Saturday. Johnny Hines in "White Pants Willy"
Monday, Tuesday, Wednesday. "Wings" with Gary Cooper
Thursday and Friday. Marion Davies in "The Cardboard Lover"

There were no shows on Sunday.

At the Sewickley Theatre many of the ushers were high school boys. They wore a suit and tie and carried a flashlight. The floor under the seats was bare wood. Twice a year it had to be oiled by all the ushers. Salary was a visit to Isaly's for the whole crew paid for by Bill Wheat, the head usher.[8] Perhaps with some connivance with the ushers, boys enjoyed the danger of sneaking in without paying. Joe Reiser said, "You could sneak in on the Locust Street side when they let people out, or ten minutes after the start of the nine o'clock show, when the ticket taker went home."

The Sewickley Theatre was a rather decorous place, according to Mr. Reiser.

You couldn't talk or whisper. You just watched. Children were not allowed in the balcony after they dangled fake spiders down on the audience. Nor were teen-agers, after one guy shot a hole through the screen. Sewickley rarely got cowboy movies or serials like Buck Rodgers. If we wanted cowboys, we went to Coraopolis.

If boys wanted more excitement, they went to the Ambridge movie on Saturday morning where there were games and talking was allowed. Sewickley did have some serials. Each episode was shown only one evening per week. Margaret Halpin remembered, "You had to go every week. I remember one time my father, my sister and I were watching one serial and it had four episodes to go. For some reason they discontinued it. My father took us to town [Pittsburgh] every Friday night until we finished it."

Going to Pittsburgh to see a ball game, or a show at the Stanley or the Penn was always a treat. Frances McElrath, who moved to Sewickley in 1904, remembered, "Mother and Dad would go to the theatre; once in a while they would take me. Dad would go to ball games and take me." The Stanley, which described itself as "The Mecca for the Amusement Seekers," had an orchestra, dancing girls, comedians, and animal acts as well as movies. John Alexander remembered:

There were 62 trains a day when I was a kid. We caught a train to Pittsburgh and went to the movie at the Stanley. It cost a quarter—Pathe News, comedy, feature and a stage show. I saw all of the stage people like Paul Whiteman and Benny Goodman in person. Then maybe we got a hot dog and came home on the train.

Special Days

Movies became a regular part of life in Sewickley. Less frequent events included the traveling circus, which was always the source of great excitement. The circus had one ring and a side show complete with bearded lady and fat lady. The Three-A Indoor Circus and Vaudeville, which came to Sewickley in 1927, raisled money for the Sewickley Valley Post of the American Legion. Helen Hegner recalled the circus when she was a child. "I remember when the circus came to town. They had a parade in Sewickley. I went to the Sewickley Hotel for lunch the day of the parade. I didn't have time to walk up the hill [to my house]. There were circus wagons with tigers." The parade of circus wagons, horses, and elephants proceeded down Chestnut, Beaver, and Walnut Streets. Children got a half day off from school. They could go down to White's field, where the Community Center tennis courts are today, to watch the tents being set up. Some even got a job. John Alexander said, "My brother got a job taking water to the elephants. He got worn out." The elephants went to Walnut Beach where they could frolic in the water.

226

Jimmy Gray in the Halloween Parade. Courtesy of The Sewickley Valley Historical Society.

A wild west show came to town on occasion. "Wyoming Bill's Wild West Combined Shows" was patterned after the original Buffalo Bill shows. Posters all over town declared it to be,

A refined, refreshing and exact portrayal of life in the far west as it really was in the early days, and as it is at present. An amusing exhibition but one that is instructive as well, and a great educator for children.[9]

Note the marketing skill employed, appealing to those wanting either entertainment or education.

Other special days were connected with holidays. The Memorial Day Parade had 200-300 participants. They marched from the old Post Office up to the Civil War Memorial at the cemetery. Probably the most colorful participants were the Washington Infantry, a voluntary military unit whose antecedents date from 1792. Their uniform is patterned after those worn by General Anthony Wayne's troops as they trained near Sewickley in 1792. The brilliant blue uniforms with white crossbelts, brass buttons, and tall brush plumes added zest to the parade. Joe Reiser said,

The Washington Infantry came and fired rifles at the memorial. They were all old men. We used to scramble around to get the empty cartridges. The Mission Brigade from Pittsburgh came; fifteen of them in uniform. A drum corps came from Butler.

Speeches at the cemetery were followed by a huge picnic which Richard McPherson remembered:

Two or three hundred people marched. My grandmother used to provide the big dinner Memorial Day. She would call up people on the Heights. When Grandmother died my mother took over. My mother sent me up. Mrs. Rea would say, "Go down to the butcher shop and pick up eight hams. I'll donate them."

Jimmy Gray, a tailor on Broad Street, was a compulsive organizer responsible for many special events. He organized a railroad excursion to Lake Chatauqua that drew an astonishing 2,500 people. The Halloween Parade was the special favorite of Jimmy Gray. Jimmy himself lead the parade on horseback dressed, in a different costume every year. He spent his spare time making costumes for the kids in the parade. Joe Reiser said, "He gave you a costume if you couldn't afford one." Following the parade, everyone gathered around a platform where the gazebo is today for a greased pig chase, a pie-eating contest, and all kinds of prizes for costumes.

[1] *Sewickley Herald*, Oct. 21, 1987, p. 5.

[2] Ibid., April 2, 1910.

[3] Ibid., October 21, 1987, p. 5.

[4] Ibid., p. 5.

[5] Ibid., July 23, 1910, p. 11.

[6] Edith Lang. *Musical Accompaniement of Moving Pictures.* Boston, Boston Music Co., 1920.

[7] *Sewickley Herald*, October 28, 1987, p. 5.

[8] Letter from Joe Rutter in the *Sewickley Herald*, Nov. 25, 1987, p. 5.

[9] *Sewickley Herald*, May 17, 1913, p. 3.

Chapter 24
There Was a Garden out Back.
Italians in Sewickley

Immigration from Italy to the Pittsburgh area swelled towards the end of the nineteenth century. In Italy peasants were unable to acquire and retain enough land to make a living. Economic necessity forced them to sell their small plots and to work for the large landowners. Typically, they lived in the village and walked several miles a day to work. Many had to supplement their wages by working seasonally in other parts of Italy. Others took up trades such as carpentry, shoemaking, fishing or tailoring. Having lost their attachment to their own land, they were willing to venture far afield, even as far as America.

Generally, an Italian immigrant did not leave his homeland with the soul-wrenching finality of other nationalities. Many came to America to earn money, planning to return home with savings to improve their lives. About three of every five immigrants returned to Italy to live. Only those who remained, obviously, were available to interview. It would be interesting to compare the histories of Italians who returned with those who remained in order to see why some did not stay. Perhaps they found it too difficult to leave family and friends.

An Irish or Scottish immigrant came with little expectation of returning, but Italians went back and forth. Eighty per cent of Italian men came alone, expecting to go back. In 1907 the Italian Commissariat of Immigration reported that emigration was often temporary. "Even emigrants to America can return to Italy to see their families and their native land for two or three years, then leave again to take part in new work."[1] First generation immigrants to Sewickley followed this pattern.

Ethnic immigrants to the Pittsburgh area settled into the special neighborhoods that are Pittsburgh's trademark. Slovaks went to the South Side, Germans to Troy Hill, and Poles to Polish Hill. Italians congregated in Bloomfield, East Liberty, and Sewickley. Italian immigrants in both Pittsburgh and Sewickley usually joined relatives or people formerly from the same village, thus benefiting from advice and help in finding housing and jobs. Having neighbors who spoke the same language eased the transition to a strange culture. So many Italians lived up on Dickson Road that it was known as Little Italy. It looked like an Italian hill town, with flower and vegetable gardens crammed into every available bit of land. It makes sense that Italians, coming from small villages, would avoid Pittsburgh with its dirt and cramped housing in favor of the more compatible environment of Sewickley. Once some Italian families settled in Sewickley, they told their relatives and friends in the old country about their new life and suggested that they come too. Jim Munizza of Sewickley remembered:

> Many years ago a few came over, then they would bring their brothers over, then they would bring their aunts over, then they would bring their brothers and sisters. Then when others came, they didn't see strange faces.

In Sewickley, Italians came from two villages in Calabria that were only about five to eight miles apart. The villages, Gizzeria and Falerna, are perched on hills on what is the instep of Italy's boot. Jerry Tignanelli said, "They came because there were a lot of Italian people from their towns here; they all liked Sewickley."

Although the census shows no Italians living in Sewickley before 1900, it is clear that there were some, according to current residents. Both Francisco Toia's and Frank and Jerry Vescio's mothers came before 1900. In that year the census taker listed 14 Italians. In 1920, there were 64 people living in Sewickley Borough who had been born in Italy. Of this number (64), 61 had Italian fathers and 57 had Italian mothers. There were also 53 people born in America who had Italian parents. Of these 53, all had Italian fathers and 50 had Italian mothers. In 1950, 224 Sewickley residents had been born in Italy. This was 44 per cent of the foreign born population of Sewickley. Figures for residents with foreign parents are not given.

The information in the following section comes mainly from talking with Sewickley residents with Italian connections.

Rossario and Concetta Flora. The Flora family typifies many of the early Italian immigrants. Rossario and Concetta Flora, who celebrated their seventieth wedding anniversary in 1989, were both born in 1900 in the small village of Falerna in southern Italy. They were married at the comparatively old age of 19. Mr. Flora's sister, for example, had "waited" until she was 15 to get married. Immediately after his wedding, Mr. Flora emigrated, leaving his bride in Italy.

Mr. Flora said that he left his homeland because, "They had nothing in Italy—no machines, no nothing." The Floras remained separated for 16 years, although Mr. Flora did visit his wife for a month every four years. The trip took 12 days each way. Nine months after each visit, a child was born.

While in America, Mr. Flora lived in boarding houses in order to save as much money as possible. By 1936, he was able to bring his whole family to Sewickley. His daughter, Teresa Flora Cortese, who was nine at the time, remembered:

> We came with a couple of other families. We landed in New York and came on the train to Sewickley and got here at night. We went up the steps and down a long corridor. Mother said, "Where did you bring me?" [That was the only time Mrs. Cortese remembered her mother complain.] It was her place to go where her husband was.

Frank and Jerry Vescio. The Vescio brothers come from one of the earliest Italian families in Sewickley. Their father arrived in the United States about 1880. Their mother, the eldest of seven Pellegrino children, immigrated in 1898 when she was six. After living in Albany for two years, the Pelligrino family moved to Sewickley. Mrs. Pellegrino never went to school.

Frank married Carmella Scalercio, who came from the same town in Italy as his family. She came to America in 1930 when she was 11 years old. Her father had been here for years, she remembered: "He worked for James Schoonmaker and boarded with relatives. Every two or three years he visited [Italy] and came back."

Jerry Tignanelli. This family moved to Sewickley bit by bit. Mr. Tignanelli's father came first in 1910 to work on the railroads. He stayed one year and went back to Italy. After returning to the States in 1913, he settled in Sewickley, joining two brothers already there. He worked for Mr. Boggs of the Boggs and Buhl department store. When Jerry and his mother arrived in 1921, they were quarantined for a week at Ellis Island. "They wanted to make sure my father had a job and could support us."

Mary Yankello and her daughter and son-in-law, Josephine and Bruno Toia. Mary Yankello's father-in-law immigrated to Amita Pennsylvania, near Punxatawny, to work in the coal mines. His son, Peter, went to school for two years in Amita before starting in the mines himself at age 14.

After the mines shut down, Peter and, later, the rest of the family, moved to Ambridge. Peter worked for the American Bridge Company for more than 40 years. The Yankellos built a house on Ferran Street, a tiny lane off Dickson Road. Bruno Toia's father is a good example of the Italian immigration pattern.

> My father was born in 1885. He came here in 1900. He went back to Italy and married in 1908, then came back without my mother. That's what they used to do in those days. They would get married, leave their wives, come back over here, make some money, go back, get their wives pregnant, come back (not even wait for the birth), go to work. My father went back twice and my mother had two sons. He sent her money every month. Finally, in 1921, he called for her. He wanted her to come before that, but she didn't want to leave. Her heart was set over there.

Life in a New Land

The most difficult problem encountered by Italians moving to Sewickley was language. The community recognized the difficulty and tried to help. Mr. and Mrs. J.P. McDonald and others organized a Free English School for Foreigners which met at the Methodist church. The school provided "a good opportunity for foreigners to prepare themselves for better advantages."[2]

Italians, like other nationalities, often had their names simplified either by officials when applying for citizenship or by employers for payroll records. Bruno Toia recalled:

> Years ago not only Italians, but many others, especially the Polish and Russians, if they had a name the judges couldn't pronounce, they changed it automatically. Mr. Flowers name was Florentino. They asked him what that name [Florentino] stands for. He said, "Flowers." So they changed the name to Flowers. Some of the children have gone back to Florentino.

Mrs. Yankello said.

> The Italian name was Ianchello. They took the way it sounded and put it in English. An i in Italian is y and ch is k. When my dad got his citizenship the judge changed it. The other Yankellos in Sewickley spell it Yanckello. The judge put c in front of the k. They changed names like you wouldn't believe!

Other names in Sewickley that were changed were Vescio to Vish; Ruperto to Rupert, Isabell-Valenzi to Valenzi, and Mastroianni to Masterani.

In general, men learned to speak English but the women did not. Mr. Flora, for example, learned English because he had to communicate at work. His wife, who spent most of her time on solitary domestic duties, had little opportunity to learn the new language. Her only chance to improve, according to her daughter, was a few times when some person who knew a little English would gather five or six people and teach them a bit. Neither Mrs. Flora nor her sister, living nearby on Chestnut Street, became fluent in English.

Jerry Vescio said:

My mother could speak English—she came over when she was six. My aunt didn't speak English but she was a genius with her hands. The only thing she could say was "Go to Hell!" She never wanted to learn English, just cuss words.

Most Italians spoke only Italian when they came to this country. An exception was Frank Vescio's wife, Carmella, because, "When my dad visited [Italy], he used to talk to us in English and after we came here, Dad always talked to us in English."

Even if immigrants became bilingual, they were often illiterate in one language. Jerry Tignanelli: "I didn't go to school in Italy. That's why I can't read or write Italian. I came at eight and had to start in first grade." Jerry's father arrived when he was over school age. He never learned to read English.

Because of language problems, shopping could be difficult, as any tourist who has tried to buy something in a foreign store knows. Mrs. Cortese used to go marketing for her mother at an A & P near the family apartment on Broad Street.

I used to go to the store and ask for stuff—at the time they didn't have supermarkets where you can help yourself. Sometimes I asked for the wrong thing. I remember the long pole they had to use to pull down what I asked for. I didn't dare say I didn't want that. [Shopping was easier at Valentes, the Italian grocery store on Beaver Street.] She had everything Italian—salami, cappicola, pasta.

Language problems caused the Italians in Sewickley to socialize with each other, as they did in Pittsburgh. In almost all cases, Italian men and women married other Italians. Bruno Toia said that in the nineteenth century, Italians married someone from their own village. Well into the twentieth century, it was a disgrace to marry outside the nationality. Not until the late 1930s did it become acceptable. "One man married a Serbian girl; it was a big thing. He broke the ice. People started changing."

In Italy marriages were arranged by matchmakers. A man picked a possible wife and hired a matchmaker to make the arrangements. Jim Munizza described what happened.

The groom went over to the girl's house with the matchmaker, who was very happy to go because every time he went to a house he would get lots to eat and drink. He was usually a good talker, a good drinker, and a good carrier of tales.

The matchmaker would say, "What are you going to give?" The man would say, "A mule, or a half acre, or an acre." "Well, we'll let you know." A couple of weeks later they came back. "Not enough." The matchmaker would love it. Then they would go to someone else's house.

They used to like to get rid of their daughters. They would call up the matchmaker and say, "Well, I've got my daughter. . . ." "I'll put you in the book." The matchmaker always made out.

In Sewickley only a few of the earliest marriages were arranged. Usually the suitor came to ask the girl's father for his permission. It was traditional for the oldest daughter to marry first. Josephine Toia remembered that this did not work in the case of her mother's family. Her aunt, the eldest daughter, did not want to marry.

My mother was disgusted. She was missing a lot of suitors. A couple of guys came, said, "I'll marry your other daughter." Grandfather said, "No, she's first." When my mother saw my dad— he was so handsome—she said, "This time you are not going to say she has to marry first. I like this guy." He said O.K. That's how my mother ended up marrying my father.

Jerry Vescio said it was unfortunate that Italians in Sewickley socialized so much among themselves:

The Italians were too clannish. They stayed together and lived like a colony. They worked together—in the summer made their gardens, in the winter made sausage. You don't see that any more.

Italian clannishness was emphasized by the women's mourning customs, which both Mr. Vescio and Mr. Tignanelli were happy to see disappearing. Mr. Vescio said,

> Every time you see someone wearing black, she's Italian. If a husband dies, or sister, brother, or child, they wear black. Over there [in Italy] they stay in black. Over here several still do. I hate black.

Jerry Tignanelli added: "My dad said, 'When I die I want you to wear red!'"

Clannishness disappears as Americanization takes over. The Floras were obviously Italian but Mrs. Cortese is thoroughly American, although she does know a lot about Italy. "Mother kept talking about it—things that went on; what she did." But the next generation has lost touch. Mrs. Cortese can still speak the Italian dialect that is her parents' native tongue, but her children cannot. She explained, "I had such a hard time that I didn't teach my children Italian. I didn't want other children to make fun of them."

Traditional Italian trades were in great demand in Sewickley just after the turn of the century when accessibility by car accelerated development of Sewickley and, especially, Sewickley Heights. Italians tended to take up trades that could be learned as an apprentice. Schools in Italian villages taught only the rudiments of reading and writing. After a few years of formal education, boys were apprenticed to a barber, a cobbler, a carpenter, a stone mason, or a farmer. Girls stayed home to help their mothers, or they might work for the nuns to learn sewing and monogramming. These trades could all be continued after coming to Sewickley. *The Sewickley Directory*, 1915 shows three Italian grocers, three shoemakers, one barber, and one confectioner.

Italians in Sewickley had a variety of jobs, according to the 1920 census which lists the native language and occupations of residents. Some of the Italians include:

Centennial Avenue
    605 James Morrow, chauffeur, taxi.
    601 Michael Maruca and son, both laborers.
    515 ? Vallon, laborer.
    501 Joseph Gariti, shoemaker, own shop.
Dickson Road
    Peter Russo, laborer in foundry.
    Joseph Pellegrino, laborer for contractor.
Ferry Street
    226 ? Pitzner, laborer, private estate.
    230 Two family heads, one a laborer in a steel foundry, the other a laborer on a private estate.

Many people today remember their childhood in the 1930s and 1940s. Josephine Toia remembered the origins of one of Sewickley's shops run by ethnic Italians, Yankello's Radio-Television Sales and Service.

> In the early 1930s, my dad purchased a radio and something happened to the radio. So my dad said, "I'll go see what it will cost to get this fixed." He came home and said he wasn't going to pay that kind of money. He was going to learn how to fix it himself. We had a small table in the kitchen, and my father took the radio completely apart until he found the part he thought was bad, a condenser. He knew a fellow who repaired them. He bought the part and my dad went home and piece by piece put the radio back together and from that day on, anyone who had any trouble with a radio, he would fix it. He worked in the mill and did it on the side. He was so proud to do it.

Many of the original immigrants, including the fathers of both Mr. Vescio and Mr. Tignanelli, worked as gardeners on estates in Sewickley and Sewickley Heights. Blacks usually worked as housemen, butlers, or chauffeurs and Italians, as gardeners. Frank Vescio said:

> Fifteen or twenty men worked for the old Jones estate (Fairacres). Most came from abroad. That's what they did. Very few worked in the winter unless they could find odd jobs. During the Depression lots of them were laid off. We worked for the W.P.A. [Works Progress Administration].

Mr. Tignanelli remembered,

> There was a line of Italians walking up Blackburn Road carrying their lunch buckets. Lew Parks had 40 Italian people working for him. He was the only one who picked his help up. It took two trips in a truck. Everyone else walked.

Later, Mr. Tignanelli worked for a family in Edgeworth. When he figured he made only 15 cents an hour, he asked for a raise to 25 cents. Because he did not get the raise, he went to work in a factory for $4 a day.

Joseph Munizza, Jim's father, worked at the Allegheny Country Club for 47 years. Jim himself worked there while still in school. First he was a caddy.

Then the caddy master asked if I wanted to wash pots and pans. You never saw so many. Then you had to wait until the party was over and wash them again at two in the morning. They gave me one dollar. I got the buck and I used to run down Blackburn Road, and I had the dollar in my hand. No one was going to take this away from me. Mom was waiting for me. I said, "Why are you waiting?" She didn't want to take it, but she could get a big bag of groceries for a dollar. I really enjoyed it—giving a dollar to my mother.

Bruno Toia was a paper boy.

I used to deliver morning papers at four in the morning. I got $1.00 a week for the morning paper, $1.00 for the afternoon, $1.25 for Sunday. I used to get a bar of candy out of that. The rest went straight home.

Frank Vescio worked during summer vacations.

I worked at the Allegheny Country Club shining shoes. The next year I was a bellboy. [After leaving school he worked three years at the club.] Then I met Mr. Burgwin at the country club and he wanted me to work for him. He owned Paddock Farm, the old Horne estate off Blackburn Road. I worked there 15 years—used to do the driving, run errands. I worked in the stable. They had 10 or 12 saddle horses and we raised our own colts. I rode horses and trained them. Later, Mrs. Burgwin bought Barberry Farm and built the big stone house on Barberry Road. The Paddock Farm was subdivided and the barn torn down.

Some of the Italian men worked for D.W. Challis, the contractor based on Centennial and Locust where the medical center is now. Challis kept 10 teams of horses to do the work now done by tractors, bulldozers, and dump trucks. When he did the excavation for the hospital foundation in 1925, he had a big steam shovel, but horses and wagons still brought the sand and gravel up from the river. All ditches were dug by hand. Mr. Tignanelli remembered earning 30 cents an hour digging ditches for pipe around the Post Office.

Other Italians worked in factories or mills. Jerry and Frank Vescio's grandfather worked for the Duquesne Foundry in Coraopolis. Jerry Vescio himself worked for American Bridge.

As new immigrants, the Italians settled in any housing that was cheap and available, hoping and usually achieving future improvements. When single men immigrated, they usually became boarders. Mr. Pellegrino stayed with relatives. Mr. Floro lived in boarding houses to save money for bringing his family to join him. The boarding system worked well for both parties. Italian women customarily did not work outside the home. It was, however, socially acceptable to take in boarders, thereby increasing family income.

Both Jim Munizza and Bruno Toia's mothers took in boarders. Jim remembered.

They [the boarders] bought a twenty-pound box of spaghetti three feet long, fifty or hundred-pound bags of potatoes, navy beans, and a whole lot of onions. Some [boarders] cooked their own or my mother or Bruno's mother would cook for them from their supply of stuff. They charged so much a month to stay there and they would wash their clothes, too.

Single men could be boarders but after they were joined by wives and families, other accommodations were necessary. When Mr. Flora's wife and children immigrated, the family had two Italian boarders themselves. The Flora family rented a second-floor apartment on 417 Broad Street above the Colonial Flower Shop. The building had 11 rooms, including six storerooms, a greenhouse, and the apartment. Housekeeping was difficult when the Floras arrived. Mrs. Flora's daughter remembered that it took all of her mother's time plus any free time that her daughters could contribute. Chores were increased because of the two boarders. The apartment was heated by a coal-burning, potbellied stove. "When we got up in the morning it was freezing. There was a quarter inch of ice on the windows." Clothes had to be washed by hand in water heated in pots on the stove. "Mother did not sew our dresses, but she did make drapes, sheets, and pillow cases from old flour sacks that she sewed together."

The Floras later bought a comfortable house on Thorn Street opposite the Borough Building. Here Mr. Flora tended his extensive gardens into his 90s.

The Tignanelli family lived on Glen Mitchell Road. Jerry Tignanelli described it:

There were 10 or 12 houses on the road, including six for Italian families. Our house had no running water. The spring was 500 feet from the house. The day before my mother washed, we carried water in buckets and filled some tubs. Everything was washed by hand. There was no electric; we had an outhouse. Glen Mitchell was a mud road with ruts a couple of feet deep. When doctors came, we used to meet them at the end of the road with a flashlight—they were scared to come up. We walked them up. It cost three dollars a visit. We used to buy groceries once a year and we got coal delivered once a year because the horses couldn't get up the road [in winter]. Everything had to be done by fall. If we came down to Sewickley to buy something, we would carry it up on our shoulders.

Mr. Pellegrino, Frank and Jerry Vescio's grandfather, had the most ingenious method of getting adequate housing. During World War I he worked in a mill in Coraopolis. Here he collected the wood left over from making concrete forms. Jerry Vescio remembered:

Every day he would leave Coraopolis carrying a two by four or two by six, cross the Sewickley Bridge, take it up to Dickson Road and stack it there. When he got enough lumber, he built the frame of the house. The house is on Dickson Road, the sixth on the left on the way up the hill.

The house had no electricity, but it was equipped with gas and a coal stove. There was a garden out back.

Gardens and their products formed a large part of Italian life in Sewickley. This was especially noticeable in the Italian neighborhood on Dickson Road, Bruno and Josephine Toia remembered:

Bruno: There were grapes, gardens, fruit trees, flowers. It was beautiful.

Josephine: Every one of the houses up there had flowers, and in the back or side, they had [vegetable] gardens.

Bruno: The men would get up early and before they went to work (most of them worked as gardeners in Sewickley Heights) they worked in their gardens. Then, they go out and work all day and come home, and after they ate their supper, they would be out there working again.

Both the Vescios and the Tignanellis produced most of their own food. The only thing they had to buy was clothes. Jerry Vescio said,

No nationality ever ate better than the Italians. Very few Italian women worked outside the home because Italian people didn't believe in sending their wives to work in those days. But they did everything themselves and lived on $60 or $70 a month for a family of up to 10. We used to go out and pick elderberries, and we picked crabapples and peeled them and made crabapple-elderberry jelly. I never ate jelly like that in my life! Everything they made. When my mother baked bread, you could smell it all over Sewickley. Our garden was where the cemetery is now. They let us use it for years and years. We lived on Dickson Road and carried the stuff down in bushel baskets. My mother used to put up 400 to 500 quarts of vegetables every year. We had a real small cellar and my mother had two fifty-gallon drums in there. Mother took all the vegetables, washed them, and she made a brine. She put everything in there. Through the winter, she took things out—peppers, tomatoes, cucumbers.

The Tignanellis and the Vescios slaughtered their own pigs. Mr. Vescio said:

We bought them off a farmer, killed them, and put them up for winter. My grandfather had the last pig on Dickson Road; when he died we didn't raise them any more. In 1932 we bought a 500 pound pig—paid $20.

Jerry Tignanelli described how they preserved the meat.

We dried it, then smoked the sausage for a couple of months in the smokehouse. Then we put it in oil or wood ashes with sassafras to give it a smell. We kept it under the porch. [Making salami was a complicated process.] You hang it from bamboo sticks. [Then] you get oak ashes, get a box, put ashes in this and cover the salami with ashes. It would keep for years. A lot [of people] submerged them in oil, but that was expensive.

The Floras, too, produced much of their own food. Mrs. Cortese said that they grew most of the vegetables, which they ate fresh in summer and canned in winter. Once a year they stuffed their own sausages. "But meat wasn't an everyday thing. It was for holidays. [For lunch and supper] we would have homemade bread, hot peppers, and a bowl of pasta or beans."

To accompany all this good food, the Italians made wine. Even during Prohibition, you could make wine for personal consumption. In October whole blocks would smell of fermenting grapes. Dickson Road (Little Italy) was particularly pungent. Bruno Toia had fond memories of winemaking on Dickson Road.

When someone made wine, some of the fellows would get together and make it, and then, when the other guy would make it, they would go down there. The only thing, every time you would make it, everybody got drunk.

Jerry Vescio said:

Dad never drank water. We bought grapes at the produce yards on the Strip. We picked them up in our Model A Ford or at the railroad station, where someone shipped all sorts of produce in one car. We used sweet muscat or zinfandel grapes. We ground them in something like a coffee grinder, but fifty times the size. Then we let it stand so many days, took it out and put it in a barrel with a spigot at the bottom. It kept bubbling and boiling off but we never let [the level] go down. We kept adding extra juice. Nothing else was added; no sugar, nothing. It has to be kept at 35 or 40 degrees. If it is in a warm place, it starts to boil again. My brother Frank makes it and keeps it on the side of the house without heat.

Social life and sports were limited by time and money. Bruno Toia said:

The only relaxation was they would work maybe a half day on Saturday and then they got together and played cards. They played cards Saturday, Saturday night, Sunday, and Sunday night. They would play for wine.

Jerry Tignanelli recalled, "There was always something going on on Sundays. They [other Italians] would come over to our house, or we would go to theirs." Men congregated at the local chapter of the Sons of Italy located in a little alley in back of the movie theater. Here they had meetings, played cards and bingo, drank, and escaped from daily routines. Other men might join the Italian band which played at different occasions all over the area.

Women's social life was more restricted. Mrs. Cortese said her mother's life centered on the family.

We went to church but did not participate in the social activities. Mother used to crochet with friends and each would teach the other. She did not even go to the movies. Mother didn't need to go out. It was not important to her and it was always in the back of her mind to save money. She didn't spend anything on entertainment.

Sewickley Valley Italian Band, 1928. Courtesy The Sewickley Valley Historical Society.

Italians living on Dickson Road had far more of the social interaction and support supplied by traditional village life in Italy. Bruno Toia's father was a great reader. "He read novels in Italian and then he would go from house to house—he was like a storyteller. Many didn't read or write." Mr. Toia told what happened in one chapter. "He went back the next week and told the next chapter. It was a continuous thing and they were expecting it." Jim Munizza said:

> We were a real close knit community. The old Italians, they used to go and visit a lot. My mother always made coffee. My mother used to bring people into the house. They would all meet and drink coffee and tell stories.

Josephine Toia remembered:

> Our neighbor lived down below us, and she had a bunch of kids. My mother would say, "Go down and give her a hand and watch the children or help do the dishes. I remember when my brother Tom was born, a family had three girls, and two of the girls came up and they ironed the clothes for my mom and washed clothes.

No money changed hands. Jim Munizza said: "You paid them by having the family over and giving them a good dinner." Bruno Toia added, "Everyone helped everyone out. If my mother got sick, the women from the neighborhood would bring food. Nobody was selfish. You don't get that anymore."

Most social life was centered on food. Any visitor to an Italian household will be offered something to eat and drink. Bruno Toia said.

> Even to this day, food is the essence of life. Everything is based on the meal. My mother-in-law brings out food and coffee. She will hound you until you have to sit down and eat. You have to accept it. If the family was eating a meal and a friend walked in, the wife would place a dish on the table for the guest. If he refused, he would be asked to go into the other room to wait.

Because there was no ethnic Catholic church in Sewickley to maintain traditions, church was not a big factor in the social life of the Italian immigrants, according to Josephine Toia. "We just went to church because it was our religion. There weren't a lot of activities. We didn't participate." Her husband agreed: "The religion was in the homes." Many holiday celebrations centered on food, Josephine Toia recalled.

> Christmas Eve you weren't allowed to eat meat; we ate fish. That was a big meal. The Italians had seven different kinds of fish: sardines, bacalhau (dried cod), squid, eel, smelts, dough with anchovies in it. At Easter every village had its own food customs: lamb, pastries, Easter bread, or cheese pie with ricotta.

Most Sewickley residents were friendly to the Italian newcomers, but, like the blacks, Italians suffered from discrimination. Mr. Toia said: "There was a lot of discrimination."

The children encountered prejudice first in school. Jerry Tignanelli's memories of school in Sewickley in the 1920s were not all happy.

> There was a little room in the back of the old school where they had the "special class" for kids that can't learn or kids that had a bad attitude about school. They took a poor little six-year-old kid who hadn't even been tested yet. They looked at him and said, "You don't belong with society. You belong in the special class." I got put in there because I was a brat when I was a kid. I was in there for a year and they had no intention of taking me out. My sister, who was five years older than me, went to the principal and begged him. He let me out. I knew colored people, the whole family in the special class. The Washington family was: Addie was my classmate, Mary, Marie, Jenny, Dorothy. And they were in there for four or five years. They would just stagnate there until they were 16. Then they quit. You know what was in the special class? A loom. You had about one hour a day in the textbooks, maybe 20 minutes of reading and arithmetic. Then everyone would be on some sort of craft preparing to go to a trade school. Kids came out of there and became bricklayers, carpenters. One was a top tailor, so he had to have intelligence.

Each grade in elementary school was divided into three sections, x, y, and z. Jerry Tignanelli remembered: "There was 6x, 6y, and 6z. I'll give you a guess who was in z. Blacks and Italians."

Mrs. Cortese had similar memories of her school days. She had been to school in Italy for a couple of years, but had to start over when she got to the Sewickley public school.

> Because we didn't speak English, we had a hard time. We were put in a school where everybody was looking at you; you don't know how to speak and nobody is going to take time. They had one class for special retarded and slow children and

that's where they stuck us. We were there until we caught up. Then we joined the regular classes, but we were old. I only went to fifth grade; then I felt too old and too big to continue.

Her younger sister, who was born in this country, was the only member of the family to graduate from high school. Even Bruno Toia and Jim Munizza, who had grown up in Sewickley, had problems in school. Bruno said:

Until we went to school we spoke very little English. If you didn't make it [in school because of language problems] they threw you into the special class. It wasn't teaching you anything—just how to make rugs, lumber. It wasn't educational at all.

Josephine Toia remembered moving to Sewickley in the fourth grade. Because of her excellent record in Ambridge, she was placed in the highest section of fourth grade.

Mrs. Wilson was the teacher. She did everything in her power to get rid of me in that class until one night she kept me after school. My father (he was young then) when he got home, that was the hour we were expected home and I wasn't home. So he paraded down to the school. I'm walking down the steps with Mrs. Wilson and my father comes in and he wants to know what the problem is. Am I not good enough to be in that class? Mrs. Wilson says, "No, I'm just afraid she'll miss her friends." My father said, "There's no friends when it comes to education. You either get the lesson or you don't." Later Mrs. Wilson said, (I can remember it to this day) "I didn't know that your father could speak English."

I was a new student in a new town. I was sick to my stomach in the morning. My dad said, "I don't understand." Then this happened, and he understood. Education was important to him. He stressed it; he didn't have it. That was the main thing in his life.

Josephine Toia did very well in school. Nevertheless, she was not encouraged to prepare for college. There were three tracks in high school: the general, the commercial, and the academic. Josephine said:

You didn't take the academic because you knew you weren't going to go to college. I had a scholarship to go to Duff's Business College, but father didn't have the money. All the scholarship would pay for was my tuition. I still had books and transportation. I was the oldest, and there were four other children.

Intolerance continued after school age. Italians suffered from many of the same prejudices as blacks. Mr. Toia remembered:

We couldn't belong to the Boy Scouts or Girl Scouts. We couldn't belong to the YMCA. In high school you couldn't belong to the gym team or the basketball team; only those who belonged to the YMCA were eligible. Mr. Winnie ran the Y and coached our gym and basketball team. He had his team all set up. You couldn't go to the prom. We had to sit on one side of the movies and were never allowed up in the balcony. They didn't want us to mingle. And we accepted it. We had one section, the blacks had another section, the middle was for everybody else.

In Sewickley Italians were not welcome to live in some parts of town, especially Beaver Street. This was one reason that Dickson Road became a heavily Italian neighborhood. Bruno Toia remembered:

Jim [Munizza] and I grew up together on Dickson Road. It was hard for us [Italians] to move in Sewickley. They kept us up there. If we tried to buy, we couldn't until after World War II. When my father-in-law moved down [to Beaver Road] from Dickson Road in 1956, the bank wouldn't give him a loan. They fought him tooth and nail. He had to go to Pittsburgh to get a loan. That was typical.

Mrs. Cortese said most Sewickley people were nice,

But then you had the ones who. . . . We lived on Logan Street, across from where my parents live now on Thorn Street. Mr. Brown lived here [in the Floras' house on Thorn]. When he learned that Italians had bought across the street, he let the hedge grow tall so he wouldn't have to see us. After Mr. Brown died, my father bought the house and leveled the hedge off again.

Sewickley was not alone in its resentment of Italians. Anti-foreign feeling was rampant in the United States in the 1920s. In Aspinwall, for example, where Agostino Zuccaro peddled vegetables, he was insulted. His son remembered,

When my father walked past the glass factory in Sharpsburg with his basket or his pushcart, people shouted, 'Dago!' and 'Garlic Eater!' and spat on him. Later, when I tried to buy a house in Aspinwall, the seller refused and took it off the market. He claimed he couldn't do that to the neighbors.

National prejudice against Italians was demonstrated by increasingly restrictive immigration. The 1917 Immigration Act rejected all persons over 16 who could not read and write. This was de facto discrimination because less than three per cent of the immigrants from northern Europe were illiterate whereas over half from southern Italy were. Later Immigration Acts continued the trend. In 1924 immigration was reduced to two per cent of the total population of each nationality residing here in 1890. By using 1890, Italians were limited because they were part of a later wave of immigration than the northerners.[3]

Italians today seem to have overcome resentments of past slights and show boundless enthusiasm for Sewickley. Jerry Vescio said,

> I love this town. Rents are high in Sewickley. I hope they keep them high—keep the riffraff out. When I'm walking, people say. "Hi, Jerry!" and I don't answer. I'm thinking. I look at the church and I'm remembering about when I was a kid and someone was climbing up putting shingles on. I'm concentrating. I'm walking along here and I can see old Anderson's garage [although it is no longer there].

America prides itself on being a melting pot of many ethnic groups. The present Italian community in Sewickley manages to improve on the melting pot. Although thoroughly adapted to America, it maintains some of its Italian traditions. This unity plus diversity is surely one of the country's treasures.

[1] John Bodnar, Roger Simon, Michael P. Weber, *Lives of their Own*. Chicago, University Press, 1982, p. 46, 123.

[2] *The Herald*, October 6, 1917, p. 6.

[3] Samuel Eliot Morison, Henry Steele Commager, and William E. Leuchtenburg, *The Growth of the American Republic*. 6th ed. N.Y., Oxford, 1969, v.2, pp. 117-8.

Chapter 25
Blacks in Sewickley

Blacks, the most obviously different group, came early to Sewickley. The 1820 census lists two free black families. Most were domestic workers. One of the best-known early blacks was David Shield's servant named either Jim or Harry Robinson. He helped clear the land for Newington and also helped the aging Eliza up the hill to teach Sunday School in the little schoolhouse. One of the early black landowners was Franklin Wetzel. In 1865 he bought one acre where Waterworks Park is and built a log cabin on the property.

Some of the early group escaped from slavery to reach Sewickley. George Marlatt came from Virginia, guiding his sister and her small son. In Sewickley, Mr. Marlatt worked for Robert H. Davis, who sent money to Virginia to buy Mr. Marlatt's freedom. Mr. Marlatt married a wonderful nurse known as Aunt Callie who took care of white families in Sewickley and Allegheny.[1]

In the 1860 census there were only 18 blacks counted. This had increased to 56 in 1870. By the end of the nineteenth century there were 48 black households in Sewickley.[2] After 1900 the black population swelled.

Population of Sewickley

	1910	1920	1930	1940	1950
Total	4,479	4,955	5,599	5,614	5,636
Black	428	570	713	776	746

Wealthy people moving to the Sewickley area and the Heights from Allegheny and the East End built large houses. Blacks worked building the houses and running them after completion. Many families had five to eight servants: cook, laundress, chambermaid, nurse, housemaids, butler, chauffeur, handyman, and gardener. Mrs. Temora Haynes explained why blacks came to Sewickley. "I remember when many folks came from Kentucky to work for Challis [a contractor] in construction. And many came from Virginia to work in the mills. But most came in droves from all over to work as domestics for the wealthy people."

Much of the information on black life in Sewickley related in this chapter is based on interviews with three key people: Charles Butler, Oliver Ward, and Virginia Hailstock. They should be properly introduced.

The Butler family has been in Sewickley since the late 1800s. The Butlers came by way of Virginia and Meadville, Pennsylvania. The family traces its lineage to Elijah and Susan, born slaves on a plantation near Richmond owned by the Stuarts. At the time slaves were known by the name of their owner, so Elijah and Susan were called Stuart. Both were house servants; Susan was a maid and seamstress, Elijah, the butler. Sometimes they were able to go to Richmond where one day Elijah was approached by a white man from Canada who said he could arrange escapes to Canada on the Underground Railroad. Both Susan and Elijah agreed to go. To avoid capture, Susan dressed as a man and they changed their name to Butler, after Elijah's job.

The couple reached Meadville in 1830. Meadville at the time was becoming both an important stop on the Underground Railroad and a haven for fugitive slaves. Many of the town's citizens were against slavery. John Brown, the nation's leading abolitionist, lived in New Richmond, only 12 miles from Meadville. Here he operated a stop on the Underground Railroad. He visited often in Meadville where he missed no chance to voice his abolitionist sentiments.

Elijah and Susan Butler had planned to continue their escape to Canada by way of the Erie Canal. They found Meadville such a sympathetic place, however, that they decided to remain, becoming the town's first black family. The Butlers settled successfully into their new community. They opened a barber shop, bought a house, and were founders of the first black church.

Their quiet life was disrupted one day when Elijah spied a slave hunter, sent to Meadville by their master to capture them. Their former owner had offered a reward of $1,000 for their return. The slave hunter saw Elijah but, because Elijah could pass for a white, he did not recognize him. Elijah did recognize the slave hunter and rushed to hide his wife, who was much darker, in the cellar of an abolitionist. The slave hunter departed empty-handed.[3]

The first Butler to move to Sewickley was John D., one of Elijah and Susan's ten children. He came in 1890 to be the chef at the Elmhurst Inn. Later he became an entrepreneur, founding the Butler Brothers ice cream store, run by his two sons, James and Carroll. James' son, Charles Butler, born in 1911, remembered the store on 514 Beaver Street.

Flatiron Building on 514 Beaver Street where Butlers had their ice cream store. Drawing by Susan Gaca.

It was in the triangle building owned by the Mateer brothers. One was a barber on Broad Street and one had a barbershop in the building. The ice cream store operated for 29 years. We made our own ice cream. The refrigeration came from a natural gas motor set up in the cellar. We lived there on the second and third floors; 10 out of 11 kids were born in that building. The ice cream fountain was downstairs. We just had the end of the building; there was a dry cleaner and a barber shop too.

My father could make 20 gallons of ice cream at a time. He used only pure cream sent in every morning from Lyonsville. There was a fellow from Haysville, John Cahee, who farmed up there.

After school Charles Butler worked in the ice cream parlor and delivered ice cream in Sewickley and Ambridge. The business grew and expanded:

You could go into the ice cream parlor and get hot chocolate, hot coffee, and sandwiches. They had oysters, taffy, and peanut brittle. They made their own Saratoga chips, potato chips cut by putting potatoes in a pot with a sharp blade on the bottom that would cut them very thin. Then they were fried in deep fat. We catered a lot of big weddings around here making frozen puddings, individual ice cream molds of chickens and different things.

In 1929, James Butler sold the business and moved to Edgeworth. Some of the larger ice cream companies were competing in Sewickley. "They used gelatin, and my dad used only cream. He wouldn't change his recipes."

The Butler family has done extraordinarily well. Charles worked over 30 years for the Internal Revenue Service, becoming chief of property management and administration for the Pittsburgh office. His brother, Basil, deafened by spinal meningitis when he was 17, attended barber school, passed the state test, and worked until normal retirement age.

Virginia Hailstock was from one of the earliest black families who settled in Sewickley. Her great-grandmother on her father's side, Mrs. William Parker, lived on the corner of Walnut and Thorn Streets. Miss Hailstock's mother came to Pittsburgh from Hancock, Maryland, on her doctor's advice.

> My mother suffered from malaria fever every summer. Her doctor told her that if she crossed water, she would get better. So, she came to visit relatives in Pittsburgh. They told her about two great aunts who had moved to Sewickley when their mother was freed from slavery. She came to visit them, liked it, and stayed.

Miss Hailstock lived on 305 Centennial Avenue, just across the street from the house where she was born in 1902. Her father, Lewis A. Hailstock, was the janitor in the Sewickley public school. "Father got up early and started the old coal furnace. Then, he came home for breakfast." Mrs. Hailstock, her mother, ran an employment agency from her house. Miss Hailstock said, "She had contacts all around the Valley and in Pittsburgh. She got cooks, maids, or day help."

Virginia Hailstock went to the Sewickley school from kindergarten through high school. She had the full support and encouragement of her mother.

> Mother went to school once a month to see how I was getting on. If my grades improved—fine. If not, she wanted to know why. One time there was a German play and I knew no German. She hired a tutor for me so I could participate.

Virginia hardly ever missed a day of school. "Once I stayed home from school and Mother gave me a big dose of castor oil. I never did that again."

Mrs. Hailstock's dedication to education was communicated to her daughter. After Virginia's graduation from Howard University, she continued her education at Bluefield State Teachers College, the University of Pittsburgh, and Duquesne University.

Oliver Ward is among Sewickley's most ardent admirers. He has always considered Sewickley his home. Oliver Ward's grandparents came to Sewickley from outside Charlottesville, Virginia. His mother and her siblings were born in Sewickley, but returned to Charlottesville to live with their aunt after their parents died at an early age. Oliver, too, lived with the same aunt for two or three years when his mother was working in Sewickley to support him. Later, when Oliver's mother was the cook for the William Tallmans, Oliver was allowed to stay with her.

> During the Depression my mother asked for more money. They said they couldn't give more but I could live with them. He [Mr. Tallman] worked in Pittsburgh. I don't know what he did. He had a chauffeur drive him back and forth in a great big Cadillac.

Besides the chauffeur and the cook, the Tallmans employed a butler, who did the grocery shopping, a laundress, who came three days a week, and a maid. This was not an unusually large staff. "The other people living around had the same."

The Tallmans had a summer house at Chatham, Massachusetts. Oliver and his mother went with them. "The Tallmans had their own beach and boat. I was a Lone Ranger up there but I loved it. The people I knew were all grown."

Despite a case of epilepsy, a disease both disabling and socially difficult, Oliver went to the Sewickley public school on Broad and Thorn Streets. When Oliver was 15 year old his mother died of what was called a blocked bowel.

> About a year after she had passed I was put in a Home in Rochester, Pennsylvania, where I stayed for six years. I was the only colored one there. Later they got a place for me in the State Home and they asked if I wanted to go there, but I wanted to stay because it was nearer home. Life was not easy at the Home. It was pretty rough at the beginning. The people who were able to do for themselves, like I was, got along very well but those who were older and not able to do for themselves couldn't work, but they were able to give me a hard way to go. I was told to ignore; so I finally got to ignore them and told them if it made them happy to call me names and all, to go ahead. It ended up I didn't have no enemies at all there.

After returning to Sewickley when he was 21, Oliver Ward lived nowhere else. For many years he worked for Conrad Cooper, chief labor negotiator for U.S. Steel, who lived on the old Woods estate at the top of Academy Avenue.

> It was really beautiful up there on that hill. When I started work there, the main house was torn down. The Coopers had turned the garage and chauffeur's quarters into a pretty big house. The house was way up the hill—you couldn't see it. They had their own private golf course along Woodland Road. All the grounds were taken care of by I don't know how many people. Seven families now live on that piece of property.

Later, Oliver Ward worked at the Sewickley Hospital where he started as a janitor and worked himself up to be the orderly in the operating room. "At first I was just to fill in in the operating room but I was there for many years."

Being black in Western Pennsylvania during these times must have been both frightening and humiliating because of discrimination. There were institutions that might have lessened the frustration but, until the Community Center opened in 1939, places for amusement and recreation for blacks were very limited. One source of pleasure for black women was the Hawthorne Club, founded in 1914 "to promote the welfare and progress of Negro women and children of the Sewickley Valley." The club met on Thursday afternoons, the only convenient time for the members who worked as servants in private homes. They traditionally were free after lunch on Thursday. Two meetings were held each month: a business meeting to handle finances and to discuss civic problems and current events; and a meeting where members produced goods to give to the poor such as canned goods or handmade knitted and crocheted items. Bettie Cole, historian for blacks, said:

> When the Hawthorne Club was started we had full-course dinners, used fine china and tablecloths. This was their time to entertain and use the best they had. They worked all during the week serving Miss Anne or Madam, so meetings were our time for ourselves. Most of these women really knew how to cook their food and set their tables because they worked for so many white families. . . .

> We've always had some kind of program at our meeting. At our early meetings we would discuss Negro leaders and current events. We now arrange our agenda so we can devote some time to black history, current leaders, and the things happening now.

The Club has been a strong supporter of women's movements, starting with women's suffrage and temperance. During World War II members worked closely with the Sewickley Red Cross. An annual card party yields funds to support several local charities.[4]

The church was the center for religious and social life. Mrs. Temora Haynes, who moved to Sewickley in 1915, remembered, "When they [the blacks] came here, especially from the South, first thing they would do is find the churches. And that's where you'd meet them."[5]

Black churches came early to the Valley. In 1857 there were enough Afro-Americans to form the nucleus of St. Matthew's American Methodist Episcopal Zion church. Its first minister, Daniel Matthews, is said to have crossed the Alleghenies, riding part of the way on a mule. When the mule died, he had to pause in his ministerial duties until he could earn enough to continue his journey. The A.M.E. Zion church has been a mainstay of the black community. Miss Virginia Hailstock was a descendant of three founders. Her great-great-grandfather and two great-great-aunts were charter members.

Outdoor services were popular in the Valley. Blacks held revivalist religious services in Waterworks Park and in McDonald's Grove on the River near Maple Avenue. In the 1860s, camp meetings on the River near Glen Osborne Station were attended by blacks from near and far, who pitched tents on the river bank and stayed as long as ten days.[6]

The St. Matthew's Church was joined by others—the Antioch Free-Will Baptist on Fife Street (now Blackburn), 1891, the American Episcopal Zion, on Elizabeth Street, 1884, and Triumph Baptist on Ferry Street, 1924.

The church played a large role in the life of blacks. Former Police Chief Walter Brannon's mother joined the St. Matthew's A.M.E. Zion Church when she came to Sewickley. Her son became an active member and served as chairman of the board of trustees. He said,

> The church is a very important part of my life. I went to church when I was young; it grows on you. I sing in the choir—did it when I was in high school. The pianist and I go back to that time.

St. Matthew's A.M.E. Zion Church. Walnut and Thorn Streets. Drawing by Susan Gaca.

Miss Virginia Hailstock appreciated the part the St. Matthew's A.M.E. Zion Church played in her life when she was a girl in the 1910s.

> All entertainment and enjoyment were centered in church. We went to church four times on Sunday: the 11:00 o'clock service; Sunday school at 3:00; Christian Endeavor [a youth group] at 7:00; and an evening service at 8:00. In addition, there were many special events at St. Matthew's. Church picnics were popular. Some were held at the Waterworks. We played games all day. People brought baskets. Sometimes we had picnics at Staunton Farm [on the other side of the Ohio River.] An old German named Mr. Menz had a livery service with a horse and buggy. He hauled all the tables and some of the people. He had a wagon we could put baskets in. There was a woman named Kirk (she was a big fat lady) and she would be on a chair in the middle of the wagon and all these picnic baskets around her. They spread the tables out and everyone threw all the meals together. People went back and forth all day. When we came home, we were led by the Wilson Band, black men from the community who marched across the Sewickley Bridge. When they hit the bridge, they would start playing "When the Saints Come Marching In." [At one Staunton Farm picnic, church rules were flouted when some members danced.] Saint Matthew's members were not supposed to dance and be a member. My mother was one of them. Each offender was brought before the church officials and punished by suspension. My mother was the last. She said, "Who saw me dance?" Nobody spoke up because she had been dancing with some of the officers of the church.

When picnics were impractical because of bad weather, dinners were held at the church. Miss Hailstock remembered feasting on pigs feet, boiled with black-eyed peas, and sauerkraut.

Each year there was a two-week revival meeting every night except Saturday to bring new people into the church, according to Miss Hailstock.

> We went every night. They sang and prayed and fell down on their knees. They called it refreshing their souls. You would go up to the Mourner's Bench at the altar and you would lean down. People would stand and pray and clap over you and shout over you. It was very emotional. Sometimes during the service, they would have a Love Feast. The deacon walked up and down the aisle while everyone sang old-fashioned hymns. When he offered bread, each member would break off a piece and eat it. The minister came behind with the pitcher. They would have a glass and you would put it in and drink it.

[Holiday events centered on the church.] On Memorial Day the women of the church made sandwiches and sold them outside the church to people going to the cemetery. On St. Matthew's Day, which coincides with the Fourth of July, both blacks and whites came to the activities held behind the church. One of the big events was Climb the Greasy Pole. The same man, Mr. Gilkerson, always won the prize. The festivities were followed by a big meal and a ball game. At Thanksgiving we didn't eat our meal at home; we ate our turkey at the church. The Christmas tree was at the church. We children would go and decorate the tree. It stayed up until Easter.

An organization especially for blacks was the Sewickley Colored Community Center, started on Division Street in 1939. Former police chief Brannon remembered, "The Center grew out of the black YMCA because blacks were excluded from the Sewickley YMCA." A former board member said, "When the center was founded, we had no place to go other than to churches for recreation. The Sewickley Y had a swimming pool, but if we wanted to swim, we either went to Pittsburgh or swam in the river." After the Center moved to Chadwick Street in 1951, it could offer many activities. Bettie Cole, the writer on black history in Sewickley, remembered, "We had our bands there, and we had club groups—girls clubs and boys clubs—that we would attend. We had arts and crafts, basketball and softball. You name it."

Blacks were not allowed in the Masonic Lodge, so they organized their own lodge about 1890. A women's Eastern Star group was formed in 1921. The Black Women's Association of Sewickley started in 1914, with Miss Hailstock as a charter member. The association continues, devoting itself to raising money for the library, hospital, and scholarships.

The Walter Robinson Post 450 of the American Legion was organized in 1922 and its Ladies Auxiliary, in 1926. The Post purchased Sewickley's railroad station in 1944 and added a pavilion a few years later. Bettie Cole said the Post became "a beehive of social activity for the black veteran and the black community." Its drill team, started in 1947, "marched its way into the hearts and the pride of blacks up until the early 60s." The Walter Robinson legion building was used by the Community Center until 1960 for dances, parties, and roller skating. Big bands came there in 1950s and 1960s, including Dizzy Gillespie, Cab Calloway, Ella Fitzgerald, and Duke Ellington. "Down through the decades of segregation and discrimination, Post 450 has always been there for the blacks when other facilities closed their doors to them. Throughout the Sewickley Valley and beyond, Post 450 was the main facility for the blacks for their social life." [7]

In 1930 the Walter E. Robinson Post made an effort to cooperate with the white post in the Memorial Day Parade.

The Walter E. Robinson Post extends a cordial invitation to all ex-service men of the Valley to parade. Start at St. Matthew's A.M.E. Zion Church. The value of racial cooperation is gradually proving its worth to the group and we trust the efforts of the same will soon be noticeable here in the borough. . . . We must formulate a worthwhile program for race advancement. To do so successfully, there must be Cooperation and agreement.

J.E. Butler, President.[8]

Discrimination and the Black Response

Much of black life in Sewickley was tainted by discrimination. Many Northerners think of segregation and discrimination as problems of the South and rather smugly think the problem in the North was solved sometime around the Civil War. Many blacks in Sewickley can refute this notion. True, public schools were integrated and blacks could vote. But other forms of segregation reigned. Charles Butler said:

A black person couldn't go no place on Beaver Street and sit and eat. And we were told that if we served blacks [at the ice cream store], whites wouldn't patronize us. So blacks had to come and take out whatever they wanted. On Beaver Street there was no place you could eat. A.C. Walker had a soda fountain on the corner of Broad and Beaver Streets. You couldn't go in there. No place could you eat; had to take out. Pittsburgh was the same. Blacks couldn't sit at Kleins or Stouffers. Everything was segregated around here, I'll tell you. Look at the YMCA up here. It is supposed to be a Young Men's Christian Association and blacks could not go. The boys, when they played football, the white boys could change up at the YMCA. The black boys changed down at the school. They had to walk clear down there, if they couldn't get a ride, and at that time there weren't many cars.

No blacks could go to Walnut Beach. To go to the movies, we took the streetcar to Coraopolis. We couldn't go to the Sewickley [movie] show. You could go once a year, when the firemen had a benefit. Later, we could sit in the balcony; then on the right side.

Blacks were offered a special Saturday evening show by one of the theaters. It promised that "every effort will be made to show pictures that are uplifting."

Wilson's Cornet Band on the steps of the Broad Street School, 1906. All bands were segregated.
Courtesy The Sewickley Valley Historical Society.

Other blacks remembered the discrimination. A letter written in 1987 from Harvey E. King, Sr. of Washington D. C. recounts what he calls apartheid in Sewickley.

Up until the day I tried to enter the theater, which was on the corner of the street I lived on, I never knew what segregation and discrimination was—I was soon to learn. The hurt and bitterness never leaves. Because of friends who were ushers, I was able to buy a ticket and see a few movies without being detected. . . . My love for Sewickley is undying, so is my hate for the Sewickley Theater.

Miss Virginia Hailstock grew up about the same time as Mr. Butler.

At first blacks were not allowed to go to the movies. Black boys took part in school athletics. Because the school had no gym, they played at the YMCA. Whites could change at the Y., but black boys had to change clothes at school.

Oliver Ward remembered Sewickley a few years later.

I went to the movies in Sewickley. Had to sit on the right hand side. We didn't like it. On the other hand, after we could sit anywhere, we still sat on the right. There was one black restaurant, Crowley's, on Centennial between Blackburn and Grimes. The YMCA was segregated, too. I used to help a caterer with dinners and parties at the Y. They had a swimming pool, golf course, tennis courts. You had to join. Blacks didn't try to join. They had a big ball field and grandstand. We did sit in the grandstand and watch the games. I didn't envy people. I accepted what I had.

Former Police Chief Brannon recalled, "We went to school together, but after school we went different ways. It was subtle discrimination." Changes started when Chief Brannon became president of the Sewickley Community Center in 1957:

The boards of the Community Center and the YMCA had a joint meeting. Some of the YMCA board members had not realized that there was a segregationist policy. Some men said, "If I had known that the YMCA was segregated, I never would have donated money to it." At least we opened their eyes that they had a policy that blacks didn't belong. It was a very amicable discussion. Gradually it [the YMCA] opened up and now, if you go up there, you see little black kids lying on the floor and swimming; you see black teachers. Some of the old folks would turn over in their graves!

There was job discrimination even for domestic workers. About half of the advertisements in *The Sewickley Herald* specified whites only.

	Whites only	*Not specified*	*Blacks only*
		Advertisements	
1923 (6 weeks)	33	38	3
1926 (3 weeks)	22	24	0

Although discrimination must have been infuriating, a more frightening phenomenon was also pandemic: the Ku Klux Klan. Charles Butler remembered,

They met at the field where Quaker Village is now. They'd have big conclaves down there. They would have readings, burned the cross first, and then sometimes they had a band playing. Sometimes the K.K.K. met over at Armory Hall in Coraopolis [and marched across the Sewickley Bridge]. Police Chief McFarland and a state policeman were down this side of the Sewickley Bridge. They [the marchers] had to lift up their masks and several of the business people of Sewickley were right in there with their robes on. I ain't going to mention no names. You couldn't have masks on going through Sewickley. They lifted the masks but kept going through town. There was a plaque for World War I veterans—the K.K.K. always put flowers there. There never was no trouble.

You know the big bend going up to the cemetery? That is where they burnt the cross. You would hear a big bomb go off. You can see it good from all over town. They burnt them in Edgeworth up on Chestnut Road, too. The K.K.K. were terrible—trying to scare people.

Others remembered the days of the Ku Klux Klan. Miss Virginia Hailstock:

They burnt a cross at the cemetery and then marched right down from the cemetery hill—down Broad Street. [The authorities] must have known they were coming because they would not allow the Klansmen to march with their heads covered. They had to uncover their heads. That is when we found out some of the merchants from Sewickley belonged to the Klan. I did not watch but I understand the Negroes stood around and laughed.

Mary Louise Johnson saw Ku Klux Klan activities in Edgeworth.

In the 1920s, Edgeworth was infected by the antiforeign and antiblack resentment which swept the nation. Many blacks left the area. Twice crosses were burned on the grass here in Edgeworth. One time the Ku Klux Klan burned a cross on the top of Poia Road. Mother got us out of bed to see what was happening. It was scary. We could see it.

James McCracken, a writer who grew up in Sewickley, was a friend and neighbor of the Butler family. He described a K.K.K. march in an article in the *Reader's Digest*, in 1980.

Sewickley's cemetery lay on a hill high above the town. One day there were rumors about. Look up at the cemetery tonight about nine o'clock. Ghosts? Never mind. Just watch. The rumor spread.

Evening came, then darkness. It was summertime. The insects hummed and whined in our ears as we all—Mother, Father, brothers and sisters—stood out in the yard. People idled along the sidewalks or stood in their own yards, eyes turned upward to the cemetery. Nine o'clock approached, then passed. I noticed the Butler family at the windows of their home above the ice-cream parlor.

Suddenly there was a burst of yellow flame, far up on the cemetery hill. We stood dumbfounded. A cross—a burning cross. And we knew what it meant: the Ku Klux Klan. As we stood, I felt my mother's hands on my shoulders. They trembled. Mother was afraid. Afraid, as was I. But no, it was not fear. "An outrage," she said, and she said it again and again.

At last the flames died. We wandered up to our porch, sat there, and talked in whispers. My mother was furious, my father less so. He tried to calm her, reason with her. The burning of the cross was dead wrong. But he could deal with it less passionately than could my mother.

Our house was on the main street of town—Beaver Street. In those days it was a joy to live on the main street. There was still the clip-clop of horses pulling wagons. There was the click of friends' footsteps on the sidewalk. And there was the clank of a few automobile engines. Otherwise, quiet. For it was a quiet time in this century.

But this night there were people about, an unusual number, talking about what had happened. A voice would rise, strident in the night, then fell.

We watched and listened from our porch. Then the voices died. People pointed down the street. There were buildings in the way, and at first we couldn't see what was happening. It was as though some cataclysmic event was about to occur. Then we saw! Up the street strode a man in a white robe and hood, carrying a torch. Behind him was another white-clad figure. Then another and another, a dozen or so in single file. They walked in silence down the main street of town.

Suddenly Mother sprang up from the swing. We hear her footsteps on the walk. Click, click, click. An angry sound. At the curb she stood and watched. Then she spoke. Her voice was quiet, but it trembled with outrage.

"I don't know who you are, under those disgraceful sheets, but I am sure I know every one of you. I talk with you in the streets, and in the stores. Even in church. And I talk to you now. You are nothing but cowards. There is not one man among the lot of you!"[9]

The Klan, like discrimination, was not limited to the Sewickley area. In the 1920s the Klan grew rapidly in Western Pennsylvania. By 1924 there were 125,000 Klansmen in Pennsylvania and as many as 250,000 by 1926. By the late 1920s the Klan had 416 individual local klaverns. Allegheny County, with 33 klaverns, had the most in the state. The Ku Klux Klan was as much opposed to Catholics and foreigners as to blacks. The most famous Klan gathering was focused against the immigrant Catholics of Carnegie. In August, 1923, the Imperial Wizard led a rally of thousands of members in Scott Township. All swore a solemn oath to the Klan. At dusk, a dozen crosses burned on nearby hillsides. Then all massed behind a white car carrying an American flag illuminated by electric lights. The procession headed for Carnegie. But the Klansmen were routed by Carnegie citizens armed with stones, sticks, and hunks of coal. The Klansmen fled, leaving one dead.[10] Over the next few months, there were many other Klan demonstrations using the slogan, "Remember Carnegie and come armed!." At West Kittanning 25,000 Klansmen gathered one night. Some nights there were 50 burning crosses across the state.[11]

Sewickley was not alone in its discrimination against blacks. It was rampant throughout the Pennsylvania. YMCA branches did not admit blacks unless there were separate black facilities. Sixty-two percent of the legitimate theaters in Pennsylvania restricted blacks, either refusing them admission or admitting them to special sections. In smaller cities and towns, two-thirds of the theaters discriminated. Movie theaters had similar rules. In Pittsburgh several publicly owned playgrounds and swimming pools denied access to blacks, even when they were in the middle of largely black neighborhoods. Some settlement houses were segregated. For example, the Soho Community House, 2358 Fifth Avenue had 15% black membership, but blacks and whites had separate social affairs, clubs, and orchestras. The Irene Kaufmann Settlement house, then located on the Hill, had a very few black children.[12]

In some cases Sewickley was less segregated than other towns in Pennsylvania. Indeed, Sewickley can be proud that it did not have separate schools for blacks as other Pennsylvania towns did. A 1929 survey found:

In many of the smaller cities and towns the school authorities have been quite frank in their segregation of the races. Such towns as Coatesville and Chester have separate schools for all Negro children. Even in communities where it was financially difficult to establish separate school buildings for Negroes, the authorities have developed what have been called "Union Rooms." In these "Union Rooms" are placed all the Negro children in the school, irrespective of grade.[13]

Housing segregation in Sewickley seems to have been less absolute than it was in other towns. Centennial Avenue, according to the 1920 census, had a mixture of families. On the 500 block, seven families were black, nine were white. The 400 and 500 blocks of Broad Street had six black and four white residents. Chestnut Street was mostly white but had four black families. The 200 and 300 blocks of Ferry Street had nine black families and seven white. Other Pennsylvania towns were completely segregated. In Williamsport, for example, most blacks lived along one unpaved, dusty thoroughfare on the railroad tracks. In Harrisburg, blacks lived in houses near the railroad tracks, packing houses, and ice plants, and the atmosphere reeked with odors from the packing plants and ammonia from the ice plants. In Coatesville the black section, again along the tracks, was so low that cellars were half filled with water for months at a time.[14]

Hospitals in Pennsylvania often discriminated. Mercy Hospital in 1930 had one seven-bed ward for Negro women and one for 20-25 men. Children's Hospital admitted blacks to the wards but, if they requested a private room, authorities did not say what they did, only admitting that they would "have a social problem." The Sewickley Fresh Air Home said, "We do not and never have admitted colored children."

It took many years for discrimination to gradually loosen its hold in Western Pennsylvania and Sewickley. In 1935 Pennsylvania passed an equal rights act which granted all persons, regardless of creed and color, equal privileges in all public places. Because the law was often ignored by restaurants and hotels, court actions were necessary to bring enforcement. The first case in Allegheny County in 1936 involved Psaras Restaurant of East Liberty. John Psaras refused to serve coffee to a black man. Psaras claimed he merely asked the man to use a booth near the kitchen, but a fellow worker heard him say, "We don't serve colored people in here."[15] In another case in Clearfield in September 1936, a drug store owner refused to serve two blacks at a soda fountain. The grand jury that heard the case ignored the charges but fined the black man who brought the case $21.75 for costs.

The cases continued. In 1938 Mrs. Sarah Filner had a party at the Penn Roller Skating Rink, 5200 Penn Avenue. She brought two black guests; they were refused admittance. When the case came to court, Judge C. D. Fetterhoof charged Mrs. Filner $125 costs because, he said, she was only trying to test the law and, anyway, "public rights always transcend individual rights." When Mrs. Filner would not pay the fine, she was jailed.

As late as 1957 Henry X. O'Brien issued an order to restrain the Lexington Roller Skating Palace from denying Negro access because, he ruled, it was not a private club.[16]

The history of discrimination against blacks and Italians has been largely forgotten in Western Pennsylvania. Remembering it will help to prevent its recurrence in greater or lesser degrees.

[1] F. Nevin, pp. 175-179.

[2] *Sewickley Business Directory, 1896-97*, pp. 86-87.

[3] Charles Blockson, *The Underground Railroad in Pennsylvania*, Jacksonville, N.C., Flame International, 1989, pp. 122-124.

[4] *Pittsburgh Post-Gazette*, Feb. 19, 1996, p. D2.

[5] *Sewickley Herald,* September 5, 1990, p. 7.

[6] F. Nevin, p. 185.

[7] Bettie Cole, *Sewickley Herald*, Feb. 26, 1992.

[8] *Sewickley Herald*, May 29, 1930, p. 2.

[9] James McCracken, "Mother is Home." In *Readers' Digest*, April 1980, pp. 203-204.

[10] *Pittsburgh Post-Gazette*, March 25, 1939.

[11] Philip Jenkins, "The Ku Klux Klan in Pennsylvania, 1920-1940." In *Western Pennsylvania Historical Magazine*, v.69, No 2 April 1986, pp. 121-124.

[12] National Urban League, *Social Conditions of the Negro in the Hill District of Pittsburgh*. General Committee on the Hill Survey, 1930, pp. 45-50, 54-55.

[13] *Negro Survey of Pennsylvania*, 1929. Harrisburg, Commonwealth of Pennsylvania, Department of Welfare, p. 58.

[14] Ibid., p. 31.

[15] *Press*, May 29, 1936.

[16] *Human Relations Review*. Dec. 1960, p. 3.

Conclusion

Studying Sewickley history is studying American history in miniature. The historian can follow the coming of the early settlers and their problems with obtaining land. The original farming community's change to a suburban town is a story told all over America. Sewickley's response to the country's wars is a sample of other communities'. And Sewickley's relations with immigrants and blacks are not unique.

The Sewickley area has changed functions through the years. Starting as a farming community and way station for travelers on the Ohio River and the Beaver Road, it became a favored abode for river captains. The railroad transformed the area into a suburban retreat for Pittsburghers.

Sewickley has developed a strong sense of community. Ask residents of Fox Chapel, Shadyside, or Squirrel Hill where they live and they will reply, "Pittsburgh." Ask Sewickleyites and they will say, "Sewickley." Current town planners are working to implant this sense of community ready-made in new communities. Attempts have been made to develop new towns with the community feel of small towns. The most famous of these is Reston, Virginia, a carefully planned venture of the Rouse Company. More recently a new town on the Florida Panhandle called Seaside has been very successful in providing the atmosphere of an older community. It is interesting, to compare the way the Seaside planners arrived at their means of developing a town like Sewickley and the way Sewickley developed on its own. The Seaside planners, architects Andres Duany and Elizabeth Plater-Zyberk were hired by the town developer. They devised a strict code for all new houses to ensure architectural compatibility. Each house had to have a large front porch, to promote easy, informal visiting. All houses had to be made of wood. There could be no large plate glass windows or doors. The architects wanted to plan a town with houses that were compatible but not identical.

Seaside appears to be a distant cousin of Sewickley Borough. In Sewickley, however, the same compatibility arrived without a code because similar people in each period tended to build in similar architectural styles. Architects and builders, by following the latest trends in building styles, abided by an unwritten code, perhaps a combination of keeping up with the Joneses and perusing books and magazines on style. The resulting houses, built in a variety of styles, blend together to make a pleasing community.

Celebration, a new planned community in Florida developed by the Disney Company, has determined after extensive study how to develop a town with a community ambiance. Compare their plans with Sewickley and you will find that many attributes deemed necessary already exist in Sewickley.

Disney plans a town center that sounds like a description of Sewickley in the early twentieth century. The center will have restaurants, shops, offices, supermarket, bank, inn, and movies. Sewickley had all. Disney requires three-story buildings with apartments in the top floors of downtown stores and offices. This is to emulate nineteenth century centers like Sewickley as opposed to strip shopping centers which are one story high. Having apartments makes downtown a busy place after shopping hours and provides affordable housing to house cleaners, store clerks and other workers with lower wages. Disney will put the school in the center of town. Children walking to school create a town with a neighborly feel. The Sewickley school was on the corner of Broad and Thorn. Parking lots will be prohibited in Celebration unless they can be tucked inconspicuously behind buildings. This will make the vista along the street attractive with no gaping holes. Sewickley has hidden lots.

Houses in Celebration will have a range of prices to attract a heterogeneous population. Sewickley has such a range. Disney will have alleys behind the houses to promote an attractive streetscape unmarred by unsightly garages. Downtown Sewickley has alleys; Beaver Road has garages, many charming former carriage houses, tucked in back yards. Disney houses must follow a pattern book of acceptable architectural designs to achieve compatible houses. Sewickley houses are naturally compatible. They were built in the styles fashionable at the time. Many of these styles are in the pattern book of Celebration. Disney plans miles of walking and bike trails. Sewickley has sidewalks enjoyed by walkers and joggers. Celebration will have a homeowners association with restrictive covenants to regulate change. Sewickley has a Historical Commission to oversee changes in the historical area.[1]

Communities like Celebration and Seaside will be pleasant places to live. One wonders, however, if they will always look fake, like a movie set trying to recreate a mythical community. Sewickley is the real thing.

---

[1]Witold Rybczynski, "Tomorrowland." In The *New Yorker*, July 22 1996, pp. 37-39.

Bibliography

Agnew, Daniel. *A History of the Region of Pennsylvania North of the Ohio and West of the Allegheny River.* Philadelphia, Kay & Bro., 1887.

Arensberg, Charles. "The Pittsburgh Fire of 1845." In *Western Pennsylvania Historical Magazine.* March, 1945, v. 28, p. 12.

Automobile Blue Book, 1913, v. 3. Chicago, The Automobile Blue Book, 1913.

Baltzell, E. Digby. *The Protestant Establishment.* N.Y., Random House, 1964.

Bausman, Joseph A. *History of Beaver County, Pennsylvania.* N.Y., Knickerbocker, 1904.

Beecher, Catherine E. and Harriet Beecher Stowe. *The American Woman's Home.* N.Y., Arno, 1869.

Binn's Justice: Digest of the Laws and Judicial Decisions of Pennsylvania. Philadelphia, James Kay, 1840.

Blockson, Charles. *The Underground Railroad in Pennsylvania.* Jacksonville, N.C., Flame International, 1981.

Boal, J. McKees. *History of the Erection of Allegheny County, its Townships, Boroughs, and Cities.* Pittsburgh, Union Fidelity Title Insurance, 1914.

Bodnar, John, Roger Simon and Michael P. Weber. *Lives of Their Own.* Chicago, University Press, 1982.

Boorstin, Daniel. *The Americans: The Colonial Experience.* N.Y,. Random House, 1958.

Boorstin, Daniel. *The Americans: The National Experience.* N.Y., Random House, 1965.

Branch, E. Douglas. "Success to the Railroad." In *Western Pennsylvania Historical Magazine*, v. 20, p. 7.

Brown, Mary Florence. *The Sewickley Valley in the Nineteenth Century.* Unpublished paper, 1970.

Buck, Solon J. and Elizabeth Hawthorne Buck. *The Planting of Civilization in Western Pennsylvania.* Pittsburgh, The University Press, 1939.

Casson, H. N. *The Romance of Steel: the Story of a Thousand Millionaires.* N.Y., A.S. Barnes, 1907.

Christy, Bayard. "Bob-White in Pennsylvania." In *The Cardinal*, Audubon Society of the Sewickley Valley, Jan., 1926, pp 7-18.

Cleland, Hugh. *George Washington in the Ohio Valley.* Pittsburgh, University Press, 1955.

Couvares, Francis. *The Remaking of Pittsburgh.* Albany, State University of N.Y. Press, 1984.

Cramer, Zadoc. "The Navigator." In *Ohio River Handbook and Picture Album.* Cincinnati, Young & Ke, 1950.

Cramer, Zadoc. *Ohio and Mississippi Navigator*, 1802. Repiir & Karl Yost Morrisson, 1987.

Crawford, Stanton C. and John A Nietz. "Old Schools of the Ohio Valley." In *Western Pennsylvania Historical Magazine*, v. 23, 1940, pp. 243-254.

Cumming, F. "Sketches of a Tour in the Western Country, Pittsburgh, 1810." In *Western Pennsylvania Historical Magazine*, March 1937, v. 20, p. 10.

Dahlinger, Charles W. "The Pittsburgh Sanitary Fair." In *Western Pennsylvania Historical Magazine*, v. 12, 1929, p. 99.

Daniel, Dorothy. "The Sanitary Fair." In *Western Pennsylvania Historical Magazine,* v. 41, 1958, p. 153-158.

Dennis, Stephen Neal. *Historic Houses of the Sewickley Valley.* Sewickley, White Oak Pub., 1996.

Downing, Andrew, J. *The Architecture of Country Houses.* N.Y., 1850.

Downing, Andrew, J. *Rural Essays.* N.Y., 1853.

Downing, Andrew, J. *Victorian Cottage Residences.* N.Y., Dover, 1981.

Downing, Antoinette F. and Vincent J. Scully. *The Architectural Heritage of Newport, R.I.* Cambridge, Harvard Univ. Press, 1952.

Elliott, J. Wilkinson. *A Plea for Hardy Plants.* N.Y., 1902.

Ellis, Agnes. *Lights and Shadows of Sewickley Life.* Philadelphia, J.B. Lippincott, 1893.

Emery, John. "The McKean Tract." In *Western Pennsylvania Historical Magazine*, v.9, No. 1, pp. 24-33.

Fiftieth Anniversary Exercises of the Presbyterian Church, Sewickley, Pennsylvania, 1838-1888. Pittsburgh, W.W. Walters, n.d.

426 Woodland Road, its History. Unpublished, 1986.

Glazier, Willard. *Peculiarities of American Cities.* Philadelphia, 1883.

Gleanings of the Harmony Society. Ambridge, 1960.

Goodfellow, Donald M. "Centenary of a Pittsburgh Library," In *Western Pennsylvania Historical Magazine*, v. 31, 1948.

Gormly, Agnes Hays, "Journey to Newington." In *Old Penn Street*, by Gilbert Hays. Sewickley, Village Print Shop, 1928.

Handlin, David P. *The American Home.* Boston, Little, Brown, 1979.

Harpster, John W., ed. *Pen Pictures of Western Pennsylvania.* University of Pittsburgh Press, 1938.

Havighurst, Walter. *River to the West*, N.Y., Putnam, 1970.

Hayes, E. L. *Illustrated Atlas of the Upper Ohio River Valley.* Philadelphia, Simmons & Titus, 1877.

Hays, George A. *Reminiscences of the Sewickley Valley.* Harmony Press of Sewickley, Pa, 1968.

Hays, Gilbert. *Old Penn Street.* Sewickley, The Village Print Shop, 1928.

Hays, Samuel. *City at the Point.* Pittsburgh, The University Press, 1989.

High School Course of Study. Sewickley, 1912.

History of Allegheny County, Pa. Evansville, Ind., Unigraphic, n.d., v.2.

History of Allegheny County, Pennsylvania. A. Werner, 1889.

History of Delaware County, Pennsylvania. Philadelphia, L.H. Everts, 1884.

History of Pittsburgh and Environs. American Historical Society, *1922.*

A History of the Presbyterian Church of Sewickley, Pennsylvania. Prepared by a Committee of the Congregation. N.Y., Knickerbocker, 1914.

Industries of Pennsylvania, 1879-1880.

Ingham, John N. "Steel City Aristocrats." In *City at the Point*, by Samuel Hays. Pittsburgh, the University Press, 1989, p. 265-294.

Jackson, Kenneth J. *Crabgrass Frontier.* N.Y., Oxford University Press, 1985.

Jenkins, Philip, "The Ku Klux Klan in Pennsylvania, 1920-1940." In *Western Pennsylvania Historical Magazine*, v. 69, No. 2, April 1986, pp. 121-124.

"Joe, Uncle." *Memories of Sweet Valley: or 40 Years Ago and Now.* Pittsburgh, Murdoch, Kerr, 1890.

Jordan, John W. *Genealogical and Personal History of Western Pennsylvania.* N.Y., Lewis Historical Co., 1915.

Kann, S. Lee. *Show Places, Know Places, Go Places.* Lee & Art Publishing, Pittsburgh, 1932.

Kelly, William M. *Edgeworth Club, 1893-1993.* Edgeworth, Pa., 1993.

Kidney, Walter C. *Landscape Architecture of Western Pennsylvania.* Pittsburgh, Pittsburgh History and Landmarks Foundation, 1985.

Klein, Philip. *Social Study of Pittsburgh*, 1938.

Kostoff, Spiro. *America by Design.* N.Y., Oxford, 1987.

Lang, Edith, and George West. *Musical Accompaniment of Moving Pictures.* Boston, Boston Music Co., 1920.

Laws of the Commonwealth of Pennsylvania. Republished. Philadelphia, John Bioren, 1810.

Laws of the General Assembly of the Commonwealth of Pennsylvania, Harrisburg, 1842.

Library of Congress. Olmsted Associates, *Papers.* MFL Reel 158, Job File #3055.

Lockwood, Alice B. *Gardens of Colony and State*, compiled for the Garden Club of America. N.Y., Scribners, 1931.

Lorant, Stefan. *Pittsburgh, The Story of an American City.* Pittsburgh, The University Press, 1964.

McCracken, James. "Mother is Home." In *Readers' Digest,* Ap. 1980, p. 200+.

Martin, Scott. *Leisure in Southwestern Pennsylvania*, 1800-1850. Thesis. University of Pittsburgh, 1990.

Mash, Donald J. *A Sequent Occupance Study of Sewickley, Pennsylvania.* Thesis, M.A. University of Pittsburgh, 1966.

Meeks, Carroll Louis Vanderslice. *The Railroad Station; an Architectural History.* New Haven, Yale University Press, 1956.

Miller, Annie Clark. *Chronicles of Pittsburgh and its Environs.* Pittsburgh, n.p., 1927.

Miller, Joseph, T. "Pittsburgh Consolidation Charter." In *National Municipal Review*, October 1929, p. 604.

Miner, Curtis. *Homestead: The Story of a Steel Town.* Pittsburgh, Historical Society of Western Pennsylvania, 1989.

Morison, Samuel Eliot, Henry Steele Commager, and William E. Leuchtenburg. *The Growth of the American Republic.* N.Y., Oxford, 1969, v. 2., p. 117-118.

Mumford, Lewis. *The City in History.* N.Y., Harcourt, Brace, Jovanovich, 1961.

Munn, M. J. *Geology of the Oil and Gas Fields of Sewickley Quadrangle.* U.S. Geological Survey, 1911.

National Park Service. Frederick Law Olmsted National Historical Site, Brookline, Mass. *Archives.*

National Urban League. *Social Conditions of the Negro in the Hill District of Pittsburgh.* General Committee on the Hill Survey, 1930.

Negro Survey of Pennsylvania, 1929. Harrisburg, Commonwealth of Pennsylvania, Department of Welfare.

Nevin, Adelaide. *The Social Mirror.* Pittsburgh, T.W. Nevin, 1888.

Nevin, Franklin Taylor. *The Village of Sewickley.* The Sewickley Printing Shop, 1923.

Ogden, George. *Letters from the West.* New Bedford, Mass., Melcher and Rogers, 1823.

Ohio River Handbook. Cincinnati, Young and Klein., 1950.

Parton, James. "Pittsburgh." In *Atlantic Monthly,* Jan. 1868.

Pastorius, Mary Beth. "Rutan Designs a Local Legacy." In *Sewickley Herald,* Oct. 23, 1985.

Paxson, Frederick L. "The Highway Movement." In *American Historical Review*, Jan, 1946.

Pennsylvania Land Office. *Report of Internal Affairs, 1892.*

Peterson, Edwin. *Penn's Woods West*. Pittsburgh, University Press, 1958.

Pittsburg and Allegheny Blue-Book, 1899-1900.

Pittsburgh. Department of Public Health. *Annual Report, 1909-1919.*

Pittsburgh and Allegheny Illustrated Review. Pittsburgh, J.M. Eistner, 1889.

Plat Book, 1897.

Polk's Directory, 1897.

Practical Receipt Book by Experienced House-Keepers. Sewickley, Methodist Episcopal Church, 1897.

The Presbyterian Church Of Sewickley, Pennsylvania, 1838-1988. The 1988 History of the Church. n.d., n.p.

Reed, John. *Pennsylvania Blackstone: Laws of Pennsylvania*. Carlisle, George Fleming, 1831.

Revised Course of Study for the Sewickley Public School. 1899.

Ritchey, S.C. and J.C. Venning. "Paper prepared at the time of the Semi-Centennial of the Sewickely Methodist Episcopal Church." Unpublished, 1902.

Rybczynski, Witold. *Home: a Short History of an Idea*. N.Y., Viking, 1986.

Rybczynski, Witold. "Tomorrowland." In *The New Yorker*, July 22, 1996, p. 37-39.

Saint Stephen's Parish Cookbook, 1912.

Saint Stephen's Messenger.

Saville, Max. *George Morgan, Colony Builder*. N.Y., Columbia University Press, 1932.

Schafer, Jim and Mike Sajina. *The Allegheny River*. University Park, Pa., Pennsylvania State University Press, 1992.

Schuyler, Montgomery. "The Building of Pittsburgh." In *Architectural Record*, v. 30, Oct. 1911.

Scott, Frank J. *The Art of Beautifying Suburban Home Grounds*. N.Y., American Book Exchange, 1881.

Scully, Vincent. *American Architecture and Urbanism*. N.Y., Prager, 1969.

Scully, Vincent and Antoinette F. Downing. *The Architectural Heritage of Newport, Rhode Island. 2d ed., N.Y., Clarkson & Potter.*

Sewickley Business Directory, 1896-1897.

Sewickley Directory, 1910.

Sewickley Directory, 1915.

Sewickley Valley Society, 1895.

Sharp, Dallas Lore. "The Commuter and the Modern Conveniences." In *Atlantic*, Oct. 1910, pp. 554-64.

Shields, Eliza Leet. "School Girls of 1850." In *Western Pennsylvania Historical Magazine*, v. 13, 1930, pp. 182-188.

Smeltzer, Wallace Guy. *Methodism in Western Pennsylvania*. N.Y., Little Valley, Stright Publ., 1969.

Social Directory for Greater Pittsburgh, 1904.

Stilgoe, John R. *Borderland*. New Haven, Yale University Press, 1988.

Stotz, Charles. *The Early Architecture of Western Pennsylvania*. Pittsburgh, The University Press, 1995.

Stuhldreher, Mary. "Autobiliousness." In *Western Pennsylvania Historical Magazine*, v. 57, 1974, p. 275+.

Tarr, Joel. *Transportation Innovation and Changing Spatial Patterns in Pittsburgh, 1850-1934*. Pittsburgh, C.M.U. Transportation Research Institute, 1971.

van Trump, James D. *Life and Architecture in Pittsburgh*. Pittsburgh, Pittsburgh History and Landmarks Foundation, 1983.

van Urk, J. Blair. *The Story of Rolling Rock*. N.Y., Scribners, 1950.

Walhauser, Fred. *Upper-Class Society of the Sewickley Valley, 1830-1910*. Unpublished paper, University of Pittsburgh, 1964.

Way, Frederick, Jr. "The Trap." In *S&D Reflector*, v.18, No. 1

Wayne, Anthony. *A Name in Arms*. Pittsburgh, University Press, 1960.

Weber, Michael. "Community and Mobility." In Samuel Hays. *City at the Point*. Pittsburgh, The University Press, 1989, pp. 373-374.

Winans, William. "Recollections of Boyhood Years in Southwestern Pennsylvania." In *Western Pennsylvania Historical Magazine*, v.22, No. 1.

"The Works of Rutan & Russell in Pittsburgh," In *The Architectural Record*, Aug. 1904, v.18, p.103.

Wright, J.E., and Doris S. Corbett. *Pioneer Life in Western Pennsylvania*. Pittsburgh, University Press, 1940.

Young, Stanley P. and Edward A. Goldman, *The Wolves of North America*. N.Y., Dover, 1944.

Manuscript Files

Gilbert Hays File. In Senator John Heinz Pittsburgh Regional History Center.

Way File. In Senator John Heinz Pittsburgh Regional History Center.

Captain Frederick Way, Jr. File. In Sewickley Public Library.

Index